NATURAL RESOURCES AND CONFLICT IN AFRICA

ROCHESTER STUDIES in
AFRICAN HISTORY and the DIASPORA

Toyin Falola, Senior Editor
The Frances Higginbotham Nalle Centennial Professor in History
University of Texas at Austin

(ISSN: 1092–5228)

A complete list of titles in the Rochester Studies in African History and the Diaspora, in order of publication, may be found at the end of this book.

NATURAL RESOURCES AND CONFLICT IN AFRICA

THE TRAGEDY OF ENDOWMENT

Abiodun Alao

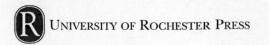

UNIVERSITY OF ROCHESTER PRESS

First published 2007
Transferred to digital printing 2008

University of Rochester Press
668 Mt. Hope Avenue, Rochester, NY 14620, USA
www.urpress.com
and Boydell & Brewer Limited
PO Box 9, Woodbridge, Suffolk IP12 3DF, UK
www.boydellandbrewer.com

Hardcover ISBN-13: 978–1–58046–267–9
Hardcover ISBN-10: 1–58046–267–7
ISSN: 1092–5228

Library of Congress Cataloging-in-Publication Data

Alao, Abiodun.
    Natural resources and conflict in Africa : the tragedy of endowment / Abiodun Alao.
        p. cm. — (Rochester studies in African history and the Diaspora,
ISSN 1092-5228 ; v. 29)
    Includes bibliographical references and index.
    ISBN-13: 978-1-58046-267-9 (hardcover : alk. paper)
    ISBN-10: 1-58046-267-7
    1. Natural resources—Africa. 2. Natural resources—Political aspects—Africa. 3. Conflict management—Africa. I. Title.
    HC800.Z65A43 2007
    303.6096—dc22

                                        2007009863

A catalogue record for this title is available from the British Library.

This publication is printed on acid-free paper.
Printed in the United States of America.

To 'Ronke, Fiyinfolu, and Ajibola, for making coming home the highlight of my day

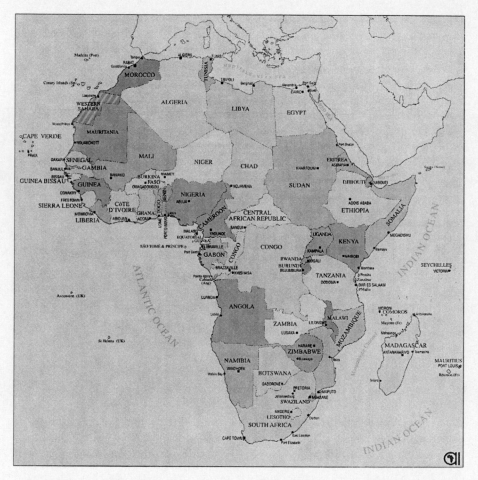

Political Map of Africa. Reproduced from *Africa at a Glance: Facts and Figures 1997/98*, compiled by Pieter Esterhuysen. Pretoria: African Institute of South Africa, 1998.

CONTENTS

ILLUSTRATIONS

PREFACE

The impetus for this book came from comments made by two people during the course of almost a decade. The first was in the spring of 1989, when a friend and colleague, Tajudeen Abdulraheem, noted during a discussion we had in his apartment at Oxford that natural resource management would be the key issue during the last decade of the twentieth century and even beyond, and that efforts should be invested into looking at how the management of these resources can affect politics in Africa. Tajudeen, then a Rhodes Scholar, was rounding up his doctoral studies at St. Peter's College Oxford, while I was then halfway through mine at King's College London. The second comment came in 1996. In an informal discussion that followed a lecture I gave at the Royal College of Defense Studies, London, one of the course participants raised a crucial point about the possible impact of natural resource management on security in Africa. Like Tajudeen seven years previously, he too opined that detailed studies into the complexities of resource politics in Africa would be crucial, if the continent was to be spared some of the conflicts that have characterized its postindependence existence. By the end of the 1990 decade, these two positions had been clearly vindicated, giving no additional need to draw anyone's attention to the obvious linkage between natural resources and conflict in Africa. What was even more frightening were the apocalyptic predictions being made in certain quarters that the years ahead would witness many more such conflicts, to further result in the weakening and collapse of state institutions in the continent.

It now seems beyond contention that the politics surrounding the management of natural resource politics has brought out some of the extremes in Africa's security complexities. Among the issues that have been thrown up are violent ethno-nationalism, acrimonious intergroup relations, youth revolts, small arms and light weapons proliferation, corruption, money laundering, warlordism, cross-border looting, mercenarism, and alleged links with global terrorism. The conflicts have raised an array of questions, most of which have been answered only rhetorically. Questions such as: How does one reconcile Africa's enormous natural resource endowment with its appalling poverty? Why is the violence associated with natural resources in the continent becoming more vicious and devastating? What are the indigenous conflict resolution principles that can help address some of these conflicts? Why have some natural resources been associated with conflict in some countries and not in others? To what extent can one consider these conflicts to be part of the inescapable process of socioeconomic and political reconfiguration of nation-states in the continent? What is the dichotomy between local claim and national interest in the politics of resource control? The questions appear endless, and the need for answers continues to challenge academics and practitioners.

This book is an attempt to contribute answers to some of the questions identified above. I use the word "contribute" deliberately, as ultimate answers are probably unlikely to most of the questions. I do not seek to reify the orthodox thinking of conflict as an outcome of clearly determinable and predictable linear patterns of cause and effect. Rather, conflict in Africa is viewed from the perspective of an outcome of contingent predisposing factors of which natural resources are central elements. Broadly, in this book I examine the ways through which the ownership, management, and control of natural resources have been linked to conflicts in the continent and the issues underlining these conflicts. To achieve this, I divide natural resources into four categories—land (including agricultural products and animal resources), solid minerals, oil, and water—and proceed to discuss some of the ways through which each one of these has been linked to conflict in the continent, especially in the last decade. Following this, I analyze the conflicts through the consequences of one phenomenon that threads through all conflicts over natural resources in Africa: governance, especially as this involves the weakness of administrative structures designed to manage these resources, the inadequacy of laws and regulations governing the sharing of the endowment, the intricacies of elite politics, and the changing role of civil society.

I argue that recent conflicts over natural resources in Africa are inextricably linked to the complete defectiveness or the selective efficiency of the apparatus of natural resource governance. By "natural resource governance," I mean the whole gamut of internal and external considerations, especially in the form of laws and practices, which come to play in the management (i.e., the ownership, extraction, processing, distribution, and control) of natural resources. Indeed, I contend that there is no direct correlation between natural resources and conflict beyond the structures, processes, and actors associated with the management and control of these resources. Consequently, contrary to conventional thinking, neither "scarcity" nor "abundance" is in itself the real cause of natural resource conflict; rather, it is the "management" of these resources. This implies that the possession of natural resources is neither a "curse" for those who have it nor is it a "blessing" (in the form of escape from conflict) for countries not endowed with natural resources. The impact of natural resources on the security calculus is mainly a function of the laws and practices guiding the exploitation of such resources. With no credible administrative structures to manage natural resources in most African states, and with the laws governing the management being either contradictory or not properly aligned with other political and social structures, issues surrounding natural resources become violently contestable.

Much more profoundly, I argue that ongoing efforts to eradicate corruption in the management of natural resources, though important, is, from the point of view of ending conflicts over these resources, inadequate. What seems crucial to ending this category of conflicts in Africa is the appreciation of the multiple domestic and international considerations that come into natural resource management, of which eradication of corruption and ensuring of accountability are just parts, even if admittedly important parts. Also important are the establishment of credible structures that can assist in ensuring equal distribution of these resources, which, as of now, is lacking in most African countries.

Against this background, I argue here for the establishment of natural resource governance as a distinct issue in the management of affairs in the continent. This sector of governance will bring together all the local and international issues relating to natural resource management. Key issues to be covered under this broad spectrum include the role of the constitution in natural resource management; the politics of revenue allocation; the process of distribution; the function of indigenization policies and the politics of expatriate involvement in the ownership, management, and control of natural resources; property rights; human rights concerns; the relationship with global market demands; the complexities of managing environmental issues relating to resource extraction, and how issues such as banking, taxation, and immigration bring together the domestic and international variables in resource politics. Indeed, it is only after this is done that the international mechanisms designed to stem the illegal exploitation and sale of natural resources, such as the Kimberley Process and the Extractive Industries Transparency Initiative (EITI), and the national and global efforts at transparency can stand chances of significant success.

Apart from this central thesis, I call for a broader approach to the studies of natural resource conflicts in Africa. While the contribution of many of the existing studies on the subject cannot be ignored, a feature that is common to most of them is that they accord too much attention to those resources that are vital to international market demands, especially diamonds, gold, and oil. This has given the conflicts in countries and places such as Angola, Democratic Republic of Congo (DRC), Sierra Leone, Sudan, Liberia, and Nigeria's Niger Delta particular prominence. In contrast, far less attention has been accorded to those natural resources that have caused communal conflicts, especially land and water resources. The links between resources in the second category and conflict have been of interest only to scholars in the region or countries specifically affected. Perhaps the only exception to this is the attention given to the land conflict in Zimbabwe and some other southern African countries, and even the interest in these conflicts can be explained by the multiracial nature of their actors and the international dimension of their politics.

I object to the above tendency on at least four grounds. First, it seems to be another addition to the stereotypical depictions that have historically governed most writings on Africa, whereby key issues that have international relevance are often made to dominate discussion at the expense of those that have a bearing mainly on local politics. With the international (largely western) demands for Africa's mineral resources, conflicts surrounding those materials have taken prominence over other natural resources, such as land, which often has far less international dimensions. The fear that these conflicts can, even if remotely, affect the global supply of these mineral resources has further intensified the interest they generate in academic literature. Second, I see the approach as reflecting another variance of Afro-pessimism, as it portrays, even if in undeclared terms, the impression that not even countries with abundant resources are spared the gradual disintegration that seems to dominate events in the continent. Third, by not giving much recognition to conflicts with communal undertones, the crucial understanding of how natural resources interlink with governance at the local level would be lost. It is my belief that recognizing the role of communal conflicts in governance is crucial to finding long-term solutions to conflicts that often lead to state collapse, especially as it is the neglect of the small communal conflicts that often converge to weaken state structures. Finally, the minimal attention accorded to conflicts with more communal undertones has contributed to many of the studies neglecting the significant role of "culture" in appreciating the complexities of natural resource politics in developing societies. Indeed, the role of "culture" in determining what constitutes "natural resources" and what determines "conflict" is an important issue that has to be addressed in any efforts to find lasting solutions to many of these conflicts.

Closely related to the above is my desire for this book to reinforce the importance of ongoing efforts aimed at changing the approach to the study of African conflicts. Until recently, when the effects of "people-power" gained some roots in the continent, scholars were wont to see African conflicts as something that concerns the "state," rather than the "people," which explains the interests in issues such as interstate conflict, armed rebellion against the state, and secessionist rebellion. It now seems established that this approach is fundamentally flawed, as it addresses issues that are essential to the survival of the state and its elite class but not necessarily to the majority of the population, who should also have a stake on how their affairs are determined. Consequently, a wider conceptualization of "conflict" needs to be adopted, so that more consideration can go into the analysis of natural resource conflicts in Africa. This should include violent civil protest, attacks on government properties, and acrimonious intergroup relations.

A word to those who think it is unnecessary to devote attention to natural resource governance and conflicts in Africa, especially as the contribution of the continent to global resource endowment is often perceived as negligible and its conflicts appear intractable. (I am hoping you are few in number.) At least three factors show the fallacy of this thought. First, contrary to what is often assumed, Africa's resource endowment is significant, and ongoing discoveries, especially as in the case of oil on the West African coast, are further reinforcing the importance of the entire continent to global resource politics. Indeed, by 2015, the United States estimates that one-quarter of its oil supply will come from Africa. Second, natural resource conflicts are increasingly important because of the significant role they play in the affairs of the region, especially as these relate to governance and the activities of civil society. Third, some of Africa's natural resources are now being linked to a number of global security concerns, including money laundering and alleged links with terrorism. This, for example, can be seen in the alleged involvement of Africa's diamonds in the activities of the al-Qaeda group. All these call for a closer look at how Africa's resource conflicts manifest.

Finally, a comment on the countries from which examples in the book are drawn and a note on my sources is appropriate. Examples are primarily drawn from sub-Saharan Africa, although there are North African countries included in some of the cited examples. This, to an extent, shows the prevalence of this category of conflicts in sub-Saharan Africa. Different aspects of conflicts over natural resources in Africa have been published in books and journals. Many of these have proved to be very helpful, even if I have had grounds to disagree with the conclusions of some of them. I have benefited from ongoing research in many universities across Africa, where several dedicated researchers are undertaking studies into aspects of natural resource conflicts. Information received from local newspapers and magazines has also been vital. Additionally, official documents and briefings of many organizations, multinational corporations, and local and international nongovernmental organizations (NGOs), have been of importance to this work. Most crucial of all my sources, however, have been the interviews and private discussions I had in all my visits across countries in the continent. Although aspects of the conflicts involving natural resources can be freely discussed, there are actors whose roles are shrouded in secrecy. Where actors have included warlords, criminal gangs, greedy politicians, and others with questionable credentials, nothing short of this could be expected. Consequently, most of my respondents spoke to me on the grounds of anonymity, which I have made every effort to respect. In a number of cases, however, informants not only waived their rights to anonymity, they actually insisted that their names be mentioned. I have refused this request out of my concern for their safety.

It is perhaps appropriate to end this preface with an expression of gratitude to all those who have assisted in the course of writing this book. The first and most important gratitude goes to the numerous people across Africa who shared their experiences with me. This should not be seen as a stylistic bow aimed at popularity. I spent four years traveling across the continent gathering materials for this book. Everywhere I visited I met enthusiastic people who wanted to share their experiences with me. It is a matter of great regret to me—and no doubt would be of some disappointment to them—that I am unable to make better use of the information they so enthusiastically gave. I hope they will forgive me.

The next gratitude goes to the Ford Foundation, whose generous grant has made this book possible. This is the second time the Ford Foundation has intervened in the course of my professional career, having first offered me a scholarship for my doctoral studies at King's College London between 1987 and 1991. The MacArthur Foundation awarded me a two-year Post-Doctoral Fellow in 1995 specifically to look at aspects of natural resource conflicts in Africa. I am grateful to these two foundations. Gratitude of special category also goes to the University of Rochester Press for all that was done to publish this book. Specifically, I want to thank the Editorial Director, Ms. Suzanne Guiod, the Editorial Assistant, Ms. Katie Hutley, and the Series Editor for the Rochester Studies on African History, Professor Toyin Falola. Thanks, too, to the anonymous reviewers for their very useful comments on the manuscript.

Readers will discover in the pages ahead that I amateurishly cut across several academic disciplines, from economics, law, and geography to philosophy, sociology, and religion. If I have not violated the basic principles of these disciplines, it is because of the assistance of those who shared their thoughts with me on the broad subject of this book. Special thanks go to my former teacher, colleague, and friend, Professor Julius Ihonvbere, who was the first person with whom I discussed the outline of the book and whose encouragement and support continued throughout. Particular mention should be made of three other people: Professor Olufemi Taiwo of Seattle University in Washington, Professor Ademola Popoola of the Obafemi Awolowo University Ile Ife, and Dr. Funmi Olonisakin of King's College London. With these three, I spent considerable time discussing the complexities of natural resource conflicts in Africa. Sometimes they convinced me; few times I convinced them; most of the time though we all remained unconvinced, but the result in every case is increased clarity. I thank them.

There is another set of people whom I must acknowledge as a group. These are the research students associated with the Conflict Security and Development Group at the International Policy Institute, King's College London. Some of them read parts or the entire manuscript, while I engaged others in very useful discussions. These include Wale Ismail, Ekaette Ikpe, Martin Kimani, Dauda Jobateh, Morten Hagen, Sabiitti Mutengesa, and Funmi Vogt. The electrifying intellect and the youthful logic introduced by these students have made me realize just how close indeed I am to the geriatric ward. I am grateful to them. Thanks, too, to other colleagues at the King's College London, especially Drs. John Mackinlay and Randolph Kent, Professor Mats Berdal, Shelly Butler, Dylan Hendrickson, and Keith Britto. Professor Jack Spence and Professor James Mayall continue to play important mentoring roles. I am grateful to them.

I also want to put on record my thanks to other academics and practitioners across the world who made helpful contributions at different stages of my work.

These include Professors Segun Ilesanmi, Sola Akinrinade, A. G. Adebayo, J. K. Olupona, Margaret Vogt, Kisangani Emizet, Sola Ekanade, and Gilbert Khadiagala. Others to whom gratitude is due include Drs. Adebayo Oyebade, Tajudeen Abdulraheem, Comfort Ero, Lansana Gberie, Adekeye Adebajo, Napoleon Abdulahi, Prosper Bani, Adedeji Ebo, Ademola Abass, Tunde Ogowewo, Tayo Adesina, Kamil Kamaludeen, Kwesi Aning, Abdel-Fatau Musa, Thomas Jaye, Wafula Okumu, Kayode Fayemi, Abubakar Momoh, Bayo Olowoake, Alex de Waal, Akin Oyetade, Akin Alao, Ozonnia Ojielo, Akin Akingbulu, Kunle Lawal, Chris Alden, Sola Akande, and Jeremy Levitt. Ambassador J. K. Shinkaiye, Dr. Martin Uhomoibhi, Ambassador Sam Ibok, Peter Obidi, and Ademola Adeyemi also offered very useful comments for which I am grateful.

I thank all those who offered friendship and support. Funmi Olonisakin again comes in here. She has remained more than a colleague and a god-mother to one of my children, but also someone in whom my family has found the steadfastness of a trusted friend. I am also grateful to other friends, including Bayo and Made Bello, Segun and Kemi Obafemi, Doyin and Wemino Sheyindemi, Dotun and Jumoke Adeniyi, Sule Baba and Zainab Ali, Danlami and Mariam Abubakar Sule, Pastor Paul and Joyce Fadeyi, Christie Adejoh, Sam and Victoria Omokan, Jide and Lola Olubode, Abiodun and Wumi Onadipe, Olaloye Badamosi, Debo Adediran, Bisi and Bola Dare, Demilade and Kemi Oyemade, and many others. I don't know what I did to deserve such dear friends, but whatever it was, I'm just glad I did it! Thanks too to my siblings, Olufemi, Kayode, Funmi, Sade, and Olusayo.

Permit me to end this preface on a hypocritical note. That is, convention places last the gratitude that in reality comes first in an author's heart—that to the immediate family. My deepest thanks go to my wife, 'Ronke, who patiently, and with great understanding, tolerated my other love affairs—that with African security, and our two delightful children, Fiyinfolu and Ajibola, who kept up with a Daddy so often away from home.

Abiodun Alao
Chislehurst, Kent

ABBREVIATIONS

ACP	African Caribbean and Pacific
ADF	African Development Foundation
AFDL	Alliance of Democratic Forces for the Liberation of Congo-Zaire
AFRC	Armed Forces Revolutionary Council
AGO	Automobile Gas Oil (Diesel)
ANC	African National Congress
APC	All Peoples Congress
APRM	African Peer Review Mechanism
ASCorp	Angola Selling Corporation
AU	African Union (formerly OAU)
CABCOG	Cabinda Gulf Oil Company
CAP	Coalition against Privatization of Water
CAR	Central African Republic
CARAT	Consumer Access to a Responsible Accounting of Trade Act
CBR	Centre for Basic Research (Kampala)
CGG	Campaign for Good Governance
CIA	Central Intelligence Agency (United States)
Cotco	Cameroon Oil Transport Company
CSSDCA	Conference on Security, Stability, Development, and Cooperation in Africa
DFID	Department for International Development (British)
DRC	Democratic Republic of Congo
ECA	Economic Commission for Africa
ECOMOG	ECOWAS monitoring group
ECOWAS	Economic Community of West African States
EEC	European Economic Community
EGPC	Egyptian General Petroleum Corporation
EITI	Extractive Industries Transparency Initiative
EO	Executive Outcome
ERHC	Environmental Remediation Holding Corporation (United States)
FAO	Food and Agricultural Organization
FEPA	Federal Environmental Protection Agency
FIND	Foundation for International Dignity
FLEC	Front for the Liberation of the Enclave of Cabinda

FNI	*Front des natioalistses et integrationiste*
FRELIMO	Liberation Front of Mozambique
GEMAP	Governance and Economic Management Assistance Program
GGDO	Government Gold and Diamond Office
GNPOC	Great Nile Petroleum Operating Company
GUPCO	Gulf of Suez Petroleum Company
HRW	Human Rights Watch
HYPPADEC	Hydroelectric Power Producing Areas Development Commission
ICG	International Crisis Group
ICJ	International Court of Justice
IDMA	International Diamond Manufacturers Association
IFI	International Financial Institutions
IHD	International Hydrological Decade (UNESCO)
ILC	International Law Commission (UN)
IMET	International Military Education and Training
IMF	International Monetary Fund
INPFL	Independent National Patriotic Front of Liberia
INYM	Isoko National Youth Movements
IPA	International Peace Academy
IYWIP	International Year for the World's Indigenous People
JDZ	Joint Development Zone
KARI	Kenyan Agricultural Research Institute
KOYA	Konkomba Youth Association
LAC	Liberian Agricultural Company
LAMCO	Liberian American Mining Company
LCBC	Lake Chad Basin Commission
LHWP	Lesotho Highway Water Project
LNG	Liquidified natural gas
LPC	Liberian Peace Council
LPFO	Low Pour Fuel Oil
LRA	Lord's Resistance Army (Uganda)
LURD	Liberian United for Reconciliation and Democracy
MAP	Millennium Partnership for the African Recovery
MDC	Movement for Democratic Change
MEND	Movement for the Emancipation of the Niger Delta
MODEL	Movement for Democracy in Liberia
MOSOP	Movement for the Survival of the Ogoni People
MP	Member of Parliament
MPLA	Popular Movement for the Liberation of Angola
MRND	National Republican Movement for Democracy and Development
NDDC	Niger Delta Development Commission
NDPVF	Niger Delta People Volunteer Force

NEPA	National Electric Power Authority
NEPAD	New Partnership for Africa's Development
NGO	Nongovernmental organization
NNPC	Nigerian National Petroleum Corporation
NOC	National Oil Company
NPFL	National Patriotic Front of Liberia
NPN	National Party of Nigeria
NPRC	National Provisional Ruling Council
NRM	Natural Resource Management
NTLG	National Transitional Government of Liberia
OAU	Organization of African Unity
OCDT	Ogoni Civil Disturbances Tribunal
OMPADEC	Oil Mineral Producing Areas Development Commission
OPC	Odua People's Congress
OPEC	Oil Producing and Exporting Countries
PAC	Pan-Africanist Congress
PFC/PFL	Procura Financial Consultants (SA)
PMS	Premium Motor Spirit
PSIRU	Public Services International Research Unit
PSO	Private Security Organization
PTF	Petroleum Task Force
RCD	Rally for Congolese Democracy
RENAMO	Mozambican National Resistance
RPA	Rwandan Patriotic Army
RPF	Rwandan Patriotic Front
RUF	Revolutionary United Front
SAPEM	*Southern Africa Political and Economic Monthly*
SADC	Southern African Development Community
SAP	Structural Adjustment Policy
SNC	Sovereign National Conference
SNNPRS	Southern Nations Nationalities and Peoples Regional State
SNPC	*Societe Nationale des Petroles du Congo*
Sonangol	*Sociedale Nacional de Combustíveis de Angola*
SPDC	Shell Petroleum Development Corporation
SPLA	Sudan Peoples Liberation Army
TDC	Tribunal Departmental de Conciliation
UDDP	United Nations Development Programme
UDF	United Democratic Front
ULIMO-J	United Liberation Movement for Democracy in Liberia (of Roosevelt Johnson)
ULIMO-K	United Liberation Movement for Democracy in Liberia (of Alhaji Kromah)
UNASIL	United Nations Mission in Sierra Leone
UNEP	United Nations Environmental Program

UNHCR	United Nations High Commission for Refugees
UNITA	National Union for the Total Independence of Angola
UNOMIL	United Nations Observer Mission in Liberia
UNRF	Uganda National Rescue Front
UPDF	Ugandan Peoples Defense Fund
UPN	Unity Party of Nigeria
WAANSA	West African Network on Small Arms
WAMCO	West African Mining Corporation
WTO	World Trade Organization
WWF	World Wildlife Foundation
ZACPLAN	action plan for the Zambezi River Basin
ZAMCOM	Zambezi River Commission
ZANU	Zimbabwe African National Union
ZANU-PF	Zimbabwe African National Union Patriotic Front
ZRA	Zambezi River Authority

INTRODUCTION

We are fighting and killing ourselves over what God gave to make us happy and comfortable. I sometimes wonder whether it would not be better if God takes away the endowment, and by so doing, spare us the tragedy it has brought to our life.

A resident of Koidu

In many African nations, the natural resources that should be used to feed and educate people are instead being used to destroy them. . . . Colonialism, which allowed Europe to extract Africa's natural resources, left behind leaders who exploit their gold, diamonds, timber, oil . . . to benefit their own regional or ethnic groups or their own bank accounts.

International Herald Tribune

The link between natural resources and conflict is probably as old as human settlement. Empires and kingdoms throughout history are known to have risen or fallen because of their victories or defeats in wars that were heavily laden with natural resource considerations.[1] History is also replete with examples of friendships and alliances forged by empires and kingdoms to defend access to, and control of, essential natural resources,[2] while efforts have always been made to appease those who might block access to sources of vital natural resources.[3] This portrays the importance of natural resources to politics, diplomacy, and intergroup relations. The formation of modern nation-states, however, introduced more complex dimensions into the nature of resource politics, with issues such as disagreements over newly drawn geographical boundaries, protests over the forceful incorporation of hitherto autonomous units into new nation-state structures, creation of new national identities, and a number of other considerations, all becoming crucial factors that consequently changed the nature of the conflicts surrounding natural resources. These complications are more profound in the states formed during the second half of the twentieth century. The efforts to build internal cohesion among the disparate groups brought together to form nation-states, the consolidation of the fragile social structures inherited at independence, the greed of the "inheritance elites" (those who took over the political leadership of these countries at independence), and the desire to ensure the state's survival in a world that had become dangerously competitive, were among the factors that combined to heighten the propensity for conflicts over natural resources

1

in developing societies. The problems in this respect were hardly alleviated, as the majority of these new states "took off" during a century colored by two global wars and an intense ideological rivalry that polarized the world. Thus, the ultimate outcome has been the catalog of resource-related conflicts that greeted the birth and early development of many of these states.

The manifestations of resource conflicts in the last quarter of the twentieth century were particularly devastating. From oil in the Middle East and solid minerals in Africa to land in Asia and agricultural products in Latin America, conflicts over natural resources shattered hopes and tore societies apart. For Africa, the implications of some of these conflicts have been profound, sometimes underlining fundamental issues such as the collapse of state structures, massive human rights abuses, the weakening of civil society, the further depression of the economy, and the disintegration of traditional institutions. On another level, however, the conflicts reinforced the need for a deeper understanding of the dynamics of conflict, social configuration, and political processes in Africa, especially as all these are crucial to the efforts to find lasting solutions to the conflicts that have bedeviled the continent. Indeed, as of the dawn of the twentieth century, 40 percent of the twenty-seven violent conflicts in the world were taking place on the African continent.[4]

Because of the diversity of conflicts over natural resources in Africa and the extent of academic literature generated by the subject, new books on the subject need to provide the analytical focus of their approach. The theme threading through discussions in this book is the primary importance of *governance* in the management of natural resources in Africa. This introductory chapter seeks to achieve three objectives: first, to introduce natural resource politics, especially the reasons for the renewed interest in the subject; second, to provide an overview of how natural resource conflicts have manifested themselves in Africa, particularly in their relations to political governance and how this subject has been treated in academic literature; and third, to explain how this book has discussed conflicts over natural resources in Africa.

Explaining the Renewed Interest in Resource Politics

Any discussion on the politics surrounding natural resources must be prefaced with the declaration that the subject does not lend itself to easy comprehension. One reason for this, as Martin Holdgate has noted, is that the environmental diversity of the world has implied that experiences are rarely universal and, consequently, societies differ in their understanding of key environmental, and by implication natural resource, issues.[5] Judith Rees expresses similar sentiments when she warns of inherent dangers in attempting to categorize the extremely heterogeneous range of natural resource problems.[6] She, however, identifies two major phases in the study of natural resource concerns, the first of which focuses on the physical environment, its limits and deteriorating qualities. During this phase, resource problems tend to be defined in physical terms. The second phase is marked by the redefinition of the central resource problem and a shift in focus from physical scarcity and environmental change to a broader investigation of the social, economic, and political dimensions of natural resource use.[7]

Public and academic interests in resource politics experienced a renaissance during the second half of the twentieth century. This was due in part to the increase in the number of academic disciplines that emerged to make a claim on the subject and, in part, to the media interest in the future of a world that was seen to be adopting a laissez-faire approach of benign neglect to the environment and its support systems.[8] The last three decades of the twentieth century, in particular, brought out some of the major complexities of the subject. Three aspects of resource politics that occurred during this period are noteworthy. The first was the concern over the future of the global ecological support system, which centered largely on the changes to the environment epitomized by such developments as the depletion of the ozone layer, the greenhouse effect, and the destruction of the rain forest. To a large extent, these concerns underlined the wide interest and publicity given to the June 1992 Conference on Environment and Development, popularly known as the Earth Summit, held in Rio de Janeiro, Brazil. Despite being one of the largest congregations of world leaders in history,[9] the conference appeared to exhibit more divergence than convergence of views on the future of the environment.[10] Although the conference established a set of broad, nonbinding principles, it also showed that the issues involved are complex, and that any attempt to oversimplify the search for solutions to environmental problems would be as unrealistic as it would be unhelpful.[11]

The second aspect of natural resource politics that manifested visibly during the last three decades of the twentieth century was the concern over the depletion of vital natural resources. This created panic and raised public attention to the politics of the environment. Although this has been of interest to academics and policymakers throughout history, the global geopolitical situation of these recent times further heightened previous concerns. Additionally, concerns and anxieties were evoked by the fear that domestic inability to meet up with increasing demand for vital materials could increase external dependence, thus exposing countries to the possibility of blackmail.

The third aspect was the interest generated by the increasing number of resource-based conflicts, especially in developing societies, which seemingly became the key issue by the end of the decade. While such conflicts have been recognized throughout history, the complexities introduced to it by successive global developments, especially the end of the Cold War and the effects of globalization, brought some renewed concerns to the ways resource conflicts manifest. The general decline in the economic fortune of many developing societies puts further pressure on the environment, and thus increases the propensity for violent intergroup relations, particularly in Africa. Indeed, by the time the Cold War ended, domestic and international conflicts with natural resource underpinnings had littered the continent, and their devastating consequences had begun to attract global attention, as were the cases in Angola, the Democratic Republic of Congo (DRC), and Sierra Leone.

Post-Cold War Resource Conflicts in Africa

The changes brought to the nature of conflicts by the end of the Cold War are now well documented.[12] While superpower rivalries receded, new crises in developing countries—occasioned by ethnic conflicts, struggle for self-determination, human rights abuses, and economic pressures—created major challenges for the international community. Nowhere has this been more pronounced than in Africa, where the fragility of state institutions and the weakness of the economy have made the consequences of conflicts more profound. In this situation, central governments and armed factions have exploited natural resources to advance their respective agendas in conflicts that have their roots in ethnic, socioeconomic, and political differences. The management and control of abundant resources have also underlined conflicts at the communal level, where groups have engaged in conflicts in their bid to maximize opportunities coming from the natural resource endowment of their communities. On the whole, it can be said that controversies surrounding natural resources led to several new conflicts and introduced new and complex dimensions to existing ones.

Broadly, natural resources can be linked to conflicts in Africa in three ways: (1) cases in which natural resources constitute a direct or remote cause of conflict; (2) situations in which natural resources fuel and/or sustain conflicts; and (3) instances in which resources have come into consideration in efforts to resolve conflicts. As a cause of conflict, natural resource considerations have become easily identifiable in many communal conflicts, especially over the ownership and control of land. On a wider national level, however, it is ironic that rarely have natural resources been blatantly evident as the sole cause of conflict, in spite of recent econometric and quantitative analysis suggesting the contrary. More often than not, natural resource issues form core considerations in conflicts that are attributable to other causes. Issues such as ethnicity and religion (in cases of internal conflicts) or boundary and ideological disagreements (in cases of external conflicts) are some of the subterfuges often exploited to conceal the crucial aspects of natural resource considerations. Once open conflicts commence, however, the importance of natural resource considerations becomes so obvious that even warring factions no longer make pretence about them.

As a factor for fueling conflicts, the role of natural resources has become one of the most controversial issues in post-Cold War Africa, especially through the increase in the number of armed groups exploiting natural resources to advance their desire for self-determination or pursue other centrifugal tendencies. While this practice is not altogether new,[13] the increase in the number of recent cases is remarkable. From Angola and Liberia to DRC and Sierra Leone, armed groups have exploited the natural resources inside their territories to prosecute wars against their respective governments. Additionally, central governments in some countries have used natural resources to consolidate their authorities against challenges from rebel forces. Furthermore, the development of this process has also benefited from some post-Cold War security complications particularly with the proliferation of, and easy accessibility to, light weapons.[14] It is the role of natural resources in prolonging conflicts that has attracted recent concerns from the international community, evidenced by the activities of the United Nations and many international nongovernmental organizations (NGOs) on the role of diamonds in Angola's and Sierra Leone's civil wars. Multinational corporations involved in the exploitation of these resources have also had to be increasingly conscious of the consequences of their involvement in those natural resources engulfed in controversies.[15]

As a consideration in resolving conflicts, natural resources have come into play in two ways. First is through the inclusion of natural resource considerations in peace agreements, especially for those conflicts in which root causes are linked to the ownership and management of natural resources. The underlying rationale is the belief that inclusion of such clauses in peace agreements serves either to pacify belligerent groups or to end willful mismanagement of these resources. An example of this was the July 1999 Lomé Peace Agreement on Sierra Leone civil war, where the management of the country's diamond resources was put under the control of the leader of the rebel Revolutionary United Front (RUF), the late Foday Sankoh. Although this did not achieve the desired result, as was evident from the January 2000 re-eruption of violence in the country, it informs on the extent to which the importance of natural resources is appreciated in recent efforts at resolving conflicts. The second way is through current efforts being made to frustrate rebel groups, warlords, and others from exploiting the resources under their control to prosecute wars. The hope in this exercise is that such frustration would assist in resolving conflicts. Perhaps Africa's most notable examples of this are the United Nations' embargo on diamonds in the rebel-held territories of Angola and the embargo imposed on Liberia's former President Charles Taylor for his alleged involvement in Sierra Leone's civil conflict and diamond trade. Other examples include the Kimberley Process, which aimed at halting the flow of "conflict diamonds" and had the desired result of enhancing the chances of peaceful resolution of conflicts. While these efforts are not always successful, their incorporation into the wider efforts at resolving these conflicts marks another initiative in conflict resolution.

On the whole, recent conflicts involving natural resources in Africa have raised a number of issues for governance, seven of which are particularly noteworthy. The first is the way in which conflicts have manifested themselves. On the one extreme, they have resulted in the collapse or considerable weakening of state institutions, and examples here are the countries of Sierra Leone and the DRC. But as will be discussed later in this chapter, although the diverse roles of natural resources have now been made to dominate discussions on the conflicts in both countries, their origins were fundamentally problems of economic and political governance, most importantly, the inability of governments in both countries to handle crucial issues such as equitable distribution of resources, management of intergroup relations, and corruption at the leadership level. This primary issue underlines the thesis of this book: natural resource governance is at the root cause of most conflicts involving natural resources. At the other extreme are those cases in which conflicts have affected intergroup relations among local communities within nation-states. The impacts of these conflicts are often ignored but are extremely crucial in appreciating politics and governance in these societies. Virtually all African countries characterize these situations, albeit in different forms and with varying impacts on national security. In this book, these two extreme manifestations are carefully discussed.

The second issue is the impact of these conflicts on the state. In all cases, the effects of conflicts surrounding natural resources have contributed to the weakening of the state. The ways through which this manifests are complex and diverse. In some cases, the inability of the state to cope with the security problems emanating from conflicts has forced the government to cede away some of its responsibilities, most especially its exclusive monopoly of force, to the private sector. The result has been the burgeoning of private security organizations (PSOs) to meet growing demands.[16] This was the case in Sierra Leone, where mercenary companies took charge of national security for a period. In some of these countries as well, multinational corporations involved in exploiting natural resources have trespassed into what should be the exclusive preserve of the state to import arms into the country for their own security. This is exemplified in the role of the oil multinational company, Shell, in owning and keeping arms in its Nigeria office during the Abacha regime.[17] Yet in others, there emerged warlords who exploited the prevailing political situation and the weakness of states to assert themselves and acquire political power and material wealth, as happened in Liberia and the DRC. Also to be recorded as contributing to the weakening of the state is the string of illegal activities, such as the bribery, corruption, and tax evasion that became pervasive during conflicts bearing on natural resources. These illegal activities, highlighted by William Reno in his "shadow state" thesis,[18] became what I have termed "permitted offenses," due to the extent of the participation of key government functionaries and the ease with which people violate the laws with impunity. This made any legal deterrence against them of little effect. Indeed, corruption was not uncommon, as top government officials entered into illegal financial arrangements that yielded personal profit to them at the expense of the state. Other forms of corruption and deliberate mismanagement of revenues from natural resource endowments were also often left unpunished. Angola, the southern African country that was at war for more than two decades, recorded several examples of this tendency with considerable implications for the state. This weakening of state institutions led to the growth in informal or black-market economy, with corresponding losses for the state in terms of taxes.

The third governance issue is the complex nature of the relationship that often exists between the opposing sides involved in some of these conflicts. Available evidence from some conflicts has shown that despite the bitterness and the brutality often demonstrated, informal understanding between opposing sides also exists, which is borne from the mutual purpose of exploiting natural resources. In Sierra Leone, for example, the distinction between soldiers and the rebels at a point during the country's civil war became extremely blurred, as both fraternized and traded in diamonds. This led to the birth of the now famous sobriquet *so-bel*, a corruption of the words *soldier* and *rebel*. Also in Angola, it has been alleged that top functionaries of the Popular Movement for the Liberation of Angola (MPLA) government traded in weapons with the National Union for the Total Independence of Angola (UNITA) rebels: both sides often orchestrated mock wars in which they avoided direct engagement but created sufficient confusion to facilitate the looting of private and public property.[19] This implies the dominance of personal interest over any advertised ideological motivation for conflict.

Fourth in our list of governance issues are the "contagious" or cross-border effects of these conflicts. It has been the case that all countries engaged in major conflicts involving natural resources have spread the consequences of these conflicts to their neighbors. In this instance, the conflict is either moved beyond borders or the neighbors have interfered for reasons ranging from altruism to selfishness. In observing conflicts that have not attracted much international interest, such as those over pastoral activities in East Africa, there have been violent cross-border contacts among communities in the countries of Uganda, Kenya, and Tanzania. Again, the implications of this have been profound. In West Africa, the multiple conflicts involving natural resources resulted in the emergence of what may be described as "mobile dissident" groups that operated in Liberia, Sierra Leone, Guinea, and Côte d'Ivoire. The alleged involvement of former President Charles Taylor of Liberia in the sponsoring of dissident movements later earned him a pariah status and an indictment by the international courts. These conflicts have violated the principle of fraternal solidarity among African states upon which expectations and aspirations were envisaged at the time of independence. Even in cases where friendship between states was considered to be time-tested, as between Uganda and Rwanda,[20] disagreements over the control of the resources of the DRC resulted in armed clashes and the support of different armed factions in the country's civil war.

The fifth issue is the nature and extent of human rights concerns raised by these conflicts, which have come in different forms. With the collapse of state structures came wanton destruction of life and property. Innocent civilians were killed in conflicts conducted by actors who do not respect laws governing armed conflicts. Those who escaped being killed had their innocence destroyed through sexual abuses and incorporation into conflicts as child combatants. Another layer of human rights concerns that has come from these conflicts is rooted in environmental human rights violations. Many resource-producing communities have suffered considerable abuses with farmlands irretrievably damaged because of mineral extraction. In many of the countries, human rights considerations emanating from conflicts over natural resources have also underlined the politics of ethnic and racial minorities, as in the cases of oil in Nigeria's Niger Delta and land in Zimbabwe.

The sixth issue is the coming to prominence of a string of external actors in the management of conflicts involving natural resources. Among these are the international NGOs and the development departments of Western European countries. The international NGOs have often worked closely with local NGOs in many of the countries, thus giving the latter's complaints international exposure. Some of the international NGOs have also adopted a name-and-shame policy against those multinational corporations believed to be benefiting from natural resources that have caused untold suffering for people in developing societies. Initially some of the multinational companies were able to ignore the criticisms of the organizations and continue their businesses as usual. The persistence of these criticisms, however, as well as the increase in the number of groups making them, alerted the companies to the potential and actual damages to their images. Consequently, many of the companies have tried to engage the NGOs in dialogues on how to ensure that basic problems are addressed. The international development agencies of Western European countries, on their part, have intervened in some of the conflicts, sometimes aiding local and international NGOs involved in managing the consequences of some of these conflicts. It needs to be added that the coming together of numerous actors involved in the exploitation of some of these resources is beginning to bring positive results, as can be seen in the establishment of the Kimberley Process.[21]

Finally is the impact of key global developments such as the end of the Cold War and globalization. For its part, the end of the Cold War has had a number of consequences. For example, it resulted in a situation in which the arms previously stockpiled by belligerents in the Cold War, particularly those in the former Soviet bloc, were introduced into local conflicts in Africa or in some cases, such as in Somalia, facilitated internal implosion. It also paved the way for regional and subregional actors to assume the roles vacated by the Cold War belligerents. Regional organizations such as the Economic Community of West

African States (ECOWAS) and the Southern African Development Community (SADC) became key actors, while subregional military powers such as Nigeria and South Africa came to the fore of security affairs in their respective regions. Other post-Cold War developments that have affected the nature and scope of natural resource conflicts include the wave of democratization whose influence encouraged some hitherto suppressed groups to raise fundamental questions about governance and the management of natural resources. Globalization, for its part, has resulted in the liberalization of international trade (including illicit trade in natural resource), increased the activities of multinational corporations, heightened the role of private security companies and others involved in resource extraction, and expanded the booming of trade in stolen natural resources and piracy on international waters. Some of the issues listed above have been discussed, even if sometimes in passing, in the ever-growing body of literature on natural resource conflicts in Africa.

Overview of Studies on Natural Resource Conflicts in Africa

Classifying recent studies on natural resource conflicts in Africa is difficult, as most studies cut across different strands, thus ensuring that the existing modes of clear categorization are somewhat insufficient. For the purpose of convenience, however, these studies can be brought under three broad headings.

1. Policy-oriented papers and reports. Three characteristics are common to most studies in this category: first, they are often sponsored projects by nongovernmental organizations (NGOs), development agencies of Western European countries, the World Bank, and other similar institutions; second, they often aim at addressing specific security concerns of targeted countries and/or resource interest; and finally, they are usually short pieces with policy-oriented recommendations. Examples of authors here include Roger Blench, who has examined a number of issues relating to pastoralists and agriculturists in Africa[22] and Mamadou B. Gueye, who discusses conflict and alliance between farmers and herders in parts of Senegal.[23] Others on specific natural resources include Peter Gleick, who considers the role of water,[24] and Mark Bradbury, Simon Fisher, and Charles Lane, who investigate pastoralism and land conflict in Tanzania.[25] Some NGOs and international development agencies have also undertaken periodic publications focusing on natural resource conflicts. In addition to Global Witness, whose sole preoccupation is the subject at hand,[26] other NGOs that have discussed recent resource conflicts in Africa include Human Rights Watch,[27] Conciliation Resources,[28] and the International Crisis Group (ICG),[29] to mention a few. The London-based International

Institute for Environment and Development, and the Diamonds and Human Security Project in Canada, have also made valuable contributions.[30] Also worth recording under this heading are reports sponsored by the United Nations on African conflicts that have a bearing on natural resources, especially the UN's Panel of Experts on Violation of Security Council Sanctions against UNITA, widely known as the Fowler Report of 2000 and the 2001 Panel of Experts Report on the "Illegal Exploitation of Natural Resources and Other Forms of Wealth of the Democratic Republic of the Congo." Although controversial in some aspects of its details, this report reviewed the activities of a broad range of actors involved in the war in the DRC. UN agencies, particularly the UN Development Programme (UNDP), have also published a number of policy papers.[31] On the whole, what threads through most of the studies is the desire to look at the causes of many of these conflicts and the attempt to offer policy recommendations to stem the illegal exploitation of these resources, especially by outside agents. Very rarely were all the ramifications of resource governance deeply considered beyond the occasional references that mismanagement has been a key issue in many of the conflicts.

2. Literature that focuses on natural resource conflicts and politics in specific countries. In most cases, research in this category identifies conflicts with natural resource underpinnings and discusses their causes, scope, and contents. With the increasing number of these conflicts in Africa, there has been a remarkable increase in the number of these studies as well, including articles in the newspapers of countries affected by these conflicts. Some of the studies in this category take a holistic view and address issues that are common to several countries in particular regions. These include land ownership disputes in West Africa; agro-pastoral conflicts in East Africa; water, land aridity, and conflict in the Horn of Africa and its immediate environs; as well as ethno-racial land distribution controversies and potential water crisis in southern Africa. Apart from specific problems peculiar to some areas, conflict-prone regions and countries have received particular attention. On the Horn of Africa, a major study by John Markakis looks at conflicts over natural resources in the region.[32] Studies on Nigeria, Angola, Liberia, Sierra Leone, and other countries have concentrated interest on resources peculiar to each country, such as oil in Nigeria,[33] oil and diamonds in Angola,[34] rubber and timber in Liberia,[35] diamonds in Sierra Leone,[36] and land in Zimbabwe.[37] In most cases, interests have been on the causal role of resources in the conflict and how resources have fueled and sustained wars. However, some of the studies have considered efforts at resolving the conflicts. An example of the latter is Ben Cousins' essay, "Conflict Management for Multiple Resource Uses in Pastoralists and Agro-Pastoralists Contexts."[38] The World Bank project on the role of economic considerations in conflicts has also cut across both causal and resolution factors in the relationship between natural resources and conflict.[39] The

approach adopted by many of these studies is to look at the specific country and provide analysis of the nature of the conflict. While in some cases references are made to the nature of governance and how this relates to the conflict, very rarely are detailed analyses made to consider the interrelated nature of the domestic and external variables of resource governance.

3. Studies that discuss natural resource conflicts as part of the post-Cold War security challenges. Some of these studies have focused largely on the actors that have emerged (or reemerged) with the changing nature of natural resource conflict. Among other points, the focuses of these studies have been on the activities of warlords, mercenaries, youths, and the unfolding patterns of the conflicts. The key authors here include William Reno, John Mackinlay, and William Shawcross (on warlords), David Shearer, Abdel-Fatau Musa, Kayode Fayemi, Funmi Olonisakin, Jakkie Cilliers, and Peggey Masson (on mercenaries), Abdullai Ibrahim and Paul Richards (on youths), Jeff Herbst, David Keen, and Mats Berdal (on the unfolding patterns of these wars, especially the motivation).[40] Although discussions and critiques of all these studies are provided in the next chapter, a summary of their arguments is provided here to highlight how well they situate the position of natural resource governance in their analysis of the subject. The writings on warlords have placed attention on how local potentates have exploited the natural resources under their control to prosecute wars that further ensure their personal wealth and consolidate their grips on political power. On mercenaries, interests have been on the reasons for their renewed activities after an initial lull. The studies on the dimension of youths in conflicts observe reasons behind their participation, such as the nature and scope of the underlying social deprivations and the socioeconomic ramifications of child combatants. For their part, studies analyzing the unfolding patterns of these conflicts tend to consider the reasons behind the brutal manifestation of the wars. In summarizing the arguments of the studies vis-à-vis the important role of natural resource governance in the explanation of conflicts over natural resources, it can be mentioned that while most of them recognize the important role of governance, they did not make much attempt to bring together and co-consider under a single framework all the issues relevant to natural resource governance. Consequently, most of the writings have succeeded in identifying some aspects, without bringing together all the multiple variables that link governance to natural resource conflicts.

Objectives and Structure

This book is primarily about conflict. The main objective is to stress the importance of natural resource governance in understanding the complex nature of natural resource conflicts in Africa. In this attempt, the book identifies and discusses interconnected themes among natural resource governance and conflicts in Africa especially since the last decade of the twentieth century. Apart from its focus on natural resource governance, this study also differs from most of the existing studies on the subject in that it is a broad survey of the themes of natural resource conflicts in Africa and not exclusively focused on specific country or region. To undertake this broad survey, natural resources are categorized into four groups: land (including agricultural practices and animal stock), solid minerals, oil, and water. Themes linking these resources to governance and conflict are then identified and examined with examples drawn from countries in the continent. This approach has the advantage of offering considered conclusions based on comparative discussions and analysis. Another consideration that underlines the preference for this approach is my belief that academic writings may never be able to keep pace with the dynamic nature of most of these resource-centered conflicts. More often than not, events in a country or region selected as a case study would have changed (sometimes significantly) before associated studies are published. Consequently, it may be more helpful to discuss the broad themes such conflicts evoke, bearing in mind the domestic and international dimensions, rather than merely focusing attention on single cases whose dynamic nature is at best indeterminate.

The remainder of this book has seven substantive chapters, which come in three clusters. Chapters 1 and 2, which form the first cluster, set the theoretical, contextual, and geographical backgrounds for the book. Chapter 1 discusses working definitions and scope of the two operational terms—*natural resources* and *conflict.* This is then followed by a discussion of the attempts to link the two topics and a conceptualization of natural resource governance. Chapter 2 considers the role of geography in the manifestation of natural resource conflicts, looking specifically at the interplay of the factors of politics, geography, and natural resources in Africa. Such a background sets the contexts for future discussions in proper geographical, geopolitical, and socioeconomic analysis. In the main, the chapter investigates the crucial question of which country has what natural resource and in what quality and quantity. In conclusion, the chapter addresses the crucial question of whether there are specific geographical peculiarities that make Africa predisposed to natural resource conflicts.

Chapters 3, 4, 5, and 6 form another cluster. In each of these chapters, key natural resources are identified and their links to conflict are discussed. Chapter 3 assesses the relationship between land and conflict against the background of political, economic, and spiritual importance of land. In this process the complexities of conflict surrounding pastoralism and agro-pastoralism are also analyzed. The conflicts surrounding solid minerals are discussed in chapter 4. This chapter is set against the controversies surrounding the conflicts in this category, as they relate to the activities of mercenaries, international regulatory policies, sanction considerations, and alleged links with international criminal gangs. Chapter 5 focuses on the conflicts involving oil, situating them within the context of the dominant influence of the resource on the politics and economy of the endowed states. Also, the chapter considers the increasing international interest in the environmental consequences of oil extraction and its contribution to the conflict situation. In chapter 6, water as a natural resource is reviewed as a factor engendering conflict, considering both the internal and the external ramifications of the conflicts. Other issues identified include the potential impacts of climatic changes, the problems associated with the construction of dams, and the modes of management of international waters that have been linked to potential conflicts.

The final cluster is made up of chapter 7 and the conclusion. Chapter 7 identifies possible factors that explain the nature of resource conflicts in Africa, especially their increase and brutal manifestations in the last decade. I look at the relevance of governance apparatus and the extent of the viability of civil society to natural resource conflicts. It discusses issues such as concerns for ethnic, racial, and gender minorities and the creation of structures that can address issues emanating from the management, ownership, and control of natural resources. Additionally, the weakness of the state in addressing key issues such as the conflict between local claims and national interest as well as the clash between international control and the local demands of natural resources as the core of many natural resource problems in Africa is analyzed. The concluding chapter summarizes the arguments of the book and glimpses into the long future of natural resource-based conflicts in Africa.

1

NATURAL RESOURCES AND CONFLICT IN AFRICA

FRAMEWORK FOR UNDERSTANDING A LINKAGE

Violence . . . is generally not a product of "ingrained" hatreds . . . but of a complex web of politics, economics, history, psychology and a struggle for identity.

Nicholas Hildyard

Africa's conflicts are diverse, complex and intractable, and it is difficult to generalize about them. One feature these conflicts have in common is that they tend to erupt in countries with limited scope for action by citizens to call their leaders to account.

Alex de Waal

Although conflicts with natural resource underpinnings have historically engaged academic interest, efforts to draw thematic links between natural resources and conflict are of comparatively recent dating. Indeed, one of the earliest efforts to draw a link between natural resources and factors that predicate conflict was Malthus' warning on the possible implications of natural resource scarcity that could come from overpopulation. The Malthusian philosophy dominated attention for generations and was to be the precursor of many subsequent writings on the subject.[1] Furthermore, that Malthus' writing came during a period when two opposing schools of thought—mercantilism and revolutionary utopianism—dominated European thinking about population enhanced its importance. The pursuit of concerted theoretical linkage then experienced a lull, only to recommence in the last few decades, largely because of the increase in the number of conflicts over natural resources.

One conclusion that seems to have emerged from most studies on natural resource conflicts is that local peculiarities and idiosyncrasies influence the ways in which natural resources intertwine with conflict. Issues such as geography, cultural traits, access to external influences, and most important, structures of governance, are some of the considerations that have an impact on the ways in which natural resource conflicts are expressed. In societies with weak socioeconomic and political structures, especially in the developing world, the link between natural resources and conflict is often connected to the state, whose responsibility it is to manage the resource endowment and to prevent conflicts. Consequently, any detailed study of a relationship between natural resources and conflict must be put within the contextual focus of the locality it hopes to address. This is what I attempt to do in this chapter, and I have four objectives: first, to put both *natural resources* and *conflict* in contextual focus; second, to investigate the circumstances under which both concepts have been linked or could be linked; third, to discuss the contents and context of natural resource governance and how it serves to explain conflicts over natural resources; and fourth, to situate the entire discussion within the context of post-Cold War Africa.

I advance three major arguments that are in line with the central thesis of this book. First, the existing methods of linking natural resources to conflict are narrow and have consequently been inadequate to address all the major strains of the problems created by the conflicts over natural resources. In this regard, I argue that any attempt to seek better understanding of this category of conflicts in Africa must discuss the ways in which natural resources are linked to the *causes*, the *prolongation*, and the *resolution* of conflicts. Second, I argue that technology, and the extent and nature of it, are crucial factors in understanding the ways through which natural resources are linked to conflicts in Africa, and that the relative weakness of technological advancement in Africa has served to explain the pattern and nature of some of the conflicts. Finally, I contend that governance is central to how natural resources become linked to conflict.

Contextualizing Operational Terms: Natural Resources and Conflict in Perspective

In its origin, the word *resources* means life. As Vandama Shiva has noted, its root is the Latin word *surgere*, which presents the image of a spring that continually rises from the ground. Like a spring, therefore, a resource "rises again and again, even if it has repeatedly been used and consumed."[2] Consequently, the concept highlights "nature's power of self-regeneration and calls attention to her prodigious creativity."[3] With the advent of industrialization, however, this principle changed and, gradually, natural resources began to lose their creative powers. They were later to become mere materials in the hands of human beings desperate to make them economic tools, with very minimal consideration for their continuity.

Natural resources have many ramifications, all of which cannot be fully discussed in this book. Discussion in this section is limited to some of the aspects of natural resources that are relevant to this study. Four of these have been identified: the definition of what constitutes a natural resource, the classification of natural resources, the evolution of natural resources in economic theory, and the process of natural resources. Concerning definition, attempts to define what constitutes a natural resource have always been of considerable concern to its students, probably explaining why no definition has yet attained wide acceptability. What seems broadly acceptable to all is the fact that a natural resource constitutes a functional relationship between man's want, his abilities, and his appraisal of his environment.[4] With the politics of natural resource management occupying an increasingly prominent position, there is a need for its students to go beyond broad conceptualization and to provide a working definition of how the concept is taken in a given study. In this book, I define natural resources as all non-artificial products situated on or beneath the soil, which can be extracted, harvested, or used, and whose extraction, harvest, or usage generates income or serves other functional purposes in benefiting mankind. Included in this are land, solid minerals, petroleum, water, water resources, and animal stock. Although there are resources not covered by this broad definition, for example, solar energy and wind, their exclusion can be justified on the grounds that they are not resources that are tangible, even if their impacts are noticeable. Consequently, they can hardly be linked to violent conflicts, especially in developing societies, which is the focus of this book. Also left out of the definition are human beings. Here again, the exclusion can be explained on the grounds that human beings exploiting these other resources are the very subject being discussed.

Many attempts have been made to classify natural resources. Perhaps the best-known attempt is by Judith Rees, who classifies natural resources into two broad categories: flow or renewable and stock or nonrenewable.[5] The flow resources are those that can be naturally renewed within a short time, such as plants, water, and animals. The process of renewal may either depend on human activity or on natural processes. The stock resources are those with fixed supply. In all cases, resources in this category have been formed over the course of many years and are often believed to have reached the peak of their availability. Resources here include solid minerals, oil, and land. This division is not watertight, however, as there are cases in which lines have been crossed. For instance, as Richard Lecomber has noted, fossil fuels, which under the above categorization would fall under "nonrenewable," can, indeed, be renewed, but at such a slow rate that may be ignored. The same applies to minerals, which despite being categorized as "nonrenewable" can be recycled.[6] But there is yet another way of classifying natural resources, which I propose to add to the existing ones, especially because of its relevance to governance. This also separates natural resources into two categories: those essential for human existence, hence, described as existence-dependent; and those whose importance is limited to making life comfortable for human beings, and as such, categorized as comfort-dependent. In the first category are resources such as water and land, while the other category comprises resources such as oil and solid mineral resources. This categorization, like others before it, may have its limitations, but it is particularly relevant for the focus of this book, as it will help to explain some aspects of the linkage between natural resources and conflict.

The process of natural resources can be described as the transition from its natural state, through the period of its first contact with man, to its final stage. This is particularly important in appreciating the politics that often surround the management of natural resources, as every stage of this process contains ingredients of conflict. Ian Simmons has identified four approaches in the study of resource process.[7] First, there is the economic approach, which follows the basic economic principle of supply and demand. The focus is on how societies match supply of resources to the demand for them. The primary issues at stake are the market forces, and emphasis is on the continued growth of production to meet increasing population. A second approach adopts an ethical dimension, judging how man ought to use the biosphere. Every element of nature is seen as having economic, cultural, or aesthetic value. The third takes a behavioral approach, looking at the sociocultural traits and psychological impulses that cause different societies to make use of its resources in different ways. The final approach is ecological, seeing each resource process as a set of interactions between the biotic and abiotic components of the biosphere. It operates on the assumption that man's manipulation of these systems has repercussions in the natural environment, and there are limits that should not be crossed without causing serious imbalance in nature.

The place of natural resources in economic theory needs to assess the extent to which governance has been taken into account in the theoretical underpinnings of these discussions. Broadly, natural resources have featured in the evolution of economic theory in two phases: classical and neoclassical. The *classical economists* were those who wrote on the subject in the eighteenth and nineteenth centuries, a period of industrial revolution and increased agricultural productivity in Europe and North America. Among the key scholars were Adam Smith, Thomas Malthus, and John Stuart Mill. A common feature of these writings is their perception of natural resources as determinants of national wealth and growth. Smith, in *An Inquiry into the Nature and Causes of the Wealth of Nations*, argues that in his attempt to employ his capital in the support of domestic industry, every individual unintentionally promotes national wealth. Malthus, as noted earlier, contends that resources may soon become inadequate to meet the demands of the population, while Mill's contention was that land would increase in its value as material conditions improve.[8]

The point of departure between the classical and the neoclassical writers centers mostly on how value is interpreted. Whereas the classical writers saw value as arising from labor power, *neoclassical economists* considered it as being determined in exchange. Geoffrey Kay has identified four characteristics of neoclassical economics. First, it asserts the existence of a universal economic problem, scarcity, which is unaffected by history in the sense that it is the common feature of every form of society. Second, it is predicated on a perspective of social harmony, and it acknowledges that conflicts can arise in practice, with the belief that they are transitory in principle and contingent by nature. Third, it identifies three factors of production—land, labor, and capital; and fourth, it takes the traditional property relations of capitalism as universal and desirable.[9] Among the key economists were Leon Walras, who stressed the efficiency of resource allocation, and Alfred Marshall, who was more interested in providing a framework within which economies can operate.

Another economic theory worth noting here is the Marxian theory, especially against the background of the controversy that emerged during the 1990s as to the extent to which the ideology considers environmental and natural resource issues.[10] In his writing, Marx places labor at the center of the people–nature relations and contends that in its basic material aspects, the labor process constitutes an external necessity enforced by nature.[11]

On the whole, implicit in the term natural resources is man's attempt to prioritize his surrounding and environment. Ciriacy-Wantrup notes that the "concept [of] 'resources' presupposes that a 'planning agent' is appraising the usefulness of his environment for the purpose of obtaining a certain end."[12] Also in line with this position, Judith Rees contends that before any element can be classified as a resource, "two basic preconditions must be satisfied: first, the knowledge and technical skills must exist to allow for its extraction and utilization; and second, there must be a demand for the materials or services produced."[13] The contention thus is that it is human ability and need that create resource value and not the mere physical presence. Erich W. Zimmermann puts this functional dimension succinctly when he argues that neither the environment nor parts of it are resources until they are, or are considered to be, capable of satisfying human needs.[14] In this regard, resources are an expression of appraisal and are thus entirely subjective.

While human needs and the availability of technical skills are primary to determining what constitutes natural resources, a dimension that should be added is what I have described as the "cultural context of resource determination." This dimension of resource politics is often ignored in most efforts to conceptualize the subject, but its importance to the natural resource equation centers largely on how culture determines what is "important" and "useful." What is taken as an important natural resource in certain societies may, under a different cultural setting, be of no economic significance. This cultural context of what determines a natural resource has been a crucial factor in explaining why conflicts emerge over natural resources and the extent of violence often associated with these conflicts.

Putting conflict in context, mankind has always tried to understand conflict, with efforts focusing on its causes, manifestations, and the mechanisms for resolution. The subject has not particularly lent itself to easy conceptualization. Nonetheless, one major conclusion that has emerged in this search is that a considerable amount could be deduced from prevailing socioeconomic and political realities against which conflicts occur. It is possibly against this background that efforts have been made to conceptualize conflicts through the geographical location of their occurrence, for example, Middle East conflict, European conflict, African conflict, or in time perspective, such as ancient conflict, mediaeval conflict, or Cold War conflict. Implicit in all this is that location and time do have impacts on the manifestation of conflict.

Not all the ramifications of conflict can be discussed here, hence, attention is focused on aspects of the subject that help illuminate discussions in this book. Three aspects have been identified: the definition of conflict, the difficulties inherent in categorizing conflict, and the levels of conflict. In defining conflict, most scholars have now agreed that two factors are central to all definitions. First, there is a presupposition of the existence of at least two different units, with agreement that something differentiates them. These units may be individuals, communities, or countries, and the demarcating factor may be personality, ethnicity, geography, nationality, race, religion, ideology, or a combination of some of these. The second is the existence, or perceived existence, of incompatible interest. Two definitions that highlight this are those by Francis Deng and Michael Nicholson. Deng defines conflict as "a situation of interaction involving two or more parties, in which actions in pursuit of incompatible objectives or interest result in varying degrees of discord. . . . The principal dichotomy is between normally harmonious and cooperative relations and disruptive adversarial confrontation, culminating at its worst in high intensity violence."[15] Nicholson, for his part, argues that conflict occurs when there is interaction between at least two groups whose ultimate objectives differ.[16] Subsequently, these groups become involved in mutually opposing and violent interactions aimed at destroying, injuring, or controlling their opponent.

Hugh Miall lists four criteria that distinguish conflict from other situations: it can only exist where the participants perceive it as such; there must be a clear difference of opinion regarding values, interests, aims, or relations; the parties may be either states or "significant elements of the population" within the state; and the outcome of the conflict must be considered important to the parties.[17] In addition, in the case of internal conflict, Miall contends that the outcome must be of great importance to the whole society and political or legal solution must be impossible, so that violence becomes the last resort.[18] While most of Miall's arguments may be valid, the point that violence comes after political and legal solutions have been exhausted seems contentious, as it is not always the case that conflicts occur only after political and legal solutions seem impossible. In some cases, in fact, the solutions may not have been attempted. Thus, contrary to his claim, it is not so often that violence comes only as "a last resort."

In categorizing conflict, two main approaches have been adopted. First, it can be categorized by casualties or intensity, grouped by degree of conflict:

Minor conflicts, in which battle-related deaths during the course of the conflict are below 1,000; Intermediate conflicts, in which more than a 1,000 battle-related deaths are recorded during the course of the conflict, and where 25 to 1,000 deaths have occurred during a particular year; and Wars, in which more than 1,000 battle-related deaths have occurred during one particular year. I disagree with this categorization on three grounds. First, it does not consider casualties in relation to the population. To categorize as "minor" a conflict that killed almost nine hundred people in a population of ten thousand is an obviously flawed analysis. Second, it makes it impossible to categorize conflict until it has ended—only after which the casualty figures can be estimated. Thus, as the duration of conflicts cannot be predicted at the outset, categorization may have to be postponed indefinitely. Third, it does not consider the impact of technology on conflict. It is possible that official casualty figures might be low whereas the conflict might witness a massive display of technology in ways that give indications of a major conflict.

The second approach at categorization is through causes, for example, ethnic conflict, religious conflict, natural resources conflict, or border conflict. This seems to be a more common form of categorization, and the advantage it has over the first method is that it can easily be pronounced from the beginning of the conflict. Its main disadvantage, though, is that conflicts are sometimes caused by complex and multiple developments, such that identifying the causal factor becomes complicated.

In discussing levels of conflict, four levels have been identified: societal, communal, interstate, and interpersonal. Conflicts over natural resources are fought on all these levels. In this book, conflicts are grouped into five levels: (1) those among communities/groups within the state; (2) those between communities across national borders; (3) those between communities and central governments; (4) those between communities and multinational corporations; and (5) those between governments. It needs to be pointed out from the outset that overlaps can occur in this categorization, but the division can assist in identifying some of the complex ramifications through which natural resource conflicts are expressed in Africa.

Because of the devastation associated with conflicts, the tendency has always been to regard conflict as unnecessary. This tendency has underlined some of the negative interpretations that have been made with regard to violent conflicts. Although living in a situation devoid of violent conflict is desirable and in some cases preferable to war, Mark Duffield has noted that war is not necessarily an "irrational or abnormal event,"[19] but rather, as David Keen has opined, could result in the emergence of alternative systems of profit and power to replace the breakdown in a particular system.[20] Lewer, Goodhand, and Hulme also reinforce this in their analysis of the Sri Lankan war, noting that war destroys as much as it creates new forms of social capital.[21] The validity of these assertions becomes clearer when natural resources are discussed in their relation to conflict.

Linking Natural Resources and Conflict

One point that should preface any attempt to establish a link between natural resources and conflict is an appreciation of the profound controversy among many disciplines as to which one would hold the ultimate "say" on both subjects. For several decades, the study of natural resources was taken to be part of geography and its affiliate disciplines such as geology, ecology, and demography. With the late 1950s introducing a decompartmentalization of disciplines, however, the study of natural resources became sliced into a number of other disciplines, ranging from environmental and soil sciences to civil engineering and hydrology. It was not until the 1960s that social sciences made a forceful entrance into the debate, with the argument that natural resources and the ramifications that surround them are inextricably intertwined with social issues. Consequently, social scientists argued that the so-called scientific facts offered by the science-based disciplines are less relevant than the societal-based interpretations that disciplines such as economics, sociology, anthropology, and law can offer.

The study of conflict, too, has experienced a similar fate. Traditionally held in the confines of historians and political scientists, a broad spectrum of other disciplines subsequently emerged to challenge this position of dominance. The impact of technological advancement on the ways in which wars are conducted further reduced the monopoly of the traditional disciplines on the study of conflicts. Disciplines historically considered remote to the subject now argue, quite justifiably it would seem, that a transdisciplinary approach is needed to tackle the complexities involved in understanding conflict. One of the conclusions of the multidisciplinary approaches to the study of both natural resources and conflict is that getting a theory that would cater for the numerous disciplines connected with both subjects has proved difficult.

In the last few decades, efforts to link natural resources to conflict would seem to have come in two major phases. The first discusses the subject under the broad theme of the environment and security whereas the other brings it under the discussion of what may be described as the "Economics of Conflicts."[22] The first, which links natural resources to conflict under the environment and security theme, had its origin in the global acknowledgment of the need to take security beyond its exclusively military scope. One of the earliest proponents of this thought is Robert McNamara who, in *The Essence of Security,* published in 1968,[23] takes the focus of security beyond the narrow confines of its politico-military axis. But one of the earliest to specifically identify the environment as posing a security threat during the period was Richard Falk.[24] Once made, this position immediately gained more disciples, resulting in a plethora of studies on the subject in the 1980s and 1990s. Among the scholars who gave the subject attention during the period were Arthur Westing, Barry Buzan, Caroline Thomas, Susan Carpenter, and W. J. D. Kennedy. Westing calls for an expansion of security to include demands on natural resources.[25] The best-known scholar of this approach at reconceptualizing security, especially during the 1980 decade was, however, Barry Buzan. In *People, State and Fear,* published in 1983,[26] Buzan opines that security, as it is often discussed, is narrow, and he then identifies the environment as one of the neglected indices of the subject. This study was to become a seminal text, such that another edition taking cognizance of post-Cold War developments was published.[27] Buzan's recognition of the importance of the environment was later followed by other scholars, including Caroline Thomas,[28] Susan Carpenter, and W. J. D. Kennedy.[29]

The interest in environmental security continued into the 1990s, when most of the studies were either subtle warning or unambiguously apocalyptic. A few of these are worth mentioning. David Wirth, for example, argues that instability and conflict could characterize the relationship between states if environmental changes shift the regional or global balance of power.[30] Peter Gleick's position is that access to resources is a proximate cause of war.[31] Jodi Jacobson contends that population explosion and the ultimate stress on land may produce environmental refugees, which can affect domestic, regional or even global stability.[32] Peter Wallensteen claims that a sharp drop in food production could lead to internal strife, especially in the developing countries.[33] Ted Gurr is of the opinion that environmental changes could cause gradual impoverishment of societies in both the north and the south which, in turn, could aggravate class and ethnic cleavages, undermine liberal regimes, and spawn insurgencies.[34] Thomas Homer-Dixon notes that environmental scarcity does cause conflicts, which tend to be persistent, diffuse, and subnational.[35] What most of these have in common is their incorporation of natural resource issues under a wider discussion of the environment.

Efforts to assess the impact of environmental stress on conflict have attained greater prominence in recent years because of the involvement of International Development Agencies in security and the desire by western countries to assess long-term security threats coming from environmental changes in developing societies. Among the development agencies that are looking at the impact of environmental stress on conflict is Britain's Department for International Development (DFID) which, in March 2002, published a policy-oriented paper on the subject.[36] A number of research institutes are also engaged in the study of the subject,[37] while there is also the U.S. Central Intelligence Agency's (CIA) project looking at the impacts of environmental stress on security. One noticeable feature of these projects and initiatives is that the interests are geared toward how changes in the environment affect security and not particularly on how ownership, management, and control of natural resources are linked to conflict.

While studies on environmental security may have contributed significantly to the body of literature, scholars have also identified major gaps in its argument. What seemed inherent at the root of the environmental security thesis is the assumption that environmental scarcity causes conflict. Jon Barnett sees this neo-Malthusian theory as being based on the ethnocentric assumption that "people in the South will resort to violence in times of resource scarcity."[38] According to him, rarely, if ever, is the same logic applied to people in the industrial North. Furthermore, it is the case that the environmental security school seems more concerned with how changes in the environment affect security and less on how natural resource management is linked to conflict.

The second phase in the linkage between natural resources and conflict came around the 1990s, and it witnessed a set of literature that can be brought under the general heading of the economics of conflicts. Some of these owe part of the interest they generate to the effects of globalization, which turned attention to the changing nature of conflict. While it is impossible to mention all the studies in this group, a broad categorization can be attempted. For convenience, these studies can be brought under four headings. First, there are studies looking at the devastating consequences of the continued pressure on the environment, sometimes linking the pressure on the environment to the consequences of the Structural Adjustment Program (SAP). Of these studies, one of the best known, if even controversial, is Richard Kaplan's "The Coming Anarchy."[39] Drawing conclusions from a research trip to a number of West African countries, Kaplan warns that poverty, hunger, diseases, and excessive strain on the environment pose a danger to the future stability of the region. He further forecasts that the undermining of central governments and the environmental, social, and political stress would lead to state collapse, with "armed bands of stateless marauders [clashing] with private security forces of the elites."[40] Kaplan's thesis immediately attracted heavy criticism. While his position that the socioeconomic and political developments in West Africa required concern was not contested, his initial conclusions, grounded on data many alleged as not being representative, have been little accepted, thus contributing to future milder conclusions.[41]

Studies in the second group look at how natural resources come into play in fueling conflicts. The focus here rests on the core assumption that the economy of war inevitably involves the management of natural resources, and that these resources are often involved in prolonging conflicts. Among the African conflicts that have attracted attention in this respect are those in Angola, DRC, Liberia, and Sierra Leone. These studies are some of the most rigorous of all post-Cold War discussions on Africa's resource conflicts. The natural resources reviewed in these cases are those with international interest and significance, notably oil, diamonds, and gold. Some of the key authors in this group include Paul Richards, David Keen, Jakkie Cilliers, and Paul Collier. Paul Richards focuses on the role of the youths in their fight for natural resources in Sierra Leone, seeing the civil conflict in the country as a "crisis of modernity" caused by the government's failure to provide employment for educated youths.[42] Keen takes a closer look at how economic motivations underline the actions of factions in civil conflicts,[43] and concludes, coining a phrase from the famous Clausewitzian concept, that "war has . . . become the continuation of economics by other means."[44] Although his focus is not entirely on natural resources, Keen identifies how natural resources have influenced conflicts, discussing, among others, the role of warlords and how natural resource endowments have been used to prosecute war. He argues that the depletion in external financial support after the Cold War has forced many of the Third World countries to look for internal means of generating funds, a tendency that has put more pressure on the environment and propelled further conflicts. Although the choice of his case studies is global, many of his examples are from Africa.

Jakkie Cilliers sees resource conflicts in Africa as a new type of insurgent wars.[45] In his words, "the concept of resource war should be treated as a recent development within the theoretical framework of general insurgency warfare."[46] He thinks that the subject would be better appreciated if it were added to the four types of insurgency earlier identified by Christopher Clapham.[47] He further identifies four factors, which serve to enhance the importance of resource wars as a new type of insurgency. These are "the increased importance of the informal polity and economy in Africa," the "continued weakening and even collapse of a number of African states," the "effect of the end of the Cold War itself that has forced sub-state actors to develop alternative resource form," and the "increased internationalization and the apparent universal salience of economic liberalization."[48]

Paul Collier's position is undoubtedly one of the most controversial. He argues that resource conflicts are caused more by greed than by grievance.[49] Using quantitative research, he contends that the main cause of conflict is the "silent force of greed" and not the "loud discourse of grievance."[50] Collier's position has attracted responses from several quarters, especially for its downgrading of the genuine ground on which many have had to go to war to seek better management of their nation's natural resources.[51] The greed versus grievance thesis also ignores the important role of charismatic leadership in the pursuit of conflicts linked to natural resources. For example, the fact that the war in Angola ended almost immediately after the death of Jonas Savimbi, when, in fact, there still existed opportunities for greed on the part of National Union for the Total Independence of Angola (UNITA) leadership, further invalidates the greed versus grievance thesis.

In the third group are studies on warlords. These are those individuals who, through sheer force of personality and charisma, get people under them to fight for a cause and, in the process, exploit natural resources under their control for their personal benefit.[52] The activities of warlords have attracted attention in recent years. Three of the scholars here are William Reno, Mark Duffield, and John Mackinlay. Reno's initial contribution to this debate was to look at how warlords exploit the natural resources under their control to consolidate their economic and political grip on their territory, and how this encourages the war and increases intransigence to peace moves. This focused mainly on Liberia, the West African nation that engaged in civil conflict between 1989 and 1998.[53] Possibly building on this, Reno later published his study on warlord politics in Africa.[54] With attention focused on four countries—Liberia, Nigeria, Sierra Leone, and Zaire—he claims that the "politics of patronage are turning into sovereignty-begging warlordism." The ability to establish and foster relationships with international organizations and global markets are some of the issues of concern to Mark Duffield.[55] He also contends that there are leaders, who, in the ways they have attempted to de-bureaucratize the state and embrace free markets, have adopted strategies similar to warlords.[56] Mackinlay, on his part, takes a panoramic view of post-Cold War warlord activities and concludes that the international community is not equipped to cope with the growing strength of these emerging actors in global politics. He identifies the main motives of warlords, listing ethnic survival, political ambition and personal gain as the key factors. It is under this that he places discussion of natural resources. Another scholar who has devoted attention to the activities of warlords is William G. Thom, even if this is sandwiched in among other considerations. He notes that in recent civil conflicts across the continent, especially Liberia, Somalia and the DRC, warlords have made economic considerations their primary objectives, going as far as targeting food aid brought in by relief agencies.[57]

In the fourth group are studies on mercenaries, euphemistically described in some circles as Private Security Organizations (PSOs). As is to be expected, the line has been drawn between those who are opposed to the activities of the mercenaries and those who offer tacit forms of support by arguing that they are either indispensable under the prevailing post-Cold War security situation in Africa, or actually beneficial. One of the earliest studies in recent years is David Shearer's *Private Armies and Military Intervention.*[58] As the work was published about the time mercenary activities were attracting attention, particularly with the activities of the South African Executive Outcome and British Sandlines in Sierra Leone, this work received considerable interest, notably in the United Kingdom.[59] Although Shearer's work is an overview of the activities of these "Private Armies," considerable attention is given to the link between the armies and natural resources. He identifies some of the private armies involved in vital resource-centered conflicts in Africa and concludes that the armies are bound to continue their "importance" in the years ahead. Others, including Kevin O'Brien and Herbert Howe, have argued along the same lines. Concluding that mercenaries will remain in Africa for some time to come, O'Brien attributes this to three factors: first, the pecuniary consideration, since mercenary companies pay more and offer better financial prospects than regular soldiers; second, the extent of professionalism, which according to him puts mercenary companies at advantage; and third, the need to get armed forces to fill a gap created by a neglect of conflicts outside western foreign policy concerns.[60] Howe, for his part, also seems to argue along the line of inevitability and indispensability, contending that the experience of Sierra Leone has shown how mercenaries can turn the tide of battle at a minimal financial and military cost.[61]

Opposed to this school are those who believe that mercenary activities in Africa are more complex than can fit them into the easy conceptualization adopted by the direct supporters. Two of these are Funmi Olonisakin and Laurie Nathan. Olonisakin opines that mercenaries are morally indefensible because of the financial cost they impose on the states they claim to assist, especially in the pressure on a country's natural resources, and because they can only provide temporary protection, as conflicts intensify after their departure.[62] Nathan contends that the absence of control—executive, parliamentary, public, legal, international, and internal—in the activities of mercenaries signals more danger to security than it purports to solve. Although he notes that some of these organizations have come up with a lot of confidence-winning proposals, this falls short of effective control.[63]

While all the studies discussed above have touched on aspects of natural resource conflicts and have drawn major thematic conclusions on the links between conflicts and aspects of resource politics, they have not attempted the establishment of theme that will bring together different aspects of resource issues to conflict. To address these conflicts, a holistic view is needed of the circumstances in which people use natural resources and are affected by socioeconomic and political variables, which can alter the supply of, or demand for, natural resources.

In seeking a more holistic way of linking natural resources to conflict, I argue for a way of making the linkage in three ways: as a *cause* of conflict, as a factor in *prolonging* conflict, and as a means of *resolving* conflicts. This proposed method offers a more comprehensive linkage that brings out the importance of governance.

In discussing natural resources as a cause of conflict, three interconnected considerations readily come out. These are the quantity and quality of availability; the politics of ownership, management, and control; and the process of extraction. The quantity and quality of availability centers mainly on the extent and the quality of the natural resource and the demand it is supposed to meet. This can be linked to conflict in a number of ways, but perhaps the most profound is scarcity. Here, scarcity is taken as "the ratio of the human demand for the resource to the environment's ability to supply it."[64] In the last three decades, students of international relations have directed attention to two kinds of scarcity: "shortages stemming from the physical limits of the earth's resources; and an uneven distribution of wealth."[65] On its part, the politics of ownership, management, and control deals with how natural resources are managed by the state, and some of the issues that arise are among the most profound causes of resource conflicts in Africa. The final part in the link between natural resources and the causes of conflict focuses on the complexities arising from extraction processes. This is the method through which the natural resource is processed to benefit human beings. Until recently, not much attention was given to the link this process has with conflict. However, interests are being generated with the consequences of extraction becoming more profound

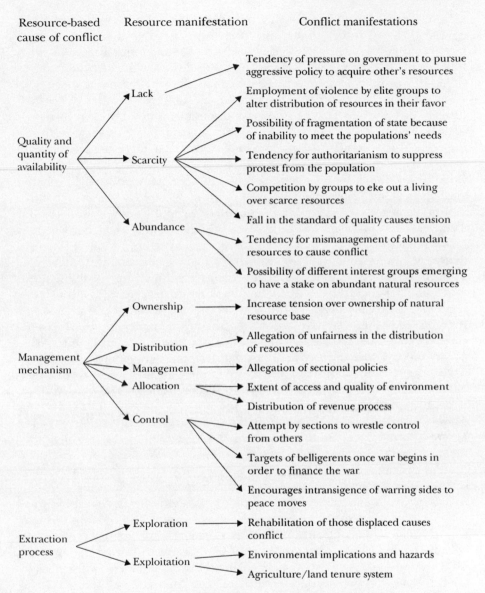

Figure 1.1 Natural resources and the causes of conflict. Created by author.

in terms of conflict, and with concerns increasing among local and international NGOs. All the discussions above will come out more succinctly later under the discussion on natural resource governance, but figure 1.1 depicts the multidimensional links between natural resources and the causes of conflict.

In discussing how natural resources can be linked to the prolongation of conflict, it needs to be pointed out from the outset that this seems to be a most important issue in post-Cold War Africa. A number of ways can be identified as the link between natural resources and the fueling of conflicts. The first is through the provision of revenue to sustain conflicts, perhaps the best-known linkage between natural resources and the prolongation of conflict. Indeed, this is where the importance of diamonds comes into play in recent African conflicts. With the end of the Cold War removing superpower funding for African conflicts, warring groups have had to resort to alternate means, and getting funds from the natural resource sites they control has provided one of the best opportunities, as in the cases of Angola, DRC, Liberia, and Sierra Leone. The second way is through the fierceness in wars to control natural resource sites. The desire to control regions endowed with natural resources has always increased the determination with which warring sides prosecute wars, resulting in an increase of casualty figures. In all major conflicts, the location of natural resources has always been a prime target for warring sides, and battles fought over these sites are often some of the fiercest. An example that quickly comes to mind here is the struggle for the control of the mineral-rich Kisangani in the DRC between the forces of Uganda and Rwanda.[66] Another example can be seen in Angola, where the northeastern provinces of Luanda Norte and Luanda Sul, the location of the country's diamond deposits, were among the most highly contested sections of the country during the civil war.[67] The third way is through intransigence to peace moves, with warring sides in control of resource-endowed sites becoming more likely to be belligerent to peace initiatives. Jonas Savimbi's UNITA in Angola, Charles Taylor's NPFL in Liberia, and Foday Sankoh in RUF in Sierra Leone provide good examples of this.[68] The fourth way is through the increase in the number of local stakeholders. Across the continent, once there is an outbreak of a conflict that has a bearing on natural resources, local stakeholders usually emerge, aiming to maximize their interests through benefiting from natural resources. To a large extent, this is what underlines the entire problem of warlordism, which has become a key feature of many recent conflicts. Examples of conflicts in which local stakeholders proliferated because of natural resources are those in Liberia and DRC. And the final way is the motivation it provides for external interests and interventions, especially from the neighboring states, Mercenaries, and International business interests, especially multinational corporations.

As a means of resolving conflicts, natural resources have recently come to play major roles. The extent of this is determined by three factors. First, the role natural resources had played in the actual cause of the conflict may be a factor. Here, chances are high that the resolution of the conflict will only come after an acceptable understanding has been reached, either voluntarily or through coercion, between the warring factions on the management of the resource(s) in question. A recent example of this is diamonds in the Sierra Leone conflict.

Second, the extent of the devastation the conflict has caused to the natural resource base of the country may be a consideration. It is to be expected that in cases in which there has been a massive environmental destruction during the course of conflict, the resolution may have to factor in the repairs of damages caused by the conflict. This can be found in aspects of the efforts to rebuild Liberia. The third factor is the nature of external involvement in the mediatory process. The nature of external involvement is also important in determining the role natural resources can play in the resolution of conflict, especially in cases in which an external mediator has sufficient power and/or goodwill to impose restrictions on the management of natural resources by warring factions in a conflict. An example of this was the role Britain played over the future of land management in Zimbabwe during the resolution of the country's war of liberation in 1978–80. Although this was to create complications in future years, Britain was able to impose some conditions on Zimbabwean nationalists regarding the issue of land in postindependence Zimbabwe.[69] Natural resources have come to play a part in implementing peace processes after conflicts. This is often the case where there is the need for some form of management control over the natural resources to ensure the survival of a peace agreement. The latest example of this was in Sierra Leone where, to ensure the survival of the July 1999 Lomé Agreement signed to end the civil war, the rebel leader, Foday Sankoh, was made the chairman of the commission managing the country's mineral resources.[70] The expectation was that by putting their leader in charge of the country's main natural resource, the rebels would allow the peace agreement to stand. It was also assumed that the rebel leader would be able to get his fighters to respect the terms of the agreement. These assumptions were to fail woefully, and the implications were to make some analysts to flaw the peace agreement.[71]

Also worth recording as one of the ways through which natural resources have assisted in resolving some of the recent conflicts in Africa is the empowerment it has given to some of the countries in the region to intervene in resolving conflicts in neighboring states. Perhaps the best example here is Nigeria and its involvement in resolving the conflicts in the West African subregion, especially in Liberia and Sierra Leone. While there are many reasons for Nigeria's involvement in these conflicts, crucial to explaining the nature and extent of the country's commitment is the wealth coming from its oil, a resource whose extraction is also important in illuminating another neglected aspect of the linkage between natural resources and conflict—the role of technology.

Technological Interfaces

How technology comes into the discussion of conflicts over natural resources is a subject that is often overlooked in academic literature, and yet, many aspects of this interface are crucial to appreciating complexities involved in the subject, including its linkage to the governance of the natural resource sector. In this section is a discussion of aspects of this interface that are particularly relevant to the discussion in this book. Broadly, there are four issues that are identified for discussion.

First, imperfection in the use of technology for exploiting natural resources can lead to conflict. This tendency is particularly prominent in developing societies where the process of extraction has resulted in considerable environmental hazards. The whole controversy here also brings to the fore other allegations and counterallegations as to the extent to which multinational corporations involved in resource extraction are deliberately exploiting the absence of clear environmental, health, and safety regulations in many of the developing countries, allowing them to use inferior technology they know is likely to cause environmental problems. One conflict that illustrates how imperfection in the use of technology for resource extraction has caused conflict is in the Niger Delta of Nigeria, where oil-producing communities have raised questions about the appropriateness of the technology being used for oil extraction in their environment. Although the details of this is provided in chapter 5, it can be highlighted here that environmental hazards coming out of the process of extraction is a crucial issue in explaining the incessant conflicts in the Niger Delta. The absence of a clearly stated mechanism to address this problem is clearly indicative of a defective management of the natural resource sector.

Second, the level of technological advancement is a strong determinant of how some natural resources can be associated with conflict. In some societies, technology has advanced to the level where specific actions that can lead to conflict over some natural resources are no longer possible, while in others, the relatively backward level of technology has made the same natural resources a major cause of conflict. For example, many of the conflicts involving pastoralism in Africa are because pastoralists move around with their stock in search of water and grazing lands, thus making them trespass on land belonging to other communities. However, the level of technological advancement in Western European countries makes such a practice unnecessary, thus eliminating one of the most important sources of pastoralist conflicts.

Third, the nature of technology involved in extracting a particular natural resource will determine how it can lead to conflict and the factors that can emerge in the cause of such conflict. In a situation where the technological requirements are basic, there is likely to be a proliferation of actors, as compared with those in which considerable technological expertise is required in the process of extraction. The link between diamonds and conflicts in Africa brings out succinctly this point. The nature of diamond reserves in Sierra Leone—the alluvial type—is such that it does not require much technology to mine. This is different from the diamonds in Namibia and South Africa, which is kimberlite and thus require considerable technology to process. The ease with which diamonds can easily be mined in Sierra Leone has made it attractive to rebel groups who often need just bare hands to become miners, as compared with the situation in Namibia, South Africa, and other places where a degree of technological sophistication, often beyond the capacity of ad hoc rebel groups, is needed before diamonds can be used to further personal objectives.

Finally, disagreements over the level of technological skills required for the management of natural resources can be a major cause of conflict. In this situation, there are often clashes between local communities who believe they should be employed to undertake certain tasks in the process of extraction and the multinational corporations who often argue that the technological skills required to undertake the specific task are beyond the capability of the locals. As will be shown later in this book, this is one of the complexities involved in the dichotomy between local claims and international involvement in the politics of natural resource control. Again, a conflict that brings this out succinctly is the situation in Nigeria's Niger Delta, where the demands by the locals for greater participation in the process of oil extraction are often met by the multinational corporation's claim that the technological skill is beyond them. This, in a way, raises the issue of how societies in Africa see natural resources and conflict. But regardless of all the various ramifications in the linkage between natural resources and conflict, central to all analysis seems to be the importance of natural resource governance.

Natural Resource Governance and Conflict

Because of its centrality to the argument that threads through this book, a definition of what is meant by natural resource governance may be in order. In this book, I take the term to mean all the internal and external considerations that come to play in the management of natural resources. These include domestic laws, constitutional provisions, cultural practices, customary laws, neo-patrimonial practices, and all the international treaties and obligations that govern issues such as the ownership, management, extraction, revenue sharing, enforcement capacity and the procedures for addressing concerns and grievances over natural resources. The central argument of this book is that how these are effectively and judiciously addressed will determine the extent to which a particular natural resource will cause or inflame conflict. I argue that it is the absence of an effective natural resource governance structure that accounts for conflicts over natural resources. In short, it is the institutional mechanisms and the political will embedded in the management of natural resources that connect it to conflict, and not the scarcity or abundance or value of a particular natural resource. As will be shown in subsequent chapters, it is the failure of states to effectively integrate all the contents of natural resource governance that is at the root of conflicts. In most African countries, the nature of natural resource governance is either completely defective or is just selectively efficient, with no efforts being made to align many of the structures to other aspects of socioeconomic and political governance. Furthermore, many of the laws governing the management of these resources are sometimes contradictory, while institutions designed to handle the dichotomy between local claims and national interest have been bedeviled with ineffectiveness and corruption.

From the analytical perspective, natural resource governance, as defined above, offers a number of advantages. In the first instance, it dispels the notions and paradox between resource scarcity and abundance in relation to conflicts, arguing that the quantity and quality of resources are less important when compared with the governance of such resources. We need to recognize, and integrate synergistically, the different components, actors, and sources of resource governance. It is, indeed, the case that conflicts in Africa since the 1990s have been related to politics, democracy (or lack of it), and the rule of law in a general, often in a manner lacking specific details, linkages, and dialectical impact. The concept of resource governance fills this gap, as it identifies a specific type of governance processes, structures, and actors that induce or reduce risks of violent conflicts, offering a potential for conflict prevention, management, and resolution. Furthermore, it captures in a holistic manner some practices that have been carried out in the last decade or so on the politics of natural resource management and conflict, including the whole concept of resource management, power sharing, and peace agreement, and takes it further by relating and integrating them—as opposed to extant isolated usages. Finally, natural resource governance as an analytical tool offers a holistic and inter-paradigm framework interrogating the impacts of local, regional, and global actors, processes, practices, and structures in the area that, until now, was thought to be the exclusive preserve of national governments. This brings together a whole range of academic disciplines, including law, political science, international relations, geography, demography, geophysics, sociology, and environmental sciences, in the effort to understand the politics of natural resource management. In other words, while not labeling it as the panacea for all the complexities in the natural resource–conflict interface, natural resource governance as an analytical tool increases and improves understanding and alerts academics and policy analysts to the primary importance of governance in natural resource politics.

Although subsequent chapters will expand this argument, this section sets out some of the key features of natural resource governance and how it intertwines with conflicts. Specifically, there is a discussion of the sources, the actors, and the tools of natural resource governance in Africa. The sources of resource governance in any African country can be divided into three: national, regional, and global. The national covers all the legal and cultural issues that govern the management of natural resources; the regional entails

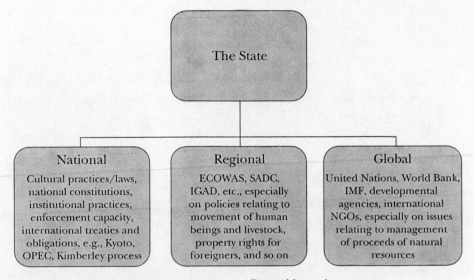

Figure 1.2 Sources of resource governance. Created by author.

the role of international organizations in the conduct of affairs of its members over issues that concern the management of natural resources; while the international covers the activities of key actors such as the World Bank, United Nations, development agencies, international NGOS, and others, on issues relating to the management of natural resources. The diversity of these sources arises because of the inherent superficiality of the typical postcolonial African state, which continues to struggle to find ways of accommodating different modes of governance in the continent. The structure highlighted above is shown in figure 1.2.

Across many African countries, managing the contents of each of these sources has been a problem. I argue in this book that the inability to correctly recognize and fully appreciate the extent of the authority of each of these sources and which takes preeminence in any given context has been at the roots of many conflicts in the continent. It is also the case that some of the conditions imposed by the regional and global sources have been at variance with aspects of local sources. The legitimacy of some of these sources and the difficulties inherent in harmonizing some of their demands have been at the roots of some of the conflicts.

On their part, the actors and players in resource governance can be divided into two sources: domestic and external. Domestic brings together all the local actors (legal and illegal) including the state, warlords, rebel groups, local segment of multinational corporations, local NGOs, and more, while the external collates all the international actors whose activities are central to the management of natural resources in Africa, especially regional organizations,

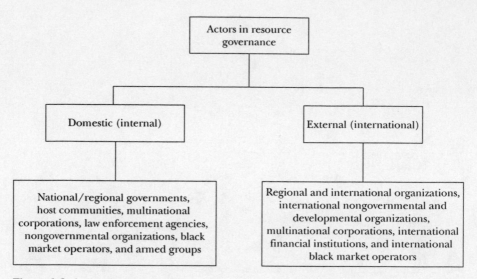

Figure 1.3 Actors in resource governance. Created by author.

United Nations, international arms of multinational corporations, international NGOs, international development sections of Western European governments, and so forth. This is depicted in figure 1.3.

Because the structures of resource governance have not been properly defined and the limits and activities of the actors have not been properly contextualized, all the actors listed above as being prominent in natural resource governance have also been those engaged in the conflicts surrounding these resources. There are sometimes difficulties in having to strike a balance between domestic and external actors, and there are also actors whose activities cuts across the domestic and external continuum.

In the last few years, the complexities of the tools of natural resource governance have been more confusing, especially as they straddled between many tendencies: legal and illegal; internal and external; formal and informal. The fact that many of the conflicts surrounding natural resources have created cataclysmic conflicts across the world has also meant that some specialized tools have had to be considered in the effort to manage these resources. Among the key tools are the use of force by governments and/or UN agencies, as in the cases of Sierra Leone and the DRC; the use of violence by non-state actors, such as rebel and militia groups, as in the cases of Liberia and the DRC; the sabotaging of resource lines as occasioned by the activities of armed groups in the Niger Delta; the administrative provisions for managing extraction and usage; the local idiosyncrasies and other cultural peculiarities of the communities where resources are being extracted; campaigns by NGOs and human rights groups; and the legal sanctions and ban imposed on

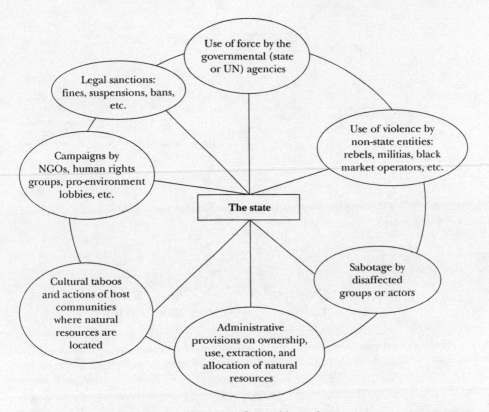

Figure 1.4 Tools of resource governance. Created by author.

individuals and countries, as in the case of Charles Taylor over the war in Sierra Leone and the suspension of Zimbabwe from the Commonwealth of Nations. All of the above, whose impacts will be assessed later in this book, are depicted in figure 1.4.

In addressing how all of these connect to conflict, it can be said that the value, quality, and quantity of natural resources are linked to conflict through the inability of natural resource mechanisms to address key issues such as the controversies over ownership, complications arising from extraction process, problems associated with revenue allocation, the procedures for addressing grievances, and the nature of the enforcement capacity, as depicted in figure 1.5.

But while all the discussions above highlight the importance of natural resource governance, everything still centers on the state, whose responsibility it is to have credible structures in place to handle natural resource governance and conflict.

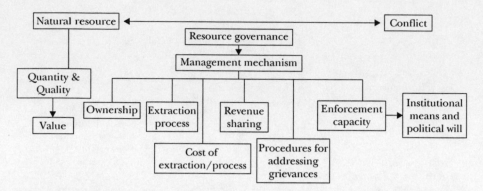

Figure 1.5 Resource governance in the natural resource and conflict continuum. Created by author.

The State, Natural Resource Governance, and Security in Post–Cold War Africa

A considerable amount of studies have been done on the nature of the state in postindependence Africa.[72] Three blurred phases can be identified in the studies on the subject. The first was immediately after independence, during which interest focused on how the state was coping with its newly attained sovereign status, especially amid the complexities of ethnic divisions. The second phase came with studies shifting to the challenges of nation building. Here, the themes that attracted attention include the military intervention in politics and democracy on the continent. The final phase came with the end of the Cold War, when interest switched to issues such as how the state was coping with the severe economic and political strains of the post-Cold War era, including controversies surrounding the governance of its natural resource base. Here, the objective is to provide background information that can guide the discussions presented in future chapters.

Perhaps the most pronounced characteristic of the state in Africa is the somewhat contradictory nature of its structures. On the one hand, states in the continent are weak to withstand some of the challenges of postindependence years, due largely to the nature of the structures they inherited at independence. On the other hand, states in postindependence Africa have strong coercive structures, especially as a result of the governing elites' suppression and manipulation of interest groups.[73] While all countries are artificial creations, African states were created with a myriad of external factors affecting their consolidation. In addition to bringing together disparate groups that had little or nothing in common, even their harmonization as states was further hampered by the complex external interference, including the Cold War.

Efforts to understand African conflicts should heed a note of caution, especially against the background of the ease with which simplistic and single deterministic explanations have been utilized. As Adebayo Adedeji has noted:

> Africa is a vast and varied continent made up of countries with specific histories and geographical conditions as well as uneven levels of economic development. The causes of conflicts in Africa reflect the continent's diversity and complexity. While some causes are purely internal and portray specific sub-regional dynamics, others have a significant international dimension.[74]

For convenience, I have grouped post-Cold War African conflicts into three major categories: communal, between communities within nation states; internal, between armed groups and central governments; and interstate, between different nation-states.

The end of the Cold War reconfigured the nature of global security. One of the most frequently cited manifestations of this change was the increase in the number of intrastate conflicts, as compared with the interstate wars that characterized the Cold War era. Grisly developments in Cambodia, Kosovo, Liberia, and Sierra Leone, to name but a few, left devastating consequences for a world that was expecting peace dividends after the end of the Cold War. One of the characteristics of these wars is their spillover effects into neighboring states. Among others, this emergent pattern of conflict is rooted in

- tensions between subnational groups stemming from the collapse of old patterns of relationships that provided the framework for collaboration among the many ethnic groups in most states;
- disputes over resource sharing arising from gross disparities in wealth among different groups within the same countries and the consequent struggles for reform of economic systems to ensure an equitable distribution of economic power;
- absence of democratic structures, culture, and practice, and the consequent struggle for democratization, good governance, and reform of political systems;
- systemic failures in the administration of justice and the inability of states to guarantee the security of the population; and
- issues relating to religious cleavages and religious fundamentalism.[75]

One reason for the extensive interest in post-Cold War African conflicts has been their devastating consequences on the civilian population, particularly women and children. In these wars prosecuted by armed groups that had no deep root in the populace and as such can afford to ignore international conventions governing the conduct of conflict, the suffering of the civilian population has evoked compassion from the international community. Also included in this display of sympathy are the refugees and internally displaced people. Although Africa has historically produced the world's largest number of refugees, the post-Cold War increase in intrastate conflicts has worsened the situation, thus increasing the pressure on those involved in managing conflicts in the continent.[76]

The downward plunge in the economic fortune of the countries also comes in for consideration in any discussion of the politics of resource conflict. At the beginning of 2000, thirty-one out of forty-two poorest countries in the world were in Africa, and in 1989, only ten out of the fifty-three countries in the continent had a per capita income exceeding US$1,000. The vast majority of the countries in Africa had resorted to loans from the International Monetary Fund (IMF) and the World Bank, with further devastating consequences to their socioeconomic and political lives. Attempts to delineate the origins of this dismal situation have been controversial in trying to disentangle the forces at play in understanding the African situation. While western financial institutions attribute the problems to "flawed economic policies and priorities," "inefficiency," "maladministration of the governments," "misuse of foreign loans," "non-productive development," "extravagant military expenditure," and "civil wars,"[77] African institutions and countries believe this explanation to be insufficient. The Addis Ababa–based Economic Commission for Africa (ECA) argues that also worth noting is the structural rigidity in the terms of trade: "failure to sustain agricultural development coupled with drought problem combined to deepen the dependency of African countries on imported food products; high cost of essential supplies, such as fertilizers and chemicals were depleted by the burden of soaring debt."[78]

Also worth noting here is the democratic status of the countries in Africa during the 1990 decade. The assumption in many quarters is that the 1990s were that of democratic awakening. On the surface, statistical figures support this: while there were just five African countries that could be described as democratic in 1989, the number had increased to twenty in 1998. Furthermore, between 1990 and 1995, "38 of the then 47 countries in Africa held competitive, multiparty national elections."[79] The figures, however, do not tell the complete story, as most of what looks like democratic transitions were mere manipulations by political leaders who recognized that continued international respectability and access to aid and credit would only come if there was an appearance of democracy.[80]

In many post-Cold War conflicts, the role of natural resources has come out quite distinctly, resulting in a catalog of devastating consequences. In their conclusions on southern Africa, which are applicable to the whole of Africa, Sam Moyo and Daniel Tarera identified key environmental problems, which underlie and define security, as:

- the resurgence of unresolved historical claims over land, including natural resources which are embedded in them;

- conflict over the definition, security and realization of rights to land, water and other natural resources; and
- conflicting authority and relations of governance between the state and civil society groupings.[81]

Although most of these conflicts are discussed in the chapters ahead, it may be appropriate to identify the key actors these post-Cold War natural resource conflicts have brought up and to mention how they come into play in the conflicts. On the whole, Africa's post-Cold War resource conflicts have raised six major actors, the distinctions between which are sometimes blurred. These are warlords, multinational corporations, criminal groups, youths, civil society, and governments.

Paradoxically, however, just as the complexities of war have changed, so also has the wish for peace increased,[82] evidenced, among other things, by the increased efforts being made to prevent and resolve African conflicts. Regional organizations, NGOs, and the United Nations have come out forcefully to explore avenues for peace. The total paralysis of governance and breakdown in law and order that have accompanied most of these conflicts have, however, meant that international efforts to resolve them have had to go beyond military and humanitarian tasks to include the promotion of reconciliation and reestablishment of effective government.[83] Another effort at managing conflicts involving natural resources in Africa comes through the activities of the African Union, formed in July 2001 from the former Organization of African Unity (OAU). Indeed, early continental efforts at addressing natural resource conflict in Africa included only broader issues, as in the case of the June 1981 African Charter on Human and Peoples Rights or the 1968 African Convention on the Conservation of Nature and Natural Resources. This trend has changed since the new millennium, with the African Union coming out more clearly on natural resource issues. At the 2nd Extraordinary Session in February 2004, the union had the Sirte Declaration on the challenges of implementing integrated and sustainable development of agriculture and water in Africa and the February 2000 Draft Protocol against the Illegal Exploitation of Natural Resources. Among other considerations, the AU adopted a Common Defense and Security Policy for Africa, and one of the issues included for consideration in the proposed policy is the management of natural resources.[84] The union also established a Peace and Security Council to promote peace, security, and stability in Africa and to promote and encourage democratic practices, good governance, respect for human rights, and the rule of law. Also worth noting here is the formation of the New Partnership for Africa's Development (NEPAD), an initiative for economic recovery and sustainable development of Africa.[85] There are debates as to the extent to which NEPAD can address the challenges of Africa's development, with some people criticizing the initiative because it came more from the leaders without much input from civil society and the population, and because it adopts the same neoliberal approach to developmental problems they believe require radical policy response.[86] Others, however, are of the opinion that the initiative should be given a fair chance, with the hope that it may, after all, provide answers that have so far eluded the continent. Perhaps the most important achievement of NEPAD is the African Peer Review Mechanism (APRM), set up by heads of states and government of NEPAD for those countries willing to be evaluated on what they are doing on good governance. It has seven panel members, with four areas of evaluation—democracy and political governance, corporate governance, economic governance, and socioeconomic development.[87]

Conclusion

In this chapter I have introduced many of the key issues in the linkage between natural resources, governance, and conflict in Africa. In this attempt, I have argued that any meaningful effort to link natural resources and conflict will require a clear understanding of the governance of the natural resource sector and the local, national, and international considerations that form the content of this sector. In Africa, where most national economies are based on the natural resource endowments, and the political institutions are frail, these considerations become more diverse. It is, therefore, not surprising that the link between natural resources and conflict in the continent is multidimensional. I have also shown that the politics of natural resource management in Africa brings together a whole range of actors—few times working together, often times working at cross-purposes, but all times working to protect their own selfish interests in conflicts that are often of zero-sum nature. On the whole, in an attempt to bring forth the conceptual and theoretical links between natural resources and conflict, I have highlighted some special considerations that introduce the peculiar circumstances underlining resource-based conflicts in Africa. This is mainly to provide a background to the discussions provided in subsequent chapters and to enable a clearer appreciation of how some of the resource-based conflicts in the continent have become linked with governance. Before going into the complexities of natural resource governance and conflicts in Africa, however, it is necessary to identify the location, extent, and nature of resource endowment of the continent. This is the main objective of the next chapter.

2

POLITICAL GEOGRAPHY OF
NATURAL RESOURCES IN AFRICA

The Ecology of Natural Resources: This country has all it needs to make it self-sufficient: rich land for agriculture, mineral resources for export; enlightened population; you name it, we've got it. God has blessed us more than many other nations. All we only need to do is to get our acts together.

A Liberian Civil Society Activist

The world's response [to Africa] has been weakened by uncertainty about the nature of the crisis. Is it economic; poor countries unable to make their way in a wicked world? Political: corrupt regimes wracked by civil wars incapable of responding to the most basic needs of their citizens? Environmental: too many people chopping down too many trees, over-farming and over-grazing pastures and causing massive ecological degradation? Climatic: shifting weather systems triggering shifting sands?

Fred Pearce

In discussing conflicts over natural resources in Africa, we need to investigate the role geography plays in the whole equation. This is particularly important because the continent's geographical attributes and limitations serve to explain the causes and manifestations of some of the conflicts. Furthermore, fundamental questions such as whether the continent's natural resource endowments are sufficient for its needs, and whether there are specific geographical features that predispose Africa to natural resource conflicts beyond the crucial issue of governance identified as the key issue in this book, need to be properly investigated. Consequently, in this chapter I look at the political geography of Africa, identifying, among other things, which country has what, in what quality and of what quantity.

From socioeconomic perspectives, African countries belong to those often categorized variously as "developing," "underdeveloped," or "Third World." While the appropriateness of some of these terms remains a matter of academic debate, there is little doubt as to the socioeconomic and political characteristics that underline the terms. These characteristics include low levels of living standards and of productivity; high population growth rate and hence dependency burdens; high and rising levels of unemployment; significant dependence on the extractive sector and primary produce export; and dependence and vulnerability in international relations.[1] Indeed, Africa, has come to symbolize the weakest link in global economic and social discourse.[2]

While Africa has some distinctive geographical features that may predispose it to natural resource conflicts, these limitations are not such that they cannot be managed. I argue that the absence of strong and resilient institutions to address the complexities emanating from the limitations, and the exploitation of the continent's vulnerabilities by local elites and a string of external forces, offer more plausible explanations than geographical limitations. I also contend that although natural resources are not equally distributed among countries, most countries in Africa have sufficient natural resources to meet their needs and cater for their population if the resources are properly managed and equitably distributed.

The Physical Background

The differences emanating from Africa's human and physical environments allow for the misapprehension of the continent. As Lewis and Berry have noted, there are numerous broad categorizations about Africa, few of which are valid when examined within the diverse realities of the continent.[3] Both authors attribute this tendency to the mistake of extrapolating a specific case to represent the entire continent.[4] As noted in the last chapter, this is a mistake that extends to assessments often made about the continent's political situation. Geographically, the entire African continent is large and diverse. Its area of about 30,328,000 square kilometers (about 11,700,000 square miles), makes it the second largest after Asia and about a quarter of the world's land surface. Its shape, however, is the most compact of all the continents, "measuring approximately 8,050 kilometers (about 5,000 miles) from north to south as well as east to west, and being bounded by a coastline which is generally straight and relatively short."[5] Like other parts of the world, its natural resource base has been determined by several million years of climatic and geological changes. Discussion in this section is on Africa's geology, relief, climate, vegetation, soil, and ecological attributes.

In terms of its geology, the larger part of the African continent consists of a great continental shield stretching between the Atlas in the north and the Cape Ranges in the south. Since the end of the Precambrian Era, the African shield has acted as a relatively rigid block.[6] Although it has been subjected to vertical movements and fracturing, it has suffered only slight folding. This description is not to be misconstrued to suppose that the structure of the continent is a simple one. Indeed, it is increasingly clear that the rocks of the African shield bear the impress of several periods of ancient earth movement, though there is now little or no topographic manifestation of these old structures because of subsequent denudation. There are, however, two areas of Africa having folding structures in later periods. These are the Atlas and Cape Ranges in the northwestern and southern extremities of the continent, respectively.

Over vast areas, the basement rocks of Precambrian age have been observed and show that they underlie virtually the whole continent. Basement complex rocks of the Precambrian times are particularly extensive over West Africa and the Sudan, much of East Africa, Zambia, and Zimbabwe. The Precambrian formations consist not only of igneous and metamorphic rocks but also include, in some places, great thicknesses of unfossiliferous sediments. This is usually the situation for solid minerals.

Some series of sedimentary rocks are found in Africa. The most outstanding of these is found in central-southern Africa. This is known as the *Karroo* System, and it is made up of rocks ranging in age from Carboniferous to Lower Jurassic, and it originally covered most of the south-central parts of the continent, from the Cape to the Congo Basin. It has since been denuded from some regions but still attains a thickness of more than 8,000 meters in South Africa. Resting with marked unconformity on the older rocks, the *Karroo* System consists almost entirely of continental sediments that accumulated under conditions varying from glacial to arid and are products of prolonged erosion of the Precambrian Basement Complex. One of the most important economic benefits of the *Karroo* series is that they contain coal deposits, especially in the southern parts of the continent.

Broadly comparable in age with the *Karroo* System are the Nubian sandstones, which are continental formations found in parts of the Sudan. Here, sediments accumulate in broad basins from the Carboniferous to the early Cretaceous. The only marine formations in Africa are of Jurassic and later periods. These formations resulted from flooding of extensive areas by Cretaceous and Eocene seas. In terms of natural resource deposits, these are the bases for petroleum and natural gas and are particularly noticeable in West Africa.

Alan Mountjoy and David Hilling have identified some key themes about the geological attributes of Africa that are important for this book. First, there is still inadequate knowledge of African geology at the local level, and substantial funds would have to be committed into geological explorations if the region is to maximize the benefit from its mineral resources. Second, the importance of the Precambrian basement is enormous in geographical and economic terms as it is the foundation of the continent's wealth. Third, the *Karroo* series are vital for the coal found in the southern parts of the continent. Fourth, the distribution of the Cretaceous marine sediments provides a valuable guide to the existence of oil in the northern and western coastal states.[7]

In terms of relief, Africa as a whole is a vast plateau of ancient rocks. This plateau has an average elevation of 425 meters in its northern part and more than 900 meters in the south. The rise from sea level is accompanied by a succession of escarpments each higher than the previous one until the surface of the tableland is reached. These escarpments often present a very steep face toward the coast. Their existence is one of the basic features in the configuration of the continent. There are also uplands that are usually less than 900 meters, as with Fouta Djalon, while in some cases volcanism has played an important part in the structure of some highlands, such as in the Cameroon and Ethiopia where peaks exceed 3,500 meters. The higher southern division of the African plateau is at its highest and is most continuous in the southeast, as with the Drakensberg where it exceeds 3,000 meters.

It is important to note that in Africa, generally, the folding earth movements of Tertiary times have been largely insignificant in the structure of the continent south of Sahara. It is only significant in the extreme south of Africa where there are some groups of less-relevant folded ranges such as Lange Bergen and Olifants Mountains.

In considering the drainage of Africa, we should bear several fundamental points in mind. The series of terraces and escarpments surrounding the plateau are responsible for waterfalls or rapids on the upper courses of the African rivers. Furthermore, many of Africa's rivers rise on the plateau edges and descend directly to the sea. The characteristically alternate dry and wet seasons of large parts of Africa are also responsible for seasonal flooding. The Great Rift Valley system introduces complexities, which may upset the normal drainage system. Furthermore, these rivers and many others have been harnessed for at least one developmental project at some point in time. Indeed, the Kariba Reservoir on the Zambezi River is one of the largest man-made lakes in the world. In addition, some of these rivers are major tourist attractions on the continent.

In broad terms, the continent's climatic characteristics are extremely important in understanding natural resource location in any environment. Indeed, writing about Nigeria, Reuben Udo made an assertion that is applicable to the whole of Africa: "the climatic factor is significant, not only in relation to its effect on the character of the vegetation, but also because climate has, by and large, played a dominant role in the ways of life, including the pattern of economic activities of the various peoples."[8]

Rainfall is the most important element of climate, as agriculture is the main occupation of the majority of the population. Roughly speaking, five climatic conditions are found in Africa: the equatorial climate, the tropical continental climate, the desert climate, the humid subtropical climate, and the Mediterranean climate. Equatorial climate occurs in areas around the equator, especially in places around the Congo Basin, Guinea coast of West Africa, and the coast of East Africa. The tropical continental climate is prevalent in the interior of West Africa, much of East Africa, and south-central Africa.

Here, rainfall levels are generally lower than those in the equatorial region, and seasonal rainfall, mostly in the second half of the year. Desert climate is more prevalent in North Africa, although sections of sub-Saharan Africa have this climatic condition, increasingly conspicuous by the extent of desertification in the continent. The main features of the desert climate are high temperature and low rainfall levels year-round. Humid subtropical climate is found around the southern African east coast, and its main features are fairly high temperatures year-round, constant rainfall all year, but generally heavier in the summer period. Mediterranean climate is the dominant climate in both the north and southern tip of Africa. It is characterized by dry summers and wet winters, and as a result, is the home of temperate fruit cultivation with many orchards across its landscape.

The climatic conditions discussed above have introduced a number of limitations for Africa. In terms of human utility, the conditions imply high levels of low productivity on the continent. Indeed, as William Hance has noted, Africa leads the world in the extent of dry climates, "possessing about a third of the arid lands of the world and having the highest percentage of any arid lands of any continent except Australia."[9] It has also been stated that precipitation is scanty in about 75 percent of Africa, with water being the principal physical factor limiting advance. Furthermore, about 90 percent of the whole of Africa may be said to "suffer" from at least one climatic condition. For instance, with water, there appears to be an abundance where it cannot be used and paucity where it is needed. As will be shown later in this book, these climatic limitations are linked to some natural resource conflicts.

Vegetation in Africa is quite diverse, ranging from the thick evergreen equatorial forest to that of sparse vegetation units in desert regions. Five categorizations have been identified: tropical rain forest, savannah, warm temperate, mangrove, and desert.

Tropical rain forest, also termed equatorial rain forest, extends from West Africa to the Congo Basin and covers about 10 percent of the total area of the continent. It is also found to the east of Malagasy. Characteristically, this forest is evergreen, usually with three layers. The trees are often very tall, reaching up to 50 meters or more in height with straight trunks. The region abounds in useful commodities such as timber, nuts, fruits, and gums. The nature of this vegetation allows agriculture to be the dominant occupation of the inhabitants, and sets up land to be a major source of conflict.

Close to the tropical rain forests is the savannah vegetation, which varies considerably and consists of tall grasses in clumps interspersed with trees. The wetter areas of the savannah woodland consist primarily of short trees; as one moves poleward the grassland becomes less wooded until the desert margins, at which point the vegetation is made up of thorny scrub. The characteristic trees of the savannah are the giant baobab and various species of *Acacias*, which support some of the largest herbivorous and carnivorous animals. The temperate grasslands are found only in South Africa and are called "veld," where the vegetation consists almost wholly of short grass and low plants. There are two types of grassland in Africa, namely the tropical grasslands, which incidentally surround the equatorial forests, and the temperate grasslands. The savannah (also called tropical grassland) constitutes the most widespread vegetation type on the African continent, covering almost 40 percent of the total area of the continent. Again, the nature of the vegetation makes pastoralism a major occupation in this region.

Warm temperate climate is found to the eastern part of South Africa, where the grass tends to be shorter than in the savannah and where there are fewer trees. Mangrove swamp is found in the fringe of the coasts, with complicated root systems, which is imperative for anchoring the vegetation in the soft mud. This occurs widely along the West African coast, as well as along the coastlines of East Africa, Mozambique, and Madagascar. Desert vegetation is found to a large extent in the northern part of Africa as well as in a small area to the western side of South Africa. There is no continuous plant cover, and many large areas are entirely sparse. There is also mountain vegetation as found in the Ethiopian highlands, East African and Cameroonian mountains, where the lower slopes are forested, diminishing at higher altitudes to make open grassland more characteristic. With regards to human use, a striking factor of African vegetation is the marginal utility of much of it. Only about 30 percent of the entire continent is classified as forest, representing a lower percentage than South America, with a landmass of approximate size.

On Africa's soil features, it should be pointed out that many exercises to classify African soils have been attempted. This section will utilize the traditional classifications. The major soil type in Africa is the characteristically red tropical and lateritic soil, which covers more than one-third of the continent. The major feature of the soil is that it has been affected by a process known as "lateralization." The process of formation of lateritic soils is complex and occurs under conditions of high temperature and abundant soil moisture. Silica is leached downward to accumulate in the lower layers, with oxides of iron and aluminum remaining behind in the surface layers, while appearing to be greatly enriched by the same compounds moving upward from the lower layers during dry periods. Mature lateritic soils are fairly permeable, and the upper clay horizons are not plastic but friable, especially in the dry season. The soil has relatively low humus contents.

Other soil types of Africa used extensively for agriculture include the chestnut-brown and the black soils. The former is situated on desert margins where grass offers a source of humus at its upper layers. The black soils are found across Africa westward from the Sudan to the middle Niger and into a few parts of East Africa and South Africa. The humus content of black soils can be high as well. These soils are usually associated with areas of low relief and are quite fertile for grain crops.

Last, there is the desert soil, which is typically lacking in organic content. The general lack of moisture leads to the soil-forming processes occurring at a slow rate with parent rock exerting considerable influence. Therefore these soils can be utilized only where irrigation is possible.

Moving finally to the continent's ecological attributes, it is noted that Africa consists of many biomes.[10] Although the attributes of each are not summarized here, the generalized descriptions outlined above are enough to show that Africa has many resources. These resources are so diverse that most countries of Africa do not depend on one main resource for their economic survival. The geological and relief attributes provide ground for many solid minerals for which some African countries lead other countries of the world in their production. Vegetation provides different kinds of valuable plants and trees, while it harbors various animals and insects that are of value. Soils are the foothold of various agricultural practices that raise crops for the continent and the outside world. The waters that surround and flow within Africa are of immense advantage to the continent. Not only do these waters provide marine resources of varied kinds, they serve as wells for petroleum in the case of some countries.

In concluding discussion on the physical background, it has been shown that it is Africa's physical condition that determines the nature and location of its natural resource endowment. Specifically, the dominant position of agriculture is determined by the tropical nature of most of its vegetation, while the presence of mineral resources in some parts of the region has been determined by its geology. With the physical presence, the crucial issues thus remain as to how to ensure that productivity is maximized and long-term exploitation made possible. This is where governance comes into the equation. The next section goes into specifics to identify major natural resources in the continent.

Major Resources

Resources in Africa are discussed here under four broad categories: agricultural, animal, mineral, and water. In each of these, there is a discussion of location, the quantity, and, where necessary, their peculiar characteristics.

Agricultural Resources

This is arguably the most important category of resources in Africa, as it is the largest source of labor employment and sustenance. Africa's agricultural resources consist of four main groups of crops: trees, roots, grains, and fibers.

Trees
Tree crops are found mainly in the forest regions of Africa. The crops under this grouping are particularly important as they form the core of the agricultural export in many African countries, which has the following implications

for the state: it is a source of foreign exchange, and its relatively sizeable scale makes it a major source of employment. Although the situation is now changing, for most of the immediate independence period, major agricultural plantations were managed by either foreign enterprise or the central government. Major tree crops include oil palm, raffia palm, coconut, cocoa, kola, rubber, coffee, and exotic timber.

Oil palm, raffia palm, and coconut: These crops are found growing widely along the coasts of Africa. In essence, all countries with coasts that lie within the tropics play host to these crops. Such countries include the Angola, Benin Republic, Cameroon, Côte d'Ivoire, Democratic Republic of Congo, Gabon, Gambia, Guinea Republic, Liberia, Malagasy, Mozambique, Nigeria, Republic of the Congo, Sierra Leone, and Togo. The current tendency is for the tree crops to be cultivated in small holdings by peasant farmers and in large plantations by large-scale farmers and government agencies.

Cocoa: Although cocoa is not native to Africa, the bulk of world production comes from this continent. Indeed, West African countries of Côte d'Ivoire, Ghana, and Nigeria are responsible for almost three-quarters of global cocoa production. Other producers include Benin Republic, Cameroon, Democratic Republic of Congo, Gabon, Sierra Leone, and Togo.

Kola: This is native to Africa, especially West Africa, with producers including Benin Republic, Côte d'Ivoire, Ghana, Nigeria, Sierra Leone, Togo, and in the southern part of Mali.

Rubber: This tree crop is not native to Africa. Its roots originate from South American forests. It is widely cultivated in large plantations in Africa. Key producers are Cameroon, Côte d'Ivoire, Democratic Republic of Congo, Liberia, Mali, Mozambique, and Nigeria.

Coffee: This is indigenous to Africa and has many varieties. It is the most important and widely grown cash crop in East Africa, playing a major role in the economy of many of the countries. Physical requirements determine which countries are successful producers as it can be cultivated only "in or near the tropics, but does not thrive in the hot low-lying parts of the tropics."[11] Producers include Angola, Benin Republic, Burundi, Cameroon, Democratic Republic of Congo, Ethiopia, Gabon, Guinea, Kenya, Liberia, Malagasy, Nigeria, Rwanda, Sudan, Togo, and Uganda.

Exotic tree crops: As a result of the depletion of natural forests and forest reserves, some trees have been introduced into the forest ecosystems of Africa. These are mainly teak (*Tectona grandis*) and pull wood (*Gmelina arborea*). The former is a hardwood whereas the latter is a softwood. They are found in Benin Republic, Cameroon, Côte d'Ivoire, Ghana, Liberia, Nigeria, Sierra Leone, and Togo.

Fruits: Many trees and shrubs produce fruits that are of immense economic value to many African countries. Such fruits include oranges, limes, lemons, figs, mangoes, vines, and almonds. Major producers are Algeria, Ghana, Guinea Republic, Liberia, Libya, Morocco, Mozambique, Nigeria, South Africa, Swaziland, and Tunisia.

Tea: This is an evergreen plant that grows in a hot wet climate and on well-drained hilly land. Producer countries include Burundi, Cameroon, Ethiopia, Kenya, Malawi, Mozambique, Rwanda, Tanzania, Uganda, and Zimbabwe.

Root Crops

These crops are found mainly in the humid tropical areas of the continent. They serve as staple foods for many Africans. The most common of these are the cassava varieties, yam and cocoyam tubers.

Cassava: This is native to South America. It is used for various food, and its leaves are used for soup. It is widely planted in Angola, Benin Republic, Cameroon, Côte d'Ivoire, Democratic Republic of Congo, Ghana, Guinea, Liberia, Madagascar, Nigeria, Tanzania, and Uganda.

Yams: Some yam varieties are native while others have been introduced. In general, yams are planted into heaps and are found in Benin Republic, Burkina Faso, Cameroon, Côte d'Ivoire, Democratic Republic of Congo, Ghana, Guinea Republic, Liberia, Nigeria, Sierra Leone, and Uganda.

Cocoyams: Like certain yam varieties, not all cocoyams are native to Africa; some have been introduced from South Pacific Islands and West Indies. It usually has a number of tubers that are attached to the corm, but they are not as big as yams. Unlike yam, it is not a climbing plant. It is mainly produced in Benin Republic, Cameroon, Côte d'Ivoire, Democratic Republic of Congo, Ghana, Liberia, Nigeria, Sierra Leone, and Togo.

Grains

These are cereals that are established on the continent but are not native. Major types are rice, maize, guinea corn, millet, wheat, barley, and sorghum.

Rice: This has become a dominant food especially in West Africa, and it is cultivated in the forest areas as well as in the flood plains of rivers in the grassland areas. Producing countries are Angola, Chad Republic, Botswana, Burkina Faso, Côte d'Ivoire, Democratic Republic of Congo, Egypt, the Gambia, Ghana, Guinea Republic, Liberia, Madagascar, Mali, Mozambique, Nigeria, Senegal, Sierra Leone, Sudan Republic, Swaziland, and Zambia.

Maize: The origin of maize remains a matter of dispute. It is a chief cereal of both forest and savannah areas, although it is planted to a larger extent in the grassland area. Producers include Angola, Botswana, Burkina Faso, Cameroon, Côte d'Ivoire, Egypt, Ghana, Kenya, Lesotho, Madagascar, Malawi, Mali, Mauritania, Morocco, Mozambique, Nigeria, Senegal, Somalia, South Africa, Sudan Republic, Swaziland, Tanzania, Uganda, Zambia, and Zimbabwe.

Guinea corn and millet: While the origin of guinea corn is uncertain, millet is known to be indigenous. These grains are grown in Botswana, Burkina Faso, Cameroon, Côte d'Ivoire, Egypt, Ghana, Kenya, Liberia, Lesotho, Mali, Mauritania, Nigeria, Niger Republic, Senegal, Sierra Leone, South Africa, Sudan Republic, Swaziland, Tanzania, Uganda, and Zambia.

Wheat, barley, and sorghum are not essentially tropical crops as they do very well in relatively cool climate and high altitudes. These constitute the main ingredients of bread. The cultivation of these crops is done mainly in Algeria, Angola, Egypt, Lesotho, Libya, Morocco, South Africa, Sudan Republic, Swaziland, and Tunisia.

Fibers

The main members of this family are cotton, sisal hemp, and flax. Cotton is an ancient crop common to almost all parts of Africa, except in the dense forest. There are both the native and imported varieties, especially the American Allan cotton. Countries producing cotton include Algeria, Angola, Benin Republic, Burkina Faso, Cameroon, Côte d'Ivoire, Democratic Republic of Congo, Egypt, Malawi, Mali, Mozambique, Nigeria, Niger Republic, Senegal, South Africa, Sudan Republic, Swaziland, Togo, Uganda and Zimbabwe. Sisal hemps are plants used in making sacks and mats of different types. They are cultivated in large quantities in Angola, Benin Republic, Kenya, Madagascar, Tanzania, Togo, and Uganda. Flax is a small annual plant found especially in temperate and sub-tropical regions. Flax seed yields linseed oil while its fibers are woven into linen cloth. The chief producers in Africa are Algeria, Ethiopia and Sudan Republic.

Other Crops

There are some crops that do not fall perfectly within the categories already discussed. These include plantains, bananas, groundnut, sugarcane, sweet potato, tobacco, beans, dates, shear butter, pineapple, and other vegetables.

Plantains and Bananas: These are crops with soft stems with outreached leaves. They are not native to Africa but rather to Asia. Their fruits can be eaten raw or fried into chips while their leaves are used for domestic purposes. The countries producing plantains and bananas are Burundi, Cameroon, Côte d'Ivoire, Democratic Republic of Congo, Ghana, Guinea Republic, Kenya, Mozambique, Nigeria, Rwanda, Sierra Leone, Somalia, South Africa, Sudan Republic, Tanzania, and Uganda.

Groundnut: This is probably native to South America. Although widely cultivated in many ecosystems, groundnut is at its highest production between 8 and 14 degrees north and south of the equator. Groundnut is produced by Angola, Benin Republic, Burkina Faso, Cameroon, Chad Republic, Côte d'Ivoire, the Gambia, Ghana, Malawi, Mali, Nigeria, Niger Republic, Senegal, Sierra Leone, Sudan Republic, Swaziland, Tanzania, Togo, Zambia, and Zimbabwe. Groundnut production is notably diminishing in some of these countries, particularly in Nigeria.

Sugarcane: This is a crop that is specific to riverine soils and often is cultivated in large plantations in some countries. The chief producers are Angola, Egypt, Ghana, Liberia, Madagascar, Mozambique, Nigeria, Niger Republic, Senegal, Somalia, South Africa, Uganda, and Zimbabwe.

Sweet Potato: This was introduced from South America. It is a spreading plant with its tubers originating from nodes that are spread over the ground.

Countries producing sweet potato include Burkina Faso, Burundi, Cameroon, Côte d'Ivoire, Ghana, Guinea Republic, Kenya, Mali, Nigeria, Rwanda, Senegal, Tanzania, and Uganda.

Tobacco: This is widely grown in Africa but is American in origin. It is used in the manufacture of cigarettes. Producing countries include Angola, Cameroon, Côte d'Ivoire, Ghana, Libya, Mozambique, Nigeria, South Africa, Swaziland, Tanzania, Zambia, and Zimbabwe.

Beans: These are a legume and a useful source of protein. They are widely grown in many ecosystems in Africa. Major producers are Angola, Botswana, Burkina Faso, Egypt, Ethiopia, Ghana, Lesotho, Mali, Nigeria, Sudan Republic, and Swaziland.

Dates: These are small, sweet, edible fruits of the palms found in semiarid areas. Dates are nutritious and are either eaten fresh or dried. Large plantations of date palms are situated in Mali and Sudan Republic.

Shear Butter: This is a product of the savannah. It is a major source of domestic oil. Major producer countries in Africa are Benin Republic, Burkina Faso, Mali, Nigeria, and Sudan Republic.

Pineapple: This has been introduced from Central America with many varieties. Countries that produce pineapple are Burundi, Cameroon, Côte d'Ivoire, Democratic Republic of Congo, Gabon, Ghana, Guinea, Liberia, Madagascar, Nigeria, Republic of the Congo, and Rwanda.

Vegetables: There are hundreds of different kinds of vegetables including pepper found in Africa, and all the countries have them. One important aspect of growing vegetables is the dry season cultivation (*Fadama*) along streams, rivers, and swamps.

Animal Resources

Africa has the most significant pastoralist activity in the Third World. In several parts of the continent, where the environment is unsuitable for agriculture, nomadic herding represents the only human activity possible for survival. As with agricultural crops, there are clearly defined livestock zones in Africa. These are primarily determined by the presence of tsetse fly, which is inimical to the rearing of certain species of cattle in the forested regions. Generally, animal husbandry is undertaken on a large scale from about 12 degrees north and south of the equator.

The major animal resources of Africa are cattle, sheep, goats, pigs, camels, horses, donkeys, mules, and fowls. There is also a growing sector in the rearing of bees and snail farming in some of the countries. Countries capitalizing on animal husbandry for export include Botswana, Burkina Faso, Ethiopia, Kenya, Lesotho, Mali, Mauritania, Nigeria, Niger Republic, Senegal, Somalia, South Africa, Sudan Republic, Swaziland, Uganda, and Zimbabwe.

Wild game are found in many of the countries of the continent, serving as a major source of foreign exchange earning in terms of tourism. The degree

Table 2.1 Pastoral activity in Africa

Activity dominant and of high growth potential	Activity significant or possessing moderate growth potential	Activity of limited importance and growth potential
Chad	Algeria	Angola
Mali	Botswana	Central Africa Republic (CAR)
Mauritania	Burkina Faso	Congo
Niger	Burundi	Democratic Republic of Congo (DRC)
Somalia	Cameroon	Egypt
Sudan	Ethiopia	Gabon
	Kenya	Gambia
	Lesotho	Ghana
	Libya	Guinea
	Morocco	Guinea-Bissau
	Nigeria	Côte d'Ivoire
	Senegal	Liberia
	South Africa	Madagascar
	Swaziland	Malawi
	Tanzania	Mozambique
	Tunisia	Sierra Leone
	Uganda	Togo
		Zambia
		Zimbabwe

Source: L. A. Lewis and L. Berry, *African Environments and Resources* (Boston: Unwin Hyman, 1988).

of development of the game reserves for these animals varies from one country to another. However, where the infrastructure has been adequately developed, this constitutes a major issue in the politics of natural resources. Table 2.1 shows a table of pastoralist activity in Africa.

Mineral Resources

Africa is generally considered the birthplace of mining activities. The oldest mining operation to be discovered (approximately 45,000 years old) was in Swaziland. Minerals such as copper, gold, and iron have been in use on the continent from time immemorial. As Europeans began to venture into Africa, they found impressive iron metallurgy.[12] Although a relatively small percentage of the population are legally employed in the mining sector of the economy, mining plays a vital role in the lives of many people in Africa by often being the primary source of wealth that sustains the economy and as such, attracting foreign investment.

Minerals have played a notable role in the history of Africa, particularly in influencing its exploration and economic development. Long before the Europeans came to Africa, many of the minerals were discovered and exploited, albeit in small quantities. Gold was known to exist in Ethiopia, Ghana, and South Africa; tin was also discovered in Nigeria and diamonds in South Africa. These minerals have been presented as a source of possible diversification of economies. Table 2.2 shows the location of mineral resources in Africa.

Table 2.2　Mineral resources in Africa

Natural resource	Location
Bauxite	Ghana, Sierra Leone, and especially Guinea Republic, where approximately one-half of the world's production occurs
Coal	Democratic Republic of Congo (DRC), Ethiopia, Mozambique, Nigeria, South Africa, Tanzania, Zimbabwe
Cobalt	DRC, Zambia
Columbite	Nigeria is the main producer
Copper	Angola, Burkina Faso, DRC, Ethiopia, Mauritania, South Africa, Uganda, Zambia
Diamonds	Angola, Botswana, Burkina Faso, Central African Republic (CAR), DRC, Ghana, Guinea Republic, Namibia, Sierra Leone, South Africa, Tanzania: Of these countries, however, only Angola, Botswana, DRC, Sierra Leone, and South Africa have diamonds in appreciable quantity.
Gold	Burkina Faso, Côte d'Ivoire, DRC, Ethiopia, Ghana, Kenya, Liberia, Mali, South Africa, Tanzania, Zimbabwe
Iron ore	Angola, Cameroon, Ethiopia, Gabon, Ghana, Guinea Republic, Liberia, Mauritania, Nigeria, Niger Republic, Sierra Leone, South Africa
Lead	Nigeria, Tanzania, Zambia
Limestone	Nigeria, Senegal, Uganda
Manganese	Angola, Burkina Faso, Côte d'Ivoire, DRC, Gabon, Ghana, Morocco, South Africa
Natural gas	DRC, Gabon, Nigeria
Petroleum oil	Algeria, Angola, Cameroon, Chad, Congo Republic, Egypt, Equatorial Guinea, Gabon, Libya, Nigeria, Sudan
Phosphate	Angola, Mali, Nigeria, Senegal, Togo, Uganda
Rutile and Ilmenite	Benin, Côte d'Ivoire, Sierra Leone
Salt	Ethiopia, Ghana, Kenya, Mali, Mauritania, Niger, Nigeria, Senegal, Somalia
Tin	DRC, Niger, Nigeria,
Uranium	CAR, DRC, Gabon, Niger, South Africa
Zinc	DRC, Nigeria, Zambia

Water Resources

Rivers and lakes remain the most important source of water in Africa. The region has some of the world's great rivers, some of whose information is provided in table 2.3. Apart from these, there are some areas of inland drainage, where the rivers do not reach the ocean. Examples of these are lakes Chad and Victoria and the Okavango Swamp. Lake Chad is on the boundaries between Chad, Nigeria, and Cameroon. It used to be one of Africa's largest freshwater lakes but has shrunk significantly in the last half-century. It now has an area of 2,400 square kilometers. The well-known floodplain sites include the Sategui-Deressia in Chad, the Yaeres in Cameroon and Chad, and the Hedejia-Nguru in Nigeria. For its part, Lake Victoria is the second largest freshwater lake in the world. Three nations, Kenya, Tanzania, and Uganda share the waters of the

Table 2.3 Major rivers and their connections in Africa

Rivers	Sources	Passing through	Flowing into	Length (km)
Nile	East African Rift Valley	Burundi, DRC, Egypt, Ethiopia, Kenya, Rwanda, Sudan, Tanzania, Uganda	Mediterranean Sea	6,485
Niger	Futa Jallon Highlands	Mali, Niger, Nigeria	Atlantic	4,184
Benue	Adamawa/ Cameroon	Nigeria	Niger	4,160
Congo	Mutumba/ Muchinga Mountains	Congo	Atlantic	4,700
Orange	Drakensberg	Lesotho, Namibia, South Africa	Indian	2,100
Limpopo	Drakensberg	Mozambique, South Africa	Indian	1,760
Zambezi	Mutumba/ Muchinga Mountains	Angola, Mozambique, Zambia, Zimbabwe	Indian	3,520
Senegal	Futa Jallon Highlands	Guinea, Mali, Senegal,	Atlantic	1,641
Kunene	Central parts of Angolan Highlands	Angola, Botswana, Namibia	Atlantic	1,050
Okavango	Central parts of Angolan Highlands	Angola, Botswana, Namibia	Okavango Delta	1,600

lake. Okavango Swamp is a large wetland north of Lake Ngami in northern Botswana. The swamp and the lake are fed by the Okavango River.

Rivers and lakes in Africa serve a wide variety of purposes, some of which are relevant for the objectives of this book. These include the supply of water for domestic, agricultural, and industrial use; water transportation; fishing; supply of hydroelectric power; irrigation; and tourism. A major feature of the rivers in Africa is that their waters are shared among a good number of states. This is especially the case in the Horn of Africa and southern Africa. As will be shown later in this book, water has played an important role in conflict and politics in these regions.

The provision of water for domestic, agricultural, and industrial use is perhaps the most important role. Although the domestic consumption of water in Africa is significantly lower than in advanced countries, obtaining the needed quantity is crucial. This often has been associated with considerable political activity and conflict, especially for landlocked countries and those dependent on a single river with an unreliable flow. The domestic need for water is principally for drinking, cooking, and washing. The industrial uses are important and more pronounced in larger economies such as South Africa, Egypt, and Nigeria. Examples of industrial water use are in breweries and soft drink manufacturers, and in companies processing coffee and sisal, where substantial quantities of water are utilized.

Second in importance is the usage of water for hydroelectric power. By the late 1960s, Africa's dependence on thermal power stations using coal was reduced considerably with the introduction of hydroelectricity. This is generated dynamically through a natural waterfall or by an artificial waterfall created by damming a valley. Many major rivers in Africa have been dammed for hydroelectric purposes. Among the main dams is the Akosombo on River Volta, which was opened in 1966. The damming of the river resulted in the formation of Lake Volta, which is approximately 400 kilometers long and covers 8,485 square kilometers. The construction has provided a source of foreign income for Ghana as it exports electricity to Togo and Benin. It has also made possible the aluminum smelting industry of the Volta Aluminum Company in Tema. A side effect has been the displacement of some 80,000 people, who were residents of the Volta Valley.

There are two dam projects on the Niger River in Nigeria. The first of these is the Kainji Dam, commissioned in 1968, with eight generating units and a total installed capacity of 760 megawatts. The second dam was commissioned in Jebba in 1985 with six generating units producing 578.4 megawatts of electricity. This dam utilizes the outflow from Kainji Dam. Another river, the Kaduna, was dammed on a high point at Shiroro Gorge, close to the confluence of rivers Niger and Diaya. Other hydroelectric power stations are situated on rivers Congo, Niger, Nile, Volta, and Zambezi. The Kariba Dam, on the Zambezi River, is generating electricity for Zambia and Zimbabwe, while the High Aswan Dam, on the Nile, provides electricity for Egypt. The Kouilou

Dam services the Congo Republic while the Kossou and Konkoure dams provide power in Côte d'Ivoire and Guinea Republic, respectively. Hydroelectricity is also generated in many other countries in Africa, such as Angola and Uganda. There are also the Sennar and Jebel Anlia dams on the Lower Nile serving the Sudan Republic and other countries in the Horn of Africa. Most of these dams are also used for fishing, irrigation, and as means of internal transportation of goods and people.

Fishing forms the third use of water. This is a very important enterprise in Africa, as it forms a major component of the diet of the populace. It is, indeed, the cheapest form of animal protein available to the greater percentage of the population, especially in the forest zone where meat is often expensive and in short supply. Fishing is also a major occupation in many coastal territories. There are two main forms of fishing in Africa: inland fishing and the creek and offshore fishing. The former is carried out on the various rivers in the countries of Africa, while large-scale fishing occurs offshore using trawlers.

The fourth use of water is for transport. Generally, water provides the cheapest form of transportation, but rivers in Africa have not proved highly effective as large-scale means of transportation. Falls are problematic; when situated near the coast they prevent connectivity with the sea and otherwise hinder the passage of boats on the inland sections. The Congo River system appears to be the most useful of African waterways with about 10,000 kilometers of route for vessels. The Nile and the Niger rivers are also relatively well used commercially. These rivers are made increasingly navigable throughout the year through the construction of dams that make the water levels stable during the dry season by releasing water stored previously during the rainy season. Residents in areas where there are no easy alternative means of transportation have had to depend on these dammed rivers to engage in commercial activity.

Ocean transport has proved more efficient in its use for import and export activities. Unfortunately, the landlocked countries have not benefited, as the road and rail infrastructures are weak and ineffective. Thus, even after goods have been transported by sea, it becomes difficult to distribute them hinterland. Furthermore, although there are seaports found along the coasts of Africa, many of the seaports are not adequate to berth big ocean liners, hence ships must be anchored in deep sea and have their cargoes offloaded by smaller boats.

Finally, water is needed for tourism. Africa presents a valuable tourism base. The industry provides jobs for a significant percentage of the population that may otherwise have been unemployed. In spite of the negative publicity coming in the wake of political instability and the spread of HIV/AIDS, a significant percentage of external earnings for many of the countries still come from tourism. Rivers and lakes in the region have contributed significantly to this industry. Perhaps the most important of these is Victoria Falls, one the largest natural waterfalls in the world, shared by Botswana, Zambia, and Zimbabwe. There are other smaller falls in places such as Erin-Jesha, and there is a warm water spring in Ikogosi, both in Nigeria.

Population

Africa's population is crucial to understanding some of the complications surrounding its natural resource conflicts for at least two reasons. First, human population is often considered the most important resource available to a nation, especially as it is needed to exploit other natural resource endowments. Furthermore, it is only the human population that can engage in the conflicts discussed in this book. Second, the key issue in resource politics has always been how long the reserve of a particular resource would last in the face of an expanding population.[13] Consequently, this section provides a brief discussion on aspects of Africa's population characteristics that are important to understanding its natural resource conflicts.

With an estimate of more than 600 million people, Africa's population is exceeded only by those of Asia and Europe. Its population growth rate is, however, the highest in the world. Africa's population characteristics raise a number of considerations for natural resource conflicts, three of which are particularly important.

The first is the disparity in the sizes of the countries, with some countries being densely and others being sparsely populated. This factor has had considerable impact on resource conflict involving land. It is perceived that the population density of some of the countries makes them particularly vulnerable to conflict, as in the case of Rwanda, where there are more than 800 people per square kilometer. Also worthy of note is the disparity in population size among countries, for example, Nigeria has about 120 million people in contrast to Gambia, which has just over a million people. This has implications on resource conflicts. For one, it gives some countries considerable clout and power with which to intimidate their immediate neighbors over the management and control of natural resources, principally those along common borders. Furthermore, it results in situations in which more populous countries have higher instances of natural resource conflicts because of the diverse interests they have had to accommodate within their geographical enclaves.

The second population issue regards the nature of internal migration, with people moving from rural areas to cities in search of a better condition of living. Migration has antecedence that goes back to the colonial period. The idea of a colonial capital began with the proliferation of ports created to handle imperial trade. With this, there emerged powerful centers of economic activity that could attract migrant labor. Hence, the development of local ports that could service exports and imports from the metropole as well as serve as colonial administrative capitals ensued. After independence, migrations to these capital cities continued such that, with very few exceptions, the largest city is often the national capital.[14] The overpopulation of capital cities has a number of consequences for resource conflicts in Africa, among which is the neglect of agriculture at the communal levels of many African countries. With the migration came a reduction of the work force that has traditionally gone to agriculture and an increase in the number of those in urban areas who rely on local food production.

The third population concern is the impact of HIV/AIDS on Africans. This presents, perhaps, the most devastating consequence for Africa, with figures showing that the continent has the highest incidence of the pandemic in the world—about 65 percent of all cases worldwide. Indeed, according to the deputy director of the UNDP Regional Bureau for Africa on HIV/AIDS and life expectancy, Elizabeth Lwanga, the rising prevalence of HIV/AIDS has driven the life expectancy in seven African countries (CAR, Lesotho, Malawi, Mozambique, Swaziland, Zambia, and Zimbabwe) below forty years of age.[15]

The prevalence of HIV/AIDS has at least three significant impacts on resource conflicts in the continent. First, there is a drastic reduction in the number of people available to take part in the exploitation of these resources, especially in the agricultural sector where the impact of HIV/AIDS is most prevalent. This inevitably lowers productivity, leading to scarcity of essential agricultural needs. The second arises out of the age bracket often affected by the spread of the virus. Available statistics show that those most affected are those of the ages between twenty-five and fifty, the most productive age group of the populace. The loss of manpower has put greater strain on the supply bases of many of the countries, with devastating consequences for the economy. The third is the impact of the spread of the virus among the military in some of the countries. Although studies to assess the impact of this are still in progress, it is widely believed that the military is one of the sectors most affected by the epidemic in Africa. For natural resource conflicts, the most important implication of this is the depletion in the number of members of the armed forces available for the protection of national security.

Constraints Posed by Geography

Before concluding this chapter, I want to discuss whether there are aspects of the physical location of Africa that particularly predispose it to conflicts over natural resources. The answer to this will clearly remain a matter of opinion, but it is believed that there are some geographical attributes of the continent, which, when considered alongside historical elements, may make it vulnerable to aspects of natural resource conflicts. However, the degree to which this explains the extent of the violence that has attended many of these conflicts is an additional subject to consider. First is the uneven nature of the distribution of these resources. While countries such as Nigeria, South Africa, and the DRC have abundant natural resources, some of the immediate neighbors are not as well endowed. In a situation where colonial boundaries are at best controversial, countries are prone to dispute the inherited colonial boundaries and exploit the possibilities of appropriating neighboring territories, especially when these are natural resource rich. While the oft-cited argument that Africa's boundaries are artificial cannot be overstretched—as, indeed, all boundaries are—the difference with Africa is that unlike in other places where wars have been fought several centuries ago in order to attain near-acceptable agreements on common borders, the relatively recent nature of African boundaries formation implies that conflicts should be expected over mineral-rich borders.

Constraints posed by nature constitute an additional issue. For example, Africa has two of the world's largest deserts—the Sahara and the Kalahari. In recent times, the Sahara Desert has been moving downward toward the humid and fertile portions of West Africa. One of the outcomes of this is that Lake Chad, once one of Africa's largest river basins, has shrunk from about 24,000 square kilometers in the 1960s to just about 2,000 square kilometers presently.

Apart from the deserts, there are parts of African countries where nature adds a paradoxical concept to the unequal distribution of natural resources. For example, while countries like Botswana, Namibia, and parts of South Africa have fairly well-endowed agricultural and mineral resources, they all suffer a lack of water, especially where most needed. Consequently, the industrialized Guateng region of South Africa is forced to import water from Lesotho, whereas the latter, with abundant water resources, suffers a major land shortage.

Another major constraint comes with the extent of population growth. However, the concern here is more for posterity. While the UN projection notes that the present world's population of 6.1 billion will grow to between 7.9 and 10.3 billion by 2050, Africa's population is expected to grow from 631 million in 2004 to about 1.7 billion in 2050, an increase of 170 percent. This projected population growth, however, varies widely with the population growth in some of these countries projected to increase by more than 200 percent by 2050 as shown in table 2.4. It should be noted that the above projection has taken into consideration the negative impact of AIDS.

Next is the extent of the fertility of Africa's land space. Africa is particularly vulnerable to soil acidity, "especially in the rain forest areas and the humid tropics generally."[16] Other climatic conditions affecting the soil include salinity and erosion. Overall, "only 18% of the soil is without major constraints, 25 countries have more than 75% of their soil with some constraints, and 6 (Djibouti, Mauritania, Botswana, Niger, Namibia, and Somalia) have more than 90% of their soil affected."[17] However, as Ian Woodman has noted, this is not unique to Africa, as comparable figures for soil affected by major constraints are 19 percent for Central and South America and 23 percent for Asia and the Pacific. There is also the degradation of agricultural land, where again Africa suffers considerably. Africa has 10 percent of its land affected by degradation, with 7 percent of Asia and Pacific and 12 percent of European

Table 2.4 Population figures of African countries, 2000 and 2050

Country	2000 (000s)	2050 (000s)	% increase
Algeria	30,291	51,180	69
Angola	4,131	53,328	1,190
Benin	6,272	18,070	188
Botswana	1,541	2,109	36
Burkina Faso	11,535	46,304	301
Burundi	6,356	20,218	218
Cameroon	14,876	32,284	117
Cape Verde	427	807	88
CAR	3,717	8,195	120
Chad	7,885	27,732	251
Congo	3,018	10,744	265
Côte d'Ivoire	16,013	32,185	100
Djibouti	632	1,068	68
DRC	50,948	203,527	299
Egypt	67,884	113,840	68
Equatorial Guinea	457	1,378	201
Eritrea	3,659	10,028	174
Ethiopia	62,908	186,452	312
Gambia	1,303	2,605	100
Ghana	19,306	40,056	107
Guinea	8,154	20,711	153
Guinea-Bissau	1,199	3,276	173
Kenya	30,669	55,368	80
Lesotho	2,035	2,478	21
Liberia	2,913	14,370	393
Libya	5,290	9,969	88
Madagascar	15,970	47,030	194
Malawi	11,308	31,114	175
Mali	11,351	41,724	268
Mauritania	2,665	8,452	217
Mauritius	1,161	1,426	22
Morocco	29,878	50,361	69
Mozambique	18,292	38,837	112
Namibia	1,757	3,662	108
Niger	10,832	51,872	379
Nigeria	113,862	278,788	144
Rwanda	7,609	18,523	143
Sao Tomé and Principe	138	294	113
Senegal	9,421	22,711	141
Seychelles	80	145	81
Sierra Leone	4,405	14,351	225
South Africa	31,095	63,530	104
Somalia	8,778	40,936	366
Swaziland	264	1,391	351

Table 2.4 (*continued*)

Country	2000 (000s)	2050 (000s)	% increase
Tanzania	35,119	82,491	134
Togo	4,527	11,832	161
Uganda	23,300	101,524	335
Zambia	10,421	29,262	180
Zimbabwe	12,627	23,546	86

Source: United Nations Population Division.

soil affected the same way. With the problem of dryland, which predisposes the land to desertification, Africa has 38 percent of its territory being dry-lands, with other continents equally or even more affected. North America has 63 percent, South and Central America, 45 percent, Asia and Pacific regions, 38 percent and Europe, 29 percent.[18]

The location in the tropics has brought some consequences, especially as these relate to diseases, and these have had implications for natural resource production. Malaria, which remains one of the largest killer diseases in Africa, schistosomiasis have been known to reduce the workforce available for the proper management of natural resources.

Although not a disease determined by geographical location, also worth noting under a general discussion of the limitations introduced by health considerations is the HIV/AIDS pandemic. All available records show that HIV/AIDS has become the biggest health challenge in Africa. By 1998, AIDS had surpassed malaria as the main cause of death in Africa.[19] Some countries are, however, more affected than others. For example, Zimbabwe and Botswana have been among the worst hit, with adult infection rates estimated at 26 percent and 25 percent, respectively. This has been damaging to development, especially as those often affected by the disease are those in their most productive years, thus further reducing the workforce available to assist in economic development. Much more disturbing in recent years has been the impact on the security forces of many of the affected countries. For example, about a quarter of the police force in Zimbabwe is HIV-positive or has AIDS.[20] Estimates of HIV infection among regional armies include 50 percent in DRC and Angola, 66 percent in Uganda, 75 percent in Malawi and 80 percent in Zimbabwe.[21]

Conclusion

By showing the nature and diversification of Africa's natural resource endowment, I have shown that scarcity and abundance of natural resources are key issues that have always been known in the continent. The fact that nothing has been done to ensure that these two extremes do not result in conflict shows a failure of governance. In debunking the scarcity thesis, I have shown there is considerable natural resource endowment on the African continent to cater for its population. These resources are useful for domestic consumption and, in many cases, vital for the global market. Indeed, in some of these resources, the continent is well-placed to influence events in the global market, especially with a natural resource such as oil. But even the euphoria of abundance, which this may reflect, is, in itself, not a requisite cause of conflict, as there are also significant challenges associated with the management of these endowments that might engender conflicts. On the whole, while I concede there are some geographical characteristics that can prompt the continent to natural resource conflict, I also argue these are neither peculiar to the continent nor are they insurmountable if the structures to govern the management of natural resources are properly instituted and they function effectively. With this, I underline the broader thesis: governance, rather than geographical peculiarities or any other consideration, holds the explanation for conflicts over natural resources in Africa. Perhaps the natural resource that shows most clearly how the problems associated with political governance intertwines with natural resource politics is land, and the next chapter discusses how this natural resource has been associated with conflicts in the continent.

3

LAND AND CONFLICT

Land means everything to us. All our life revolves round it. We cannot fold our arms while other people take our land. To be passive while others are encroaching on our land is like mortgaging the future of our children. Even the ancestors would turn angrily in their graves and rebuke us in no small measures. The implications are just too far-reaching.

A peasant farmer

My country, my government, my party and my person are labeled "land grabbers," demonized, reviled and threatened with sanctions in the face of accusation of reversed racism. . . . but our conscience is clear and we will not go back.

Robert Mugabe

Land is undoubtedly the most important natural resource in Africa. Its importance transcends economics into a breadth of social, spiritual, and political significance. Among other things, it is considered as the place of birth; the place where the ancestors are laid to rest; the place which the creator has designated to be passed down to successive generations; and the final resting place for every child born on its surface. Consequently, every society in Africa sees land as a natural resource that is held in trust for future generations, and the sacredness of this trust lies behind most of the conflicts over land in the continent. What further makes land vital to any discussion on conflict is that it is the abode of most other natural resources—a characteristic that means the controversies surrounding these resources often manifest through conflicts over the ownership, management, and control of land. In recent years, the nature and scope of conflicts surrounding land have been further widened, thus making the conflicts crucial to understanding security and development in Africa.[1]

Reduced to broad generalization, all conflicts over land can be summarized as clashes among "bodies" for "spaces." "Bodies" in this context come in different forms: ethnic or racial groups, local communities, nation-states, professional groups such as pastoralists and agriculturists, gender or age groups, and so forth, while "spaces" are the geographical boundaries within which these "bodies" have to compete for coexistence. This bodies and spaces dichotomy explains some of the features exhibited by conflicts over land, especially their widespread zero-sum nature, their links with governance, the deep interest shown by the elites, and the international dimensions that are sometimes associated with them.

In this chapter I discuss the ways through which land has been linked to conflict in Africa, identifying in the process the themes these conflicts raise and their primary link to natural resource governance. The central argument is that most of the recent conflicts over land in the continent are rooted in the inability of governments to manage the conflicting legacies bequeathed by the different land tenure practices that have existed in the continent over the precolonial, colonial, and postindependence periods, and the determination of governments and political elites to ensure effective grip over the ownership and control of land. These two issues once again, have brought into focus the role of governance in the handling of land conflict.

Conflict Associated with Ownership, Management, and Control of Land

Conflicts under this category are some of the most profound in Africa. Although many of the considerations are interwoven, the conflicts can be traced to nine main sources: problems associated with land scarcity; difficulties arising from conflicting laws governing land tenure; boundary disputes and rival claims to specific portions of land; demands for a review of "landlord–tenant" arrangements over land ownership; complexities arising from racial imbalance in land ownership; the clash of spiritual considerations with political and economic realities; complaints over government's land regulatory policies; complexities of massive human influx; and conflicts arising from land and labor relations. The centrality of natural resource governance in all these cases comes out distinctly as these issues are individually discussed.

Problems Associated with Land Scarcity

Scarcity as a factor in land conflict comes in two forms: natural and artificial. More often than not, natural scarcity comes when overpopulation or other environmental considerations result in an imbalance between the population and the land available for agricultural and other domestic needs. Artificial scarcity arises when forced migration, often arising from land acquisition, leads to overcrowding and reduction in the lands available for agricultural and settlement purposes. Although natural scarcity still leads to violent conflicts, it seems that societies across Africa have accepted, even if with some form of fatalism, the problems associated with natural scarcity. Artificial scarcity, however, is posing far greater challenges, with local communities rising to protest against perceived injustices associated with the forced migration that often follows massive acquisition of land by elites and governments. In some countries, however, the inability to manage scarcity emanating from both artificial and natural circumstances have come together to bring about conflict of cataclysmic proportions.

Rwanda has been cited as one of the most vivid examples of an instance in which complexities associated with land scarcity have been linked to conflict on a genocidal scale.[2] Here, natural and artificial considerations seem to have coalesced. In a recent study on land scarcity in the country, Jean Bigagaza and others have provided statistics that are particularly stunning. Rwanda has an annual growth rate of 3.3 percent and an average of 271 persons per square kilometer, making it the country with the highest population density in Africa. The population density in the rural area is up to 843 persons per square kilometer.[3] Furthermore, 95 percent of the overall population inhabits 43 percent of the total cultivated land. In terms of family holdings, the study also revealed that while the average family held "3 hectares per family in 1949, it reduced to 2 hectares in the 1960s, 1.2 hectares in the early 1980s and 0.7 hectares by the early 1990s."[4] But the problem here was further complicated by elite greed, which would have been prevented if a credible structure for managing land had existed in the country. As of 1984, it was believed that 43 percent of poor families owned 15 percent of cultivated lands, while 16 percent of rich families owned 43 percent of cultivable lands.[5] Rwanda may have presented the extreme, however, a number of other countries have recorded similar experiences, albeit on a much lower scale.

Although natural scarcity of land remains a major issue in Africa and has caused conflicts in some of the countries, it is still not a problem that exists in all African countries, and despite the predictions based on the continent's rapidly growing population, available data do not indicate that natural scarcity would be a general concern for all the countries in the continent. While countries such as Rwanda, Burundi, and Eritrea, where just about all the land suitable for rain-fed agriculture is already in use, may continue to experience problems of land scarcity, the continent as a whole is still in a fairly good shape, even well into the future. Of the 2.4 billion hectares that comprise the total area of Africa, the Food and Agricultural Organization (FAO) estimates that only 7 percent is currently under cultivation, while another 40 percent of uncultivated land is suitable for agriculture. Indeed, for a country such as the Democratic Republic of Congo, only 0.7 percent of land suitable for cultivation is being used.[6] This shows the need to have a credible arrangement in place for managing land in the continent.

Even though academic literature has recorded numerous examples of conflicts linked to natural scarcity, artificial considerations in the causes of land scarcity are now attracting interest, thus increasing the relevance of their recent patterns. One common method that results in artificial land scarcity is for social and political elites to dispossess the less-privileged segments of the society of their land in order to acquire a wide expanse of land for various private uses, notably mechanized farming and the construction of elite private housing estates. For example, an underlying aspect of the conflict in the Nuba Mountains of Sudan was the expansion of large-scale mechanized farming schemes, which resulted in devastating social and ecological effects on the less privileged of the community. While not reducing the importance of the political and ethno-religious considerations in the war in this region of the Sudan, the role of land is now widely recognized as a key factor.[7]

Another contentious land use situation is the acquisition of wide expanses of land in exclusive areas to build private residential apartments for social and political elites. This often forces out the original occupants of the land, moving them into overcrowded areas. Although the practice of preserving exclusive residential areas for elites began during the colonial rule, postindependence elites have furthered and expanded this far beyond pre-independence schemes. Presently, there are very few major cities in Africa where there has not been forceful evacuation to facilitate the construction of residential homes for local elites.

Conflicts emanating from the kind of artificial land scarcity identified above have been fought on two levels. Ironically, the first is often between different segments of those dispossessed of their lands. More often than not, the conflict here is between those who are willing to accept government's directive dispossessing them of their land and those determined to fight it. It is not uncommon for those who want to fight against losing their land to allege that those advocating a pacifist reaction have been bribed by the government. Local clashes are known to have occurred as a result of this. For example, the divergence of opinion over how to respond to Benin government's takeover of some local land around the capital, Cotonou, in 2001, resulted in a minor conflict between the displaced populations.[8] The second level of conflict is between the dispossessed community and the political or social elite group trying to take over their lands. Conflicts come in the form of violent protest and property damage. For example, in Nigeria, there were clashes among local communities whose land was usurped when the Lagos State Government acquired land in the Ajah area of Lagos.[9]

On the whole, conflicts emanating from land scarcity have exhibited a number of features. First, they are often fought at the local level, with warring factions being ethnic or social groups who live together in the same community. Second, in the case of conflicts emanating from environmental considerations that have caused scarcity, the nature and extent of conflicts often vary, depending on ecological and seasonal conditions. It is thus the case that there may not be any conflict over a period of time, when the climatic conditions satisfy the diverse interests of different segments of the population. This implies that the occurrence of such conflicts is unpredictable, and factions often oscillate between harmonious and acrimonious relations. In another situation, conflicts arising from artificial scarcity of land often develop alongside the opposition of the affected population to laws made by the government to acquire land. As I will show later in this chapter, governments across Africa have devised legislation to ensure authority over the control of land. Consequently, land conflicts in this class are often spontaneous, usually ignited by an unexpected court decision or the promulgation or enactment of new laws or decrees. It can be argued that many of the conflicts associated with artificial scarcity are linked to ad hoc arrangements by governments and political elites to use extra-constitutional means to acquire land from local populations, whose sentimental attachments to their land have impressed on them to resist advances by governments and political elites, a tendency that is clearly linked to the ineffectiveness of the nature of natural resource governance across countries in the region.

Difficulties Arising from Conflicting Laws Governing Land Tenure

Discussions here may need to be prefaced with the identification of various laws governing land tenure in Africa. Broadly, these come under three headings: customary, western, and religious.

The customary system is the practice that had been in operation before colonialism, and its principles are still widely respected across the continent. Although local idiosyncrasies may introduce variations, the main characteristics of this system include absence of formal registration of land; predominance of user rights; overlapping of rights, with a single individual or family having the rights, and other members of the family also having some form of control over the land; preservation of land within the clan or ethnic group; and restriction of ownership or control to women. Under this arrangement, traditional institutions handle disputes.

The western legal system came into existence during the colonial rule, and it was formally adopted by most of the countries at independence, with minor modifications to suit national peculiarities. Among the basic characteristics are formal registration of land; exclusivity of ownership; holding of title deeds, and equal opportunity for the population, regardless of gender. The handling of disputes is mainly through the law courts.

The third legal system comes under religion; here, the Islamic jurisprudence is perhaps the only prominent system. Major characteristics of this include strong concept of individual ownership and clear rules concerning transfer and inheritance.[10] As would be expected, the application of these principles is mostly done in countries that have adopted the Islamic legal system, and institutions, such as the Sharia courts, are used to resolve disputes that emerge over land ownership and control under this arrangement.[11]

Recent conflicts coming from the application of the laws identified above can be traced to three sources, all of which are related to the governance of natural resource sectors. The first arises from the objections by sections of the populace to the contents of these laws and the extent to which they are willing to violently oppose them. For example, traditional law governing the ownership of land has been widely criticized for what is considered its gender insensitivity. The restricted opportunity to women is seen as unfair, especially as they form the greater percentage of those engaging in farming. With the emergence of many gender-based NGOs in Africa, women are now encouraged to oppose the discriminatory arrangement, even if it is by peaceful means. Aspects of the western legal system too have been criticized as being subtly discriminatory against women. For example, in many African countries, the Marriage Act does not specify who should own what property in a subsisting marriage. Upon dissolution, there is no provision in the Divorce Act as to how property is to be allocated. Women thus tend to be the losing party on land, which is often their main source of livelihood. In addition, the religious laws have been violently opposed by those who see it as outdated and unrealistic. So, in all cases, there are groups in most of African societies who oppose the principles of these laws, and encourage their supporters to protest, even if not always violently, against them.

The second source of conflict arises from the inconsistencies, contradictions, and corruption in the implementation of the laws. This is due largely to the efforts by elites to manipulate the systems to their advantage thereby perverting the course of justice. Consequently, the local population is inclined to adopt extrajudicial methods to seek redress, especially if they believe that elites have corrupted the judicial process. In order to get the jurisdiction of land out of the control of the (theoretically) independent and formal courts, and thus have greater opportunity to manipulate the outcomes of disputes over ownership and control, governments across the continent have set up ad hoc groups—committees, commissions, tribunals, and such, for this purpose. In some cases, the decisions of these groups cannot be formally challenged in law courts, therefore, the disaffected populace has resorted to extrajudicial ways of seeking redress.

The third source emanates from the multiple adoption of varying law regimes. In most of the countries, there are at least two systems being adopted simultaneously. Apart from the confusion involved in this practice, there is also the problem of which of the laws would take precedence in a certain situation. While it is often the case that the western law takes precedence officially, realities at the grassroots level often give recognition to traditional principles over western. Consequently, a claimant may have "legal" victory in the court without having "social" victory to operate on the land. This incoherent means of law administration in most countries has resulted in situations where land trespassing crimes are committed unwittingly.

On the whole, apart from their linkages with the nature of natural resource governance, most of the conflicts arising from the different laws governing land tenure have exhibited three general characteristics, the first of which is the close link to the extent of the independence and effectiveness of the judiciary, whose role it is to interpret laws, thus clarifying the distinction between social and legal ownership of land. Another is that conflicts are often fought at the local level, where belligerents are, as in the aforementioned case of scarcity, mainly ethnic groups. A final factor is that they are often spontaneous, with elites' sponsorship and encouragement to advance selfish economic and political interest.

Boundary Disputes and Rival Claims to Specific Portions of Land

The conflicts brought together under this heading are those in which two different communities take up arms to pursue their claims to a parcel of land. Broadly, conflicts such as these have been fought on local, provincial, and national levels but, in recent years, the majority of the devastating consequences have been felt mostly at the local level, where the lack of clarity over borders has created conflicts among families, clans, villages, and ethnic groups. At this level, the causes of conflicts include inheritance disagreements, historical rivalry, breakdown in social hierarchies, and boundary difficulties. The increasing number of these conflicts can be explained by the greater interference by governments in local disagreements over land between local communities, while the increasing violence in their construct can be explained through the introduction of sophisticated weapons hitherto unused in African communal conflicts.

Before identifying the themes underlying conflicts in this category, a few recent examples are noteworthy. In eastern Nigeria, two communities—the Umuleri and the Aguleri—were at war between 1995 and 2000 over the control of a parcel of land along their common border.[12] This resulted in the deaths of several hundred people. Also in Nigeria, the Kuteb and the Chamba, in the northern part of the country, engaged in conflict in 1995 over the ownership of land along their borders.[13] Many examples of this type of conflict have also been recorded in Kenya, where the Kikuyu, Masai, Kalenjin, Kissi, and Luo, among others, are involved in interwoven conflicts: Kikuyu versus the Masai, the Kikuyu versus Kalenjins, the Kissi versus Luo, in the coastal region between the Mijikenda and the non-coastal people, and the Kipsigi and Kissi on the Bomet and Nyamira district border in the southwest.[14] Neighboring Tanzania also has a number of ethnic-based conflicts over land ownership, most pronounced in the north, the Kagera region, where the Haya and Sukuma are engaged in internecine conflict. In the south, conflicts exist between African coastal ethnic groups and the Arabs.[15] Other countries that have recorded clashes of this nature, though on a comparatively low scale, include Ghana, where the Gonja and Nawuri were at war in May 1992,[16] and Guinea, where there have been clashes between the Peul and the Soussou.[17]

Changes to land tenure brought about during conflicts can create long-term land ownership problems between different ethnic groups in a community. An example of this can be found in the DRC. During the political upheavals in 1973, emigrating Belgians, who had leased land from the Lendu people, left the land in the hands of their managers, mostly from the Hema ethnic group. Over time, the Hemas secretly registered the land in their names. This sparked off a land dispute in 1998 between the Hemas and the Lendus, with the Lendus rising up in revolt and destroying property belonging to the Hemas.[18] In a retaliatory attack, the Hema militia attacked the Lendus in August 2002 and May 2003. The conflict between the two groups also has wider implications, as it also fits into the Rwandan and Ugandan involvement in the Congolese conflict.[19] Apart from conflict, famine has also been known to create long-term land ownership controversies between neighboring communities, as in the Sudanese famine in 1974–76, which resulted in long-term conflict among a number of communities, notably the Arab ethnic groups and the Fur in the Jebel Marra Massif region.

At the communal level, conflicts in this category have exhibited six major characteristics, all of which again underscore the importance of natural resource governance. First, many of the conflicts are often ignited by issues that may not focus on natural resources, such as politics and socioeconomic relations. Second, they have been heightened by the democratic agitation that became prevalent in the 1990s. This is a further confirmation that political aggregation in Africa is often woven into resource consideration. Third, they are usually difficult to resolve permanently, as sides in such conflicts often hold strongly to the underlying ownership sentiments. Fourth, resolution efforts often bring conflicting judicial mechanisms into play, as the traditional methods often clash with the western judicial system. Fifth, the weapons used in such conflicts almost always include local charms and witchcraft, which may not be recognized in western societies but still hold powerful force in most African societies.[20] Finally, the conflicts are often exploited by local elite for political advantage with an outcome that may reflect less on historical claims than local power politics.[21]

In the countries where this category of conflicts is quite prominent, the impacts of local politics and elite manipulation further show the difficulties inherent in the absence of credible structures to manage natural resources. Kenya and Nigeria present good examples here. In Kenya, the ethnic groups of former President Moi and his one-time deputy, George Saitoti, the Kalenjin and Masai, respectively, allegedly used the advantages of being close to the corridors of power to acquire land belonging to other ethnic groups, especially the Kikuyu, the Luo, and the Luhya.[22] The acquisition of the Kikuyu land shows the irony of power shift in the country. From independence to 1978, when Jomo Kenyatta was the president, his ethnic group, the Kikuyus, was also alleged to have taken over land belonging to other minority groups.[23] As a result, the reacquisition of Kikuyu lands during President arap Moi's tenure was seen by some as a way of getting back land that had been unfairly acquired. With Mwai Kibaki, also from the Kikuyu, now the president, the Kikuyu may well reassert dominance over land, with the Kalenjin experiencing some retribution for the benefits they were accorded under Moi. In

Nigeria, it is believed that the outcome of the conflict between the Kuteb and Chamba has been influenced by the powerful connections the latter have in an indigene, Lt. General Yakubu Danjuma, a retired army chief and former Minister of Defense, who has allegedly manipulated factors to the advantage of his ethnic group.[24] The outcome here is the development of vicious cycles in land conflict due to elite manipulation and the absence of credible structures to manage the resource.

The second level where direct land-ownership conflicts manifest is at the provincial level where, depending on the layers and structures of governance of a country, units like provinces, states, or local government areas clash over the control of land. The disputes are often complex because the units involved are artificial creations, made merely for administrative convenience. Conflicts often arise when groups believe that provincial boundaries have not correctly reflected ethnic and historical realities of the population. This is due to governments' preoccupation with boundary adjustments to satisfy selfish political interests. Also connected with the set of conflicts here is the politics often associated with the distribution of national resources, revenue allocation, and the disbursement of social amenities. In this connection, the objective of the units engaged in conflicts is to attract the attention of central governments, with claims of superior land space and population.

This set of conflicts is common in countries that are constantly making boundary adjustments, as in Nigeria, where there have been six attempts at dividing the states and numerous attempts at creating local governments. In almost all of these exercises, there have been conflicts over land boundaries between communities. For example, in July 2003, there were conflicts between Edo and Kogi states of Nigeria over land, forcing the deputy governors of both states to have a meeting to resolve the crisis.[25] Ebonyi and Benue states also have conflicts of this nature between the Ngbo and Agilla clans, respectively.[26] Another country where attempts to redefine provincial borders has resulted in conflicts is Ethiopia. In May 2002, the government changed the status of Awasa, the regional capital of the Southern Nations Nationalities and Peoples Regional State (SNNPRS), as well as the zonal capital for the Sidama people. The reaction of the Sidama to the transfer of the zonal capital to Aleta Wondo was vigorous and widespread, as the Sidama feared that the change in Awasa's status would have impacts on their rights to the land they had cultivated for decades.[27]

At the third level—national—land ownership conflicts continue to remain extensions of boundary disputes. These have receded considerably following the end of the Cold War, and the few remaining conflicts are often woven around three factors: historical claims, prestige, and control of borderline mineral resources. A widely reported example of this is the conflict between Namibia and Botswana, over a piece of land on their mutual borders—Kasikili to the Namibians, and Sedudu to the people in Botswana. Although tension between the two countries over the land has been ongoing, it gained intensity in the second half of the 1990s. This resulted in both countries moving to the brink of war prior to taking the case to the International Court of Justice, where the territory was given to Botswana in 2001.[28] Another prominent case is the conflict between Ethiopia and Eritrea over the border town of Badme. This was at the root of the war between the two countries that claimed more than 70,000 lives between 1998 and 2000. Ethiopia has rejected the ruling by an independent boundary commission, although the country has ruled out any further war with Eritrea on the disputed land.[29] In December 2003, the UN appointed the former Canadian foreign minister, Lloyd Axworthy, as a special envoy to the crisis.[30] A conflict of a lower profile exists between Kenya and Sudan over a portion of land known as the Ilemi triangle. The land is claimed by Sudan, but it is presently under Kenyan administration, where it has become the natural grazing ground for the Kenyan Turkana herdsmen. Nigeria and Cameroon have debated the ownership of some villages around Lake Chad.[31] Like Botswana and Namibia, both countries took the dispute to the International Court at The Hague, which ruled in favor of Cameroon. Nigeria complied and, in October 2003, more than thirty villages were handed over to Cameroon.[32]

Three characteristics seem to thread through many of the land-ownership disputes at the national level. First, they have reduced considerably in recent years. This is probably because, after more than thirty years of independence, countries in the continent have accepted the boundaries inherited at the time of independence. Second, apart from that of Ethiopia and Eritrea, recent conflicts in this category rarely resulted in outbreaks of war, even though there are often threats of military action. This is probably because African countries have a variety of unifying factors, and there are several fora where disputes among them can be resolved, in addition to the now defunct OAU. For example, Nigeria and Cameroon both belong to the Commonwealth of Nations, while Botswana and Namibia are both members of the Southern African Development Community (SADC) and also of the Commonwealth. Third, there is an increasing role of international mediation, especially the International Court of Justice (ICJ). Many states now present their disputes to the court for arbitration and consequently comply with the decisions of the court, even at the expense of public opinion.[33]

Demands for a Review of "Landlord–Tenant" Arrangements

Let me first define what is meant by "Landlord–Tenant Arrangement" in land ownership. This is a system whereby ethnic groups who resettle in a new abode after fleeing from war or natural disasters enter into some form of agreement with their new hosts. In most cases, this arrangement places the "guests" at the mercy of their new "hosts," and requires the new settlers to pay tribute for the land they occupy. In the past, this was done either by giving a fraction of their agricultural harvest on an annual basis to their hosts or by providing labor on the farms of the "landlord." The tenants were expected to affirm their loyalty to the paramount ruler of the host community on a regular basis. Depending on the arrangement, tenants may be allowed to have a traditional ruler, who would be expected to pay homage and constantly reaffirm his loyalty to the paramount ruler of the host community. The paramount leader of the host community in turn provided land and protection to the new arrivals. This practice was more prevalent in West Africa, where the colonial control of land was less stringent and, as a result, precolonial arrangement of ownership remained largely intact. For most of the time during the colonial era, this arrangement was typically well respected by both sides, though sometimes after an initial conflict.[34]

After independence, demands began to come from the tenants for a review of this arrangement. This was predicated largely on the changes that had come to their social, economic, and political status. These changes ensued from the hard work that the contractual arrangement had imposed, and subsequent generations of the tenants thus acquired wealth and property, often at the expense of their landlords, due to increasing complacency on the latter's part. In addition, the descendants of the tenants had acquired western education. Thus, not long after independence, the level of the socioeconomic standing of the former tenants had improved, both within the community and sometimes in national politics, and, expectedly, they began demanding a review of the old contractual arrangement. Moreover, in many cases, the national political situation placed both sides in different political camps, and in situations where ethnicity often influences politics, political parties have exploited the situation for political gains.

The crux of the tenants' argument is that they have lived long enough on the land to cast off their tenant status and that intermarriages between them and their landlords should transform the relationship to one stronger than the original landlord–tenant arrangement. Often at the vanguard of this call are the youth, many of whom consider with aversion the scorn with which their contemporaries, who are indigenes of the host community, relate with them. The landlords have always rejected the tenants' demands, insisting rather that the contractual arrangement is for life. Paramount rulers of the host communities are often wont to fight to retain control of all tenant territory in order to avoid the unpleasant stigma that control of the land was lost during their reign. Inevitably, this results in serious conflicts over land.

Two recent conflicts have brought out clearly the complications in this arrangement. The first is in northern Ghana, between the Konkomba on the one hand and the Dagomba, Gonjas, and Nanumbas on the other. Under the precolonial arrangement, the Konkombas were settlers, while the other groups were their landlords but, since the 1980s, the Konkombas have been calling for a review of this relationship. They also want their own traditional ruler, having occupied the land for many generations. At the forefront of this struggle is the Konkomba Youth Association (KOYA). The landlords have objected to this, and over time, tension has heightened between the Konkomba and their landlords. There are at least two other considerations that serve to inflame tension. The Konkomba are mostly farmers, whereas their landlords are predominantly herdsmen and, while the other groups practice traditional religion, the Konkomba are mainly Christians—mostly Roman Catholic.[35] The attendant closeness with the church made the Konkombas better beneficiaries of western education.

This tension reached its peak in February 1994, when an apparently trivial disagreement in a marketplace resulted in the killing of a Nanumba woman by a Konkomba man.[36] Full-scale conflict later ensued, leading to the burning of villages, the destruction of property, and the killing of people. Up to 2,000 people were believed to have been killed and about 100,000 people displaced.[37] In response, the government sent in the military force of a two-infantry battalion unit to quell the fighting, and a cease-fire was achieved within two months. The government then set up a permanent negotiation team, which visited the area and made frequent reports to the government on how to ensure harmonious relations between the two groups. A skeletal military presence remained for some time in places like Salaga, Yendi, Kpandai, Saboba, Konkomba, and Bimbilla, with the government still addressing the problems of property ownership and chieftaincy supremacy.

A second example of conflict under this category is that between the Ife and Modakeke people in southwest Nigeria, home of the Yoruba people.[38] Here, the Modakeke people, with ancestral linkage to the Oyo Yoruba, migrated to Ife during the Yoruba civil wars of the 1830s.[39] The reigning *Ooni* (the paramount ruler of Ife) allotted land to the new Oyo arrivals. Alongside tilling their own land, they worked as laborers in Ife villages and, for almost a century, remained loyal to successive *Oonis*, albeit with occasional tensions. Most of the first two decades of independence were also peaceful, especially because the reigning *Ooni* during this period, Oba Adesoji Aderemi, enjoyed tremendous respect from all across Yorubaland and the country.[40] With his demise in 1980, tension began to rise between the two groups, as the Modakeke people began making greater demands. They argued that by the country's Land Use Decree of 1979,[41] all land belongs to the government and as such they saw no further reason for payment to their Ife landlord. Conflicts between the two communities have been recorded as occurring in 1981, 1997, 1999, and 2001.[42]

Although the Ife–Modakeke conflict is essentially over land, its manifestation has come mainly through political differences and disagreement over structures created for administrative governance, especially local government headquarters.[43] During the country's Second Republic, when the first in the series of conflicts occurred, the Ife people belonged to the Unity Party of Nigeria (UPN), the party that controlled the state, while the Modakeke people pitched their camp with the National Party of Nigeria (NPN), the ruling party at the center. Elite politics also served to influence the complications, with the Modakeke people believing there was a deep personal friendship between then governor of the state, late Chief Bola Ige, and the reigning *Ooni*, Oba Okunade Sijuwade. Furthermore, the national leader of the Unity Party of Nigeria and undoubtedly the most powerful Yoruba politician of the time, late Chief Obafemi Awolowo, was perceived as having sympathy for the Ife cause. The Modakeke allegation seems to have some justification, as the two politicians never hid their aversion to the Modakeke cause.

The Ife–Modakeke crisis has a number of important features. First, it shows the complexities that could engulf resource-based conflicts, especially in circumstances where they envelop historical rivalries and politics. Immediately after the lines of the conflict became distinct, the Modakeke people received sympathy from other Oyo Yorubas, including places such as Gbongan, Ikire, Ode Omu, and other neighboring areas. Although these other groups did not take part in the conflict, they provided important psychological support. Eventually, the conflict merged with the historical rivalry between the Ooni of Ife and the Alaafin of Oyo, the two paramount rulers in Yorubaland.[44] Second, the war demonstrates how elite solidarity can continue even in times of conflict, especially when economic interests are at stake. Despite the intensity of the conflicts, local elites were still selling land, using proxies in the opposing side. Ife elites who had plots of lands in Modakeke had informal arrangements with Modakeke elites to sell their land, and the Modakeke elites with lands in Ife were doing the same, with both sides making correct returns for the transaction.[45] Third, the conflict shows that ethnic-centered conflict of this nature manifests more distinctly under democratic dispensation than autocratic military rule. Of the four conflicts, three—and the most devastating— occurred during civilian rule. This is not necessarily because of the relative freedom of expression associated with civil rule but more because civil rule offers more opportunities for political elites to exploit and manipulate ethnic differences for selfish motives.[46] Finally, the conflict benefited from the effects of globalization, as both sides were alleged to have set up websites on the Internet to solicit for financial contributions for arms procurement from their respective indigenes in the diaspora.

There is, however, a way through which this practice of landlords oppressing tenants can be reversed: the former tenants, through the acquisition of power and position, become landowners and subject the former landowners into playing second fiddle. An example of where this has resulted in conflict is in the DRC, where the Hema and Lendu conflict discussed earlier also serves as an example. The Hemas were originally tenants, which is why they were able to serve as farm managers to the Belgians. With the exit of the Belgians and the ascendance to dominance of the Hemas, the Lendus have been dispossessed of the land that originally belonged to them.[47]

Apart from the distinct absence of mechanisms for handling rivalry in ownership claims, recent landlord and tenant land conflicts demonstrate at least five characteristics. First, they are intermittent, with economic and political developments occasionally igniting latent resource differences. Second, like most conflicts, they are often exploited by local elite, especially to advance economic and political interest. Third, more often than not, there are other divisions that reinforce the original landlord–tenant differences. These divisions may be along political or religious lines or over farming patterns. Fourth, the conflicts are frequently championed by youths who are determined to remove the contempt with which their contemporaries from the opposing side treat them. Finally, the resolution often involves the intervention of central governments. But beyond all these, conflicts associated with landlord–tenant relationships are inextricably linked to governance as it is indicative of the inability of governments to effectively address the crucial issue of identity and its linkage with property rights.

Complexities Arising from Racial Imbalance in Land Ownership

The land conflicts in this category have been some of the most controversial in recent years, with developments in Zimbabwe and, to a lesser extent, Kenya, South Africa, and Namibia, dominating interest and attention.[48] The aspect of the problem that has attracted attention is the implication of the racial imbalance in land ownership, and the controversial methods governments in some of these countries have adopted in managing the problem. However, there are other natural resource governance issues that are important in discussing the complexities of rectifying the problems these countries inherited at the time of independence. The key issues that have predicated conflicts in these countries, as Donna Pankhurst has noted in the case of Namibia, include whether the land taken back from the whites be given to the families that had the land before white's appropriation; those whose labor has been exploited on the commercial farms; those who now have little or no access to land; those who fought in the war of liberation; or still, the state.[49] All these are crucial issues of natural resource governance whose management determines whether there would be conflict in the management of land.

Often at the root of this category of land conflict are efforts by postindependence governments to redress imbalanced racial allocation of land inherited at the time of independence. Four key questions, again, all associated with natural resource governance, are particularly crucial: How much land should be taken back from the former white settlers? How is it to be taken? How is it to be redistributed? Who is to bear the brunt of paying any compensation that could arise from the process? In addressing these issues are a litany of intricate local and international politics and intrigues, all with serious implications for governance, economics, and the management of political and racial relations in the affected countries.

The country that best demonstrates these complexities of conflict is Zimbabwe. Because land was crucial to the war of liberation, at independence the British and American governments promised money for land distribution on the basis of "willing seller–willing buyer." This was, however, not particularly generous, but further constraints came because the new Mugabe government did not want to go all out to reclaim land in order not to frighten the whites who already expected retribution from a Mugabe-led government.[50]

The history of the nation's land politics has been recorded in several instances, such that a brief recap will suffice.[51] Three phases of the controversy can be identified: first was the period immediately after independence, when concern was more on how to obtain enough land from the white minority for the blacks, both to ensure equitable distribution and to satisfy the aspiration of blacks who equated the armed struggle with land redistribution;[52] the second phase came after the government had acquired some land from the whites and concern shifted to how fairly the government would ensure an equitable redistribution among the population; while the third phase came when political opposition against the Mugabe administration brought the land issue to the forefront of national political debate.

At the core of the Zimbabwean controversy are three main actors: the government, the white commercial farmers, and the local population. Despite ephemeral alliances, which sometimes bring segments of these groups together, there has in reality been no love lost among them. During the first phase, the battle line was drawn mainly between the white commercial farmers and the government, with the local population supporting the government. The main issue during this phase was how much land the whites were willing to give up and how they were to be compensated for it. The government rejected any claim for compensation on the grounds that a country coming out of the throes of war cannot afford to pay the huge compensation demanded by the white landowners. An undeclared position though was the belief in many government circles that the initial acquisition of land by whites was illegal, and as such there were no moral grounds to discuss compensation. On the contrary, however, the position of the white commercial farmers, and one which was shared by foreign governments and international financial institutions, was that the law of property rights was applicable on the commercial farmlands, and that market-value compensation had to be paid in case of acquisition. The local population did not see land strictly in the economic perception of either the government or the white farmers, but their inclination to get more land forced them to support the government.

The second phase came in the early 1990s, when the dissatisfaction of black Zimbabweans at the speed with which the government was tackling the issue of land redistribution brought land to the forefront of public interest, forcing the government to promulgate the 1992 Land Acquisition Act. This act seeks to administer a "swift process for acquiring selected lands for minimizing legal contestations over land designated for acquisition, while clearly articulating the reasons for land designation."[53] The government's argument for this promulgation was that a law was needed to disentangle it from the legal encumbrances that made land redistribution difficult. While this was in itself controversial, as some saw it as an attempt to forcefully recover land from the whites, greater controversy came when it was realized that the land acquired was allegedly distributed among the senior members of the ruling Zimbabwe African National Union (ZANU) party, cabinet ministers, and others close to President Mugabe.[54] This increasing concern over land came at a time when domestic opposition against Mugabe was rising, especially because of the weakening of Zimbabwe's economy, and the land problem fed on (and into) other aspects of domestic politics. After 1993, black Zimbabweans began to revise their views about the government's land policy, as white farmers and political opponents of Mugabe also began an informal alliance that was to develop later in the land saga.

In February 2000, the land politics in Zimbabwe reached another phase when the ruling Zimbabwe African National Union Patriotic Front (ZANU-PF) party lost a national referendum.[55] Although the referendum was on constitutional reform, land issues played an important part in its campaign and subsequent outcome. The government based its campaign for a "Yes" vote for constitutional reform on the need to acquire more power to complete its land reform. It claimed that it intended to acquire approximately 5 million hectares of the 12 million currently being held by the whites.[56] However, the opposition argued that the referendum was a political ploy by the government to divert attention from the political situation, and that the process was being managed by a government department whose competence and independence were widely questioned.[57] The opposition further argued that the clause "was bad in law and calculated to sabotage [the] country's economic prospects."[58] The referendum indeed brought together an unlikely alliance—white farmers and radical black politicians, both united in their opposition to Mugabe's continued stay in power. The outcome was a defeat for the government—the first in its twenty years in power. With this, Mugabe and the ruling ZANU-PF party realized that the parliamentary election, which was then three months away, could not be taken for granted. As a result, from the moment of the electoral defeat, the government brought the land issue more fully into politics.

An unprecedented turn came on February 26, 2000, when a group of people describing themselves as the "War Veterans" began seizing white farms in the country. Although War Veterans had been active in Zimbabwe before the referendum and had, indeed, been campaigning for land reform,[59] the increase in their activities and the level of violence after the government's referendum defeat was viewed by many as Mugabe's ploy to intimidate the opposition ahead of the May 2000 election. It was also seen as a means by which to break the alliance between the opposition Movement for Democratic Change (MDC) and the white farmers. Mugabe gave open support to the takeover of the farms, even after the country's High Court declared the occupation as illegal.[60] By the end of March 2000, the situation had become such that many believed Zimbabwe to be on the road to anarchy. On April 6, 2000, the first white farmer in the spate of controversy gave up his land and emigrated to

Australia,[61] and by April 15, the first white farmer casualty had occurred. By the end of May 2000, the government had produced a list of the first 804 farms to be seized without compensation.[62] The situation continued to deepen racial tension within the country and a food crisis further compounded the unstable political situation. Although Mugabe was to concede in May 2004 that some mistakes were made in the land controversy,[63] he maintained that he had no regrets.

Once the Zimbabwean crisis became pronounced and white farmers began considering leaving the country, other African countries extended arms of invitation to the expelled farmers. One such country was Nigeria, where a governor of one of the states (Kwara) invited the farmers to come and assist his state's efforts at revolutionizing agriculture.[64] Indeed, by July 2004, a Memorandum of Understanding had been signed between the Kwara State Government and the Zimbabwean farmers.[65] Here again, the seeds of future controversies seem to have been laid,[66] although the government thinks it has done the best to reduce the political fallout of the experiment.[67]

Understanding the events in Zimbabwe between March and April 2000 is a difficult task. It was alleged that government and army trucks were used to transport the War Veterans to the white farms and that the government kept them supplied with food while they were on the farms.[68] Having lost the referendum, Mugabe and the party's cloak of invincibility seemed to have disappeared, thereby placing future elections in a precarious disposition. Thus, the takeover of the farms was almost certainly designed to intimidate the white farmers and browbeat them into conformity. It was also clear that most of those who took part in the seizure of the farms and the intimidation of people were not war veterans, as many of them were too young to have participated in a war that ended twenty years previously.[69] Obviously included were party thugs loyal to President Mugabe and the ZANU-PF party. Even the credential of the leader of the group, late Chenjerai Hunzi, was later questioned, as it was revealed that he did not fight in the war of liberation.[70]

There was an irony in the entire controversy as Mugabe, who later became the champion of the landless, was being forced a few years earlier to act on land issue. Indeed, there were also those who opposed Mugabe politically, but nevertheless supported the forceful occupation of land.[71] Many black Zimbabweans wanted land, and few were interested in how the land redistribution would come about. In many parts of the country, the land occupation was described as the *Chimurenga* 3.[72] The intimidation carried out against the whites also had racial undertones. The frustration felt by black Zimbabweans at the racism of some of the white farmers cannot be ignored. While some of the whites were kind and considerate to their black staff, there were those who grossly maltreated them, as if their employees were no better than hired chattels. Having said this, it is believed that the little resistance made by some of the black workers was not to save their white employers but to ensure that in the eventuality of the white farmers exit from the country, the land would not go to the War Veterans. By early 2003, another phase seemed to have emerged distinctly in the Zimbabwean land saga with Zimbabwean elites, especially those close to President Mugabe, allegedly driving landless black Zimbabweans away from the land occupied.[73]

Britain was the western country that was most critical of Mugabe's handling of the land conflict. The Zimbabwean government alleged that compensation for the acquisition of white land could not be paid because Britain did not fulfill the promise it made at the Lancaster House Agreement to provide funds. The British government argued that as of April 2000, it had spent £44 million to assist the Zimbabwean government buy back land for redistribution among the blacks.[74] However, it claimed to have stopped when the black peasants got little of the land, as most went to Mugabe's cronies. The former British Foreign Secretary, late Robin Cook, later noted that Britain was willing to put £36 million into the land distribution program in Zimbabwe, but this would come only after war veterans had vacated the occupied land.[75] The next years were to witness intense diplomatic tension between Whitehall and Harare.[76] This later had an impact on the Commonwealth, from which Zimbabwe was suspended in 2002 for what was seen as fraudulent conduct during the general election. In the end, Mugabe pulled Zimbabwe out of the organization after the Commonwealth meeting in Abuja, Nigeria, in March 2004, where it was decided to extend the suspension.[77]

Britain's involvement in Zimbabwe's land controversy raises a number of considerations. First, there are those who believe that the policy did not help the situation, as it further enraged Mugabe and made it easy for him to depict the crisis as a war against colonialism. The position of Peter Hain, a junior foreign office minister, depicting Mugabe's position as the "outburst from the President that bears little or no semblance to reality," was particularly seen as being unhelpful.[78] Second, there are those who see the involvement as indicative of the inconsistency of Britain's policy toward developments in Zimbabwe. Indeed, some read racial meaning into it, wondering why Britain's sudden interest in Zimbabwe was ignited when interests of the white settlers in the country were threatened, and nothing was done to call Mugabe to order when he unleashed terror on Matabele province of the country between 1983 and 1987.[79] Third, the conflict raised a fundamental question as to the extent to which a country should remain obliged to the international agreement it has signed, if it has reasons to believe that respecting such an agreement may not serve the interest of the majority of the people whose interests are to be protected. As aforementioned, Britain claimed it refused to give more money to the Zimbabwean authorities because land was not going to the Zimbabwean masses. However, it would not be the first time Britain would respect an international agreement it had signed, even when there are grounds to question the appropriateness of such a decision. A recent example of this was the decision to hand Hong Kong back to China, despite apprehensions in Britain of the possible implications of Communist rule in Hong Kong.

Land controversy in Zimbabwe shows the problems that could come from accumulation of defective natural resource governance. The structure inherited by the country at independence was unsustainable because of its glaring racial imbalance, but the attempts by the Mugabe administration to create new structures have been sectional, defective, and unhelpful. The outcome was the general confusion that has characterized the country's land sector. Nevertheless, beyond all the media euphoria, the Zimbabwean land crisis raises four important themes: first is the nature and extent to which resource conflicts can be exploited by the incumbent administration for political advantage; second is the extent to which resource conflicts in Africa can attract western political interest, even at short notice; third, is the impact resource conflicts could have on socioeconomic and political developments of a country; while fourth are the consequences such conflict can have on regional stability.

Faced by serious economic difficulties, Zimbabwe had begun to modify its position by the middle of 2005. Indeed, government officials such as vice presidents Joseph Msika and Joyce Mujuru both pointed out that the war against white farmers was over, and that farmlands were to be given to the farmers on a 99-year lease.[80] The governor of the country's Reserve Bank, Gideon Gono, added that white farmers would be provided with guarantees of uninterrupted tenure backed by government security forces.[81]

The land politics in Zimbabwe created panic in other countries with similar ethno-racial land arrangements, especially South Africa, Kenya, and Namibia. In South Africa, for example, the rand fell by 3 percent in the period following the crisis in Zimbabwe. South Africa's land situation, although less controversial than Zimbabwe's, has a potentially explosive ramification. Indeed, by the middle of 2001, some form of land invasion had been attempted in the country.[82] In South Africa, about 60,000 white farmers own more than 200 million acres of land, with 1.2 million black farmers eking out a living on 40 million acres. A number of reasons, however, give South Africa some respite, even if temporarily. First, the ANC Government is determined to ensure that the situation is peacefully managed, especially to protect the racial harmony in the country and to safeguard investment and the foreign respect it has earned since the peaceful transition from apartheid. Second, unlike Zimbabwe, South Africa has other natural resource endowments, which reduce the economic and social pressures on land. Third, international interest in South Africa is such that the country is in a better position to obtain external support to address its economic problems, and as such provides a cushioning effect on some social problems that can aggravate land crisis.

At independence, the South African government found itself in a dilemma. While it wanted to satisfy the aspirations of the blacks deprived of their land during apartheid, it was concurrently determined to prevent the massive emigration of whites, which might have followed a massive and instantaneous acquisition of land. A balance was thus struck between these two conflicting tendencies, so that while there was a constitutional protection for land owner-ship, there was also provision for a land reform program. This land reform program included neutral arbiters of land claims, buyouts of landowners and giving state-owned property to the poor and dispossessed. A Land Claims commission was set up in 1994 to consider the problem of land reallocation to blacks. This has, however, been bogged down in bureaucracy and in fight-ing such that, as of April 2000, only 4,000 out of more than 70,000 claims before it had been settled.[83] All along, South Africa has always adopted a "will-ing buyer–willing seller" policy, under which both the buyer and the seller agree on a price. This, however, has its own problems, as white land owners allegedly inflate the prices of their land, making it difficult for blacks to have access to land.

Tension over land in South Africa has manifested in three contexts. First, there were encroachments on white commercial farms, particularly in the provinces of Kwazulu Natal. Second, people dispossessed of land under apartheid reoccupied the land in a desperate bid to force the resolution of their claims, and third, people whose houses were destroyed by flood invaded and occu-pied lands outside Johannesburg and Cape Town.[84] However, more disturbing is another trend of land-related protests, which is the spate of rural murders. A report by the New York–based International Peace Academy (IPA) in February 2002, noted that more than nine hundred white farmers have been murdered since independence.[85] The report further noted that spatial analy-sis of the attacks indicates "they have been clustered in areas where commer-cial farms are adjacent to former homelands characterized by overcrowding, landlessness and immense poverty."[86]

The Zimbabwean crisis put political pressure on South Africa. In the after-math of the former's land crisis, 54 percent of black South Africans supported a Zimbabwean-style land invasion. By the middle of 2001, the land crisis in South Africa had become more serious with cases of land invasion in places like Mangete in KwaZulu Natal province and Kloof, just outside Durban. Indeed, the manager of Land-Invasion Control for Durban, Neville Fromberg, confirmed that such land invasion had become a big problem.[87]

To a large extent, the politics of land reform in South Africa initially fol-lowed the politics of the armed struggle for independence and intra-party division within the ANC. One of the independence movements, the Pan-Africanist Congress (PAC) had always made land a major political issue, even during the liberation war.[88] When the crisis in Zimbabwe began, the PAC acclaimed Mugabe's position and urged Mbeki to follow suit. While the Mbeki government could afford to ignore the PAC, especially as the party itself had become a politically spent force inside South Africa with just one member of Parliament, it had to consider the radical calls for reform coming from the black population, who, though not supporters of the PAC, found in the organization a convenient umbrella to vent their opposition to the govern-ment's slow actions on land reform. This, indeed, led to the increase of the

PAC activities over land. In July 2001, for example, the party organized an illegal occupation of private land at Bredell, Kempton Park, about fifty kilometers from Johannesburg, and sold parcels of the land to squatters for twenty-five rands.[89] This sent a message to the government of the politicization of the land problem. There were also local organizations, such as Mpumalanga Labor Tenants, the Land Services Organization in the Transkei, and the Restitution Forum in the Cape, which had undertaken some form of land seizure, even if unsuccessfully. More disturbing, at least initially, was the intra-party division that was apparent within the ANC on the issue. Some of its members, notably Mrs. Winnie Madikazela Mandela, appeared to have supported the policy of the Mugabe government.[90]

In managing its land policy, South African government distanced itself—particularly diplomatically—from the Zimbabwean government, and this explains why the outcomes in both countries have been different. The South African President, Thabo Mbeki, told the South African Parliament on May 11, 2000, that he would not tolerate a similar land grab.[91] As late as August 2002, the governor general of the South African Reserve Bank, Tito Mboweni, noted categorically that his country "is not Zimbabwe" and further asserted that South Africa "handle[s] things very different . . . [believing] in property rights . . . [and] in the importance of the Rule of Law."[92] This was in the wake of the South African rand hitting its lowest in four months, at R10.95 to the U.S. dollar. Subsequent developments, however, brought land to the forefront of attention, and the extent to which the government can keep the land issue under control will be further tested in the future. There are growing demands among landless blacks, particularly hastened because of the brutality of white farmers to their black employees.[93] The casualty figures also do not support the optimism of the leadership. The spokesman for Agric-South Africa, Kobus Visser, noted that 144 white farmers were killed in 813 attacks in 1999, and in 2000, there were 119 murders from 804 attacks.[94] It needs to be noted though that some of these were the activities of criminal gangs picking on isolated farmsteads, with robbery as the main intention.

The South African Land Reform process has three components: registering land rights to those dispossessed by segregation and apartheid through a Land Restitution Program served by specially constituted Land Claims Court; securing and upgrading the rights of those with insecure rights to land through a Land Tenure Reform Program; and changing the racially skewed land ownership patterns through a Land Tenure Reform Program. In August 2006, however, the Minister for Agriculture and Land Affairs, Lulu Xinqwana, announced that her department had done away with the willing buyer–willing seller policy, and that negotiation would last for only six months, after which, land whose prices were believed to be inflated would be expropriated. This, according to Xinqwana, was to meet the government's target of land resettlement set for 2008.[95] This position won immediate acclaim from the South African Communist Party.[96]

Kenya, with the experience of the Mau Mau Rebellion behind it, also has a complex ethno-racial land arrangement, and the Zimbabwean crisis seems to have re-evoked some of these sentiments. Indeed, shortly after the outbreak of violence in Zimbabwe, a member of the opposition Social Democratic Party and member of Parliament for Juja Central Province, Stephen Ndicho, called on black Kenyans to invade white-owned farms. Support for this position came from some Mau Mau veterans and the little-known Umma Patriotic Party. In June 2000, sixty-four squatters who invaded a white-owned farm in central Kenya were jailed for one month. What makes this invasion worthy of note is that the jailed people included two policemen. Although some opposition members of Parliament have called for the occupation of white-owned farms and some Kenyan pastoralists have moved onto white-owned cattle and camel ranches in Laikipia,[97] these remained isolated cases. Generally, however, land issues in Kenya have not reached a crisis stage, for four immediate reasons. First, the Mau Mau Uprising has solved some of the basic land problems that Zimbabwe seems to be addressing with its current land revolts, as it afforded blacks the opportunity to demonstrate the determination with which they can assert their claims to land. Thus, the urgency for immediate redress has been reduced. Second, unlike Zimbabwe, the KANU government in Kenya is opposed to forceful land acquisition. Indeed, the country's attorney general, Amos Wako, specifically warned against such tendency. This thus denied those who might want to forcefully acquire land the kind of official support that proved crucial in Zimbabwe. Third, land ownership in Kenya has less intense racial undertones. In fact, there are few white farmers in the country, and they don't own the type of large estates as those in Zimbabwe. Finally, whites in Kenya have remained removed from the kind of politics that may incur the displeasure of the ruling party.

Namibia seems to be oscillating between two tendencies. While a significant percentage of the black population would seemingly prefer a situation of land occupation—*a la* Zimbabwe—and while the leadership has been known to be sympathetic to the Zimbabwean President,[98] nothing has been done to give the impression that land occupation of the Zimbabwean sort is imminent. Indeed, official statements have indicated otherwise. As of the end of 2000, Namibia, with a population of about 1.8 million people, had about 6,000 commercial farms, 65 percent of which were owned by whites and 35 percent by blacks.[99] Of the 65 percent owned by whites, 2 percent belonged to foreigners. Also during this period, commercial agriculture was contributing N$810 million per year (about 6 percent of GDP) to the national economy.[100]

Like Zimbabwe and South Africa, land was a crucial issue in Namibia during the independence struggle and, within a year of independence, in March 1990, the government convened a land reform conference to discuss land-related issues. What was considered somewhat strange about the outcome of the meeting was that it decided not to entertain the most controversial aspect of land politics in the country—the ancestral land. This led to calls from many for another land conference that would abrogate completely the willing seller–willing buyer concept that makes it difficult for black Namibians to have access to land.[101] This practice also makes things difficult for the government as whites are not willing to sell their land and the few who want to do so are hiking their prices. So far, land remains a thorny issue in Namibia. Unlike Zimbabwe, farm invasion has not happened, but unlike Kenya and South Africa, the extent to which the leadership would violently oppose a land invasion is not certain. For now, though, the leadership has maintained a no-invasion policy. How far the landless people in Namibia can go without forceful occupation remains to be seen.

On the whole, conflicts emanating from attempts to rectify colonial land allocation anomalies have shown five features. First, their racial underpinnings often evoke international interest, as western countries are wont to intervene to protect the interest of the white minority. Although this is often hidden under a general guise of protecting property rights and maintenance of law and order, it is widely believed, especially in Africa, that the deep interest shown by the West in these conflicts is predicated by racial considerations. Second, the magnitude of such conflicts is determined by the position of the incumbent's government on land matters. In cases where the government has taken a clear policy that is distinctly against the racial minority group, as was the case in Zimbabwe, government's implicit endorsement of the violence may further inflame passion. Third, such conflicts have often had an impact on racial relations within the affected countries. Fourth, depending on their extent, such conflicts could lead to political division within the country, allowing those with ideological and political differences against the government to form alliances with the racial minority group. Finally, the impacts of such conflicts would depend on the influence they can impose on local politics and the place of land in the politico-economic equation of the country. In Zimbabwe, for example, the black population was not reaping the dividends of majority rule and had consequently become restless. By the beginning of the millennium, the slight concession granted to the whites at the time of independence because of their dominant position within the economy or the need to stabilize the political equation were no longer strong enough arguments to placate the blacks regarding demands for land. More profound than all these is the link of this category of land conflict with natural resource governance. While the inherited land-tenure structure had been defective, the extent of political stability over land politics has been determined by the policies adopted by immediate postindependence governments. This explains, to a large extent, why land has caused conflict in postindependence Zimbabwe but not in South Africa.

The nature of natural resource governance explains why racial imbalance in land ownership has caused conflict in Zimbabwe and not in other countries with similar problems. While the governments in these other countries were determined to ensure that the crisis did not go overboard, the Mugabe administration in Zimbabwe, for the reasons discussed above, was willing to give the crisis active encouragement, with the attendant implications for socioeconomic stability and racial relations in the country.

The Clash of Spiritual Considerations with Political and Economic Realities

This category of land conflict is not commonly discussed, but it is nevertheless one that is worth recording as a known cause of land conflict, especially as it shows another dimension of the selectively efficient nature of natural resource governance in the continent. This manifests in two ways. The first manifestation is when leased land is put into use in ways that offend the religious sensitivity of others, especially the original landowners. The problem arises because land is often leased without a clear stipulation as to the way it can be used; consequently, conflicts often arise when the leased land is used in ways landlords consider unsympathetic to their spiritual and cultural beliefs. An example of this happened in 1996 in Oru, in southwest Nigeria, where the Nigerian government situated a camp for refugees from the first round of Liberian civil wars.[102] Although the local population accepted, even if reluctantly, the settlement of the refugees and allowed them to farm and produce food, conflict soon emerged when some of the refugees decided to raise poultry. The local population claimed that chicken feces on the land desecrates the burial places of their ancestors, particularly that of Ijagbolu, who is reputed to be the founder of the town.[103] This resulted in conflicts between the local population and the refugees, and it took the intervention of the state government to resolve the conflict.

The second way by which conflicts of this nature have arisen is when the desire by a group of people to take over land considered sacred is opposed by those who see themselves as custodians of the land. Situations in some parts of Ghana present examples of such conflicts. Here, those attempting to violate sacred land come in three groups: those who want to acquire these lands for purely economic use or for building of residential homes; religious groups who consider as fetish and backward any segregation of land for animist practices; and common criminals who want to exhume the bodies of ancient rulers buried on the land and remove gold that is believed to be buried with these rulers.[104] Opposed to all these groups are members of the traditional communities, especially the elders, who consider themselves as repositories of local tradition. More often than not these conflicts are nipped in the bud although on a number of occasions things have escalated, resulting in violent confrontations among these groups.

The Ghanaian example reflects another growing tendency over land usage in Africa. This is the increase in the number of religious groups, Christian and Islamic, who object to what they see as animist exploitation of land by the traditional societies. Although not many conflicts have emerged as a result of this, it is a possible source of conflict that is likely to be inflamed in the years ahead, as many religious groups are now emerging to wrest land from the traditional users. In short, social realities are clashing with tradition over the ownership and usage of land, thus exhibiting the failure to create a credible intergroup relation that can address the identity differences that come into the politics of land tenure.

Complaints over Government's Land Regulatory Policies

Virtually all governments across Africa have introduced policies to control the ownership and usage of land. The main motive for this is the determination to consolidate the grip on land, considered crucial to the control of socioeconomic and political power at the local base, although several ostensible reasons have been proffered, including the desire to acquire land for development, to partition warring factions from fighting, and to ensure proper recreational usage of land for games, parks, and such. As in most discussions over land, national peculiarities often color how these policies are formulated and implemented. However, a feature that is consistent in all cases is that an arm of the government, often the executive branch, has control over land and can acquire, through executive power, control over any portion of land throughout the country. In some countries, these executive powers are acquired constitutionally, while in others they have come through military decrees and other authoritarian processes. An example of each of these processes is noteworthy. In Kenya, there is the Land Act, which empowers the president to allocate land to anyone, irrespective of whether the land is occupied or not. There is also the Compulsory Land Acquisition Act, which gives the government powers to take over land from its owners for development. In Nigeria, executive control over land first came through the Land Use Decree, promulgated by the military administration in 1978. This vested land rights in the hands of the head of state or state military governors. Even though this was instituted under military rule, essential clauses that ensure the executive grip over land were subsequently included in the constitution after the country became democratic.[105] Although technically the law made it clear that the government holds the land as a trustee, everything seems to confer de facto ownership on the government, as it has the power to issue Certificates of Land Occupancy and to revoke them for what are deemed reasons of "overriding public interest." This vague term includes acquiring land for mining or oil exploration activities.[106] And in Mozambique after independence, land was nationalized, and rural families were put in areas where they were to provide the labor force or to participate in agricultural cooperatives. The government gave individuals the right to use land through title deeds. This, however, changed during the second half of the 1980s, when economic restructuring led to the regulation of land law, which recognized title deeds as the only legal proof of transmission of land rights from state to foreign nationals. The situation changed again in 1990 when the impending end of the war resulted in the search for land. Conflicts subsequently emerged between the owners of the title deeds given by the state and the rural owners returning to cultivate the farms they fled during the war.

Governments' land management policies have resulted in conflicts in many countries. The first cause of conflict arises when the population opposes the process through which these laws have come into operation. This often occurs when the process is believed to be associated with corruption, with government officials benefiting at the expense of the local population whose land is being forcefully taken. Kenya presents examples of how such policies can be corrupted and made to benefit elites. For example, in the Kisii district of the country, land belonging to the Kenyan Agricultural Research Institute (KARI) was allocated to sixteen individuals, including two cabinet ministers, Zachary Onyonka and Simon Nyachae. Even when there were oppositions against this in the Parliament, the assistant minister of land and settlement, Japheth Ekidor, justified the allocation.[107] Also, there are political considerations that governments ignore but that local populations consider important. However, perhaps the most objectionable of these is that with ownership of land comes the control of all the contents therein.

The nonpayment of compensation for land acquired for resource exploitation also remains a core cause of conflict between central governments and local communities. The resource that has resulted most often in land acquisition by governments continues to be oil. Apart from the Nigerian oil-producing communities (discussed in chapter 5), another recent example is Chad, where the population displaced over the construction of the Chad–Cameroon pipeline from Doba Basin in Chad to Kribi in Cameroon have yet to be fully compensated.[108]

Another problem has arisen because of inconsiderate eviction of inhabitants by governments without providing reasonable alternatives. In 1995, for example, the Kenyan government evicted sixty households in the Korogocho area of Nairobi, who had been living in the area for twenty years. Also, in the Kanyakwar area of Kisumu, about three hundred people were displaced in 1992 after the government acquired the land for industrial development. This attracted criticism from radical MPs, including Anyang' Nyong'o, the MP for Kisumu rural.[109]

Kenya again presents an example of how government's control of land can be exploited to punish political opponents. In the Enoosupukia region of the country, Kikuyu farmers and Masai pastoralists had lived together for decades, but this area was to become a region of controversy when, in 1977, the government declared the area a land adjudication area and allocated title deeds to the owners. As the 1992 multiparty election was approaching, the Kikuyus were accused of supporting an opposition candidate over the ruling KANU party contestant, William ole Ntimama. In the eventual election, Ntimama won, and eight months after his victory, he changed the status of Enoosupukia region into a Trust land, and people who had been living in the area as legal owners became trespassers.

Across Africa, what seems common with most of the attempts by the government to ensure control over land is that the laws conferring the control of land on government are often confusing and contradictory. Indeed, commenting on Nigeria's Land Use Law, a Nigerian academic, Ademola Popoola, notes: "it is a notorious fact that the Bench, Bar and academic community are still battling to unravel the mystery of its interpretation and operation."[110] It is, however, worth noting that in recent years, many countries have tried to review the land management policies that have been in practice since the time of their independence, with the ostensible intention of making more land available to the general population.[111] There are fears that elite greed and bureaucratic hiccups are still rearing their ugly heads to frustrate these initiatives. In Tanzania, where Issa Shivji chaired the process, such problems have been highlighted, with the chairman confessing to the government's cheating its citizenry as it passed over the process to the ministry officials, who drafted a position paper that formed the basis of the Tanzania National Land Policy.[112] Ghana is undertaking similar steps with assistance being provided by foreign development agencies.[113]

In some countries, governments have signed agreements with big companies that allow these companies to take over lands from local communities, with the local communities often unaware of the risk of losing their land to the government and these companies. With the depressing nature of the economy of many African countries and the attempt to attract foreign investors, this tendency has increased. Countries recovering from the throes of war are more vulnerable to entering into such agreements with foreign companies as it would be thought that such action would assist in postwar recovery. A recent example in which the attempt to acquire land resulted in tension is Liberia where, in August 2004, the Liberian Agricultural Company (LAC) issued an eviction notice to inhabitants of a number of communities on the basis of a concession agreement the company had signed with the Government of Liberia.[114] The company promised to pay an "ex gratia payment based on purely humanitarian consideration" for the crops and structures on the land.[115] The affected communities have resisted this move, as they were not willing to migrate to another community to live as displaced people, and local NGOs are considering taking up their case.[116]

Another government policy that has generated conflict is the mass relocation of ethnic groups into areas different from their traditional abode. While the reason often given for this is the need to make room for modernization, critics of this policy have often cited less altruistic reasons, including the need for the government to exploit natural resources in lands belonging to traditional communities. Perhaps the most widely reported occurrence is the case of the San Bushmen in Botswana, who were removed from the traditional abode they had inhabited for several thousand years to camps outside the

Central Kalahari Game Reserve.[117] The official explanation was that the people need to be in a place where they can benefit from basic infrastructures. The local population refused this forced resettlement, and their protest was supported by sections of the international civil society, especially the London-based Survival International, which argued that the primary motive was linked to diamond exploitation. When the population refused to move, the government cut off basic and essential services.[118] Tension continues to exist between the San Bushmen and the government.

Evidences across the continent show that laws by governments to control the usage of land have been confusing and guided mainly by elite interest. The ostensible reason of acquiring land for "overriding public interest" has been exploited to offer local elites the opportunity of taking expanses of land for private uses. Although there were attempts to make land reforms, many of these have ended up creating far greater confusion, making this category of land conflict one with profound ramifications for natural resource governance.

The Complexities of Massive Human Influx

The best example of the manifestation of conflicts in this category comes as a result of refugee influx, creating clashes between hosting communities and the refugees. While there may not be a monopoly in Africa, the situation on the continent is particularly profound, mainly because of the size of the refugee population. At present, there are about five million refugees on the continent, with another twenty million people internally displaced. With the obviously weak capacity of the continent to host refugees, the consequences of the problem on land management have been profound. The reduction in international concern for an African refugee crisis, occasioned by the drastic reduction in financial assistance, and the simultaneous increase in internal conflicts in Africa, have further aggravated the problem.

The ramifications of these conflicts have been discussed in United Nations High Commission for Refugees (UNHCR) policy papers.[119] Here, attention is focused mainly on how refugees have been linked to land conflicts and how the conflicts can be traced to lack of credible governance mechanisms. The link with conflict comes in at least two ways. The first and perhaps more pronounced is the conflict that often arises as a result of scarcity of available land. In many cases, the massive and uncoordinated influx of refugees automatically means they have to eke out a living on land hardly sufficient for the local community. Clashes have inevitably occurred as a result of this, with the intensity seeming to be on the increase in recent years. For example, in 1998, some refugees were killed at the Acholi-pi refugee camp in Uganda in clashes with the local population over land.[120] In neighboring Kenya, the problem is more demonstrable in both the northeastern and northwestern parts of the country, the parts hosting refugees from Somalia and southern Sudan, respectively.

Refugees from northwestern and southern Somalia were also flooding into Ethiopia in the early 1990s, especially those from the Aware Province of Eastern Hererghe Administrative region, resulting in the heightening of tension between the groups.[121]

The second problem arises from the environmental consequences of hosting refugees. The provision of shelter inevitably leads to the cutting down of vegetation and hence, the destruction of the environment. Although host nations appreciate the need to shelter refugees, they sometimes find the magnitude of the assault on the environment unacceptable, which it is felt, leaves them vulnerable to environmental problems. For instance, the refugee problem that came along with the crisis in Rwanda affected all the neighboring countries. In Tanzania, the environment around the camps in Benaco, Lumasi, and Murungo were destroyed, with deforestation resulting in erosion. The same can be said for the environmental situation in the DRC, Uganda, and Burundi,[122] which, although not leading to conflict, generated resentments that were barely contained by the respective national governments.

Land problems that emanate from hosting refugees can continue even after the political instability that created the refugee crisis has ended. This may happen when refugees refuse to return to their home state after the conflict that drove them out has subsided. Consequently, the hosts find that the release of their land to the refugees, initially understood to be for a temporary period, may be longer in duration. In western Uganda, which for several decades served as the home of Rwandan refugees, this problem seems ongoing. There are subtle conflicts among the Rwandese who have stayed back in Uganda and the traditional owners, the Toros and the Acholis.[123]

Rwanda also presents an example of how envisaged scarcity as a result of the return of hitherto displaced people can aggravate conflict. It has now been established that one of the factors that contributed to the 1994 genocide was how to cater for the returning Tutsis who were coming from the Ugandan refugee camps. After the Tutsi's departure in the early 1960s, the Hutus occupied the farmlands left behind. With the advance of the Rwandan Patriotic Front Army indicating the likelihood of the return of the Tutsi population in Uganda, the Hutus at home orchestrated resentment against the Tutsis still based in Rwanda. This is believed to have further heightened the mass killing of the Tutsis.[124] In recent years, conflicts in this category have become more violent, largely as a result of the easy availability of weapons in many refugee camps. It is noteworthy, however, that institutions managing refuges have tried to address most of these resource-based conflicts between the refugees and their hosts.[125]

The relevance of natural resource governance is again apparent. First, many of the conflicts that result in refugee crises can emerge because structures to ensure effective management of resources do not exist. Consequently, groups have found recourse to war as the only alternative to a defective structure for managing political and economic governance. The second point relates to the nature of the structures put in place for disaster management. While African countries are often willing to assist neighbors in need and are willing to share their resources, most countries in the continent do not have structures in place to cope with long-term disaster assistance, and many of the problems that have arisen over land have been because of the magnitude of the burden.

Conflicts Arising from Land and Labor Relations

In Africa, the interconnection between land, labor, and conflict has occurred in two ways. The first, which is more prevalent in traditional societies, especially in West Africa, often takes the subtle form of ethnic conflict. In many societies across the region, it is common to have people from specific ethnic groups migrating to other areas to provide land labor. It is often the case that these workers live together in particular sections of the city, thus making the establishment of informal ethno-labor unions relatively easy and strengthening them beyond conventional trade unions. It has thus been possible for them to have informal codes of practice that include fixing prices for the labor they provide and relationship conduct with their employers and the local community. In many cases, local people are resentful of this behavior and make efforts to break these ethno-professional unions. Further complicating this problem is the contemptuous undertone that sometimes characterizes this relationship. It is a common tendency for ethnic groups employing the migrant laborers to treat them as inferior, which has often resulted in violence. Examples of this can be found in southwest Nigeria, where laborers from the Middle-Belt region of the country are employed.

Another type of land-labor conflict that emanates from the above is between the migrant labor workers and local providers of land labor. More often than not, migrant workers are willing to take on jobs that local laborers consider degrading. In a market-driven economy, clients often favor migrant laborers as they tend to undercut the local wage rate, thus creating resentment and hatred from the local producers of labor. Violent clashes have taken place between the migrant and local laborers, and it is not uncommon for the local laborers to go to farms to prevent foreign laborers from carrying out contracted work. Examples of this are also common in southwest Nigeria.

The second connection between land, labor, and conflict is distinctly different from the preceding. Here the underpinning is racial, and it is common in societies where white farmers with large plantations employ black laborers. The conflicts have centered on the relationship between white farmers and black laborers. While in the colonial period, black employees had accepted whatever conditions they were offered by their white employers; postindependence black employees have been more empowered to demand better conditions. This has sometimes resulted in minor conflicts. Examples of these are found in countries such as Kenya, Namibia, Zimbabwe, and South Africa. Also behind conflicts over land in South Africa is the Land Tenant system, a semifeudal arrangement in which blacks living on white-owned farms provide labor for the land they use. This is particularly prominent in Kwazulu-Natal and Eastern Transvaal regions.

In South Africa, there have been cases of maltreatment by whites of their black employees, and this has become a source of racial tension in the country. Perhaps the worst manifestation of this was when a white South African, Mark Scott-Crossley, ordered that one of his black workers, Nelson Chisale, be fed to lions in the Kruger National Park in February 2004. Chisale, who had earlier been dismissed by Scott-Crossley for running personal errands during official hours, went back to the farm to take his personal belongings and was apprehended and tied to a stake for several hours. He was later put in the back of a vehicle, driven to the park, and thrown into the lion's den where he was killed and eaten by the animals.[126]

The relationship between white farmers and black laborers also can be complicated when black employees of white-owned farms are treated as sympathizers of white farmers by the war veterans, as evidenced in the developments of the Zimbabwean land dispute. Although many black laborers voted along with whites in the February 2000 referendum and some joined the opposition party, this did not imply that they supported the labor relation situations on the farms.[127] Indeed, many of them supported the opposition either because their employers instructed them to do so or because they pragmatically calculated that their future would be better if tied with the continued land occupation by whites. They were thus willing to protect it in all ways possible. It is also believed that many were against the farm invaders because they saw them as coming to take over what they anticipated could be theirs in a possible future transfer of land rights. The absence of effective resource governance mechanisms is relevant to land and labor conflicts because fundamental issues such as wage relations, land management, intergroup relations, and other related issues that have been at the roots of conflicts would have been effectively addressed under credible natural resource governance structures.

From the above, it can be seen that most of the conflicts over land in Africa can be traced to the absence of clear policies on issues such as land ownership rights, wage relations, nationality and identity, and a host of others. Because many of the countries had to address principles emanating from three conflicting land-tenure systems—traditional, western, and sometimes religious, conflicts have been inevitable.

In concluding this section on the conflicts surrounding the ownership and control of land, I need to address two crucial questions. Why have these conflicts increased in recent years? A number of issues would seem to account for the increasing spate of these conflicts. First, there is an increasing level of awareness on the part of the population, which has increased queries about the management of land and other natural resources. Second, economic pressure put further strain on land and consequently re-invoked latent land problems in many African countries. Third, there is an increasing level of elite greed.

Fourth, climatic changes have reduced the amount of viable land available for productive farming, and fifth, a general freedom of expression has come with the democratization of the political landscape.

And why has there been increasing violence in the manifestations of these conflicts? Here, three reasons can be identified. First, the effect of globalization has manifested in the ease with which information relating to land conflict spread and how deregulation in the global economy has been exploited in the transfer of money from abroad to aid land-related conflicts in Africa. Second, further manipulation continues by elites, who, in some cases, ensure that weapons are procured to prosecute these conflicts. Third, there is general disenchantment of the youth population, with a consequent increase in violence within these conflicts. However, while the ownership, management, and control of land have been crucial in explaining conflicts in Africa, also important has been the role of agricultural resources and practices.

Agricultural Resources and Conflict

Agricultural practices and products have always been linked to conflicts in Africa, and here again the governance of the natural resource sector has been a crucial issue in explaining these conflicts. For greater clarity, issues linking agricultural resources to conflict can be brought under five categories: conflicts emanating from the management of agricultural resources; disenchantment from the national breadbasket, that is, conflicts from regions providing the agricultural products that form the mainstay of national economy; how agricultural resources are being exploited to prosecute conflict; financing of conflict from agricultural resources; and the linkage between conflict and the destruction of wildlife. Discussion of each of these and how they are linked to governance are presented below.

Conflicts Emanating from the Management of Agricultural Resources

This category of conflict is more profound in countries where a major cash crop dominates national economy. Conflicts of this nature have emerged when the government fails to honor contractual agreements with the farmers responsible for the production of the produce. Since governments are often the sole marketers of these resources in the international market, local farmers have had to rely on governments to negotiate for them in processes that are often complex and laden with potential indices of conflict. An example of this is the conflict that erupted in Kenya in 1999 over coffee production. Coffee had been the country's major export earner, but by 1998 the decline in production had reduced this product to third place after tea and horticulture. The Kenyan Coffee Board has the sole monopoly to buy and sell the product. On the international market, Kenya's processed coffee fetched US$5/kg, but farmers were paid as little as US$0.08/kg, with the highest amount earned for the top grades being US$1.25/kg. There had been allegations of corruption leveled against the Coffee Board, and a government audit confirmed that US$4 million was paid to "ghost" farmers, and another US$1.5 million purportedly paid to the Coffee Research Foundation was not accounted for.[128] Furthermore, the board lost US$3.21 million because of milling inefficiencies.[129] Fed up with what was considered unjust treatment, groups of Kenyan Coffee farmers armed with bows and arrows, machetes, and other weapons invaded the Agree Coffee Factory in the Nero District of Kenya in December 1999, injuring several people. The rioters requested that the giant coffee industries believed to be responsible for their poor treatment be split up, and the situation is still ongoing. Even as of May 2003, when Kenyan Coffee was fetching between $10 and $30/kg, growers were earning $2/kg or less, resulting in calls for the new government to reform the entire process.[130] In Ghana, workers at the National Palm Oil Limited at Prestea, near Takoradi, went on violent protest in September 1991 on similar grounds.[131]

Apart from the role of governments in managing the export of these commodities, cooperative activities by farmers also have resulted in violent conflicts, especially when fall in international demand put strain on domestic production. For example, the heightened global supply of coffee and the attendant drop in price fostered considerable conflict in Kenya. Also, in October 2000, violent conflicts ensued during a meeting to discuss internal problems within the Othaya Coffee Farmers Cooperative.[132] At the Kagari Central Coffee Farmers Cooperative Society, members threatened to lynch officials who were sacked for allegedly embezzling the cooperative money.[133]

How agricultural products are managed and how to ensure that just and equitable payment is made for products sent abroad through government organizations have been at the center of many conflicts. While it can be conceded that international market prices do vary, thereby making it difficult for governments to be precise as to how much would go to producing communities, many of the conflicts in this category would be prevented if there had been a transparent policy of accountability in the entire process. It is the absence of this that gives local producers the impression that they are not receiving the best for their labor. This is a clear problem of governance, reflected in the lack of trust between the producers and the government.

Disenchantment from the National Breadbasket

Brought under this heading are those conflicts involving a particular region within a country that believes its role is important in producing the major agricultural products—domestic food or the main source of foreign earnings for the country. Conflict manifests either with the desire of the resource-producing region aspiring secession and the central government trying to maintain the existing national structure, or in the producing region preventing the export of agricultural products from their region. The Casamance Province of Senegal provides an example of a conflict of this nature. This can be traced to the colonial period, when Senegal was confined to groundnut trade and rice growing. At present, the Casamance region is Senegal's most fertile, producing half of the country's rice, cotton, and corn. However, the widespread perception in Casamance is that other parts of the country, especially in the north, have sprinted ahead of the south in education, business, and industry.[134] Since the independence of the country, the Casamance region has been fighting to secede. The war now has complex ethnic and geographical underpinnings, but at the core of the conflict is the management of the agricultural production of the country.[135]

The picture then, is that local claims clash with national interests. The fundamental question of how much should be given to the resource-generating region is a crucial issue of governance. It is a problem that is present in other natural resources, exemplifying the weakened nature of efforts to manage natural resources in the continent.

Conflict Impeding Agricultural Production

Conflicts have impeded agricultural production in many African countries. At the most elementary level, it prevents farmers from going to farms. In situations where the duration of the conflict has been short, the economic consequences have been less severe, and as such, easily managed. National economies, however, have been affected in cases of prolonged conflicts. This is often through the decline of vital agricultural sectors. This has been the case with Senegal as annual production of groundnuts fell from 10,000 tons in the 1980s to 1,000 tons by 2001, while rice production during the same period fell by 66 percent as a result of the conflict in the Casamance region.[136]

The second concern is at the national level. Here the conflict is with the government at the center, and the extent of such tensions is such that they have affected national and subregional supplies of agricultural resources. Two recent examples involve Zimbabwe and Côte d'Ivoire. In the former, conflict and political instability affected the production of key agricultural resources that were vital to the national economy, especially tobacco. The inability of the white farmers, who form the backbone of growers for the country's agricultural export, to attend to the farms resulted in severe shortages, and this has contributed to the economic problems that have confronted Zimbabwe in the last few years. The situation in Côte d'Ivoire, where a civil war has been ongoing since 2001, has adversely affected not just the country but neighboring countries.[137] This is because Côte d'Ivoire was vital to regional agricultural trade prior to the crisis. Its position as the world's largest producer of cocoa has meant that the effects of the conflict are far reaching in its global implications as well.[138] The conflict has affected agricultural production in three ways. First, military operations have resulted in the closure of vital production centers. For example, in October 2002, the rebels captured the cocoa capital of Daloa, forcing an end to the production of cocoa and related activities there. Second, this had an impact on West African migrant laborers. For generations, Côte d'Ivoire has attracted laborers from other West African countries, many of whom come to the country to provide labor in cocoa plantations. With the war, many of these laborers have been forced to leave, leading to a significant reduction in productivity.[139] Third, there is an impact on the day-to-day economic activities of the population, especially as the livelihood of up to six million people depend on coffee and cocoa production.

In Congo Brazzaville, the civil conflict between the Cocoye militias, loyal to the ousted President Pascal Lissouba, and the Ninjas, supporting his Prime Minister Bernard Kolelas on the one hand and the national army on the other, has affected the exploitation of timber—the country's second most important export after oil. For most of 1999, the rebel operations affected farming. The areas most affected were Niari, Bouenza, and Lekoumou, as well as Pool, near the capital, Brazzaville. Before the conflict, these regions made up a third of Congolese production, which as of 1998 was 500,000 cubic meters of rough fiber.[140]

It should be noted that in countries where conflicts have offered opportunities to make quick and large sums of money from illegitimate businesses, there has been a mass exodus from agriculture, especially from subsistence farming, further weakening the local economy. Emizet Kisangani notes that in the Kivu and Oriental province of the DRC, the massive exodus to the Coltan and diamond trade resulted in the additional weakening of subsistence agriculture.[141]

Another way by which conflict has been linked to agricultural production is by the reduction in the amount of land that can be available for farming as a result of land mines. Perhaps the conflict where this has manifested most is that in Angola, where it is estimated that more than fifteen million mines were laid under the soil surface. As an extension of this, adults who could have taken to farming and thus reduced the economic hardship that often aggravates civil wars or weakens the pace of postwar reconstruction, have been directly affected by landmines. It is no surprise that Angola has the highest percentage of quadriplegics in the world. Additionally, the fear of rape during conflicts has often prevented women from attending to their farms.

Financing of Conflict from Agricultural Resources

Apart from solid minerals, agricultural products have been the most important source of revenue for financing conflicts in developing societies, and there is a well-established link to this in Africa. The determination to control the local capacity for agricultural production has traditionally been a major objective during civil conflict. Although such control may not bring as much yield as the control of mineral resource sites, control of agricultural resource sites in conflict situations has the unique advantage of producing food to feed the teeming fighters, while the surplus can be sold to the international market. This aside, control of the agricultural base has often assisted in gaining local grip of the conflict, especially because of the sentimental attachments that local populations have to land. Among the key governance questions this raises are whether the government has the powers to mortgage agricultural products for weapons, and who has the power, under the constitution, to cede out land and agricultural resources to foreign companies and individuals.

Although interest has often concentrated on how agricultural resources come into play in civil wars, there are ways in which agricultural resources also play an important role in the politics of communal clashes. For example, local tyrants often emerge who control the management of agricultural commodities to their economic and political advantages. These people exploit communal clashes to demand payments in cash and agricultural products in exchange for the protection for local farmers. Like warlords, they attain this position through imposing personality and brute force; but unlike warlords, they do not have the desire to attain any political power, or to use the wealth they have accumulated to advance any immediate or long-term economic and political objective. One example of this was in the Ife–Modakeke crisis in southwest Nigeria, where a number of local tyrants emerged, especially in the suburban farmlands of the two communities.[142]

Another way through which control of agricultural resources comes into focus during periods of communal conflict is when control of land and agricultural resources is placed under temporary central control. This is often to ensure equitable distribution and adequate compensation for those whose farmlands are lost or destroyed in the course of conflict. In this situation, the central control is temporary and its main objective is to ensure that those whose farms have been destroyed or have had access to their land blocked by war, do not have to suffer for what is seen as a communal struggle.

Agricultural resources come out most distinctly in conflict, however, when they have been used to finance civil wars. Conflicts across Africa have examples of warring factions exploiting agricultural resources to finance their military objectives. For example, one of the National Union for the Total Independence of Angola's (UNITA) earliest sources of income was coffee. Indeed, by the late 1980s, the organization had established control over most of the coffee-producing northwest province, which it sold to Zairian traders.[143] In post-Cold War Africa, however, the Liberian Civil War (1989–95) exposed the ramifications of this conflict most distinctly. As soon as it became obvious to the government of the late President Doe that a conflict was impending, the administration began the process of using agricultural resources to prepare for war. As early as February 1989, Doe had entered into an agreement with a southwest London company to supply military weapons worth US$60 million. In return, the company specifically demanded timber concession in the following areas:

- 173,448 acres located in Grand Gedeh County, lying to the northwest of Pyne Town;
- 150,240 acres also located in Grand Gedeh County, lying to the northwest of Zwedru; and
- 59,304 acres located in Grand Cape Mount County, lying to the east of the town of Congo and immediately bordering the Mano River.[144]

These were acceded to by the Doe administration, which had in fact agreed before the requests were made that the government "would grant a waiver of all taxes or fees normally payable to Government entities by the beneficiaries of such a concession."[145]

Once the Liberian Civil War broke out in December 1989, two agricultural resources—rubber and timber—were the main products that featured prominently. Rubber was Liberia's main agricultural product, and the country is the world's largest producer of the commodity. Before the outbreak of the war, rubber accounted for $111.6 million and supported 20 percent of the Liberian population.[146] Rubber plantations were owned mainly by foreign multinationals, especially from the United States and Europe, and the main corporations were Firestone, which owned the plantation in Harbel, and the Liberian Agricultural Corporation, whose plantations were in Grand Bassa and Guthrie in Bomi County.

In Liberia, the (mis)management of resources is also linked to the outbreak of the war in the first place, as the corruption of the Doe administration had created a disenchanted operational base that was exploited by the rebel factions. The mismanagement also weakened the economic base of the country and made the regime incapable of mounting an effective response to the guerrilla insurgence. Apart from corruption, Doe's policy of granting rubber concessions to foreign countries and corporations in exchange for military support to suppress opposition further affected the economy and weakened civil society.[147]

With renewed outbreak of conflict in the country, and with the pariah image of the former President Charles Taylor, the role of agricultural resources in the Liberian and other regional conflicts assumed renewed interest and attention. The rebel movements that fought the government of Charles Taylor specifically targeted regions of timber production. For example, by May 2003, one of the rebel forces, the Movement for Democracy in Liberia (MODEL), had captured the key timber port of Haper, close to the Ivorian border.[148] Greenville, Liberia's main timber port had fallen to the rebel force earlier in the same month, while the main rebel movement, the Liberian United for Reconciliation and Democracy (LURD), also targeted agricultural bases.[149]

While the rebel forces were making the exploitation of timber difficult for the government of President Taylor, another blow came for the administration in May 2003, when the United Nations Security Council extended sanctions against the government to include a ban on timber export.[150] The sanction, which took effect from July 7, 2003, was to force Taylor to stop his alleged involvement in regional conflicts. Timber was a main source of revenue for the Taylor government, especially since the imposition of sanctions on the administration, with Chinese, Indonesian, and Malaysian logging companies being the key trading partners.

In the DRC, agricultural resources also come into the complexities of the conflict, with resources including coffee, tea, quinine, and hardwoods playing prominent parts. There is a tendency to ignore this aspect of the country's conflict because of the concentration of attention on solid minerals. DRC coffee production is officially estimated at 60,000 metric tons of robusta and 8,000 metric tons of arabica per year, almost all of which is being exported via Uganda and Rwanda. There are also reports of increased hardwood cutting and export through the occupying states, with Thailand-based investors fueling operations and working closely with DRC warring factions. The DRC conflict also shows how instability in a country can be exploited by outsiders to support different sides in land-ownership conflicts. For example, the Ugandan troops in the DRC have supported the Hema ethnic minority in their land war against the majority Lendus.

Countries that have intervened in the civil conflicts of their neighbors are known to have used this interaction opportunity to benefit from the agricultural resources of the war-afflicted state. What determines how this is done is the nature of the conflict itself. In a situation where the state has collapsed completely and is helpless to prevent the illegal exploitation of its agricultural resources, pillagers often adopt a free-for-all approach and the country is forced to appeal to the international community to assist in stemming the tide of the looting. This has been the case in the Democratic Republic of Congo (DRC), where the Ba-N'Daw Commission set up by the United Nations indicted Rwanda and Uganda in the illegal timber smuggling business. It is the case that the countries' alleged involvement in solid minerals has obscured the timber connection. It is, however, ironic that the DRC, which complained about Rwanda and Uganda, turned a blind eye to the involvement of Zimbabwe and other countries supporting the cause of the Kabila government, which was also involved in timber smuggling.[151] Perhaps this symbolizes that regime-protection takes precedence over long-term misuse of natural resource endowment.

Conflict and the Destruction of Wildlife

Largely because factions involved in conflicts in Africa do not respect the laws governing the conduct of conflicts, there is little or no consideration for wildlife, whose destruction in the course of a conflict comes as a result of two major factors. The first is the desire of members of the warring factions to trade in endangered species and animal parts, especially tusks, ivory, and rhino horns. During the Angolan civil war (1975–2000), an estimated 100,000 elephants, thousands of black rhino, and great herds of buffalo were slaughtered by the warring factions and their external supporters.[152] Another victim of the Angolan conflict was the Sable Antelope, considered to be one of Africa's rarest and most spectacular animals.[153] Indeed, it was thought that the animal had been completely wiped out, until an expedition team from South Africa to the country succeeded in finding five of them alive. Another major example is with the gorillas of the Parc National des Volcans, in northern Rwanda, where it has been estimated that up to 75 percent had been killed as of March 1993.[154]

The second factor is the killing of these animals for food. While this cannot be separated from the above, in the sense that the animals are often eaten after the removal of their tusks and ivories, there are also cases in which other animals were killed specifically for the purpose of feeding. During the Liberia civil conflict for example, the country suffered depletion in some of its key wildlife, while the Rwandan gorillas, globally known as a national treasure, were greatly affected by the war that bedeviled the country.[155] Liberia also presents a case of how the destruction of wildlife can be linked to conflict. Since the end of the war in the country, ex-combatants have been converging around the National Park in Zwedru to kill animals and sell the meat to passengers driving through the area. This has caused tension between the ex-combatants and the local population who have historically relied on the killing and selling of these animals as means of livelihood. These issues call for a deeper discussion on the place of animal stock in conflict.

Pastoralism and Conflict

It is perhaps appropriate to begin this section with a working definition of pastoralism. *Pastoralism* is seen as a practice with the main ideology and production strategy of the herding of livestock on an extensive base. Pastoral-related conflicts are some of the most controversial aspects of natural resource conflicts in Africa. It is difficult to demarcate the theater of these conflicts, as belligerents often do not recognize national boundaries. Consequently, it is not unusual for conflicts to extend to neighboring countries. Although pockets of pastoral conflicts exist in many countries, the problem is most prevalent in the northeast region of the continent, notably in the Horn of Africa, Uganda, Kenya, Tanzania, and Ethiopia.

Conflicts surrounding animal stock are of interest in Africa for reasons that include the importance of these animals to other socioeconomic realities of the affected societies, and the effects of these conflicts on the political realities of the affected countries. This section has two objectives: to identify the issues determining pastoralist conflicts and to discuss recent cases of these conflicts and the themes they evoke.

Issues Determining Pastoralist Conflicts

Broadly, issues underlining pastoral conflicts can be brought under two headings: perception and culture. The role of perception may be observed on three levels. The first is at the level of governments across the regions and focuses on how governments perceive the lifestyle of the pastoralists; the second is at the level of agriculturists and how they perceive the lifestyle of pastoralists, while the third is at the level of the different pastoralists themselves and how they see other segments of the pastorals group.

Across Africa, pastoralists are perhaps some of the most misunderstood participants of the natural resource sector. As Leif Manger has noted, they are victims of "conscious policies of marginalization based on the simplistic assumption [accusing them] of desertification, of managing their stock according to irrational economic principles and of being technically stagnant and backward, of wandering about destroying nature, and of adhering to conservative social structures and cultural notions."[156] In short, they are often seen as being antithetical to development. Consequent to this perception, governments across the continent have condemned pastoralists' ways of life, and have tried, though often unsuccessfully, to force them into rigid administrative structures. In response, the pastoralists have resisted every attempt to impose an "alien" way of life on them, and the mutual distrust this breeds is crucial to understanding many of these conflicts.

Perception has underlined conflicts between agriculturists and pastoralists. This again has been the focus of several detailed studies, and the post-Cold War increase in their occurrence has only added new impetus to the academic interest in this phenomenon. Agriculturists perceive pastoralists as people who have no respect for crops, and who place the interests of their livestock ahead of all else. In a way, they share the government's view that pastoralists are backward and unwilling to progress and move with civilization. For their part, pastoralists see agriculturists as an ally of the government in its various attempts to force them into conformity. Both pastoralists and agriculturists have different attitudes to land tenure, and this has further intensified problems in the ways they comprehend each other. All across Africa, agriculturists have a more "settled" perception of land. It is seen as a place of abode and a source of livelihood. The pastoralists see the functionality of land as transient, due to their nomadic lifestyle. They therefore do not have the kind of ownership mentality that agriculturists have. Land is seen as a place where the animals can graze as they proceed on their journey. This also explains why these conflicts often cut across national boundaries.

Among pastoralists themselves there is often rivalry and tension among herders of different animals. Under an unwritten pattern of rivalry, those herding cows have a superior attitude toward herders of camels and goats. Their attitude is determined by the economic and cultural importance of a cow, as it is used in some societies as means of settling bride price. This further shows the importance of culture in the complexities surrounding pastoral activities in Africa. Hence, in all the conflicts surrounding pastoralism in Africa, this problem of perception has remained a crucial consideration.

In concluding this discussion on perception, I should note that a number of the conflicts involving pastoralists emerge from a lack of adequate appreciation for their thinking and the principles that govern their actions. In many societies, they are viewed as being impervious to change and uncompromising in their positions. While it is presumptuous to generalize, it is the case that pastoralists live in a state of "increasing precarious economic insecurity, with many factors contributing to the fragility of their existence."[157] As Belay Gessesse and others have noted, there is an orthodox view that pastoralists live in a subsistent economy characterized by total absence of economic rationality and that they accumulate animals only for prestige."[158] We need to go beyond this argument, as often pastoralists are reluctant to sell stock because "they have to maintain a certain level of production for current needs as well as hedge against the vagaries of uncertain climatic and epidemiological conditions."[159] Furthermore, they see their stock as representing not only their saving but also their contingency reserve for drought, sickness, and retirement.

The second issue determining conflicts is what, for want of a better term, can be called cultural considerations. This is perhaps the most publicized cause of pastoralist conflict, and at the core of discussion here is the practice known variously as "rustling" or "raiding." Originally a cultural practice that later assumed violent ramifications, it involved men raiding the animal stock of neighboring societies. There are two types of raiding: redistributive and predatory. Redistributive raiding, as the name suggests, is a process of reallocating pastoral resources between rich and poor herders, and it involves rebuilding herds after livestock have been killed by drought or seized in raids. This, to an extent, ties the practice to climatic conditions and the prevailing state of intergroup relations.[160] Predatory raiding is distinguishable from redistributive in two ways. There is the use of sophisticated weapons and the growing involvement of actors outside the pastoral system, which has undermined the socioeconomic integrity of pastoral activities.[161] Its main motive is commercial, and cattle are taken either to feed warring armies or to sell on the market for profit. Over time, the practice later assumed more violent dimensions, and the introduction of arms into the equation further aggravated the associated level of conflict. The practice has significant cultural importance, as it is also used as a rite of passage for young men, means of paying dowry, and as a mark of prestige. However, in this respect, the practice has now been transformed "from a quasi-cultural practice with important livelihood-enhancing functions, into a more predatory activity."[162]

On the whole, scholars of pastoral conflicts have divided the causes into two aspects: long-term and immediate. The long-term causes are due mainly to the difficulties of geography and the nature of national boundaries. Unpredictability of rainfall and the population expansion in most African societies, often forces encroachment to pastoralists' grazing areas, thus resulting in the hindering of animals during migratory seasons. Other issues that often stay in the background of these conflicts include drought, management of water resources, land management policies, government discriminatory policies, and the activities of varying interest groups. The nature of national boundaries contributes to conflict because of the artificial national boundaries erected to debar the movement of pastoralists and their herds.

The immediate causes can be brought under three headings, namely, crop destruction by the pastoralists in the process of their movement, blocking of access by agriculturists to prevent movement of pastoralists and their animals, and the retaliation to earlier clashes. All the clashes in these cases have been the subject of several detailed studies, and the post-Cold War increase in their occurrence has only added new impetus to the academic interest in this phenomenon.

Post-Cold War Pastoralists Conflicts

There are few new cases of pastoralist conflicts in Africa, as most of the current clashes have been going on for several years, in some cases from the time of independence. However, while there have been few new cases, the accompanying scale of destruction has become more profound. This has been attributable to the climatic changes in some of the countries, which has put further strain on both agriculturists and pastoralists. Furthermore, the upsurge in democratic agitation, which permits freedom of expression and dissent, has allowed disenchanted groups to challenge injustices that have been persistently imposed on them. The easy availability of weapons to a large extent explains the violence behind the manifestations of these conflicts.

Some recent conflicts that present evidence for some of the themes discussed above are worthy of note. First to consider is the multidimensional pastoralist conflict in the Karamoja region, in the northeastern part of Uganda, inhabited by the Karimojong. There have been many studies on the Karimojong, most of which have centered on the numerous conflicts that have characterized their history.[163] As is often assumed of people with a long history of conflict, the general impression about the Karimojong is that of a backward people whose social structures are impervious to change. In this section, attention is focused on the ramifications of the conflict and the underlying mechanisms and the government's response to them.

Three factors are important in understanding the roots of the conflicts involving the Karimojongs. First is the nature of their geography, ecology, and history. Like most pastoralists, the livelihood of the people is dependent on water. As water sources are seasonal and unreliable, however, the people are persistently in search of water, a process which, inevitably, leaves them at loggerheads with other groups. Second was the attitude of the colonial government, which further heightened intergroup tensions. Despite the limited land available to the people for grazing their cattle, the colonial government still constructed a national park, the Kidepo National Park, on the most fertile lands in the region.[164] Again, the colonial attitude toward the people was that they were congenital troublemakers who were impervious to change.[165] Thus, by the time Uganda became independent, the Karimojongs had learned to exist with little or no government assistance. They were thus set in their opinions of the central authority. Third is the impression successive governments have of the Karimojongs as being uncompromising. This may be backed by their perceived lack of willingness to cooperate with the country's cattle market established in 1948. Although the government saw this as irrational, the Karimojongs' rationale was that it was more reliable to save in stock than in fluctuating Ugandan shillings.

The Karimojong conflict has both national and subregional ramifications. Within Uganda, the conflict can be placed in two broad categories: within various subclans of the Karimojongs and between the Karimojongs and neighboring ethnic groups. At the base of the crisis is the increasing inability of the area to economically sustain its people, further affected by the drought of recent years. The conflicts between the Karimojong subclans have focused mainly on cattle, especially with the Bokora, Matheniko, and Pian engaging in cattle raids. One of the most violent in recent years was in September 1999, when up to one hundred people were killed in a raiding battle at Kalosarich, between the Motoro and the Kotido, both subclans of the Matheniko and Bokara clans.[166] One feature of the interclan clashes among the Karimojongs is that they are often retaliatory attacks, sparked off by earlier raids or clashes. For example, the September 1999 clash was a revenge attack by the Bokora against Matheniko, who had attacked about a month earlier. This incident had itself been sparked by an earlier attack in which Jie warriors had raided Matheniko cattle.

Conflict between the Karimojongs and neighboring ethnic groups center largely on cattle, watering grounds, and the control of the mineral trade in a corridor stretching through Somalia, Sudan, northern Uganda, and northwest Kenya. The worst of these is between the Karimojongs and Itesots, who are largely agriculturists. The Itesots accuse the Karimojongs of destroying their farmlands. This has resulted in the death of several people from both ethnic groups, and with the wider conflict in the northern part of Uganda, the implications have become widespread with heightened security and political ramifications.

The international ramifications of the crisis in northeast Uganda brings the Karimojongs into conflict with people in neighboring countries, especially the Turkanas of Kenya and the Toposas of Sudan. These conflicts have centered on cattle raiding and agro-pastoralist conflicts. The roots of the Karimojong–Turkana conflict are deep. While harmonious relations existed even after the imposition of colonial rule, the colonial veterinary department's attempt to restrict the movement of cattle between Kenya and Uganda first introduced strains in their relationship. The subsequent killing of a Karimojong student by the Turkanas in 1952 eventually brought full-scale conflicts between the two groups.[167] Conflicts have underscored the relationship between the two groups since then and, in recent years, has reached disturbing proportions. Between January 31 and February 2, 2000, as many as forty-three Dodoth Karimojong were killed and many cattle taken by the Turkanas of Kenya and the Toposa of Sudan in a raid on Kapedo subcounty in the Koido district. The raiders are said to have numbered up to 1,000, and the attack was in retaliation for a series of raids by the Dodoth (one of the clans of the Karimojongs) in November 1999. The Turkanas were enraged also because the Dodoth failed to return 1,500 Turkana animals raided the previous year, as was agreed to in a meeting in Kenya.[168] The pattern of regional alliance that has now emerged is that the Dodoth have linked up with the Didinga ethnic group, a group that fell out with the Sudan Peoples Liberation Army (SPLA) of southern Sudan. This group has introduced sophisticated military skills and contacts for the acquisition of weapons for use in the conflict. To meet this challenge, the Turkanas of Kenya and the Nyangatum and Merile of Ethiopia have teamed up with the Toposa.[169]

Conflicts in this region have shown how state weakness can affect resource conflicts. This, for example, has been manifested in the process through which the Karimojongs gained access to arms. For a long time they fought with bows and arrows but, in recent decades, they have switched to the use of sophisticated weapons such as the AK-47. The first set of sophisticated weapons availed them were those hurriedly abandoned by the late President Idi Amin's soldiers during their flight from the invading Tanzanian forces in Moroto Barracks.[170] Over time, they were able to trade cattle to buy more weapons. The political situation in Uganda has helped the Karimojongs to also secure weapons. After President Museveni assumed power, he was disinclined to attempt dispossessing the people of their weapons as they served as a buffer against the Ugandan People's Army and the Lord Resistance Army, two of the armed wings fighting against the Museveni government.

A more controversial decision was taken by the Museveni administration in 1999 in the distribution of arms to the Teso. This was justified on the grounds that the Teso people needed arms to defend themselves against the armed Karimojongs, and that their location made it difficult for government's law enforcement agencies to protect them from attack. Although the government set up criteria for the issue of the weapons, it was hardly followed. However, in May 2000, the government set July 1, 2000, as the date for the removal of illegal guns in the Karamoja region.[171] Not much success attended this, and another firearms disarmament exercise was launched in Karamoja in December 2001. This showed initial signs of success as, by January 2002, the government had recovered a total of 9,873 guns from the Karamoja region.[172] During the same period, a total of 107 Karimojong warriors had been prosecuted.[173] The government promised to send in national troops and local defense units, to protect the inhabitants from cross-border raids from the Kenya Turkanas and the Pokot and Toposa from Sudan.[174]

Ethiopia has also recorded conflicts involving pastoralists. This, in a way, should be expected, as pastoralists constitute about 10 percent of the population and the country is believed to have the largest concentration of domestic herds in Africa.[175] Some of the causes of the conflicts involving pastoralists in Uganda are also present in Ethiopia. For example, as Melakou Tegegn has noted, almost all the national parks in the country are situated on lands belonging to the pastoralists.[176] This has resulted in a situation where grazing lands had to be confiscated for the creation of wildlife parks. This aside, more lands had been taken from the pastoralists through various machinations, including the construction of commercial cotton farms. The implications of this have been most profound in the Afar region, where the land taken is along the main river basin.[177]

Another country that has recorded conflicts of this nature is Mali. The differences over land usage in Mali are complex as well, as it involves not only farmers and herds but also forest users and fishermen. The control over agricultural and pastoral resources has resulted in armed clashes, especially in the country's Fifth region, also known as the Mpoti region. This region, with an area of about 75,000 square kilometers, has a population of about 130,000. Its topography is important in understanding the nature of its resource-based conflicts. As Idrissa Maiga and Gouro Diallo have noted, "in this . . . landscape, the Niger divides into many channels, which flow into a vast depression: the basin of lakes Debo and Waladou. A vast area of land . . . is watered by the river's network of channels. This provides agricultural, pastoral and fishery resources."[178]

In the post-Cold War era, one of the first major agricultural–pastoralist conflicts was the 1994 Koino conflict in Mali between the largely agricultural community of Noima and the pastoralists in Sirabougou-Peulh. This had its roots in the controversial decision of August 1982 to withdraw a plot of land, which the Noima people had used for more than a century, to create a livestock-raising area. At the time the decision was made, the Noima people had no serious objection, as it was a "drought time, and flood waters were not reaching a level which would make it profitable to grow crop on the land."[179] When the climatic condition changed making the land more favorable, however, the Noima wanted the land returned. The livestock farmers of Sirabougou-Peulh refused to do so. An amicable solution was later arrived at to share the piece of land between the two communities, but conflict broke out later in July 1994, when the Sirabougou occupied and began grazing the whole area. Although another understanding was later reached, the conflict shows how initial mismanagement by a government, evidenced in this case by the withdrawal of a plot of land already occupied by a group of people for more than 150 years, can lead to conflict. Also in Mali, the historical conflict between the Sossobe and the Salsabe over Townde-Djolel, a flood-plain grazing land, broke out again in December 1993.[180] This conflict was over a land tenure dispute. The Sossobes had occupied a disputed piece of land for three days to the objection of the Salsabes. All the effort made by the local security force, the gendarmes, to calm the two groups that had been armed with guns, spears, and knives failed, and a few days later conflict broke out.

Conflicts like these are not always within national borders. They could also be international, as was the case between Niger herdsmen and Benin republic farmers in 1999. Crisis erupted when Niger herdsmen took cattle into the neighboring Benin Republic for grazing, and the animals fell into local trapping devices that a farmer had set to protect his farm from invading herdsmen. In retaliation, the herdsmen hid in the bushes and killed the farmer when he returned to his farm the following day. The wife of the murdered farmer alerted the local population. They pursued the herdsmen, who succeeded in fleeing the scene, but were eventually caught and killed. The ensuing conflict resulted in the intervention of the governments of the two countries. Cross-border pastoralist–farmer conflict also exists in northern Nigeria between the Fulanis from Niger Republic and the inhabitants of Jigawa State in Nigeria.[181]

Clashes between pastoralists and agriculturists are, in some parts of Africa, a fairly recent development. Indeed, in Nigeria, the problem is largely a post-1980 phenomenon. Although livestock production began in the northern part of the country, by the colonial period it had reached the south as a result of the peaceful atmosphere that prevailed after the Fulani Jihad and the eradication of tsetse fly. Thus, by independence, pastoralists were moving into southern Nigeria during the dry season thereby making contact with farmers. Prior to 1989 violent pastoralist conflicts rarely occurred, apart from Tivland, where it was reported as an ethnic conflict. Peaceful co-existence was highly beneficial to both groups, where the waste products of crops provided feed for the livestock and the waste products of animals nourished the soil for crops. Problems as a result of animal destruction of cropland are acknowledged but never resulted in violence. Where animals destroyed crops, pastoralists paid compensation under a mutually agreed arrangement. Where it was not possible to come to an agreement, community leaders stepped in to handle the situation. In the post-Cold War era, however, there were increasing clashes between the two sides, resulting in casualties. Most of these have been in the northern part of the country, as in July 1999, when herdsmen invaded villages in the Karim Lamido Local Government area of Taraba State and allegedly killed ten villagers.[182] Also, Fulani cattle herdsmen supposedly clashed with farmers in the southwestern town of Iwo.[183]

The problem between the pastoralists and agriculturists in Kenya has also had ramifications both within and outside the country. On the wider regional level, it is connected to the crisis in the Karimojong area of Uganda, as it links the Karimojong people with the Pokot people in Kenya. Because of the severe drought ravaging the Pokot area, herdsmen from the west divisions of Pokot, especially Arlale, Kachelia, and Kasai divisions, often crossed the border to Uganda, and the Karimojong also moved to Kenya border towns. Both the Karimojong and the Pokot have, however, been in dispute over grazing lands. A recent conflict between both sides took place in January 2000, when the Karamojong attacked Pokot herdsmen in Morita hills.

The internal ramifications are, however, more complex within Kenya. The Pokot have been in conflict with other ethnic groups within Kenya, including the Turkana. The harsh dry season drove Pokot and Samburu herdsmen into Laikipia district, where there were conflicts with the local farmers. The problem also touches on the complexities of local politics. The Pokots are largely associated with the ruling party, while the Laikipia support the opposition Democratic Party. Indeed, many people in the country believe that the Pokot have exploited their link with the ruling party to oppress their neighbors, especially the Turkana, Samburu, and the Marakwet. Pokot indigenes who hold powerful positions in government have also been accused of fanning the conflict in the area.[184] As in Uganda, the Kenyan government has been trying to disarm these groups, especially the Pokot,[185] with little success.

On a much lesser scale are a number of countries where there are agriculturist–pastoralist clashes. In northeast Tanzania, the Masai, mainly pastoralists, have for years been fighting with the Chagga and Meru, who are agriculturists. Nigeria has also recorded a number of similar conflicts. Between June and July 1999, more than one hundred people were believed to have died in clashes between the herdsmen of the Fulani stock and the Tiv over-grazing areas. The affected areas of the state stretched between Bali, Gassol, and Ardokola local governments.[186] Governments can also exploit local differences to fuel conflicts between agriculturists and pastoralists. Along the Senegal River, different ethnic groups in Mauritania and Senegal are at war over grazing land.[187] In Sudan, for example, the central government in Khartoum is known to be using the local Baggara Arab Pastoralists against the Nuba people. The Baggaras, who have lost their grazing lands to commercial farming, have been armed and trained by the government forces and have been encouraged to take over Nuba lands.[188] There are also disputes over grazing and farming rights in the country's Darfur region.[189]

Pastoral conflicts in the whole of northeast and central Africa have been affected by the general political instability in the region. Many of the countries face deep-seated internal crises, which have introduced large numbers of weapons into the region. For example, the government in Uganda is facing at least two armed factions fighting against it.[190] Sudan has been embroiled in civil war for more than two decades; Ethiopia has had years of political instability, and there is still war in some parts of the country, while Somalia has to a large extent experienced state collapse. Kenya, which borders all these countries, has been inescapably affected.

One example of a "new" case of conflict involving the pastoralists is the one in Oke-Ogun part of Oyo State in southwest Nigeria. The Fulani pastoralists who had been living together peacefully with the Yoruba farmers went to war in early 2000.[191] While the causes of the conflict include, allegedly, the destruction of farmlands by Fulani nomads and the refusal of the Fulanis to pay compensation, there are other indices of the conflict that show the impact of prevailing political and social conditions on the manifestation of agro-pastoralist conflicts. Among others, the key issues that emerged include the insensitive and partisan role of the police, who allegedly took sides with the Yoruba farmers, and the role of the Odua People's Congress (OPC), a militant ethno-nationalist group that also supported the Yorubas against the Fulani herdsmen.[192]

Nevertheless, just as conflicts involving pastoralists and agriculturists persist, likewise, countries in the region are looking for ways to address them, and structures and institutions are being erected to meet the challenges posed by these conflicts. In Burkina Faso, for example, a central institution responsible for handling these disputes is the Tribunal Departmental de Conciliation (TDC).[193] The West African subregional organization, ECOWAS, has also taken interest in the conflict between livestock and crop farmers. In January 2003, the Council of Ministers adopted a regulation and a number of recommendations on the social conflicts between livestock breeders and crop farmers.[194] Part of the resolution deals with effective implementation of the rules governing transhumance and the establishment of a regional framework for consultation in the area of pastoral resource management. In April 2004, ECOWAS delegation on trans-border pastures made visits to three countries— Burkina Faso, Ghana, and Togo.[195]

Conclusion

With examples drawn from across the continent, this chapter has shown that land, agricultural, and pastoral activities are sources of inexhaustible controversies in Africa, and the conflicts associated with them are some of the most profound. While the causes of most of these conflicts have been diverse, I have identified the weakness, and in some cases, the complete absence of mechanisms for resource governance as being central to all. For example, across the continent, the land tenure arrangements are laden with potentials that can engender acrimonious intergroup relations, especially as they have been unable to resolve the contradictions that have been bequeathed by traditional, western, and sometimes religious land tenure systems. The management of agricultural products, especially those central to national economy too has been defective, with producers alleging that central governments have been less than honest with the ways they have acted as intermediaries between them and the foreign market, while policies to manage relationships between pastoralists and other segments of the society have caused acrimonious intergroup relations. But apart from specific problems created by the land itself, other resources embedded in it are also major causes of conflict. The next chapter looks at how some of these resources—solid minerals—have been associated with conflict in post-Cold War Africa.

4

THE CONFLICTS OVER SOLID MINERALS

> The conflicts and political instability that have characterized the country's history cannot be separated from its abundant natural resources. Copper, diamonds, uranium, cobalt, silver, gold, etc., have all contributed to the conflict in the DRC.
>
> Tajudeen Abdulraheem

> Diamonds . . . have been implicated in terrible wars, and have compounded the corruption and misrule that have had such corrosive effects [on states].
>
> Lansana Gberie

Discussions in this chapter may have to be prefaced with the identification of the group of natural resources categorized here as "solid minerals." Put simply, these are resources whose finished products come in solid form. Included here are natural resources such as copper, diamonds, gold, and iron. Two considerations justify a separate discussion of this class of natural resources. First, some of them, notably diamonds, have featured prominently in many of Africa's recent conflicts, making them perhaps the most controversial natural resource in the continent's post-Cold War conflicts. Second these resources evoke peculiar characteristics in their recent linkage with conflict, particularly because of their association with a number of post-Cold War security developments, including the reintroduction of foreign mercenaries, the increasing prominence of warlords' activities, and the deep involvement of external actors, especially multinational corporations and international nongovernmental organizations, in African civil conflicts.

In this chapter, I discuss how solid minerals have been linked to recent African conflicts. The central argument in the chapter is that this class of mineral resources has assumed the negative reputation it has because the structures of governance have not taken into consideration how the ease of the disposability of these resources and their high profit margins could attract the attention of an array of interest groups, including armed groups, international business interests, political elites, criminal gangs, local and international civil society, and multinational corporations, to encourage and sustain conflicts. The pursuit of divergent interests by these groups has launched a sustained assault on some countries, thus resulting in a domestic political climate of a willingness to exploit the international demands for the resources and vice versa. I also contend that fundamental governance issues such as injustices in the management of these resources, particularly as these relate to the neglect of the societies producing them, and the mismanagement of revenue coming from them, have created a defiant attitude in the local population and instilled in them the determination to wrestle and control these resources for their direct advantage.

Linking Solid Minerals to the Causes of Conflict

Across Africa, solid minerals have been linked to the causes of conflicts in three circumstances: when the land bearing these resources is a subject of rival claims between different communities, ethnic groups, or nation-states; when the population or sections of it protest violently against government's management policies; and when political alliances disrupt the activities of local artisan operators.

Rival Claims to Land Bearing Solid Mineral Resources

Disputes over the ownership of land bearing solid mineral resources have caused a number of conflicts across Africa. The way these conflicts have been expressed has given them the characteristics of a land ownership conflict. In theory this category of conflicts can manifest at both national and international levels, however, the relative stability in Africa's international boundaries in the last decade has meant a prevailing tendency to the former, where belligerents are often local communities fighting over portions of land known or believed to be rich in solid mineral resources.

The logic behind many of these conflicts symbolizes the complexities inherent in the politics of natural resource governance in Africa, as the intention of most of the local communities engaged in such conflicts is not to exploit the resources for their direct benefit—a prerogative often left exclusively to governments—but rather, to derive the benefit of physical developments that sometimes accrue to areas the governments recognize as being endowed with vital natural resources. The development here includes good roads, schools, hospitals, and so on. Consequently, at the root of such conflicts is the desire to reap the developmental benefits and the minimal compensation governments might pay for the land acquired for the purpose of extracting these resources.[1] As discussed later in this book, this raises a crucial question in resource politics as to whether the local inhabitants or the government should have greater control of the natural resource endowment of a particular area.[2] The whole phenomenon also raises the issue of what formula is to be adopted in the event of local communities and central governments having to share the profits accruing from these resources. A situation in which ethnic communities have to violently contest ownership of resource-rich land in order to attract the attention of the government is indicative of a fundamental problem in governance.

Two recent examples of the aforementioned category of conflict can be noted here. First is in southwest Nigeria between two communities, the Igbojaiye and Ofiki in Oyo North.[3] Both sides cite conflicting historical claims to a portion of land rich in mineral resources, and they began warring in 2002. It took the intervention of the government to pacify the situation.[4] The second example is in the Gambella region of Ethiopia, where the discovery of mineral resources have prompted the Anuaks, who consider themselves to be the original settlers of the land, to assert their claims against rival claims from other ethnic groups, particularly the Highlanders.[5] In December 2003, conflict broke out between the Anuaks and the Highlanders and about three hundred people were killed.[6]

One characteristic of conflicts among local communities over the ownership of lands on which solid minerals are deposited is that they are often unreported outside the country of their occurrence. Generally, they are low-intensity in nature, and central governments are often determined to ensure that news of such conflicts is nationally contained. Such conflicts may receive wider recognition only when foreign multinational corporations invited to exploit these resources are prevented to do so by means including protests and kidnapping of their workers.

Disagreement over Management Policies

A far more profound linkage between solid minerals and the causes of conflict in Africa arises in the objections from the populace to the government's management policies. Indeed, it is the set of conflicts in this category that has brought solid minerals to the fore of politics in regions such as Liberia, Sierra Leone, and the Democratic Republic of Congo (DRC).[7] Since the conflicts in these countries are vital to the discussions in this chapter, a brief summary, especially on how they relate to governance and the management of natural resources, may be necessary. It is also important to identify specific solid minerals whose mismanagement is linked to the causes of these conflicts.

Liberia, the first of the three countries to experience civil war, has had its conflict come in two phases: 1989–96 and 1999–2004.[8] The first took off as a war against the late President Samuel Doe but later became a multidimensional civil war,[9] while the second saw two armed groups, the Liberians United for Reconciliation and Democracy (LURD) and the Movement for Democracy in Liberia (MODEL), fight against the Taylor administration.[10] The solid minerals whose management has been linked to the conflict were diamonds and iron, of which the former was far more pronounced. Diamonds were discovered in Liberia shortly before World War I, but it was not until much later that a discovery of any meaningful significance was made, and even this was not of comparable scale to those in neighboring Sierra Leone. All mining activities in the country are artisanal, and they are almost entirely alluvial (found in waterborne deposits of gravel).

Different aspects of the war in the West African nation of Sierra Leone have also received considerable attention.[11] Within the country, a rebel force, the Revolutionary United Front (RUF), under the leadership of the late Foday Sankoh,[12] fought four successive governments between 1994 and 2002, resulting in up to 100,000 casualties and several more thousand displaced persons.[13] The war in Sierra Leone has brought out an array of actors, including the national army, local civil defense units, known as the *Kamajors*,[14] regional peacekeeping force, Economic Community of West African States' monitoring group (ECOMOG), the United Nations military team, mercenaries, and members of the British army.[15] The mineral resource whose mismanagement has been linked to the Sierra Leone conflict is the diamond, which is the country's main mineral resource. Since its discovery in the 1930s, the country has produced more than 50 million carats of diamonds.[16] The diamond deposits in the country are commonly the alluvial variety.[17] There are also highly prized Kimberlite dyke concessions (underground rock-formation deposits). These are found in Sierra Leone's three main fields—Koidu-Yengema (Kono),[18] Tongo,[19] and Zimmi.[20] For most of the 1960s and 1970s, diamonds accounted for approximately 70 percent of Sierra Leone's foreign exchange earnings. However, corruption, collapse of state infrastructure, and smuggling had considerably reduced the country's diamond exports by the mid-1980s.[21]

The conflict in the Democratic Republic of Congo is more complex than those of Liberia and Sierra Leone. Indeed, the incessant instability that has characterized the country's postindependence history seems to have arisen from the efforts by local and international interest groups to control its enormous resources as well as from the corruption of its governing mechanisms to handle the resources in ways that would benefit the population.[22] At one stage in the war, there were more than ten interrelated conflicts simultaneously taking place in the country.[23] In 2003, a peace initiative championed by South Africa's President Thambo Mbeki resulted in the signing of another peace agreement between the Joseph Kabila government and the main rebel factions. Under this, Kabila maintains his position as the president, with four vice presidents.[24] This has not brought lasting peace to the country. As noted in chapter 2, the DRC is endowed with large reserves of solid mineral resources, including copper ore, tin concentrates, cola, zinc concentrates, cobalt, uranium, industrial diamond carats, gem diamonds, silver, gold, tantalum, and niobium.[25]

A close look at these three countries has shown three major ways through which the management of solid minerals has been linked to the causes of conflicts. The first is due to the corruption of the governing elites. Across the continent, confirmed cases of corruption have been consistent features in some of the countries endowed with abundant solid mineral resources, and in two of the countries—Sierra Leone and DRC—where a solid mineral resource (diamond) has played a key role in the civil conflicts, the period preceding the actual commencement of the conflict was characterized by massive corruption in the management of these resources. In Sierra Leone, successive administrations mismanaged the proceeds from diamonds. The government of the late Siaka Stevens (1968–85) was perhaps the greatest culprit in this respect. Stevens' greed was likely to have benefited from his deep knowledge about the internal workings of the mining business as the country's pre-independence minister of mines. Although there was a Government Gold and Diamond Office (GGDO), established to oversee the collection of revenue,[26] the vast majority of annual production was smuggled out of the country. Local politicians and resident Lebanese entrepreneurs colluded with external business interests and petty criminals to bypass official channels in order to smuggle the diamond resources. In the words of Victor Davies, the administration "institutionalized corruption through a patrimonial system of rationed favors, theft of public funds, illicit payment and bribes, rent from allocation of access rights in the exploitation of diamonds and other natural resources and individual exceptions to general rule."[27] These nefarious activities continued under subsequent administrations of Momoh, Strasser, and Bio[28] to such an extent that despite the country's enormous potential, it had, by the early 1990s, become one of the poorest countries in the world.[29] This catalog of corruption reduced the respect the populace had for the government and thus created a fertile ground on which the rebel force was to base the appeal at the commencement of its activities. Indeed, the RUF anthem specifically demands for accountability from the government on the management of natural resources.[30]

Mismanagement of proceeds from solid minerals was also a major cause of the war in the DRC, (formerly Zaire). The years of Mobutu's mismanagement of resources resulted in the collapse of the country's economy. By early 1997, the Zairian economy barely existed. Despite its enormous resources, the GDP was just over half of its 1988 level and the per capita income was about $125. Infant mortality at 142 per thousand live births was one of the highest in the world, and the International Monetary Fund (IMF) had declared the country as "off-track."[31] Disenchantment with the government was widespread, and it was not difficult for the rebel movement to gain sufficient recruits from the largely unemployed and malnourished population. Even those who did not join formally became sympathizers of the rebel movement. The army, which had been weakened by decades of nepotism and corruption, could not meet the determined challenge of the rebel forces and their regional backers, and it was not long before the government collapsed.

The situation in Liberia was similar to those in Sierra Leone and the DRC. After more than a century of economic mismanagement by the Americo-Liberian oligarchy, the late President Samuel Doe continued the corruption that had existed in the country's iron and diamond productions.[32] Doe personally took over the management of some of the key resources in the country. As Reno has noted, Doe's corruption and his desire to appease his domestic base led to chaotic tax policies.[33] Exports fell drastically and multinational corporations responsible for mining in the country, especially the Liberian American Mining Company (LAMCO), the National Iron Ore Company, and the Bong Mining Company left the country in 1989, 1985, and 1988, respectively.[34] The result was the further worsening of the country's economic situation, which further paved the way for rebellion. During his administration of the country (1999–2003) Taylor also continued the mismanagement of the country's natural resources.[35]

In all the cases discussed above, the extent of the corruption was to be a crucial factor in latter years when the political climate in these countries changed and the populace emerged to challenge the corrupt tendencies of their political leaders. As will be shown later in this book, the extent of corruption in many of the countries endowed with natural mineral resources, and the reckless abandon with which this is demonstrated, are factors that have underlined the violent conflicts surrounding solid mineral resources. The local population in many African countries is often indifferent to corruption of their political leaders. However, the appalling insensitivity demonstrated by some of these leaders was such that the populace was willing to adopt violence in opposition to the corruption that was reducing them to abject poverty in tandem with the unsympathetic demonstration of affluence by their leaders.

The second way in which the management of solid minerals has been linked to the causes of conflicts is through the neglect of resource-producing areas. This comes mainly in the form of inadequate infrastructures. While this factor is noticeable in all three countries, albeit in varying degrees, the situation in Sierra Leone was the most pronounced. Here the country's southeast province, which is the main diamond-producing region, suffered neglect from successive governments, such that the people in the region had little to show for being the residents of the resource-rich land that is the mainstay of the national economy.[36] This ultimately created a disenchanted operational base for rebellion in the locality. It was thus not surprising that the rebel leader Foday Sankoh spearheaded his rebellion from this region, in spite of the fact that his ethnic base was in the north, where one would expect him to have the requisite support for such a rebellion.[37] It is also noteworthy that in the 1980s, the Ndogboyosoi War in Pujehun district (Southern Province) was the first rural rebellion against central government.[38] In the DRC, the situation was slightly different, as the neglect was widespread through most of the country. However, while most regions of the country fatalistically accepted the situation, those from the resource-producing communities were more prone to violent reactions. This exploitation of a disenchanted base by Taylor also manifested in a slightly different way in Liberia, as Nimba County, from where Taylor launched his rebellion, was not vulnerable because of the earlier mentioned neglect but from the victimization Doe inflicted on them for their political views.[39]

In the above cases, a consistent pattern arises in that antigovernment sentiments are often rife in communities that do not see visible impacts of hosting solid mineral resources on the quality of their lives, providing disenchanted bases that were thus exploited for dissident activities. With the depression in the economic fortune of many African countries, the tendency for these neglected societies to feel further aggrieved has increased considerably, and the ease with which they can gain access to violent weapons has further heightened the propensity for violent conflicts.

The third way of linking the management of solid minerals to the causes of conflicts comes through the neglect of rural communities in favor of urban dwellers. Across Africa, evidence of rural neglect is rife. In Sierra Leone, for example, access to safe water and sanitation in urban areas in 1990 was 83 percent and 59 percent, respectively, compared with 22 percent and 35 percent for rural areas. As a result, rural dwellers increasingly became indifferent to the security problems confronting the central government. Thus, when rebel forces took up arms against the Momoh government, there was apathy from the rural areas. Although the Kamajors, largely from the rural areas, became the backbone of the government security forces, their involvement was more visible after the rebel force took to brutalization. A similar pattern of neglect was evident in Liberia where, apart from the victimization visited on the Nimba people by the Doe government for supporting his opponents, the neglect the people experienced from the national wealth was a major factor in their support for the rebellion. Across Africa, this tendency has been linked to the causes of conflicts surrounding solid minerals in two ways. First, it further adds to the provision of an aggrieved operational base, waiting to be exploited by those intending to challenge the government. Second, it makes the rural communities become indifferent to the security plight of the urban dwellers, even when the rebellion is externally sponsored against the government at the capital. It is vital to note that a consistent pattern in much of the conflict is that people living in rural communities have indeed given support, in varying degrees, to the cause of the antigovernment forces, largely based on their perception that they are the neglected majority in an unjust social setup.

While the neglect of rural communities is common across Africa, the residents of communities in mineral-rich countries failed to comprehend why they were denied the most basic of amenities. Further, the post-Cold War political climate has raised questions about issues that had hitherto been taken for granted, inclusive of the neglect of the rural community. The failure of governments to provide timely valid responses led to the adoption of violent methods by rural communities. The extent of their determination to use this opportunity to seek redress is clear in the ways that members of these communities are at the vanguard of scouting and marketing the resources for personal enrichment after the breakdown of the structures for resource-extraction and management. The scale to which this was pursued was also motivated by the realization that such an "opportunity" may never avail itself again.

Disruptions to the Activities of Local Artisans

While this class of conflicts over natural resources is quite common, they are often unrecorded. This is possibly because they are usually intertwined with other considerations in natural resource politics. At the root of the conflicts are a number of considerations that bring local artisans into disagreement among themselves, international mining consortiums, and the government. Among the issues at stake are the determination of local artisans to continue operation in areas governments have allocated to international organizations for mining purposes; the attempt by foreign companies, often with the support of governments, to displace local artisans from mining sites; and the determination of local artisans to reject any attempt by the government to regulate their activities. In short, at the roots of the conflicts are the clashes between local claims, national interest, and international demands.

Across Africa, local artisans have often seen themselves as victims in a purported conspiracy of the alliance between the government and international mining consortiums. They also see their direct involvement in the mining process as the only opportunity to directly benefit from these resources. The government, on the other hand, argues that it is difficult to regulate the activities of these groups and hence, it has been impossible to monitor them for taxing purposes and for the prevention of smuggling.

The relationship between local artisans and big multinational corporations in the diamond trade is far more complex. In all of Africa's producing countries, artisan producers play an important role in diamond production. In the DRC, estimated figures claim there could be up to a million artisan miners, while the Sierra Leone minister of mineral resources, Mohamed Deen, has noted there may be up to 200,000 artisan miners in the country.[40] The activities of artisan miners are largely unregulated, operating with very crude equipment. While there are no known cases of violent conflicts between artisan producers and major diamond companies, artisan production raises a string of security considerations, especially as only the indigenes are officially allowed to operate as artisans. This has become problematic in regions where nationality and citizenship are contentious issues. Presently, Angola is facing more criticisms from human rights groups, especially Human Rights Watch (HRW), that the country is committing "acts of barbarisms" against foreign diamond diggers, commonly known as *garimpeiros*. These people are mainly from neighboring countries such as Namibia, Zambia, and Zimbabwe, with some coming from as far as DRC, Mali, and Burundi. In the process of expelling these people, HRW claims that the Angolan army committed acts of atrocities. While admitting that excessive force could have been used in some cases, the Angolan Interior Minister, Osualdo Serra Van-Dunem, argued that this was in legitimate pursuit of national interest.[41]

Worth recording at this juncture is the role of Lebanese traders in the diamond politics in Africa, especially in Liberia, Sierra Leone, and the DRC. While some of these may be involved in legitimate trade, a far more significant percentage is involved in dubious trading methods. Over the years, they have developed complex networks of relationship with successive government functionaries at the expense of the state. The most important characteristic of the dubious segment of the Lebanese traders' activities is their ability to develop formal and informal business arrangements with all actors that emerge in the diamond business. This has seen these traders work perfectly well with successive government functionaries, rebel groups, and peacekeeping missions, among others. More often than not, the relationship between the Lebanese traders and these actors is based on their mutual desire to exploit the natural resources of the country. As Lebanese traders control a string of other businesses in the region, they can afford to undercut the market and sell at a loss, since they can make up for the shortfall in other businesses. This is coupled with a knack of operating business during conflict.[42] Corrupt African leaders have also preferred to deal with them because of their somewhat unethical business practices.

In the aftermath of wars, local artisans and illegal miners have also exploited the prevailing weak structures to loot solid minerals. For example, in the mineral-rich Grand Kru region of Liberia, illegal miners have refused to pay taxes on the gold and diamonds they smuggle to Guinea, Côte d'Ivoire, and Togo.[43] The problem is particularly prominent in the town of Genoyah, where illegal miners have bribed their way through to escape payment of taxes.[44]

Solid Mineral Resources and the Fueling of Conflict

The main attention solid minerals have attracted in recent years has been due to its association with the fueling of conflicts. Indeed, a June 2000 World Bank Report asserts that diamonds were prime factors in conflict. The key countries whose conflicts have been fueled by solid mineral resources are Sierra Leone, DRC, and Angola, and in all cases, diamonds have been a key resource. Since there has been an overview of the wars in Sierra Leone and the DRC earlier in the chapter, there is the need to provide a summary of the Angolan war, especially as it relates to the discussions in this book.

Like Sierra Leone, Angola's main solid mineral resources are diamonds. The country's diamonds account for more than 50 percent of its foreign earnings and, along with Botswana and South Africa, Angola has been Southern

Africa's major diamond producer. The concentration of diamonds in Angola is in the Cuango Valley and Lucapa, with the latter source being the origin of the larger and purer diamonds.[45] Diamond mining in Angola dates back to 1912, and dominated the country's export income until World War II brought coffee into prominence.[46] The discovery of oil in 1973 further reduced the importance of diamonds, but by the 1980s, diamonds, along with oil, were the main natural resources in the country. However, Angola's natural resource endowment was beclouded by its civil war (between the National Union for the Total Independence of Angola [UNITA] and the Popular Movement for the Liberation of Angola [MPLA] government), which had the unpleasant distinction of being one of Africa's longest and most bloody civil conflicts. A major opportunity for peace, however, came in 2001, when Jonas Savimbi was killed.[47] Both UNITA and the MPLA governments have diamond deposits in the territories they held, but the greater percentage of the resources fell under UNITA's control. The organization's control over Angola's diamond territories had become established by the end of the 1980s, especially in the northeast region, as it had begun exploiting the resource.[48] Although battle vicissitudes changed the nature of control, with government forces making greater inroads into UNITA territories, the organization still held greater control of diamond sites for the entire duration of the war.

In Liberia, Sierra Leone, Angola, and DRC, the countries where solid minerals have been crucial to fueling civil conflicts, control of territories with resource endowment is often the prime target of belligerents. In Sierra Leone, the RUF had initial control of the main mines, and it took the involvement of mercenaries and the Nigerian-led ECOMOG force to dislodge them. In Angola, UNITA concentrated attention on diamond-rich regions. The situation in the DRC was, however, more complex because, unlike Angola and Sierra Leone where there was only one rebel movement each, several warring factions contested for the future of the DRC. During the first phase of the conflict, the politics of resource control was less ambiguous, due largely to the limited number of the sides involved in the conflict. With most of the resources still under the central government, Mobutu exploited these in order to prosecute the war. However, as the rebel force advanced and took over control of the mineral-resource sites, they too exploited these resources in prosecuting the war.

In discussing how solid minerals have been linked to the prolongation of conflicts in Africa, four interrelated factors could be identified. These are: through their use as a source of revenue used for arms procurement; through their encouragement of intransigence to peace moves; through their encouragement of greed on the part of the political elites; and through their attraction for external interests. Since there is a separate discussion of the activities of neighboring countries later in this chapter, discussion in this section is limited to how solid minerals have been linked to arms procurement, how control of territories with mineral resources has encouraged intransigence to peace moves, and how solid minerals have served the greed that has encouraged the prolongation of conflicts.

Concerning the link to arms procurement, it has to be noted from the outset that this is perhaps the most pronounced of the ways through which solid minerals have contributed to the prolongation of conflicts. It is also one that has attracted considerable attention. In Sierra Leone, it is believed that apart from the initial arms the RUF obtained from Liberia's NPFL at the beginning of the conflict in 1992, most of the weapons used in the civil war were those obtained through the direct sales or barter of diamonds. Most of these arms came from Eastern European countries, then anxious to dispose of weapons made redundant by the end of the Cold War, and were transferred to the Sierra Leone rebels through countries such as Libya, Côte d'Ivoire, Burkina Faso, and Liberia. At the beginning of the war members of the Sierra Leone armed forces connived with the rebels to supply them with weapons and uniforms in return for rough diamonds. According to Paul Richards, this kept the RUF alive in military terms "and served to confirm its belief that Sierra Leone is still plagued by corrupt tendencies that . . . 'require revolutionary cleansing.' "[49] While the role of diamonds in the RUF's arms procurement has been widely reported, it needs to be noted that the government also used money from diamonds to procure arms to fight the rebels. It provided additional opportunity for rent seeking especially during the National Provisional Ruling Council (NPRC) government, as top members of the administration had family members participate in arms trade.[50] Both Taylor and the RUF swapped arms for diamonds with other arms dealers and diamond merchants involved in the arrangement.[51]

However, the conflict that most demonstrated the link between solid minerals and arms procurement was the Angolan civil war, where UNITA relied almost entirely on the sale of diamonds to provide the arms used in prosecuting the conflict. For example, between 1995 and 2000, buying offices purchased up to US$36 million worth of stones yearly from UNITA sources without paying tax. All the offices were closed in January 2000, in a bid to end the flow of UNITA diamonds into the international market. Earlier in December 1999, the Angolan Council of Ministers revised diamond law and had set up a new parastatal, Sodiam, which reserved the sole right to buy diamonds within Angola. A 51 percent state-owned marketing venture, the Angola Selling Corporation (ASCorp) was also set up within two *diamantaires*—Israel's Lev Leview and Antwerp-based Sylvain Goldberg. It was envisaged that this new marketing system would control the internal buying of gems, boosting tax returns to more than US$50 million from US$22 million. The new system also uses unalterable Certificate of Origin with a control system in place of each serial-numbered certificate.[52] The difference between Angola and other countries is that, in the latter, the arms procured were mainly light weapons that suited the nature of the conflict, whereas UNITA's purchases were more sophisticated, including warplanes and missiles. For example, between 1994 and 1998, UNITA purchased military hardware from Eastern Europe, particularly Ukraine and Bulgaria. This is believed to have included "50 T-55 and T-62 tanks; a significant number of 155 mm G-5, B-2, D-2 and D-30 guns; medium and long-range D-130 guns; BMP-1 and BMP-2 combat vehicles; ZU-23s anti-aircraft weapons; and BM-21 multiple rocket launchers."[53]

The encouragement of intransigence to peace moves, which constitutes the second way through which solid minerals have been linked to the prolongation of conflicts, has also gained interest and attention in recent years, as factions holding control of areas rich in mineral resources during the course of conflicts are usually more predisposed to continuing the conflict. In Sierra Leone, it is believed that one of the reasons why the RUF reneged on all the peace agreements signed in the course of the country's conflict was the financial benefits accruing to its leadership from the illegal sale of diamonds.[54] Indeed, some of the documents recovered from Foday Sankoh's house after the January 2000 raid on his residence showed that exploitation and sale of diamonds increased immediately after the signing of the agreements.

However, the intransigence to peace moves that can be linked to control of solid mineral resources features prominently in the case of Angola, where UNITA, even at the risk of losing all the external support that had historically sustained its rebellion remained intransigent to local and international efforts to end the war. This shows how the desire to retain the financial privileges coming from control of solid minerals can becloud careful assessment of battle fortune, as it should have been obvious to UNITA and Savimbi in particular that they could not sustain the war for long without the support from apartheid South Africa and the United States.

The nature of the conflict in the DRC introduces a different dimension to the manifestation of this problem. The intransigence to peace moves has been both from the different warring factions and from the regional countries that were involved in the war. The armed groups have been party to many agreements signed in order to end the conflict, most of which were not successful. War later broke out again, ultimately necessitating deeper threats and involvement of the United Nations. One characteristic of the war is that the nature of regional interest was so complex that the extent of the local factions' capability to dictate developments was severely limited.

The third way, which is through whetting the appetite of greed, has manifested in different ways, the most important being the emergence of a multiplicity of actors. As a result of the existence of single rebel groups in Sierra Leone and Angola, the focus of interest was on the key players in the RUF and UNITA, respectively, and Liberia, in the case of Sierra Leone. However, the multiplicity of the fighting force in the DRC and the extent of regional involvement have meant that the centers of authorities are diffused, and so there is an increase in the number of greedy interests to be satisfied. There have been allegations of direct involvement of many of the key Congolese politicians in mining deals. It is probably impossible to get to the roots of these controversies. Although most of the attention has been on the leaders of these factions, the rank and file are also known to have taken deep interest in acquiring resources for personal gain. Indeed, it is believed in certain quarters that one of the reasons Laurent Kabila fell out with Uganda and Rwanda was that his wealthy local allies felt uncomfortable with the role being played by these two countries in the management of the Congo's mineral resources.[55]

The role of mineral resources has come out more distinctly in the controversy between the two factions of the Rally for Congolese Democracy (RCD). Both sides have traded accusations of mining deals. It has been alleged that a key RCD Goma's official established a company known as Sonex, which was supposedly owned in conjunction with South African–based Anglo-American firms that have had substantial mineral interests in Congo since the Mobutu era. Another company, Saropa, also allegedly controlled by RCD Goma, was purported to be mining diamonds in Banalya, about sixty miles north of Kisangani. The RCD Goma, has in turn accused the Wamba faction of the RCD of being involved in mining deals.

Also worth recording under this section is the role of the members of the national army of these countries in personal financial enrichment through the provision of security and protection for foreign companies engaging in mining during the periods of conflict. Sierra Leone and Angola present notable examples in this respect. In the former, members of the security forces, especially during the period of the NPRC, were providing protection to those undertaking illicit mining, while at the top echelon of the government, members of the ruling council were issuing licenses to foreign concessionaires involved in diamond mining. The political situation in the country during this time was such that diamond mining could only take place alongside the protection of members of the security forces.[56] There was a similar arrangement in Angola, with generals from the national army engaging in private arrangements to provide security for foreign companies involved in mineral extraction. This arrangement completely excludes the state, as the military officers undertook this in their private capacities, even though the rank and file soldiers they use to provide the protection for these companies were members of the national armed forces. This example was particularly common in the Lucapa area, where the military provided security for diamond companies and casual diggers involved in illegal mining.[57] A clearer picture of the nature and extent of greed is revealed, however, when the activities of warlords and the immediate neighbors of the countries affected in this category of conflicts are discussed.

Warlords and Conflicts Involving Solid Minerals

As noted in chapter 1, implicit in the notion of warlord is the desire to maximize the incidence of wars for economic and political gain. In this context,

Duffield's definition of a warlord seems appropriate. He sees a warlord as "the leader of an armed group, who can hold territory locally and operate financially and politically in the international system without interference from the state in which he is based."[58] All across Africa, it is believed that most of the warlords who have led rebellions against central governments have exploited the resources for personal gain. Solid minerals have offered some of the greatest attractions to warlords in times of conflict, largely because of the ease with which they can be sold or bartered to procure weapons. The methods of operation in most cases are similar. With an outbreak of conflict, warlords target the main mineral resource base of the country in order to capture and market the produce. The proceeds are used to procure weapons, which are then used to acquire more political powers. Complex networks are developed, either through the neighboring states or international criminal gangs, and warlords are able to penetrate international markets to dispose of these resources and ensure the regular supply of weapons. Apart from direct involvement in the mining of these resources, another source of income for the warlords is through "protection" fees that are extorted from foreign multinational corporations. For the multinationals, it fulfils mutual interests with the warlords. Although, on the surface, it often appears that the multinational corporations are losing income because of the protection payments, in actuality, with those payments, they are able to go beyond the agreed extraction limits that are in their contract. Consequently, they were able to make up for the loss through the increase in their exploitation.

Going now into the history of warlord activities in these countries: in Liberia, while it was only Charles Taylor at the commencement of the first phase of the conflict in 1989, other warlords later joined. In Sierra Leone, the situation was a little more complex. While the leader of the only armed faction against the government, Foday Sankoh, remained the key warlord, the nature of the conflict was such that a number of key supporters of Sankoh became major actors in their own right, especially as they assumed the leadership of the group on his behalf while he was incarcerated in Nigeria.[59] Hence, an individual such as the late Sam Bockarie (Mosquito) could be effectively described as a warlord.[60] Even members of the armed forces who later left the force to join with the rebel movement, such as the former leader Johnny Paul Koroma, represent, to a large extent, warlords. The nature of the war in Sierra Leone has served to alter the existing categorization structure of a warlord.[61] The same applies to Angola where, although the late Jonas Savimbi remained the main warlord, the duration of the conflict and its complexities resulted in the emergence of several sources of alternative authorities and control, resulting in the creation of other actors who could be described as warlords. Although they were largely loyal to a central authority, they also had individual political and economic ambitions, which they advanced under the single UNITA fold. In the DRC, the history of warlords remains a very confused one, as there appears to be more warlords than the number of warring factions.

Four factors have determined how successful warlords can be in benefiting from solid minerals in periods of African conflicts. These are: how weak existing governance structures within the state are; how strong and determined the alternative structures advanced by the warlord are; the extent of external involvement in the conflict; and the time the external involvement was introduced into the equation. Where the existing structures are weak and the warlord provides a stable, even if oppressive alternative, with little on no direct involvement from outside countries, it is likely that the grip of the warlord on the economy will be strong. This was the case with Charles Taylor in Liberia. If, however, the situation is otherwise, an alternative may be the case.

In post-Cold War Africa, one of the first conflicts that created distinct warlord–solid minerals connections was the Liberian Civil War, and the first major warlord that emerged was Charles Taylor. Although the structures in the country were weak and Taylor provided a strong and determined leadership, the nature and extent of regional intervention, and the timing of the intervention, prevented him from maintaining his dominant position as the sole warlord in the country. Although there had been disagreements within the force even before the regional force ECOMOG came into the conflict, as has been evident in the split of Prince Yomie Johnson from the National Patriotic Front of Liberia (NPFL), the wrangling would seem to be more of divergence of views over how to fight the Doe government, than over the management of natural resources. However, by the time ECOMOG came into the country and Taylor's strength was diluted, other actors with the sole intention of exploiting the mineral resources in the country began to emerge. There were also some founded allegations that the regional peacekeeping force, ECOMOG, encouraged and even assisted in the formation of some of the factions that ultimately created more warlords.[62] These new sets of warlords and members of their armed gangs later joined Charles Taylor and his NPFL in pillaging the mineral resources under their respective controls. The nature of the conflict was also that even within these armed groups, there were those who could be termed as "mini-Warlords," who operated as local actors in resource exploitation. For example, one William Toe of the NPFL arrested miners at Jlodah and ordered them to mine under his command, confiscating regular taxes and demanding four ounces of gold every month.[63] In most cases, the main warlords were aware of the activities of these mini actors but were inclined to overlook such activities, provided, of course, these were not overdone in ways that could affect the "returns" they make to the main warlord. All these mineral resources were sent to European markets through conduits provided by countries such as Côte d'Ivoire and Burkina Faso. In Liberia, Charles Taylor was specifically well placed to maximize his benefit, as he was able to use the contacts he had previously established with foreign companies as a senior procurement official in Doe's government.[64]

The situation in neighboring Sierra Leone was similar, as the corruption and maladministration of successive All Peoples Congress (APC) governments left the country's structures weak. Although it was not the case that Sankoh provided any credible alternative at the beginning, the assistance he obtained from Taylor disguised this fact until he was strong enough to make independent existence. Sankoh was quick in establishing his leadership over his troops, and with the control of the resources, he was able to gain and retain their loyalty, at least initially. The exact amount of how much he made during the conflict is unlikely to be ascertained, but a record of diamond transactions that was discovered at his residence during the 2000 raid shows that between August 1999 and January 2000, Sankoh received 2,134 pieces of diamonds, amounting to 347 carats of gem and 95 carats of industrial diamonds from his fighters operating in the eastern mining towns of Kono and Tongo. The regional involvement in Sierra Leone had a lesser impact on Sankoh's activities than it did in the case of Taylor in Liberia. There are at least two reasons for this. First, unlike Liberia, the extent of regional involvement in Sierra Leone was weak, and it had little impact on the rebel forces. By the time the regional peacekeeping force responded to the situation in Sierra Leone seriously, Foday Sankoh and his troops had taken effective control of most of the main mining sites, leaving the international community with little option but to negotiate with him. Second, Sierra Leone's mineral resource base is more extensive than that of Liberia, and it was therefore not easy for the regional force to take effective control. This gave Sankoh the continued financial backbone to prolong the war. His detention in Nigeria resulted in the loss of considerable authority over his forces. This shows that warlord authority, even after it has attained a somewhat mystic image, must be constantly strengthened to ensure a continued grip over economic and political influence. Indeed, economic and political initiatives had broken into several groups, with the late Sam Bockarie maintaining the dominant position. Sankoh's delay in returning to Freetown after the Lomé Agreement was influenced in part by the desire to obtain greater financial support from Côte d'Ivoire and Liberia, the two countries with whom he maintained regular business contacts.[65]

Angola presents a slightly different scenario, as the warlord politics in the country are not purely a post-Cold War phenomenon, so the factors that have shaped it have been of a complex hybrid. Over the years, Jonas Savimbi and his key officials established a strong network through which they were able to exploit and market the resources under their control. As of 1986 and 1987, it was alleged that diamond trade revenue was in the range of US$50,000 and US$4 million a month for Savimbi and UNITA.[66] Angola's proximity to South Africa, a major base in the international diamond market, and the years of support that apartheid South Africa gave UNITA, made it possible for the leadership to maximize its gains from diamonds. This survival was not devoid of difficulties, especially in the threats that came after the organization lost American support. Savimbi was able to entrench himself more easily because at the time the war began, there were indeed no state structures. He thus had the advantages warlords in other recent conflicts did not have—starting with a clean slate and establishing "structures" in the territories he controlled. For example, UNITA had a "Ministry of Natural Resources," which handled diamond sales. Savimbi was also able to put in place a complex relationship structure with a number of African leaders to whom he made generous donations in exchange for assistance with money laundering and the provision of end-user certificates for his arms.[67] Over the years, Savimbi became entrenched in the international diamond trade and was thus able to continue with the war, even after South Africa and the United States stopped assisting his movement.

Warlord politics in the DRC has also been largely determined by the nature of the war. Although there were weak structures in the country that could have given warlord politics a strong base to survive, especially if it were to be under a strong leadership, the attempt to fill the gap was largely externally driven. Even Kabila, who was later to replace Mobutu, was more of a regional initiative. This strong regional influence in the commencement of the war reduced the influence of local warlords, at least initially, and made them mere individuals making money from the sale of the resources but with no commensurate power and influence. All the key players in the conflict have a major regional power determining, even if only to an extent, their activities. Furthermore, the geographical expanse of the country means that it is difficult to establish control over its entire space. Also, with many factions involved in interwoven conflicts, having local warlords with considerable strength became all the more difficult. The ultimate outcome was a situation in which many warlords emerged to carve the country into spheres of economic and political influences, a tendency not made easier by the deep involvement of neighbors in the conflict.

In concluding this discussion on the involvement of warlords in conflicts involving solid mineral resources, a number of conclusions may be drawn. The first is that solid minerals are vital to warlords because the international demand for them carries considerable financial benefits. Second, the degree of the success that attends the efforts of warlords in benefiting from solid minerals depends on the extent of the weakness of the state, especially as it relates to the management of these resources. Third, the extent of the grip of the warlords over the control of solid mineral sites can be vital in the political outcome of the conflict, especially in the ultimate resolution of the dispute.

External Involvement in Solid Mineral Conflicts: The Roles of Neighbors and Mercenaries

In most of the African conflicts where solid minerals have featured, a common factor is the involvement of the countries bordering the affected states. As mentioned above, this has been a crucial factor in prolonging the conflicts. This section discusses the reasons and the nature of the involvement of neighbors in the major conflicts highlighted in this chapter. While reasons vary from country to country, four determining factors can be identified. First is the genuine desire of the neighbors to end the conflict and thus get the affected country "up and running" again; second is the desire to protect their own security, especially against the possible fallout of the conflict, such as refugee influx; third is to carry out the international mandate that may have been imposed to end the war; while the fourth is to benefit economically from the conflict. It is often difficult to explicitly demarcate these factors as the altruistic intention of ending these wars tends to be beclouded by the desire to seize the economic opportunities emanating from them.

During Angola's civil conflict, immediate neighbors were unable to benefit much from the country's solid mineral wealth for at least two reasons. First, the stakes in the conflict were quite high, such that beyond platitudinous condemnation of UNITA, the neighbors were not strong enough to play any decisive military role in the conflict. Although apartheid South Africa and Namibia were active participants, they played smaller roles in carrying out instructions from their Cold War backers. Thus, the limited involvement of the neighbors denied them active participation after the Cold War ended. Second, the nature of the war, which, owing to its level of sophistication, meant the weak economies of many of the countries in the region could not afford to be active participants.

The neighbors' involvement in the DRC seems to be the most extensive. Indeed, in a recent edition of *Diamond Industry Annual Review* published by the reputable Diamonds and Human Security Project, the country is said to be located in a bad neighborhood where diamonds are concerned.[68] Nine countries surround the DRC, and with porous borders it has been difficult to monitor its regional trade. Although the smuggling of DRC diamonds has been going on for several years, the civil conflict in the country has worsened the situation. The general assumption has been that many of the external actors in the conflict intervened for the sole purpose of profiting from the country's mineral wealth. However, other factors have served to explain the extent of the involvement of neighbors in the conflict, such as the weakness of the state and the number of factions involved in the conflict. As noted earlier, five countries have been involved in the DRC conflict: Angola, Rwanda, Uganda, Namibia, and Zimbabwe. Critics of the neighbors' expansionism have argued that the economies of most of these countries do not justify the "adventurous" foreign policies being pursued. Consequently, they have argued that the war could only have been economically profitable if the country's mineral resources are exploited and looted.[69]

External actors in solid mineral extraction in the DRC tend to fall into either those supporting the different rebel factions or those assisting the government. Although there are many factions involved in the DRC conflict, the RCD have come out prominently. For most of the war, Uganda controlled two of these factions, albeit unsuccessfully, while Rwanda essentially controlled the

RCD faction led by Adophe Onu-sumba. However, as Emizet Kisangani has noted, the Congolese rebel groups do not share the same agenda with their stakeholders.[70] The three other countries—Namibia, Angola, and Zimbabwe—supported the Kabila administration.

Uganda gave five reasons for its involvement in the DRC: (1) to deny the Sudanese government an opportunity to destabilize Uganda through the eastern Congo; (2) to deny habitation to Ugandan dissidents, especially the United Democratic Front (UDF); (3) to ensure that the political and administrative instability arising from rebel-government clashes in eastern Congo do not destabilize Uganda; (4) to demobilize elements of the *Interahamwe* and ex-FAR and thus prevent them from terrorizing Uganda and Rwanda;[71] and (5) to protect Uganda's territorial integrity from invasion by the Kabila forces.[72] Rwanda's reasons are similar. They were all related to the determination to seek out and incapacitate members of the *Interahamwe* and ex-FAR, who fled into the DRC after the genocide, from attacking the country.[73] This determination became more profound after the alliance that brought Kabila to power collapsed, and he was allegedly assisting the Rwandan dissidents based in the DRC. Thus, to varying extents, both Uganda and Rwanda believed there were direct military threats to their respective countries emanating from the DRC. Some are of the opinion there was an exaggeration of the aforementioned factors in order to conceal less altruistic motives. There are also arguments that making an incursion of several thousands of miles into a country, just as Rwanda did, cannot be explained under the desire to protect borders.[74]

On the other hand, the three countries that intervened on the part of the Kabila government—Zimbabwe, Angola, and Namibia—did not make any claim to any direct military threats against their sovereignty. The roots of their involvement date to the invitation the late President Laurent Kabila sent to the SADC to assist him in meeting the security challenges poised by Uganda and Rwanda. Consequently, the three countries maintained that they went into the country in the name of the SADC. It needs to be mentioned, however, that this intervention split the SADC, as the decision to intervene in the DRC was taken at a meeting that was not attended by all the members of the organization. Indeed, South Africa was not present at the meeting at which the three countries decided to intervene in the DRC conflict, and this is despite the fact that President Mandela was the chair of the body that should ratify such an intervention. It is, indeed, consequent on this that many believe there are hidden motives behind the intervention of Angola, Namibia, and Zimbabwe in the DRC conflict. It is believed that Mugabe in particular wanted to demystify the reputation being attributed to both Museveni and Kagame as the new set of African leaders around whom future patterns of leadership on the continent would be woven.[75] For Angola, there was also the reason of national interest for supporting Kabila, as the MPLA government aimed to puncture the alliance allegedly growing between UNITA and the rebel groups in the DRC. This network seemed to be linked to complex diamond sales allegedly going on between rebels in the diamond-rich towns of the DRC and UNITA, also in control of the diamond provinces of Angola.

Certain background considerations need to be borne in mind in appreciating the complexities involved in the neighbors' involvement in the DRC civil war. From its outset, all the countries seemed to have realized that their intervention would be an expensive enterprise, and there was thus an implicit understanding among all parties including the Congolese factions that the war would have to pay for itself. The Ugandan and Rwandan involvements in the DRC have been most controversial for a number of reasons. First, the general assumption that the expansionist tendencies of the two countries was seen as being incompatible with the growing status of "radical leaders" being enjoyed by the respective leaders. Second, the rapid process of transition from loyal supporters of the late President Kabila to his ardent opponents was viewed as suspicious and not devoid of the expectation of personal gain in the involvement in the DRC conflict. Third was the ultimate disagreement between the two countries on the policy in the DRC. After being trusted allies for several decades, the open display of antagonism between both governments raised questions as to what ulterior motives may exist. Finally, the two countries operated in some of the richest portions of the DRC and, therefore, international attention on their activities was profound.

The region of the country most affected by the activities of Uganda and Rwanda in the DRC is eastern Congo, especially Province Orientale, North and South Kivu, and Maniema. There are significant reserves of good quality gemstones in Province Orientale and in northern Maniema. These include diamonds, gold, and manganese. The Ugandan and Rwandan involvement in the exploitation of the DRC mineral resources is somewhat complex. While it is widely believed that illicit trade in mineral resources occurred with their tacit and open support, it is often difficult to obtain accurate information of all the ways through which this occurred. One way that has been identified is through the various local officials under the patronage of the two countries. This pattern is a reorientation of the clandestine and fraudulent trading mechanisms of the Mobutu years.

The conflict between Uganda and Rwanda presents one of the main ironies of the Congo crisis, and the extent to which this has been rooted in resource considerations can be seen in the various clashes between both sides in the DRC town of Kisangani. The town is in the eastern part of the DRC and is one of the main mineral-rich provinces of the country. The Kisangani war has different sides to it, but all can be traced to the unresolved issues of divergence of objectives and priorities of conducting the war in the DRC, further compounded by uncoordinated orders from Kampala and Kigali. The roots of the controversy surrounding Kisangani can be traced to the early stages of the war when both Rwanda and Uganda were allies supporting the rebel forces against Kabila. Rwanda captured Kisangani, with assistance from the rebel force that was based in Goma, but handed over the administration to Uganda, while it continued its daring pursuit of blistering attacks on Kinshasa, Lubumbashi, and Mbuji-Mayi. The attacks on these other towns suffered setbacks, largely due to the regional support that came for the Kabila government, and it was under this military stalemate and continued Rwandan attack on Mbuji-Mayi that the Lusaka Peace Accord stalled all further military moves. So, without the control of Kinshasa, Lubumbashi, and Mbuji-Mayi, and with huge military commitments, Rwanda had to fall back on Kisangani and seek joint control with the Ugandans, who also needed the resources from the town to sustain and justify their involvement in the war. Both countries thus had to administer Kisangani, and it was inevitable that conflict would ensue. Indeed, for a long time, Kisangani became the reference point of the extent and greed of regional desire to profit from the Congo conflict.[76] The irony is rooted in the fact that both countries are regional allies, who had worked together through four rebellions, genocide, and two decades of turmoil in the region. It will take a long time for the whole story of the conflict to emerge, and some aspects may remain unknown. However, most independent observers of the conflict believe that mineral resources played a major part in the debacle between the two countries, even though both sides often try to de-emphasize the importance.[77]

Differences in the policies to be adopted toward the DRC form another source of problem between the two countries. Uganda claims that Rwanda did not share its stance that the Congolese should be empowered to administer the area, and that they (Uganda and Rwanda) should assist them in this respect. It was alleged that Rwanda wanted to dominate the events in the region and prevent the involvement of any local initiative.[78] Rwanda dismissed this allegation and condemned Uganda's claim as cheap publicity.[79] Regardless of what the position was, it was clear that both sides had different interpretations of what the policy toward the DRC should be. There were additional unresolved military issues linked to the issues of divergence of objectives and priorities of conducting the war in the Congo. This in turn was complicated by issues of organization and strategy among the allied forces in Congo. The matter was left to the whims of operational commanders and the noncoherent orders from Kampala and Kigali. At the beginning of the war, a joint operational command by both the Ugandan Peoples Defense Force (UPDF) and the Rwandan Patriotic Army (RPA) was agreed upon by the political leadership in Kampala and Kigali, but this was rejected by the UPDF officers in Kisangani. The UPDF officers preferred two operational sectors, with the northern sector (Kisangani sector) to be under UPDF and the southern sector under RPA. This was unacceptable to the Rwandan Patriotic Front (RPF) government in Kigali, thus leading to the inevitability of conflict.

Apart from this, there was the issue of each country's ego. Rwanda complained bitterly at the tendency of Ugandan authorities to consider them "small boys" who should treat them (Ugandans) with respect. Uganda allegedly remembered the time when many of those presently in the leadership of the

RPA were junior officers in the NRM rebel force, and thus the Ugandans still had a condescending perception of some of the Rwandan leaders. Indeed, it was rumored that some members of the UPDF described the commander of the Rwandan Army in the DRC, Brigadier Kabarebe, as a "small Corporal" in the Ugandan Army. This was viewed with great aversion by the leadership in Kigali and, with all these differences unresolved, it was clear that a total breakdown of the relationship was only a matter of time. Closely linked to this is the issue of what the Ugandans see as an act of "betrayal" on the part of the Rwandan leadership. It is widely believed that Museveni specifically chose Kagame to lead the RPF after the assassination of the organization's leader, Fred Rwigyema. The Uganda leader, however, was said to have felt uncomfortable with Kagame's presidential ambitions, especially as he (Museveni) preferred a Hutu president in order to prevent any suspicion of his trying to build his own Tutsi empire in the Great Lakes.[80]

Beyond these operational disagreements were major differences over the exploitation of DRC's mineral resources. By the time the war broke out, fighters from both sides had become deeply aware of the enormous potential that could come from Kisangani. The senior officers had been involved in arrangements with RCD members on how best to maintain monopoly of mineral resource sites. Allegations and counterallegations abound on the management of Kisangani resources. An example of this was the case known as the Pikoro case, which centered on the ownership of the Banalia gold mine. Following the overthrow of Mobutu, the Alliance of Democratic Forces for the Liberation of Congo-Zaire (AFDL) government arrested one Mr. Pikoro on charges of murder and assault of some mineworkers. He was taken to Kinshasa, where the government revoked his licenses and repossessed the mines. Pikoro, however, regained the mines after the defeat of the Kabila forces in Kisangani and continued mining. The action brought him in direct conflict with the local administration, especially the governor of Kisangani and the RCD leadership in Goma, who challenged his possession rights, deciding to handle the case in accordance to law.

In an effort to secure possession "rights," Pikoro sought the protection of the UPDF top commanders in Kisangani. The governor and the RCD leadership who needed revenue from the mines to run the state felt blocked by the Pikoro–UPDF alliance. This divided the UPDF, RPA, Congolese Forces Commanders, and the Congolese Civil Administration, with the UPDF on the side of Pikoro and the RPA on the side of the governor. It also created a dilemma for the governor who did not want to antagonize his two allies (RPA and UPDF), thus referring the matter to the RCD leadership in Goma. When eventually an attempt was made by policemen to arrest Pikoro, the UPDF officers intervened and whisked him away. The governor formed a five-man commission to "care-take" the mines, but the UPDF commanders blocked their access to the site. The governor called another meeting, involving Major Ruvusha of the RPA, Lt. Col. Geoffrey Muheesi of the UPDF, and a Congolese officer, in order to arrive at a resolution. The meeting again came to the conclusion that the mines belonged to the state, but Lt. Col. Muheesi insisted that the decision would not apply until after the war. Also important in understanding the role of mineral resources in the conflict between the two countries is the dispute over the Bamaliya diamond mines, where both countries are believed to have deep commercial interest.[81]

The first open clash between Rwanda and Uganda over Kisangani occurred in August 1999. Inevitably, accounts of events leading to the clash differ. Uganda claims that Rwanda attacked UPDF bases to prevent the verification exercise agreed upon under the Lusaka Peace plan which, according to the UPDF, it was helping to facilitate. This was denied by the RPA, who claimed that it was the UPDF that attacked their position. The clash lasted between August 6 and 7, 1999, and by August 17, 1999, both President Museveni and Major General Paul Kagame, then Rwandan vice president, met to demarcate Kisangani. In the ensuing demarcation Rwanda was to control west and south, while Uganda was to take charge of north and east. The RPA was also to keep one company at Bankoka airport, which was in the UPDF sector, while the UPDF was to station a company at Simsim airport, which remained under the RPA. All troops were to be deployed out of Kisangani city center, which was to be exclusively patrolled by joint military police of Uganda and Rwanda. A number of joint committees were also set up to ensure that tensions were nipped in the bud.[82] These, however, did not prevent future conflicts, as there were two further clashes between Uganda and Rwanda in Kisangani.[83]

Zimbabwe, which was the first to enter the conflict on the side of Kabila, had invested an estimated $47 million in military and economic partnerships with Kabila, as of 1998, even before hostilities broke out, including $5 million allegedly given to fight Mobutu.[84] The initial number of troops committed was 3,000, but this eventually grew to 11,000.[85] Zimbabwe's Mugabe never hid his intention of financial benefits in his involvement in the DRC. He confirmed that he had discussions with Laurent Kabila on how Zimbabwe's involvement would be financed. According to Mugabe, after suggesting to Kabila that DRC should bear the cost of Zimbabwe's involvement, Kabila had instead suggested a partnership to exploit the natural resources of the DRC and to share the profit.[86] Other senior officials have followed this line. For example, the justice minister, Emerson Mnangagwa, confirmed that he had been introducing Zimbabwean businessmen to Congolese officials, and declared that there was "a deliberate effort to push Zimbabwean business interest into Congo."[87] Another government spokesman, Mr. Chiyangwa, confirmed that one of the reasons Zimbabwe was keen to get into Congo was that it had missed other lucrative opportunities in the region. Citing the Mozambican civil war, where Zimbabwe had earlier committed troops,[88] Mr. Chiyangwa claimed that despite his country's sacrifice, it was South Africa, fighting on the side of the rebels, who picked up the gains at the end of the war.[89] He thus made it clear that Congo was not to be a repeat experience. Indeed, concluding on

Zimbabwe's involvement in the DRC, Michael Nest noted that the government "prodded . . . an initially private sector to establish commercial units and engaged in business, while rich entrepreneurs with close links to the Zimbabwe African National Union Patriotic Front (ZANU-PF) inner circle did business in the DRC using military personnel as a cover to avoid Congolese customs."[90] A point that is noticeable about Zimbabwe's business deals in Congo is that it has not concentrated only on natural resources but on a wide range of sectors, including transportation, banking, and defense. However, two solid minerals that allegedly caught the interest of Zimbabwe were cobalt and copper.

Inevitably, the entire business sector in Congo has resulted in names of key Zimbabwean politicians and military officers being involved in extensive business deals. Zimbabwe's former information minister, Chen Chimutengwende, denied President Mugabe's involvement in the Congo's business sector, but maintained there was nothing wrong with ministers' and politicians' involvement in government or party-owned companies or even their own companies to do business in Congo. However, key names that have been mentioned include President Mugabe himself; Mr. Emerson Mnangagwa, the justice minister, who, though denying the allegation, confirmed that he might have introduced businessmen to Congolese ministers; and the army commander, General Vitalis Zvinavashe.[91] Apart from key politicians and senior military officers, other ranks of the armed forces were encouraged to profit from the conflict in the DRC. A Zimbabwean national army officer, Colonel Thinga Dube, was alleged to have said on national television that "there are fortunes to be made in the Congo . . . so why rush to conquer the rebels."[92]

The controversies over Zimbabwe's involvement in Congo's resources also resulted, again expectedly, in domestic opposition. While the crux of the criticism was on the justifications for the country's involvement in the Congo, it later became more specific as to the allegations of fraudulent mining deals in Congo. For example, a vocal independent member of parliament, Margaret Dongo, raised the issue and demanded an explanation from the government on whose interests the alleged deals were serving.[93] In recent years, Tanzania also has been mentioned in allegations of gem smuggling with the focus being on the alleged involvement of Tanzanian officials with their Zimbabwean contingents and businessmen.[94] In what was later called the Dar-Harare Axis, the growing ties between Tanzania and Zimbabwe were believed to be disturbing western donor institutions, who see Tanzania as a faithful pupil of the IMF reform.[95]

But by the far the greatest indicators that neighbors are exploiting the conflict in the DRC to smuggle out diamonds can be seen in the activities of the Republic of Congo (Congo Brazzaville). The country is not known to be a major actor in the diamond trade, but has, in recent years, exported diamonds of significant magnitude. The conclusion from most diamond analysts was that these were smuggled diamonds from the DRC.

Neighbors' involvement in the exploitation of Sierra Leone's diamond resources also has become an issue of major international controversy. Some of the countries surrounding Sierra Leone were involved in profiting from the country's diamonds and have, in different ways, encouraged the prolongation of the conflict. Of all these countries, however, the most prominent was Liberia. While it was always believed that the country had been involved in diamond deals in Sierra Leone, evidence remained largely anecdotal. But by 1997, anecdotal graduated to circumstantial, when Liberia exported 5,803,000 carats of diamonds to Belgium. At this time, the estimated production of diamonds in Liberia was only 150,000. This aside, the country's diamond export increased sharply from US$8.4 million in 1988 (before the wars in both countries) to US$500 million in 1995. The final confirmation came in May 2000, after the collapse of the Lomé Peace Agreement forced many Sierra Leoneans to invade Foday Sankoh's house. During the search of the house, evidence of diamond transactions with Taylor, which Sankoh had documented, was uncovered. Other countries such as Côte d'Ivoire and Guinea also have been indicted. The former, which is not known to be as substantial a diamond producer, sold 150,000 carats of diamonds in 1997, while Guinea had its modest annual expectation of 295,000 carats increased to 533,000 in 1998. The believed assumption here is that these were utilized opportunities to conceal Sierra Leone's diamonds.

A somewhat different dimension of regional involvement in the exploitation of natural resources in conflict is the role of the regional peacekeeping force, ECOMOG, in Liberia and Sierra Leone. This peacekeeping force has been accused of entrenched involvement in the exploitation of natural resources of both countries. Some have even accused the leadership of Nigeria during the period, especially Babangida and, more important, Abacha, of various business deals in mineral resources. There is evidence to support the allegation that some members of the peacekeeping mission took active part in illicitly benefiting from the solid mineral endowments of both countries.[96] The desire to benefit from the resources was, however, not the main reason for intervening in these conflicts. This is explained in Nigeria's desire to maintain its position as a regional superpower and to keep the military engaged.[97] While occasional lapses in military activities might give the impression of connivance with the warring sides to exploit the resources, the main reason has to be sought in the poor treatment of the members of the regional force and the political problems in Nigeria, especially in its military. When it was necessary for Nigeria to act decisively, it always did so, as evidenced on many occasions, the last being the attempt to reinstate Kabbah after his overthrow by Koroma.[98]

A more complex stage in the ECOMOG involvement in Sierra Leone came in May 2001, when the commander of the UN force (UNAMSIL), Major General Vijay Jetley, implicated four Nigerians—Brigadier General Muhammad Garba, Major General Gabriel Kpamba, the late Major General Maxwell Khobe, and Ambassador Olu Adeniji,[99] of collaborating with the RUF in diamond mining.

In a letter written to the UN, Jetley claimed that ECOMOG and the RUF had formed a strategic relationship over time, which included:

> non-interference in each other's activities, the total absence of ECOMOG deployment in RUF held areas is indicative of this. Keeping Nigerian interest was paramount even if it meant scuttling the Peace Process and this also implied that UNAMSIL was expendable. To this end the Representative to the Secretary General (SRSG) and the Deputy Force Commander (DFC) cultivated the RUF leadership—especially Foday Sankoh—behind my back.[100]

This was emphatically denied by the accused, who were supported by the Nigerian government.[101] The allegation leveled by General Jetley needs to be explored in greater depth, especially because it was the first formal allegation since ongoing suspicions from the beginning of the war in Sierra Leone. From the moment he assumed command of the Sierra Leone operation, Jetley had major problems with Nigeria. The friction had a story of its own: when the UNAMSIL was formed, Nigerians expected that a Nigerian officer would be made the commander. This expectation was grounded on the local knowledge Nigerian officers had acquired from their years of operating in Sierra Leone. Furthermore, Nigeria had more troops in the mission than India, Jetley's home country. However, Jetley's appointment was because a Nigerian diplomat, Olu Adeniji, had been the UN secretary general's special representative, and it was considered inappropriate for the special representative and the force commander to come from the same country. Consequently, the relationship between Jetley and those of his immediate subordinates—Kpamber and Garba—was not cordial.[102]

It was thus not long before things began to go wrong with the operation. The worst case was the abduction of five hundred UN peacekeepers by the rebel force. Jetley blamed his inability to free the peacekeepers on moves by the Nigerian officers to circumvent his efforts. He said this was a result of Nigeria's General Kpamber not being made the commander of UNAMSIL, and he based his allegations against Nigeria on three grounds: messages of RUF intercepted at the Sierra Leone Defense Headquarters; total absence of ECOMOG deployment to the RUF-held areas; and the refusal of Nigerian troops in NIBATT 2 to fight the RUF at Lunsar, Rogberi, Rokel, Masiake, and Lara junction.[103] Jetley's accusation against the Nigerians created considerable diplomatic furor. In response, Nigeria refused to allow its forces to serve under Jetley, and India later withdrew its forces from Sierra Leone.

Going now to the role of mercenaries, allow me to point out from the outset that recent involvement of mercenaries in African conflicts is attributable to four factors: the end of the cold war that created new opportunities and challenges; the increase in the number of conflicts, especially resource-based in post-Cold War Africa; the emergence of a more "organized" professional outfit of mercenary companies; and the effects of globalization, which lessened the difficulties traditionally experienced by mercenaries, especially in relation to payment for services rendered.

Any writing on the linkages between solid mineral resources and mercenary activities must, of necessity, concede to the fact that the clandestinity that is a strong feature of mercenary activities makes the validation of available information very difficult. At the helm of mercenary activities is the expected financial reward. This has indeed given rise to a host of terms that associate it with financial returns, including "soldiers of fortune" and "dogs of war." In the post-Cold War phase, mercenary companies have attempted to put on a new face, as they employ new methods, but the principle motive of making fortune out of conflict has remained. Shortly after independence, when there were a number of conflicts in the efforts to consolidate their independence, the activities of mercenaries were minimal. There are at least two reasons for this. First, Africa, fresh after independence, was still an unfamiliar territory, making it necessary for mercenaries to be cautious of venturing into its terrains. The importance of this is clear as even after the end of the Cold War when a new phase emerged in the relationship between African conflicts and mercenaries, those who first took active interest were white South Africans who had considerable experience on Africa's sociocultural and geopolitical terrain. Second, in the immediate postindependence period, most of the countries on the continent had some form of defense arrangements with their erstwhile colonial masters. This made the activities of mercenaries less lucrative, as the former colonial masters were at the beck and call of their former colonies without any financial implications. Attendant to this were the prevailing Cold War politics, which dictated caution in intervening in African conflicts, especially as not to offend interested Cold War actors.

Toward the end of the Cold War, the interest of mercenaries in natural resources began to take shape. Although their focus remained on the ability of the inviting nations remitting financial pay for services, they were willing to consider other means of payment apart from money. This brought in the era of payment in-kind, with concessions being granted in lieu of payment. Angola was the first to perfect this mode of payment in Africa through diamond concessions, and others followed in the post-Cold War era. There were two main reasons for this shift. First, the international market was getting tighter, and accessibility to trade for factions in war-torn societies was difficult. The demand for cash was high as arms were procured on this basis, hence, all parties were open to some degree of payment in-kind. Second, payment in resources was considered more profitable by the mercenaries. The more they realized their indispensability, the more they were willing to make more demands, and obtaining mineral concessions became one of the key attractions to mercenary companies.

After the end of the Cold War, things changed significantly, and the linkage between mercenaries and resources became more prominent. The considerable increase in resource-based conflicts was a contributing factor to this.

While during the Cold War most of the conflicts were political, and resource consideration stood in the shadows of politics, the guise was completely removed in the post-Cold War period, and the competition over resources assumed greater prominence. Additionally, some of the economic contradictions and injustices that had been suppressed under Cold War politics erupted, leading to the collapse of a number of states in Africa. With this, mercenaries had more interest in African conflicts as the politics of state collapse often linked them in some form of alliance with the warlords who emerged to dominate economics and politics during the civil conflict. Another issue has been the changes in the global political scene, as mercenaries during this period became better organized. Against this background, a new phase emerged in the link between mercenaries and resources in conflict management.

In Sierra Leone, mercenaries took center stage in 1995, when the government of Captain Valentine Strasser brought in the services of the Gurkha Security Guards. This arrangement was allegedly made by a British weapons manufacturer, J&S Franklin.[104] The main tasks given to Gurkha were to protect the U.S.-Australian Mining Corporation, Sierra Rutile, and to offer special training to special forces and officer cadets of the Sierra Leonean military. The fifty-eight–member team that subsequently came to Sierra Leone was led by Robert Mackenzie. Before long, the operation fell apart, and on February 24, 1995, seven members of the group including Robert Mackenzie were killed in an RUF attack.[105] After the incidence, Gurkhas refused to participate in direct operations again and eventually left Sierra Leone in April 1995.

The exit of the Gurkhas and the continued insurgence from the RUF forced the government in Freetown to hire the services of another mercenary company. This was what eventually led the government to the agreement with the South African mercenary group, the Executive Outcome (EO) in April 1995. By the following month, the EO had dispatched one hundred troops to Sierra Leone. This was to reach three hundred at the peak of its operation in the country, and through their close working relationship with the Kamajors, the EO was able to turn the military situation around against the RUF. In financial terms, the EO was paid US$13.5 million for the period between May and December 1995. After Tejan Kabbah assumed power, he extended the contract for twenty months from April 1996 for the sum of US$35.2 million.[106]

But apart from this obviously favorable deal, the EO, through its fronting agents, allegedly gained access into Sierra Leone's diamond market. By July 1996, the diamond mines in the Kono district and other mineral assets along the Sewa River in Koidu had been granted to Branch Energy, one of the organizations linked with the EO. This continued even after EO left Sierra Leone in January 1997. In terms of the military situation, the EO turned the situation around in favor of the government. By May 1995, the RUF had been defeated outside the capital, Freetown; by August 1995, the mercenaries had cleared the rebels from Kono and, by December 1995, the EO had taken over the Sierra Rutile site, a major diamond site in the country.[107]

After the departure of the EO, there was a lull in mercenary activities, and the void was filled temporarily by the Nigerian-led regional peacekeeping force, until the infamous Sandline International controversy in 1998. Sandline International, with Tim Spicer at its head, is a British mercenary organization, which first entered global controversy with its involvement in Papua New Guinea.[108] The company was allegedly introduced to the Sierra Leonean authorities by the former British High Commissioner to Sierra Leone Peter Penfold.[109] A deal was agreed upon with the Kabbah government in exile in February 1998, and it was to supply arms to the Kamajors and ECOMOG to enable them to fight the Koroma government that had overthrown Kabbah in May 1997. Controversy, however, arose when it was alleged that Sandline imported arms in violation of the UN sanction. The company insisted that its activities were known to the British government. This was particularly an embarrassment to the Labor government, who was then trying to establish its "ethical foreign policy." The Sandline controversy ended mercenary activities in Sierra Leone.

The situation in Angola was similarly complex. The country's latest relationship with mercenaries began in January 1993 when Luther Barlow, a mercenary with known links to the Executive Outcome, was commissioned to recruit mercenaries with combat experience in Angola, to secure Soyo, a major oil base which, as of January 1993, was in the hands of UNITA. Barlow succeeded, although UNITA repossessed the town shortly after the mercenaries left. This brought about a new era, as not long after this some Canadian companies with oil interests in Angola hired mercenaries to protect their installations. Apart from the $30 million allegedly allocated by the company for this task, speculation is that oil and diamond concessions were also made. At the end of the operation, mercenaries were believed to have assisted the Angolan government in reclaiming the diamond field of Saurino and Cafunfo. These two fields were major sources of UNITA's funding for the war, and it is possible that their loss was a principal reason why UNITA acceded to the 1994 Lusaka Peace Agreement.

This overview of post-Cold War mercenary activities in Africa shows a number of consistent features, most notably in their link with resources. Perhaps the first has to do with the type of resources involved in the conflicts. In each case, the resources for which the mercenaries have been invited to protect are primary to the national economy, and hence, a major determinant of the invitee's ability to pay the mercenaries. Consequently, often implicitly agreed in most contractual arrangements with the mercenaries are clauses that payment could also be made with resources. This guaranteed the mercenaries that their services would be paid for either in cash or in resources.

A second factor, in the post-Cold War years, some of the mercenaries operating in African conflicts were invited by the central government who, in most cases, had legitimate control over the natural resources of the state. This has caused many of the mercenary companies to argue that they only operate in conflicts where they have been invited by central governments as they would not support rebel forces.[110] While this may be exaggerated to reflect some principled commitment to democratic ideals, it is obvious that the position is largely based on the greater natural resource capacity of the so-called democratic countries.

The fact that some of the post-Cold War mercenaries are invited by the central governments to fight the rebel forces shows clearly the weakness of the state in the post-Cold War dispensation. It is evidence that rebel forces have been able to launch successive rebellions that could not be addressed by the national military forces. The main danger here is that resorting to the usage of mercenaries further weakens the state structures and gives opportunity to external influences, which further erodes the state's ability to cope with a host of post-Cold War challenges. The weakness of central government in the management of its affairs, especially its economic affairs, is also evidenced in the fact that in some cases, the mercenaries were brought into the countries by multinational corporations. This implies that the government was unable to provide the security needed by these companies. It also shows that the government has no serious objection to "leasing" one of its major obligations to the multinational corporations. In all cases, the government is at a disadvantage as multinational corporations often extract the extra expense they incur in hiring mercenaries from the host nation by overexploiting natural resources.

Finally, some of the companies that have emerged in recent years have had some form of association with apartheid South Africa. There are a number of reasons for this. First, because of its peculiar history, South Africa has an abundant supply of residents with marketable military skills. With the end of apartheid, there was limited use for these skills within the region, necessitating going beyond the region to find need for their services. Second, as most of those ex-South African soldiers had no other marketable skills after they were demobilized, mercenary activity was a most viable option. Third, the postapartheid government did not, for a long time, change the laws governing the creation of mercenary companies in the country, thus making their emergence more viable. Finally, unlike mercenaries from outside the continent, they have greater knowledge of the cultural and socioeconomic contexts of the continent.

The involvement of neighboring countries in the affairs of many of the countries involved in conflicts believed to be heavily linked to solid minerals raised a number of key issues for governance, both for the intervening countries and the affected countries. Issues include the implications of such intervention for regional governance, the legality of the intervention, and the extent to which the intervening countries passed the process of intervention through constitutional channels in their respective countries. In all the cases identified above, these problems existed, and they all underline the subregional components of natural resource governance in Africa and the wider global connections.

Solid Mineral Conflicts, International Market, and Global Concern

A number of actors and issues have emerged in the link between solid mineral conflicts, international markets, and global concern. Before discussing these, however, it is worth pointing out that four aspects of solid mineral conflict's linkage with international markets have attracted global concern. The first is the brutality of those engaged in the conflict, which has been largely responsible for the birth of the much-quoted phrase, "blood diamonds"; second is the issue of money laundering; third is the alleged link with global terrorism; and fourth is smuggling. These are somewhat interrelated, especially in the association with the activities of international criminal gangs. Many of the activities are carried out with uttermost clandestinity, consequently, factual evidence for some of the claims may be difficult to find.

The brutality associated with the conflicts has been present in almost all cases. It has been highly documented, thus this book will only summarize the consequences. Sierra Leone and Angola present some of the most gruesome examples, with several cases of children and elderly people killed or brutalized by the armed functions in a desperate bid to maximize their gains in the natural resource linked wars. The publicity given to the brutalization has attracted the attention of the international community and has ignited some of the most passionate campaigns against the illegal trade of gemstones that has fueled this greed.

Money laundering is a crime that has gained international recognition in the last few decades. While initially the practice was linked to the drug trade, in recent times, the trade in gemstones has become the most important means for money laundering. Furthermore, the weakness in the banking structures in Africa has allowed for the increased prominence of this practice. Put in lay terms, money laundering is the process through which money acquired from illegal business transactions is "purified" and thus allowed to enter the banking network as "clean" proceeds from legitimate business arrangements. As a result of its complexities, it has become intertwined with many other activities, including terrorism and corruption. In this practice, money launderers who are able to pay above the market prices for diamonds operate under the cover of a buying office. Typically, they operate on an irregular basis, buying small quantities officially and large quantities unofficially. The official parcels are thus exported through the regular channels with the remainder being smuggled. The official diamond parcels are often sold on the market at a loss with the sale proceeds channeled through the banking circuit.

Smuggling takes different forms, from the highly sophisticated activities with strong political backing to the occasional casual and less well-organized practice. Because of their high value and low volume ratio, diamond trade is considered a most ideal opportunity for smugglers. However, the practice in a more complex form has gained international attention, especially as it is now widely alleged to involve leaders of a number of African states. While this may still be open to debate, what now seems to be beyond contention is that a number of African states with no known records of substantial gem production now trade ample quantities of gemstones in the international market. These countries enable diamond dealers to purchase and re-export gemstones smuggled from neighboring countries as original local productions, or at least to export them with proper documentation. The entire practice affords the smuggling groups other opportunities, including dealing in stable currencies and payment of lower export duties than those applying in producing countries.[111] As noted earlier, Liberia was an important center, serving as a conduit for diamonds originating from Sierra Leone and Guinea. Although it has the capacity to produce only 100,000 karats of diamond annually, it exported more than 30 million karats during the period 1995 to 1999.[112] Congo Brazzaville too has been the center for "legalizing" diamonds smuggled from Angola, CAR, and DRC. The process through which UNITA smuggled Angolan diamonds to the international market was diverse. Dealers from Belgium and Israel would go to UNITA territory with funds to obtain and export diamonds. Another route was through the Portuguese business people with aircraft bases in South Africa who would fly in with oil and arms in exchange for diamonds.[113] UNITA diamonds were also smuggled to Europe via Congo, Namibia, South Africa, Rwanda, and Zambia.[114]

Low-level smuggling is less complex. As a diamond digger receives less than 6 percent of the export value, he will be tempted to sell to an illegal buyer who often pays more. Illicit buyers are numerous around digging areas; they range from the "harmless" unregistered field brokers who sell to buying offices, to serious operators with considerable resources. These are often Lebanese traders, operating on a cash and barter basis, exchanging diamonds for household things.

Five different actors have come out distinctly in the controversies over the concern for conflicts involving solid minerals. These are international NGOs, multinational companies involved in the mining of these resources, the United States, the EU countries, and the United Nations. A number of international NGOs have been involved in the efforts to stop all illegal trade in solid minerals, especially diamonds. The main interest of these NGOs is to ensure that the resources do not continue to encourage the brutalization of the local population in these countries. Hence, the concern about the effects of smuggling and money laundering is predicated on the extent to which these can further result in the killing and mutilation of innocent civilians in these countries. This position was spearheaded by a British NGO, Global Witness. In December 1998, the organization published *A Rough Trade* and followed this up with an effective media campaign that attracted global attention. In September 1999, another NGO, Human Rights Watch, published a report entitled *Angola Unravels: The Rise and Fall of the Lusaka Peace Process*. Although this was on the political and military situation in Angola, it also confirmed UNITA's funding of its war efforts through the sale of diamonds. By October 1999, Global Witness had stepped up its media activities by joining forces with other NGOs to launch an umbrella group known as Fatal Transaction. The first act of this organization was to distribute information to jewelry retailers on the whole issue of conflict diamonds. By January 2000, a Canadian NGO, Partnership Africa Canada, added its voice and called for a comprehensive review of diamond trading regulations. Specific concern was focused on the role of diamonds in the Sierra Leone conflict, and international industries were accused of encouraging the trade in smuggled gems.[115] In April 2000, a group of European NGOs launched a public awareness campaign over the role diamonds can play in conflict. The NGOs claim that in Angola, between 1992 and 1997, nearly 500,000 people died while UNITA earned US\$3.7 billion in the illegal sale of diamonds, and that trade in diamonds between 1991 and 1999 earned the RUF of Sierra Leone US\$200 million per year.

The second set of actors is the multinational corporations involved in these resources and, quite expectedly, the company that has been at the forefront of this is De Beers.[116] The company has exclusive buying rights with some governments in Africa,[117] so it is the diamonds not bought by the company at source that ultimately end up in Antwerp, Belgium, often regarded as Europe's diamond capital.[118] When calls began to mount on the need to place a ban on UNITA's diamonds, the initial response from De Beers was vigorous opposition. Its argument rested on the difficulty in ascertaining the origin of diamonds.[119] Although the company argued that it never knowingly bought UNITA's diamonds, it also claimed there were complications, which made it possible for UNITA's diamonds to end up in the company's bulk. In this regard, De Beers argued that diamond traders are wont to mix up parcels of diamonds from different sources to disguise their origin. They further argued that some of UNITA's main buyers were government officials who bought the diamonds and gave them the official certificate of origin.[120]

All the negative publicity surrounding diamonds forced De Beers to change its position on the issue. While it condemned the ways in which rebel factions have exploited diamonds to prosecute conflicts, it argued that calls for a global boycott of diamonds would be counterproductive, as it would affect other countries that depend on diamonds and are not at war. Specifically, the company identified Namibia, South Africa, and Botswana. It further argued that Angolan diamonds account for only 1.5 percent of global production.[121] Statistically, the company further noted there is only a 1 in 100 chance that a diamond bought by a consumer would have come from Angola, 1 in 3 from Botswana, and 1 out of every 2 from southern Africa as a whole.[122] De Beers insisted that it had not bought any UNITA diamonds (even through a third party) since July 1998, when sanction came into effect. In February 2000, De Beers announced that it would guarantee that any uncut gem it sells through the Central Selling Organization did not originate in rebel-held territories. In June 2000, the Israeli Diamond Exchange added its voice by declaring that it would revoke the membership of any diamond dealer who knowingly sells conflict diamonds that have originated from rebel territory.

In July 2000, the International Diamond Manufacturers Association (IDMA) agreed to implement a system that would provide documentation showing where a diamond has been mined. A meeting was later held in September 2000, in Windhoek, Namibia, bringing together many of those involved in the diamond business. Despite the difficulties involved in the fight against "blood diamonds," it is certain that an appreciable level of public awareness has been raised in the linkage between diamond and civil conflicts in Africa. While there may still be blood diamonds in circulation, it is no longer through "respectable channels." This subsequently forced UNITA to sell the stones at 30 percent discount.[123]

There has been a subtle disagreement between the NGOs working to put an end to conflict diamonds and the multinational corporations involved in their exploitation and marketing. The companies accuse the NGOs of irresponsible overreaction, especially in overgeneralizing their condemnation of multinational corporations involved in the diamond trade. They also believe that the search for funding and the desire to gain new headlines have encouraged NGOs to make unsubstantiated claims that sometimes border on being libelous. The NGOs, for their part, argue that the secrecy with which the companies operate indicates that some of their activities are not straightforward, and that despite their claims to transparency, they are still using legal loopholes to endorse illegal trade in diamonds. Without specifically mentioning NGOs, De Beers came up with what it described as the "Problems with the Conflict Diamonds Campaign" in the case of Angola, listing inaccurate and unsubstantiated estimates; negative effects on legitimate and economically critical trade; persistent confusion over the political history of Angolan diamond fields; lack of appreciation of the complexities of the diamond industries, among other points.[124]

The activities of international corporations involved in solid mineral extraction in Africa again entered international attention when, in June 2005, the world's second largest gold mining company, Anglo-Gold Ashanti, confirmed that it had been paying one of the rebel factions in the DRC to ensure regular access to resource sites and for importing cargoes—something it now claims to regret doing. The company operates in Mongbwalu, in the Ituri district, one of the richest parts of Congo, and the rebel faction the company had been having regular discussion with, the FNI, has been involved in gross human rights violations. The NGO, Human Rights Watch, has been at the forefront of investigating the activities of the companies, and the entire disclosure further supports the claims by the NGOs that there are multinational corporations involved in resource extraction that are less-than-truthful in their claims. The meeting between the company and the rebel group began in 2003. The director of Anglo-Gold Ashanti tried to explain that the nature of the environment made it difficult for him to confirm some key details of the transaction with the rebel groups but did confirm that payment was made to the rebel group as late as January 2003.[125]

The third actor consists of the United States and some Western European countries. Contrary to what is often assumed, America's involvement in the fight against conflict diamonds precedes the September 11, 2001, terrorist attacks. As far back as May 2001, President George Bush had made clear his decision to prohibit the influx of all rough diamonds originating from Liberia.[126] However, America's participation in the war against conflict diamonds became more pronounced after there had been alleged links with the activities of Osama bin Ladin.[127] For the United States, the whole involvement has been necessitated with the supposed association between solid minerals and terrorism. With regard to Western European countries that are involved, especially Britain, the interest has been rooted both in the effort to combat terrorism and the drive to pursue the proclaimed effort to assist in the establishment of good and accountable governments in some of these countries. In October 1999, a U.S. Democratic Congressman for Ohio, Tony Hall, introduced the Consumer Access to a Responsible Accounting of Trade Act (CARAT), which required diamonds coming into the United States to be accompanied by a Certificate of Origin. This was later replaced by the Clean Diamonds Act.

A subtle disagreement also seems to be brewing among key western countries involved in the diamond business over the nature and extent of conflict diamonds in Africa. Belgium and Canada are notable actors in this disagreement. Many key people in the Belgian diamond trade, including the managing director of the Diamond High Council,[128] Peter Meeks, believe that the controversy over conflict diamonds has been inflated and that as of early 2004, the problem barely existed.[129] He thus views the whole issue as part of a "Canadian plot to damage Belgian diamond industries."[130] He also argues that the regular monitoring suggested by the Kimberley Process Certification Scheme is economically motivated. This is a claim categorically denied by Canada, with Ian Smilie of Partnership Africa Canada disagreeing with Meeks' claim that conflict diamonds barely exist.[131]

By far the greatest efforts have been made by the United Nations, whose main objective initially was to ensure that these resources cease fueling the wars that have caused untold sufferings to the population. Over time, though, other issues, such as the linkages between these resources and the global security issues of terrorism and money laundering, have become key considerations, albeit on a lesser scale. Mainly, the United Nations' role has been through the establishment of commissions to investigate and identify culprits in the politics of resource extractions in countries involved in civil conflicts. The first of such was the Fowler Commission, set up in 1998 to investigate the sanction bursting in Angola.[132] The committee submitted its report in March 2000 to the UN Security Council, in which it found a number of African leaders guilty in the UNITA diamonds-for-arms deal. The alleged chief culprits in the report are the late President Mobutu Sese Seko of Zaire, the late President Gnassingbe Eyadema of Togo, and President Blaise Compaoré of Burkina Faso. The report confirmed that Eyadema had, from 1993, begun collaborating with UNITA in providing end-user certificates for the organization to purchase weapons and was also providing a safe haven for UNITA equipment. The deal also allegedly included Eyadema playing host to some of Savimbi's children and receiving diamonds in exchange.[133]

According to the report, Eyadema kept a share (normally within the range of 20 percent) from each consignment of the arms and military equipment that were imported for UNITA. In each case, Eyadema could decide whether Togo would take its share in-kind or as cash. It was further alleged that Eyadema made a personal fortune in deals with UNITA in both monetary terms and the diamonds given to him by Savimbi. With the fall of Mobutu, Eyadema, for a period in 1997, became the recipient and "storekeeper" of UNITA's military weapons and equipment, also replacing Mobutu as the primary supplier to UNITA of end-user certificates.

The report established Burkina Faso as a transit point for arms originating from Eastern Europe and destined for UNITA. It was revealed that arms were unlawfully diverted to UNITA through Burkina Faso in breach of the UN sanction. The Burkinabe capital, Ouagadougou, was a particularly favored safe haven for transactions between UNITA and diamond dealers based in Antwerp, London, and Tel Aviv. It was also indicated in the report that Savimbi would inform Compaoré in advance of a delegation from him arriving for a diamond sale. Such delegations were usually met on arrival by Compaoré personal aides and provided with protection and escort, to ensure the safety of the diamonds or cash during the delegation's stay in the country. Other countries identified as having participated in sanction bursting are Côte d'Ivoire and Rwanda.

In its conclusion, the Fowler Commission came up with thirty-nine recommendations, including Security Council sanctions against governments breaking sanctions; compliance with UN sanctions as a consideration by NATO and the EU when evaluating candidates for membership;[134] DNA-type analysis to establish the origin of fuel captured from UNITA; forfeiture penalties on those who cannot prove the origin of their rough diamonds; sanctions against those breaking UN sanctions on UNITA diamonds; offending states should be noted as sanction-breakers and their nationals barred from senior positions in the UN, with international organizations discouraged from holding meetings there.[135]

The determination of the international community to carry out the dictates of the UN resolution on the culprits first came when Togo was isolated in the May 2000 African Caribbean and Pacific (ACP) states' negotiation with the EU for a new Lomé Convention. A more profound showdown was threatened when a number of African countries, particularly from southern Africa, threatened to boycott the July 2000 OAU Summit in Togo, and further opposed Eyadema's assumption of office as the organization's chairman. Angola, in particular, was vehement in the call that Togo should not be allowed to host the summit, and for ethical reasons that Eyadema be prevented from becoming the OAU chairman.[136] The clampdown on blood diamonds by the Fowler Commission received the endorsement of De Beers. The corporation benefited from the tightening of control on blood diamonds as it would allow for more effective control over diamond prices.[137]

The United Nations also became involved in Sierra Leone, where it imposed sanction on Liberia's Charles Taylor for his involvement in the conflict, which he persistently denied. A United Nations Special Court later indicted the former president for complicity in the conflict. In March 2001, the UN Security Council passed Resolution 1343, imposing sanctions on Liberia for its role in the illicit trade of diamonds in Sierra Leone.[138] However, the civil war that re-erupted in Liberia further added complications to the efforts by the Special Court to arraign President Taylor for his role in regional destabilization. Taylor's exile to Nigeria seems to have provided him a respite but only temporarily.[139] In March 2004, the UN Security Council passed Resolution 1521, freezing the assets of former President Charles Taylor, members of his family, and close associates. In July 2004, the U.S. government threw its weight behind this by blocking all assets belonging to Mr. Taylor and his associates.[140] In March 2006, the newly elected government of President Ellen Johnson-Sirleaf in Liberia requested the extradition of President Taylor from Nigeria, and the Nigerian President consented after discussions with the South African President Mbeki and the Chairpersons of Economic Community of West African States (ECOWAS) and the African Union (AU). Before he could be deported from Nigeria, however, Taylor and some members of his family allegedly made an unsuccessful attempt to escape from Nigeria.[141] They were arrested by Nigerian custom officials at the country's border with Cameroon.[142] Taylor was immediately deported to Liberia, from where he was first transferred to Sierra Leone and later to The Hague for a war crime trial.

The UN has shown considerable interest and concern also in the DRC, where two commissions—the Ba-N'Daw and Kassim—were set up. The outcome of the two reports has been widely quoted, especially because of their confirmation that some of the key countries that have gone into the DRC have done so with the sole intention of benefiting from the country's natural resources. Specifically, the report indicted key individuals in Uganda and Rwanda, and indicated that their governments have participated in exploiting these resources to fund the war efforts. The Ba-N'Daw report pointed out that while Uganda officially spent 2 percent of her GDP on defense, which should have been about US$110 million, about US$126 million was spent on the military in 1999.[143] During the same period, Rwanda's calculated expenses far outstripped its official budget by US$63 million.[144]

Key individuals in the two countries were named as having benefited from the involvement in the Congo. Among those indicted in Uganda were the army commander, James Kazini; the director of military intelligence, Col. Noble Mayombo; Lt. General Salim Saleh, who is also President Museveni's younger brother; the minister for regional affairs, Col. Kahinda Ottafire; and Col. Peter Kerim. Private individuals indicted include Sam Engola, Jacob Manu Soba, and Mannase Savo. In Rwanda, the panel found the army commander, General James Kabarebe, and the military intelligence chief, Col. Jack Nziza, guilty. Apart from the specific individuals, the report also criticized Uganda of signing a deal with one of the rebel factions in which a battalion of the UPDF would be stationed in Congo, in exchange for a $25,000 reward.

The reactions of the two countries were swift. Uganda's Foreign Affairs Minister James Wapakhabulo dismissed the report and accused the UN panelists of relying on hearsay. Specifically, the accusation that the UPDF was into a pact with a rebel faction in exchange for a $25,000 reward was considered insulting. The individuals accused also denied the allegation, with one of them, Noble Mayombo, promising to look into the possibility of suing the UN for defamation of character.[145] The Ugandan government also set up its own internal inquiry to investigate the indicted officers,[146] and found some of them guilty. Rwanda described the UN panel report as tragic and absurd, finding the allegation that it collaborated with fugitive Interahamwe militias to plunder Congolese resources ridiculous. The country's Director of Cabinet Theogene Rudasingwa argued that the report was false.[147]

What seems more serious, however, was the report's indictment of elites from both countries in the pillaging of Congolese resources. It noted that although the armed forces of both countries had been withdrawn, there existed "elite networks" running a self-financing war economy centered in pillaging the DRC. It also indicted a number of foreign companies, including Anglo-America, Amalgamated Metal Corporation, and Barclays Bank. While the UN reports have been widely quoted, there are clear indications that the reports are inaccurate on many of the findings, some of which are based on unsubstantiated information.

Another level of UN involvement in the DRC was demonstrated through the dispatch of a peacekeeping mission. The dispatch of the mission was to ensure general peace in the country, yet solid mineral resources have again played a key role in the activities of the mission, as fighting between the peacekeepers and the insurgent forces have been more prevalent in regions rich in natural resources. The worst of these clashes was in February 2005, when nine Bangladeshi peacekeepers were killed in Ituri, a part of the DRC that is rich in diamonds and gold.[148] This raised international condemnation for the DRC militias and, in retaliation, the UN force mounted a counterattack that led to the death of more than fifty members of one of the rebel forces, the *Front des natioalistses et integrationiste* (FNI). The following month, the leader of the FNI, Floribert Ndjabu Ngabu, and several of his aides were arrested. Under the UN program for bringing peace to the country, demobilization was to have ended by March 31, 2005, but as of the beginning of April, only

6,800 militias had been through the disarmament process, with an estimated 15,000 still roaming around the resource-rich Ituri.[149]

Solid Mineral Resources and the Efforts at Resolving Conflicts

Once it became recognized that diamonds and other solid minerals have become indispensable in insurgent wars, attempts to end such wars have had to consider this reality. The three post-Cold War African conflicts discussed in this chapter have approached resolution in different ways. The first is to ensure that sides that remain recalcitrant to peace moves are placed under sanctions to prevent them from using these resources to continue the war. This has, however, been difficult to implement, as the nature of the international market ultimately enables even those under international sanctions to gain access into the market. The second way is to incorporate clauses into peace agreements that would ensure the management of the mineral resources for a specific period, while the third is to threaten outside actors believed to be involved in such disputes for economic motives with sanctions. These were meant to ensure that such conflicts are either starved of the impetus that gave them life, or that all sides are sufficiently pacified to ensure peace.

An example of the first method came when UNITA went back to war after losing the election. The Security Council passed Resolutions 865 (1993) and 1237 (1999). Among others, the resolutions instructed that all states shall take necessary measures to

- prevent the entry into or transit through their territory of all senior officials of UNITA and of adult members of their families;
- suspend or cancel all travel documents, visas, or resident permits issued to senior UNITA officials and adult members of their immediate families;
- prohibit flights or aircraft by or for UNITA, the supply of any aircraft components to UNITA and the insurance, engineering, and servicing of UNITA aircraft;
- ensure that all states except Angola in which there are funds and financial resources, including any fund derived or generated from property of UNITA as an organization or senior officials of UNITA or adult members of their immediate families, shall require all persons and entities within their own territories holding such funds and financial resources to freeze them;
- prohibit the direct or indirect import from Angola to their territory of all diamonds that are not controlled through the certificate of origin; and
- call upon states and all international and regional organizations to act strictly in accordance with the provisions of the resolution not withstanding

the existence of any rights or obligations conferred or imposed by the international agreement or any contract entered into or any license or permit granted prior to the adoption of the resolution.

Also in December 2000, the United Nations General Assembly adopted unanimously a resolution on the role of diamonds in fueling conflict, thus attempting to break the mutually reinforcing link between illicit transactions of rough diamonds and armed conflict as a contribution to the prevention and settlement of conflicts.

The second way—incorporation of clauses into peace agreements—is reflected in the case of Sierra Leone, where the Lomé Peace Agreement specifically recognized the importance of diamonds to the resolution of the conflict. It then named Foday Sankoh, the rebel leader, as the chairman of the Commission for Strategic Mineral Resources and Development with the status of vice president and an amnesty for all the crimes he committed before the peace deal. This was an office that gave him control of the country's diamond resources. Under the agreement, the rebel movement also had four cabinet positions.[150]

The developments in Sierra Leone in May 2000, however, shows how concessions granted to a warlord over mineral resources may not forestall another outbreak of conflict. This is particularly so if, as in Sierra Leone, the warlord believes that political realignment of forces can make him lose relevance, or alternatively, he could gain total political power through continuation of the war. Although the Lomé Peace Agreement granted concessions, the RUF still went to war with a purely political motive. Sankoh had lost some of his key supporters, including his military commander, Sam Boukarie (Mosquito). The fear was that these people could form their own rebel group, thereby dispossessing him from the position of attention he had occupied as the main rebel leader. With the bulk of the Nigerian ECOMOG contingent out of Sierra Leone and the respected ECOMOG Commander Maxwell Khobe, the RUF calculated that it could run over the UN troops before they could consolidate in the country. This was viewed as giving the RUF the opportunity to gain ground against potential rivals and thus prevent a Liberian scenario where seven factions ultimately emerged to wrestle for the country.

The relative peace that came with the establishment of a transitional government in Liberia has again brought the whole controversy over sanctions and natural resource exploitation to the fore. The transitional government of Gyude Bryant called on the UN Security Council to remove the sanction that was imposed on the country under Charles Taylor, and in this he seemed to have the support of the country's Ministry of Land, Mines and Energy. However, several people in his government and sections of civil society believed it was premature. For example, the immigration officer for the country pointed out that any removal of sanctions would result in illegal exploitation of resources, as many of the border posts were still under non-state actors.[151] After the UN turned down this request, the government went ahead with an agreement with a Canadian company, Diamond Fields International Limited. Under this agreement, the company is to undertake reconnaissance of a 2,000 square kilometer of land in Nimba County along the Ya Creek.[152] The government was, however, quick to point out that this was a mere survey and does not give the company rights to mine diamonds or interfere with local mines.[153] Greater controversy came in March 2005, when a UN Expert Panel discovered a secret deal made by the transitional government committing all the country's diamond resources to the West African Mining Corporation (WAMCO), a company the UN experts describe as being of "unknown provenance," for a period of ten years.[154] This company was allegedly financed by the privately owned London International Bank Limited. The agreement also allegedly allowed WAMCO to set up a private security service.[155]

The efforts to resolve the DRC conflict have adopted a somewhat different approach. Here, attention has been focused on the regional countries that are believed to be stirring the conflict. In June 2000, the UN Security Council threatened to invoke Chapter 7 on Rwanda and Uganda if they did not withdraw their troops from the DRC. This gives the UN Security Council a wide range of options to take against any country considered to have threatened peace and undertaken acts of aggression. Although the UN did not put any date on it, the impression was clear that an urgent compliance was required from the two countries. The United States also came up with the threat of sanction against Rwanda and Uganda over Kisangani, describing the clashes as "unacceptable and a violation of the peace process."[156] A few days before the UN sanction, the U.S. spokesman Richard Boucher said that the United States would "hold the governments of Uganda and Rwanda responsible for the death of innocent Congolese and the extensive damage of Kisangani."[157]

Perhaps the most important international effort to stop the flow of illegal trade in gemstones, in this instance diamonds, is the Kimberley Process, which came into effect in 2003, after three years of negotiation. The process specifically aims to eliminate opportunities for warlords and terrorists to use diamonds for arms purchase and money laundering. Under the arrangement, all participating countries would provide every diamond with a government-backed certificate of origin. (See Box.) All the countries outside the agreement are not allowed to sell or trade in diamonds.

From the outset, critics have noted gaps in the efforts, as the Kimberley Process relies more on the goodwill of participating countries and thus does not possess strong enforceable regulations. It has also been criticized for not having enough local civil society input. As William Wallis has noted, nothing shows the flaw in this scheme as much as the relationship between DRC and Congo Brazzaville.[158] While the DRC has one of the world's largest reserves of industrial diamonds, Congo Brazzaville has no diamonds. With the admission of the latter into the Kimberley Process, both have been licensed to trade in diamonds. In 2001, Congo Brazzaville traded US$223 million worth of diamonds,[159] most of which are believed to have come from DRC and Angola—two countries at war. However, in July 2004, the Kimberley Process published a new list of participants from which the Congo Brazzaville was removed.[160] The Kimberley Process team sent to the country concluded that the Republic of Congo "cannot account for the origin . . . of rough diamonds that it is officially exporting."[161] The country was also prohibited from importing or exporting diamonds to or from countries that are members of the Kimberley Process. Another country that is believed to have violated the terms of the Kimberley Process was Liberia, under Taylor's administration. According to the UN Security Council Expert Panel, as late as August 6, 2002, less than a week before Charles Taylor was forced out of office, Liberia was still swapping diamonds for weapons.[162] A third country, Togo, is believed in a number of quarters as being in violation of the Kimberley Process, although attention for now seems to be more on Congo Brazzaville.

The Kimberley Process Certification Scheme

Each participating country should have the following internal controls:

- establish a system of internal control designed to eliminate the presence of conflict diamonds from shipments of rough diamonds imported into and exported from its territory;
- designate an importing and exporting authority(ies);
- ensure that rough diamonds are imported and exported in tamper-resistant containers;
- as required, amend or enact appropriate laws and regulations to implement and enforce the Certification Scheme and to maintain dissuasive and proportional penalties for transgressions;
- collect and maintain relevant official production, import and export data, and collate and exchange such data in accordance with the provision of Section V;
- when establishing a system of internal controls, take into account, where appropriate, the further options and recommendations for internal controls as elaborated in Annex II;
- provide to each other through the Chair information identifying their designated authorities or bodies responsible for implementing the provisions of this Certification Scheme. Each Participant should provide to other participants through the Chair information, preferably in electronic format, on its relevant laws, regulations, rules, procedures and practices, and update that information as required. This should include synopsis in English of the essential content of this information;

(*continued*)

- compile and make available to all other participants through the Chair statistical data in line with the principles set out in Annex III;
- exchange on a regular basis experiences and other relevant information, including on self-assessment in order to arrive at the best practice in given circumstances;
- consider favorably requests from other participants for assistance to improve the functioning of the Certification Scheme within their territories;
- inform other participants through the Chair if it considers that the laws, regulations, rules, procedures or practices of other participants do not ensure the absence of conflict diamonds in the export of that other participant;
- cooperate with other participants to attempt to resolve problems which may arise from unintentional circumstances and which could lead to non-fulfillment of the minimum requirements for the issuance or acceptance of the Certificates, and inform all other participants of the problems encountered and of solutions found;
- encourage, through their relevant authorities, closer cooperation between law enforcement agencies and between custom agencies of participants.

The Kimberley Process has brought an impressive degree of sanity into the diamonds trade, and some of the countries are now beginning to see significant changes in their fortune. For example, there has been a remarkable improvement in the diamond export sectors of Sierra Leone and the DRC between the time preceding the introduction of the Kimberley Process and the time it was introduced in 2003, as shown table 4.1.

DRC has also recorded significant progress since the introduction of the Kimberley Process as shown in table 4.2.

However, it needs to be pointed out that the DRC government has also undertaken a number of steps to ensure that its diamond resources are protected from external manipulation. For example, it has signed agreements with some of its neighbors to ensure its diamonds are not smuggled through their countries.[163] Apart from this, the government now has new political structures in place and a new national army. Efforts are being made to work closely at the grassroots level to get information about diamond smuggling.

Although the Kimberley Process has significantly changed the nature of trade in diamonds, there are now growing concerns that the scope has to be expanded if it is to stand the pressures of the future. For example, there are those who argue that the objectives of the Process as it stands, only prevent

Table 4.1 Sierra Leone diamond export data, 2003–5

Month	Export $ 2003	Carats 2003	Export $ 2004	Carats 2004	Export $ 2005	Carats 2005
Jan	4,612,174	37,853	6,732,551	55,347	9,676,953	57,349
Feb	7,087,005	40,612	9,956,715	67,192	8,829,145	42,153
Mar	4,827,357	29,566	12,186,650	61,730	9,857,565	47,966
Apr	7,363,137	45,259	12,219,747	72,589	12,950,368	63,982
May	5,526,897	41,334	9,824,063	49,712	12,440,447	54,986
Jun	7,673,862	56,612	17,371,974	89,560	21,573,844	77,155
Jul	5,417,475	37,191	12,925,172	59,194	13,180,714	54,372
Aug	7,527,192	49,182	9,689,861	50,172	13,543,472	62,980
Sep	6,828,932	50,068	9,897,734	51,781	7,123,957	34,101
Oct	6,789,034	44,032	9,588,852	46,014	10,607,968	51,528
Nov	5,868,077	35,121	9,215,901	51,310	11,873,960	54,248
Dec	6,465,401	39,903	7,052,411	37,152	10,281,845	68,015

Source: Diamond Industry Annual Review, Special Edition on Sierra Leone (2006), p. 9.

Table 4.2 DRC diamond export data, 1996–2003

Month	1996	1997	1998	1999	2000	2001	2002	Average 1996–2002	2003
Jan	19.7	20.1	21.5	18.3	10.7	11.6	18.8	17.2	42.4
Feb	21.6	18.8	25.9	16.2	10.7	15.2	17.5	17.9	40.4
Mar	27.3	23.3	34.0	21.3	12.4	10.9	23.0	21.7	41.0
Apr	29.2	4.2	25.8	18.1	11.9	17.1	21.6	18.3	34.0
May	29.3	—	24.7	16.4	11.1	9.0	27.3	19.6	36.7
Jun	25.4	19.2	33.0	22.9	19.4	11.8	21.0	21.8	34.7
Jul	29.2	42.0	36.2	20.2	22.7	22.9	28.1	28.7	48.9
Aug	26.8	37.7	31.6	17.8	17.5	24.3	32.2	26.8	45.0
Sep	27.1	40.9	28.1	12.2	7.4	16.8	35.4	24.0	56.7
Oct	28.6	38.3	35.8	5.7	11.6	22.8	28.9	24.5	48.7
Nov	23.2	32.3	31.8	13.2	14.7	23.1	30.4	24.1	48.6
Dec	24.9	32.4	27.8	9.9	17.9	16.5	33.2	23.2	46.5

Source: Diamond Industry Annual Review, Special Edition on DRC (2004), p. 9.

rebel groups from dealing in diamond trade without looking at how governments abuse their people. In a recent report on Angola, there have been calls that the Kimberley Process should expand its definition of conflict diamonds to include cases in which "diamond mining is based on the systematic violation of human-rights."[164]

Conclusion

Efforts have been made in this chapter to discuss the conflicts surrounding solid mineral resources, especially against the prominent role they have played in recent African conflicts. Because of the high degree of profitability and the absence of credible arrangements to manage issues relating to extraction, ownership, and distribution of opportunities coming from these resources, individuals and groups have hijacked initiatives and have turned most of these valuable gems into instruments of destruction. Most of the civil wars that have brought Africa into international attention have all been linked to solid minerals, as in the cases with Liberia, Sierra Leone, Angola, and the DRC. The extent of the tragedy associated with these resources has also meant that of all resource-centered conflicts, this seems to be the one to which the international community has diverted attention, evidenced in the ways the United Nations has tried to get countries and leaders believed to be benefiting from the resources to change their behavior. There are, however, degrees of skepticism in the efforts to end conflicts in this category. The nature of the international market, the extensive formal and informal networks that had been developed and perfected over the years, and the globalization of conflicts that has increased the number of actors intent on maximizing the "benefit" from this category of natural resources only indicates that the extent of conflict can only, at best, be reduced.

The nature and extent of solid minerals in conflict shows clearly the extent to which governance comes into consideration in the linkage between natural resources and conflict. Because the control and management of these resources fall under the exclusive control of central governments in many of the countries, governments and individuals involved have seized the opportunity created by conflict to benefit from its proceeds. The sides involved in conflict have exhibited all the security complexities prevailing in post-Cold War African security, including mercenary activities, warlordism, proliferation of light weapons, and collapse of state institutions. The only other natural resource that shows these tendencies, albeit on a lesser scale, is oil, whose link with conflict is the topic of discussion in the next chapter.

5

CONFLICTS INVOLVING OIL

I have to confess that, if in the past, I ever thought about oil at all, it was
only when filling up the car. . . . But [after my visit to Angola] I now think
about oil all the time. There are images from Angola, which I will never
forget. Images that are direct consequences of the oil curse. . . . it is clear
that for the curse to become a blessing, people of oil-producing communities must be able to see how much money there is, where it is coming
from and where it is going.

Joseph Fiennes

I come from an area where 25% of oil is produced. I should be like a
Kuwaiti or Saudi Arabian Prince, moving round Europe and America in
beautiful suits and buying gold watches. But who are those doing that: the
many compatriots from the arid zones and we are most deprived.

Hope Harriman

Next to solid minerals, the natural resource whose linkage with conflicts has
generated perhaps nearly as much interest and attention in Africa is oil. This
is due to a number of factors, including the resource's high degree of profitability, the environmental consequences of its exploration, the international
nature of its politics, and its role in the ethnopolitical and socioeconomic
affairs of the endowed countries. In recent years, however, also important in
explaining the recognition accorded to oil, is the string of "sympathies" that
seem to be coming to local communities believed to be suffering from the
consequences of oil exploration. These sympathies have come from an array
of sources: environmentalist groups, who oppose the degradation that often
follows oil exploration; civil society activists, who want greater participation
for the indigenous population in the decisions surrounding the management
of their countries' natural resources; and international pressure groups clamoring for good governance, who want governments in developing countries to
be more accountable to their populace on the whole management of natural
resources. The outcome has been that by the turn of the twenty-first century,

Africa features prominently in discussions on how global energy issues intertwine with conflict. Furthermore, many observers believe that the growing import-ance of Africa in global oil production will further increase interest in this continent's role in energy politics.[1]

In all oil-endowed countries, management of the resource has been at the core of socioeconomic and political governance, although, not all of them have succeeded in evolving credible structures to manage the resource in a way that will ensure fairness and to strike an acceptable balance between local claim and national interest. Because of the centrality of the resource to national economy, cognizance has not been given to other issues that can fos-ter harmonious intergroup relations.

In this chapter, I discuss the various ways through which oil has been linked to conflict in Africa, situating the subject within the local and international signifi-cance of the resource. In the main, I argue that oil has attained such a promin-ent position in African conflicts because of the coalescing of four main factors: the high global demand for energy resources, notably oil, which encourages for-eign multinational corporations to exploit the internal weaknesses of natural resource governance in African oil-producing states and consequently interfere in their domestic politics; the high rents that accrue from the resource, which in diverse ways, can be linked to the corruption and greed on the part of the ruling elites of some of these countries and the heightening of expectations of the local population in oil-producing communities; the changing nature of politics, which has increased awareness on the part of civil society for accountable governance; and the effects of globalization, which raised a new set of considerations in the nature of a global response to energy politics.

African Oil-Producing Countries and Global Oil Politics

The nature of the global oil business is such that oil-producing countries in Africa cannot remain indifferent to its politics. The reverberations from these politics have influenced oil-related conflicts in the continent. The extent of the dependence of these states on oil revenue has further increased their vul-nerability to wider global considerations. Three aspects of this are particularly important. The first involves the complexities that arose from the high degree of external involvement in the prospecting, production, and marketing of oil in Africa. The extensive capital and technological skills required for prospect-ing and processing oil are often beyond the capacity of most oil-producing African countries, thus necessitating the involvement of foreign multinational companies. Furthermore, the fact that oil discoveries in some of these coun-tries occurred during the colonial period meant that local input had initially been almost nonexistent. As a result, by the time local entrepreneurs gained an inroad, the foreign companies had made significant headway, such that the exploration and marketing of oil in most of these countries has remained foreign dominated.[2] Among the key companies involved are the Anglo-Dutch Shell, Italian Agip, American Chevron,[3] French Elf, and British BP Amaco.[4] Apart from these large corporations, there are a number of medium-sized firms making advances into the oil industry in Africa. These include Malaysia's Petronas Karigal, South Africa's Energy Africa, and companies from Brazil and China. These organizations are also partnering with others to prospect and trade in oil. For example, Energy Africa is in partnership with Australia's Hardman Resources in Mauritania and Uganda.[5]

This external involvement has three identifiable impacts on governance and oil-related conflicts in Africa.

1. It creates a catalog of "we" versus "them" politics in oil management, most of which ultimately end up in confrontations. Some of these dichotomies occur between the foreign oil companies and local communities; the foreign companies and their indigenous counterparts; the local employees and the foreign companies; and between governments and multinational companies. Second, the extent of foreign involvement in the oil production also implies that most of the attendant conflicts get internationalized, as the home states of most of these foreign companies are apt to interfere in potential melees. As the experience of Venezuela has shown, local conflicts surrounding oil become more complex where substantial external interests are involved.[6] Third, as will be shown later in the chapter, the nature of the arrangement between these companies and the host state has often been problematic, putting pressure on the oil-producing countries to negotiate better deals with the foreign oil companies.

2. It is linked to the international politics that surrounds oil pricing and marketing, and this relates mainly to the Oil Producing and Exporting Countries (OPEC), the cartel that controls most of the world's oil resources.[7] Indeed, as Michael Feyide has noted, "OPEC was the first producer-grouping of developing countries to impact on international trade."[8] At the formation of the organization, members declared their intention to pursue three objectives: to stabilize oil prices and ensure that no future changes are made without due consultations; to look at ways of achieving assured income through, among other things, the regulation of production; and to support each other against possible "divide-and-rule" tactics by oil companies.[9] Presently, the organization accounts for the management of more than 70 percent of the world's reserves. Although very few African oil-producing nations are members of OPEC,[10] the cartel's overriding influence sometimes imposes constraints even on nonmember states, and its dominant role in influencing the global production and price of oil has been a factor that even nonmembers have had to consider in formulating their policies. However, it can be conceded that the organization's grip on its members has reduced,[11] but even the volatility this brings into the

market is a crucial factor in understanding the nature of conflicts over oil in Africa.

OPEC politics has been linked to conflict in at least two indirect ways. First, the mere existence of the organization is controversial. While oil-producing countries that are not members of the organization object to the dominating influence of the cartel, non–oil-producing countries have often accused it of blackmail, especially because of its supposed role in monopolizing the market.[12] Furthermore, even for Nigeria, one of Africa's OPEC members, the continued membership has created considerable controversy, with sections of the population calling for the country's withdrawal of membership from the organization.[13] Even those who do not call for the country's withdrawal from OPEC have sometimes clamored for ways of freeing the country from some of the stringent measures of the organization. For example, there have been calls that the country should keep aspects of its production, especially those from deep waters, out of OPEC quotas. This, they argue would give the country more revenue to implement its economic reform programs.[14] Second, the relationships among members of the organization are sometimes uneasy, and conflicts that have ensued on a number of occasions have had reverberating consequences for other states. For example, Iran and Iraq, two founding members, fought a bitter civil war in the 1980s, and Iraq invaded Kuwait, another OPEC member, in 1990.

3. Another aspect of international politics noteworthy is the political instability that seems to be a dominant factor in the main oil-producing region of the world, the Middle East. This has two major bearings on oil conflict in Africa. First, there is an effect on the price of oil, and consequently the budget forecast of many African oil-producing countries. Once conflict breaks out in the Middle East, African oil-producing states have often had to put pressure on the local capacity to produce, either to meet up with the shortfall in their budgetary projections or to maximize profit because of reduced supplies coming from the Middle East. As will be shown later, the attendant pressure the sudden increase in production has on the oil-producing environment has been linked to conflict. Second, the incessant political instability in the Middle East and its effects on oil supply to western capitalist countries has resulted in a situation in which the West, especially the United States, has begun to consider alternate sources of oil and, as noted earlier, West Africa has featured prominently in American calculation.[15] Consequently, the prominence Africa would assume as a result of this is likely to put greater pressure on local capacity to produce—a tendency that can further predispose some of the countries to conflict. On the whole, the wider global development to oil politics in African oil-producing nations often means that conflicts associated with oil have had this external dimension to them. Indeed, in all cases, it is when these external dimensions get intermingled with domestic variables that the complete picture of oil conflicts becomes clearer.

A discussion of the impact of oil on the national economies of the oil-producing states needs to be put into perspective. On the whole, Africa currently produces about 9 million barrels of oil per day, accounting for about 11 percent of global supply. Although the continent is proven to have close to 10 percent of the total global reserves, this is set to increase with new discoveries being made across the continent. In all oil-producing countries, the impacts of the resource on the economy, politics, and social life are phenomenal. In spite of the presence of other natural resources, oil remains the dominant one.[16] In this section, I provide an overview of the position of oil in the socioeconomic structure of the host countries. There are two reasons for this discussion, the first of which is to help in understanding some of the hidden politics that often characterize the oil sector, while the other is to provide a background that will illuminate one of the wider objectives of this book, which is the role of governance in natural resource conflicts in Africa.

Nigeria is Africa's largest oil-producing nation and is the seventh in the world. It is also the country with the most complex oil-related politics in the continent.[17] Oil exploration in the country began in 1908 when a German company, the Nigerian Bitumen Corporation, was granted license to exploit bitumen deposits around Araromi, in the country's southwest province. It was not until 1956, however, that oil in commercial quantity was discovered in Oloibiri.[18] Interest proliferated, with oil companies coming from the United States, Western Europe, and Japan. Even though at independence the economy relied on its agricultural exports, notably cocoa, palm oil, and groundnuts, oil had assumed a dominant position by the end of the first decade of independence. After the country's civil war (1967–70), the importance of oil was consolidated and the country embarked on a catalog of developmental, if sometimes wasteful, projects. This predominance continued, such that by the mid-1990s, oil was accounting for about 90 percent of Nigeria's annual foreign exchange earnings and about 80 percent of the revenue of the federal government.[19]

As of 2005, Nigeria was producing 2.5 million barrels of oil per day.[20] The country also has the highest rates of oil discoveries.[21] The proven oil reserves are estimated at approximately 22.5 billion barrels. Nigeria's latest offshore oil explorations include the Agbami fields, where there is speculated to be about one billion barrels of recoverable hydrocarbons, Akpo 1, Amenam/Kpono fields, and Bonga fields. The country also has an estimated 124 trillion cubic feet of proven natural gas. This is one of the largest in the world.[22] However, the fields' development costs in Nigeria are high in relation to the global average.[23] While no detailed study has been conducted to explain this peculiarity, it has been suggested that the most likely explanation is the contribution to the Niger Delta Development Fund, which adds about 5 percent to the overall cost of developing fields in the country.[24] Nigeria, with the development costs of about $4 per barrel of oil equivalent for a field coming on stream since 1996, ranks fourth after the United Kingdom, Australia, and U.S. Deep Water Gulf of Mexico.

The vast majority of Nigeria's oil deposits are located in the country's Niger Delta region.[25] The region is home to several subethnic groups, including the Ogonis, Andonis, Ikwerres, Ekpeyes, Ogbas, Egbemas, Engennes, Obolos, Urhobos, Isokos, Itsekiris, among others.[26] Apart from oil, the Niger Delta is also rich in other natural resources. For example, it is the third largest mangrove forest in the world and is known to have great biological diversity. Considered within the ethnopolitical classification in the country, however, the Niger Delta is considered a "minority area." This is because it is not one of the three major ethnic groups—Hausa/Fulani, Ibo, and Yoruba—that have historically dominated politics and economy in Nigeria. Under the present administrative structure in the country, the oil-producing communities are within eight states: Rivers, Delta, Edo, Bayelsa, Akwa Ibom, Cross Rivers, Abia, and Ondo. The management of Nigeria's oil is vested in the government-owned Nigerian National Petroleum Corporation (NNPC). The corporation works with a number of foreign oil-prospecting companies, including the multinational companies Shell, Mobil, Texaco, BP, Elf, Chevron, and others. As mentioned earlier, a number of indigenous companies have emerged in the prospecting for oil, but their impacts remain comparatively low as their work is in managing marginal fields.[27]

Libya, Africa's second largest oil producer, remains one of Africa's most controversial oil-producing nations. While the relative political stability in the country and its nearness to Western Europe qualify it as a most attractive source of oil supplies to western markets, the controversies that often surround the country's foreign policy positions, especially the alleged links to radical activities in the Middle East and other parts of the world, have brought caution to the West's links with Libya. The years of sanctions against Libya have had impacts on the management of its oil resource. For example, it resulted in the massive reduction in the number of foreign multinational corporations involved in oil explorations in the country. It has also meant that Libya remains largely unexplored, and as such has the possibility of considerable potential. During the sanction period, the state-owned National Oil Company (NOC) controlled the entire oil industry, working with thirty-three subsidiaries. By 1979, the NOC was allowed to enter into agreement with foreign companies, and many oil multinational companies entered into partnership with the company. With the removal of sanction in 1999, more than fifty oil companies signified intention of moving into Libya. The total proven reserve of the country is about 30 billion barrels. Like Nigeria, Libya is also a member of OPEC.

Algeria is another key oil-producing nation in Africa and a major OPEC member. With an estimated 11.8 billion barrels of proven reserve and a daily production in 2004 that averaged 1.9 million barrels per day, the country is the sixteenth largest producer in the world. Oil was discovered in Algeria in 1956, in the town of Hassi Messaoud. The main oil-producing regions of the country are located in the east-central and central regions. Presently, there are thirty major producing fields in the country, and the major multinational corporations involved in the exploration include Agip, Andarko, Arco, BP-Amaco, Cepsa, Exxon-Mobil, Lundin, Petrol-Canada, Petronas, Talisman/Burlington, and Total. The management of Algerian oil is through the National Oil Company (Sonatrach) Enterprise Nationale Sonatrach, and its role is encompassing, including exploration and production, transport, refining, processing, marketing, and distribution. Although the government is planning to privatize and deregulate the organization, it also maintains that certain aspects of the organization will not be privatized. The political unrest in the country has not had any significant impact on the Algerian oil industry, and the resource accounts for the greatest percentage of national revenue.

Angola is the largest oil-producing country in southern Africa. Oil was discovered in the country in 1955, mainly in the Kwanza valley. Expansion in oil production came in the late 1960s, when further discoveries were made in the coastal enclave of Cabinda.[28] The Cabinda region has an approximate area of 2,800 square miles and an approximate population of 600,000. There is a geographical characteristic that underlines the politics of oil in Cabinda as the region is separated from the rest of the country by a sixty kilometer wide strip. This, as will be noted in more detail later, remains a key issue in the politics of resource ownership in the country. Cabinda accounts for almost "60% of Angolan oil production, estimated at approximately 900,000 barrels a day."[29] Further discoveries in the area led to oil becoming Angola's principal export by 1973, with the annual range of its income from oil oscillating between US$1.8 and $3.0 billion.[30] Oil installations remained unaffected for most of the war period, and the country's largest oil field in the north coast region of Cabinda remained under the control of the MPLA government. However, in October 1992, following the resumption of war after the 1991 truce, oilfields became primary military targets. In February 1993, the installations in Soyo, at the mouth of the Zaire River, were captured by the National Union for the Total Independence of Angola (UNITA) but were later recaptured by the government forces.

The management of Angolan oil was invested in the state-owned *Sociedale Nacional de Combustíveis de Angola* (Sonangol), which was established in 1976 as the sole concessionaire for oil exploration and development. Foreign companies were allowed to participate with Sonangol and, in 1990, the structure became one of the state-owned holding companies with autonomous or semi-autonomous subsidiaries handling production, distribution, research, and other functions. There is also a Ministry of Petroleum, which oversees the oil industry, and with the Ministry of Finance and the country's central bank, supervises the operation of Sonangol. It was the largest and most important mining sector under the control of the MPLA government for most of the war, thus enhancing its importance. Ironically, the main purchaser of the country's oil has been the United States. Even during the decades of the Cold War tensions between the two countries, major U.S. oil companies, especially Chevron, continued drilling Angolan oil. Other active companies include Petrofina (Belgium), Elf Aquitane (France), with companies such as Agip (Italy), Hispanoil (Spain), Svenska Petroleum (Sweden), Petrolbras (Brazil), Mitsubishi (Japan), and British Petroleum playing a lesser role. By 2000, Angola was producing about 800,000 barrels per day, almost six times higher than the 1980 production level.[31]

Oil was discovered in Sudan in 1978, and its impact on national economy has been remarkable, especially as estimates put its oil reserve as one of the largest in Africa.[32] Oil has, however, been linked to the civil conflicts between the central government and the Sudan Peoples Liberation Army (SPLA) and a number of other smaller conflicts that have characterized the country.[33] Sudan's oil deposit has attracted international interest because of its civil war. Although the first discovery was made in western Sudan, the bulk of oil deposits are found in the south, which has been in conflict with the northern-dominated government. However, shortly after the oil discovery, the Nimeri government transferred the oil refinery that was initially planned for Bentiu in the south to Kosti in the north. This was done with the excuse that "Kosti was closer to the centre of major industrial and agricultural development schemes, whereas Bentiu was in the middles of nowhere (*sic*)."[34] This was seen by many as a way of depriving the south of its endowment.[35] The government of former President Nimieri also altered the administrative map of the coun-try to put the oil deposit under the northern section of the country. Furthermore, in order to reduce the capacity of the south to fight these alter-ations, the Nimieri government divided the south into three regions. The companies involved in the field have also become embroiled over the owner-ship of the oil—between the rebel and the government and between the for-mer government militia and government forces.[36]

In Sudan, the oil multinational Talisman was the first to commence com-mercial exploitation in September 1999. Sudan's oil fields are operated by the Great Nile Petroleum Operating Company (GNPOC). Talisman acquired its 25 percent stake in GNPOC when it bought out cash-starved Arakis Energy. It shrewdly calculated that U.S. economic sanctions against Sudan would ensure there was little competition from the big American oil companies. Talisman's other partners in the GNPOC are Chinese National Petroleum Company (CNPC) with 40 percent; Malaysia's state-owned oil companies, Petronas, with 30 percent; and the Sudan's state-owned oil company with 5 percent. This arrangement saw "the Chinese and the Sudanese supply manpower; the Malaysians supply the Muslim credential necessary to do business with radical Islamic regime and Talisman supplies the oil-field expertise."[37] Despite the war, oil continues to substantially contribute to the national economy.

Egypt's discovery of oil was accidental. In 1868, the Sulphur Mines Company discovered oil in Gamasa while they were digging tunnels in search of sulphur. This led to concerted efforts, and more sites were discovered in subsequent years: Hurghada in 1913, Ras Gharib in 1938, Surd, Materma, and

Assal between 1947 and 1949, and Abu Redees and Balaeim in 1952. A major discovery was made in 2003 when the British oil company, BP, discovered oil in the Saqqara field.[38] In terms of geographical location, Egypt's oil is situated in four main areas: the Gulf of Suez, which accounts for about 50 percent; the western desert; the eastern desert; and Sinai Peninsula. Offshore production possibilities are also being explored in the Mediterranean. As of 2003, Egypt was producing about 620 barrels per day. Most of the oil companies operating in Egypt are joint ventures between foreign multinationals and Egyptian main oil companies. For example, the Gulf of Suez Petroleum Company (GUPCO), which produces oil in the Gulf of Suez, operates under a production-sharing agreement between BP and the Egyptian General Petroleum Corporation (EGPC). The second largest company, Petrobel, is a joint venture between EGPC and Agip; the Badr el-Din Petroleum is an arrangement between EGPC and Shell; and the Suez Oil Company, between EGPC and Deminex.

Apart from these main oil-producing countries, there are a number of other countries, including Congo, Equatorial Guinea, Gabon, Cameroon, Chad, and Sao Tome, with substantially less oil deposit. As a result, the impact of oil politics has been less acrimonious. Although the deposits in these countries may not be as substantial as in the aforementioned countries, the impact on their relatively smaller population is potentially significant. Furthermore, given the increasing interests in African oil deposits, the future of these countries' role in global economy is likely to increase.

In Congo, oil came to the forefront of national economy in 1957 with the discovery of an offshore field at Point-Indienne. However, it was not until the late 1970s that its impact began to manifest so that by the end of the 1980s it had become a key resource in the country. The main oil fields in the Congo are the Emeraude field, Kitina, N'kossa, Senji Tchibouela, Yanga, and Zatchi fields, and the majority of the production is located offshore. In April 1998, the Congolese government established a new national petroleum company, the *Societe Nationale des Petroles du Congo* (SNPC). The main multinational corporations involved in the exploration are Total, Agip, and Heritage oil, and exports are mainly to the United States and France. Oil exports in the country grew from $820 million in 1994 to around $2.8 billion in 2002. It is also worth recording that Congo has an estimated 3.2 trillion cubic feet of natural gas—the third largest in Africa after Nigeria and Cameroon.

Equatorial Guinea's oil deposit was discovered during the early 1990s, with the first offshore oil platform being inaugurated at Punta Europa near Malabo in April 1992. It was, however, the discovery of the Zafiro field in 1995 that made oil the most important export for the country. As of 2001, oil was accounting for nearly 90 percent of total export,[39] as from a modest 17,000 barrels per day in 1996, production had increased to 210,000 barrels per day in 2002, and to 350,000 by 2004. Currently, the country already produces more oil per capita than in Saudi Arabia. In May 2003, Equatorial Guinea approved plans by Marathon to build a liquidified natural gas plant on Bioko

Island to supply 3.4 million tons of liquidified natural gas (LNG) per year to the United States alone once it is completed in 2007.[40] Natural gas was first exported in 2001, when Marathon commissioned a $450 million plan that converts gas into methanol. The new discoveries have resulted in the country having a gross domestic product (GDP) per capita reaching almost $7,000.[41] In 2001, a state-run oil company, GE Petrol, was established to manage the country's oil sector alongside the multinational corporations, namely, Chevron, Der Energy, Exxon Mobil, and Petronas.

Although oil exploitation in Gabon began in 1956, it was not until 1967, with the discovery of the Gamba-Ivinga deposit and the offshore deposit in Anguille, that it assumed primary importance in the country's economy. After this initial period, the focus remained largely on offshore deposits until 1989, when the deposit in Rabi-Kounga made onshore operations of increasing significance. By 1990, Gabon was producing 135,000 barrels per day and, by 1999, petroleum and petroleum products were accounting for 74 percent of foreign exports earnings.[42] For a long time, the main producer was Elf-Gabon, but this position of dominance was overtaken by Shell-Gabon in 1993. Other companies participating in the sector in Gabon include Occidental, Marathon, Conoco, and Total. A South African company, Energy Africa, entered the sector in 1995 with its acquisition of a 40 percent stake in three of the satellite fields of Rabi-Kounga. Gabon's only oil refinery is the SOGARA refinery at Port-Gentil, jointly owned by the government, private investors, and a consortium of international oil companies. The bulk of the export goes to the United States, France, Argentina, and Brazil.

Cameroon has one of the smallest deposits of all the oil-producing countries in Africa, although the international ramifications of its deposits make it a key actor in subregional oil politics. The story of oil exploitation in the country began in 1976, when Elf began operation in Cameroon. By the end of the 1990 decade, oil was on the decline in economic importance. However, two developments reemphasized the prominence of oil in the strategic calculation of the country. The first was the decision of a consortium involving Petronas of Malaysia and America's Exxon and Chevron to construct a 1,070 kilometers long pipeline to transport 250,000 barrels per day from Doba basin in southern Chad to the southern Cameroonian port of Kribi. The project is expected to fetch about $13 billion over the next twenty-five years.[43] Of this, Chad is set to earn at least $2 billion, which was calculated would increase its income per capita from US$250 to US$550 per year by 2005.[44] The second development was the 2002 victory of Cameroon over Nigeria at the International Court of Justice over the disputed Bakassi Peninsula. This is discussed later in this chapter; suffice it to say here that the victory introduced an impetus to the declining relevance of Cameroon in the subregional oil politics.

In Chad, the discovery of oil came in 1977, in Sedigui, in the Kanem region, north of Lake Chad. This was a welcome development, as the country was completely dependent on Nigeria for its oil supplies. Chad is a landlocked country and this made drilling for oil extremely expensive. Although construction of a refinery began in N'djamena, the fragile political situation, which led to the kidnap of some foreign oil prospectors, halted this process. Between 1978 and 1989, there has been an intense search for new reserves by a consortium of Exxon, Chevron, and Shell, especially in the southern part of the country and the surrounding areas of Lake Chad. This led to further discoveries, such that it was calculated that the Sedigui field would supply oil to N'djamena for domestic use, while Doba crude would be for export via pipelines across Cameroon.[45] The Chadian–Cameroon oil pipeline remains one of the most ambitious programs in the continent. The project was sponsored by the World Bank, Exxon Mobil, Chevron Texaco, and Petronas of Malaysia. In 1999, Anglo-Dutch Shell and French Elf pulled out of the project without explanation. Oil revenue is purported to be reaching between $80 and $140 million.[46]

Sao Tome's oil deposit is offshore, and this has added to the controversies that have saddled the country's oil sector. Prospecting for hydrocarbons began in the late 1980s, and by 1997, considerable deposits had been found. This justified the government's entering into contractual agreement with the United States Environmental Remediation Holding Corporation (ERHC) and the South African Procura Financial Consultants (PFC). Under the agreement signed in May 1997, the government was to collect an initial payment of $5 million from the ERHC, while the ERHC and the PFC were to finance the evaluation of the petroleum reserves.

A number of factors have colored oil exploration in Sao Tome. The first was the breakdown in the contract between the government and the ERHC, and the implications this has on oil politics in the country. By mid-1998, the ERHC had only paid $2 million of the $5 million it was to pay under the 1997 agreement, and by October 1999 the government had rescinded the agreement with the corporation. The second is the relationship the country has had to foster with neighboring countries over its offshore oil deposit in the Gulf of Guinea region, where oil reserve has been put at 4 billion barrels. Under a Joint Development Zone (JDZ) signed with Nigeria in 2001, Nigeria was to have 60 percent of the profit while Sao Tome would have 40 percent. This agreement was to last for forty-five years, however, the agreement and the implementation have had a lot of hiccups. First was Sao Tome's complaint over Nigeria's non-implementation of a compensation package that was supposed to be part of the treaty. These were that Nigeria would offer Sao Tome 10,000 barrels of oil per day, funding of a deepwater port, an oil refinery, and 250 scholarships. The complaints by Sao Tome were followed by Nigeria's objection to Sao Tome's unilateral agreements with third parties over interest in the zone. Furthermore, Sao Tome was embroiled in controversies with oil firms it had engaged in data gathering in the country.[47]

In July 2003, there was a military coup in Sao Tome and Principe, believed to be linked to the country's oil resource. While the country's elected president,

Fradique de Menezes, was visiting Nigeria, he was ousted by the military, in connivance with a small opposition party, the Christian Democratic Front. The deposed president confirmed that oil was at the center of the coup plotters.[48] The coup plotters were then invited to Lagos where they were instructed by the Nigerian president to reinstate their president. It is noteworthy that because of the joint oil exploration, Nigeria has a mutual defense pact with Sao Tome and Principe.

There was also the belief in Nigeria that the United States, in its desperate desire to secure hydrocarbon assets for U.S. companies, wanted to use the Sao Tome authorities to scuttle the investment drives being made by some Nigerian companies.[49] Indeed, a report signed by the attorney general of Sao Tome requested the U.S. authority to investigate contracts awarded to Houston-based ERHC Energy. The report, which indicted the Nigerian government, alleged that Nigerian-controlled ERHC made improper payments to officials and their families during the award of oil blocs in the JDZ.[50]

In recent years, discoveries along the West African coast have further heightened the importance of the region in global energy supply.[51] A 2,000-kilometer pipeline, which will stretch from Nigeria to Senegal, is planned.[52] On the whole, it now seems clear that Africa is poised to influence global oil politics, especially with the instability in the Middle East. Although President George W. Bush (Jr.) declared in 2000 that Africa has no strategic importance to the United States, some of his advisers are beginning to appreciate the strategic role of the region's natural resources, and especially oil. The Assistant Secretary of State for African Affairs, Walter Kansteiner, noted that while Africa is currently producing 15 percent of US oil needs, the supply from the continent may soon go to 25 percent.[53] This was further confirmed in the May 2001 National Energy Policy Report, when U.S. Vice-President Dick Cheney recognized that West Africa is experiencing the fastest-growing source of oil and gas for the American market.[54] Consequent on all these, major oil companies operating in the continent revealed during their 9th Annual African Upstream 2002 that they are investing $45 billion over the next few years on African oil reserve.[55] Indeed, as Ike Okonta has noted, with Iraq and the entire Middle East in freefall, and the investments of transnational oil companies in the region in jeopardy, the oil fields in the Gulf of Guinea and the new finds in Sudan have become of great geostrategic importance to the industrialized countries.[56] This has given the Gulf of Guinea a major strategic relevance in global energy politics.[57] Table 5.1 shows oil production in Africa for 2000 and the projected figure for 2010.

Before concluding this section, I need to identify the main actors in African oil conflicts. These have varied, depending on the countries concerned. However, generalizing broadly, nine actors can be identified. These are national governments; state or provincial governments; local population in the oil-producing communities; oil multinational corporations; armed-resistance groups; mercenaries; global civil society; local civil society; and multilateral

Table 5.1 African oil production, 2000 and 2010

Country	2000 (in million barrels per day)	2010 (in million barrels per day)
Nigeria	2.105	3.20
Libya	1.475	2.40
Algeria	1.580	2.10
Angola	0.735	1.40
Egypt	0.795	0.90
Congo Brazzaville	0.275	0.40
Gabon	0.325	0.30
Cameroon	0.090	0.15
Equatorial Guinea	0.115	0.15
Others	0.325	0.20

Source: Africa Confidential 43, no. 5 (March 8, 2002), p. 7.

agencies. Discussions in the chapter will illuminate the activities of each of the above identified actors.

Oil and the Causes of Conflict

Obtaining a complete picture of how oil has been linked to the causes of conflict in Africa is difficult, as the importance of the resource to the economy often introduces considerations that are peculiar to specific countries. Looking across the continent, however, six considerations appear to link oil to the causes of conflict, and here again, they are all connected to the governing of the structures managing the resource. These are: controversies over the ownership of oil-bearing sites (land and marine); disagreements over the management of the proceeds from oil; complications arising from the process of exploration; protests by local inhabitants against the government and multinational companies' insensitivity to indigenous practices of culture and religion; secessionist desires by oil-rich provinces; and crisis emanating from inability to meet up with domestic petroleum needs. Discussions of each of these are presented below.

Controversies over Ownership of Oil-Bearing Sites

Conflicts of this type are fought at three levels: local, where the belligerents are often different ethnic or subethnic groups within a country; national, often between the central government and other segment(s) of the country, including armed dissidents and rebel groups; and international, between independent nation-states. At the local level, the conflicts are always linked to land, with different factions laying claims to the portion of land where oil has been discovered or is being prospected. What most motivates these conflicts is the belief that acquiring ownership of the land rich in oil deposits will attract the attention and interest of the central government, and consequently result in greater developmental benefits for the community.[58] As noted in the last chapter, it often takes the discovery of a vital natural resource to alert governments to their responsibilities of providing basic infrastructure for local communities. This explains some of the many communal clashes in Nigeria's oil-producing communities, details and ramifications of which are discussed later in this chapter. Conflicts also arise in situations where communities have lost their lands as a result of oil exploration. In Chad, disputes have been recorded over springs that were destroyed in the process of constructing the oil pipeline from Chad to Cameroon as people have been deprived of access to drinking water.[59]

Another dimension of ownership controversy at the local level arises over the issue of compensation for the land acquired for oil exploration. The conflicts here are fought on three fronts. The first front pitches rival local communities against each other and often centers on how to distribute the compensation that has been paid by either the government or the multinational oil companies. As lands acquired for such purposes are often extensive, they inevitably cut across different communities, making equitable distribution of compensation difficult. This again is best manifested by the situation in Nigeria's oil-producing regions. The second front is often within the affected communities and revolves around the distribution of the compensation between/among families and between/among demographic structures, due to cultural and traditional mechanisms. As will be discussed later in this chapter under the discussion on oil and communal conflict, youths from many of Nigeria's oil-producing communities have accused their local chiefs of diverting compensations paid by government to private, personal use. Indeed, the emergence of youths as vanguards for protest in the Niger Delta province owes a great deal to the belief that the older generations have not accounted for monies collected from government and foreign oil companies as compensation for lands acquired for exploration. The third front in which compensation links oil to the causes of conflict at the communal level is between governments and local communities. As governments have unilaterally taken over the control of land, the issues of ownership vis-à-vis compensation from the government becomes complicated. The problem here often centers on how much is to be paid, who is to pay it, and to whom should it be paid. This again finds the best set of examples in Nigeria.

At the national level, conflicts over ownership of oil sites can be traced to two sources. Conflict may arise when ethnic groups within a state come together to challenge the ownership claim of the central government over oil deposit sites. In this situation, they are not contesting the legitimacy of the government but rather its hold on natural resources. An example of this can be seen in Nigeria, where, despite the disagreement between oil-producing communities, they sometimes come together to contest the federal government's ownership claims. The second way is similar, except that the group fighting the central government over oil is also challenging the government's legitimacy. Perhaps an example of this is the situation in the Sudan. Although the dispute in the country is not primarily over oil, it is now a prime target for both sides in the civil war. It is believed that one of the reasons the northern part of the country was reluctant in agreeing to the secession attempt by the south is because of the oil deposit in the latter. Although a UN-sponsored peace agreement was signed by the SPLA and the Sudanese government in November 2004, with the hope that this would address the attacks the SPLA has continually threatened on oil installations, the political situation remains unstable. This is discussed in more detail later in the chapter. What, however, remains certain is that the future political stability of the country will depend to a large extent on how the ownership and management of the oil reserve is addressed.

At the international level, disagreements over ownership of oil-bearing land have led to conflict between nations, and perhaps the best example here is the conflict between Nigeria and Cameroon over the Bakassi Peninsula. This peninsula, which lies at the border of the two countries, has been a cause of tension between them for more than two decades, with both sides stationing troops on their respective sides of the peninsula. Cameroon lays claim to the territory on the basis of an agreement signed in 1975 by Nigeria's former military leader, General Yakubu Gowon, arguing that through the agreement known as the Maroua Declaration, Bakassi was ceded to Cameroon. Nigeria, however, claims that Gowon had no right to do this under the constitution, and that the agreement was never ratified, especially as Gowon was overthrown shortly after the signing the agreement. Controversies over the Peninsula reached its peak in 1981, when Cameroon killed five Nigerian soldiers. This brought the two countries to the brink of war until an apology from Cameroon ended the tension.[60] The case was later taken to the International Court of Justice for adjudication. At the court, Christian Tomuschat, the lawyer representing Cameroon, countered this argument by noting that Gowon "could not be said to have acted alone, even when he attended one of the meetings (where the agreement was signed) with 18 senior officials of the administration, including technical experts and bureaucrats who were in the best position to advise him."[61] Nigeria has maintained its position that the Maroua Declaration is not recognized, as Gowon had no power under the constitution to cede any part of the country.[62] In its judgment, the ICJ ceded the territory to Cameroon.[63]

Another example of a conflict of this nature is between Equatorial Guinea and Gabon, and the disputed territory in this case is the Mbagne Island in the Gulf of Guinea. Here too, both sides cited opposing historical claims to back up their ownership of the territory. The situation reached a dangerous height in February 2002, when the Gabonese government seized control of the island. This forced both countries to seek an amicable solution to end the dispute. There was also disagreement between the two countries over the Corisco Bay Islands. These are three small islands, which lie north of the Gabonese capital of Libreville, near the border with the continental territory of Equatorial Guinea. The dispute dates back to 1972, and it arose out of different interpretations of maps dating back to 1900.[64] In 2003, the two countries appealed to the UN to help resolve their dispute, and the UN secretary general appointed a former Canadian Ambassador to the United Nations, Yves Fortier, as his special adviser and mediator on the issue. By the following year, both countries had signed a Memorandum of Understanding to jointly explore oil in the disputed region.[65]

Across West Africa, there remain disputes over offshore discoveries, even though efforts are continually been made to ensure that the differences are contained. For example, the Nigerian government still has contentions with the government of Equatorial Guinea over the Zafiro field. The field is Equatorial Guinea's main field and the country argues that it is a separate field, while the Nigerian government maintains that it saddles the territorial waters of both countries. After subtle tension, in September 2000, both countries signed a pact delineating their maritime boundaries and in April 2002, a treaty was signed on the joint exploration of oil in the region.

On the whole, increase in oil conflicts rooted in ownership controversies can be traced to at least three factors: first is the depression in the economic fortune of many communities that increases the propensity to search for territories embedded with natural resources; second is the decline in the power of the state in Africa, which makes it incapable of "nipping" minor conflicts in the bud; and third is the increasing strength of civil society, which has led it to challenge governments over the ownership of oil-deposit sites.

Disagreements over Management of Proceeds

This seems to be the most important consideration linking oil to the causes of conflicts in Africa. The causes of the conflicts here can be traced to three main roots, and once again, Nigeria presents the best set of examples. The first root is one in which the ownership of oil reserve sites does not translate to any infrastructural development of oil-producing communities. This is somewhat linked to the general problem of infrastructural development in Africa, where, as noted earlier, governments have tied development of infrastructures to the resource endowment that can be derived from the specific communities. Thus, with such discoveries in a community, there naturally arise expectations on the part of the community that there should be some form of infrastructural developments. When this does not come, the inhabitants feel shortchanged, and resorting to violence has been one of the ways through which they express their disappointment. In actuality, oil-producing communities appear to have suffered more underdevelopment than their non-oil-producing counterparts, as is evident in Nigeria's Niger Delta region. Basic amenities such as electricity, pipe-borne water, hospitals, and schools were for a long time not available in most oil-producing areas.[66] For example, as of November 1998, it was reported that there was not a single petrol station in all the riverine areas of Ijaw, Itsekiri, and Ilaje in Bayelsa, Delta, Edo, and Ondo States.[67] This picture serves to explain why the inhabitants feel short-changed, given that it is the wealth of their land that sustains the nation.

What the people of Nigeria's oil communities find most objectionable is that in spite of their deprivation of the benefits to the resources, those from the dominant ethnic groups are monopolizing its benefits. Although the inhabitants hold the three dominant ethnic groups responsible, the main culprits, in their views, are the Hausa/Fulani stock in the northern part of the country. This is the group that has held political power for most of the postindependence years.[68] Indeed, the two other major ethnic groups—the Yorubas and the non-oil-producing sections of the Ibos—were, until recently, perceived merely as opportunistic accomplices.

Nigerian government, in seeking to address the aforementioned plight of the indigenes, has set up a succession of institutions to manage the development of the areas. However, corruption and poor management of these institutions have resulted in situations in which the people have found themselves somewhat worse off. It is ironic that many of the agencies set up to administer these funds have been headed by indigenes of the oil-producing communities. This has supported the government allegation that even local people cannot be trusted to protect the interest of their own people. However, the local population has countered this by arguing that successive governments have often handpicked indigenes they know would serve the interest of the establishment. In so doing, they also claim the government sometimes discredits the appointed people in order to give the impression of the Niger Delta oil-producing communities at war with themselves.[69] This was, indeed, the case of a head of one of these institutions, who looted the money for the department and escaped from the country. He was officially declared wanted but has not been brought to justice. This may be viewed as a further confirmation of the assertion that local elites have persistently placed personal interests before group interests, and that ethnic solidarity, even in the face of clear persecution, can be sacrificed for personal greed.

Before 1992, the government allocated 1.5 percent from the federal accounts to mineral-producing areas. These funds were channeled to a presidential task force set up to execute development projects in the area. When this failed, the government set up the Oil Mineral Producing Areas Development Commission (OMPADEC), through a decree in 1992. The revenue accruable to the oil-producing areas for their development then rose to 3 percent. Another clause in the OMPADEC bill was that only indigenes of oil-producing communities would be qualified to be appointed as the head of the commission. While some in the oil-producing communities saw this as a major development in the right direction, it failed to satisfy their aspirations, due to political engineering and underfunding. Out of the N85,489.56 million due to the commission from 1992 to 1996, only N13,164.26 million was actually disbursed.[70] It is a startling revelation that the same government gave N100 billion to the Petroleum Trust Fund in its three years of existence.[71] OMPADEC was later replaced by the Niger Delta Development Commission (NDDC), which despite having improved on the efforts of the previous bodies, still offers less than the population of the Niger Delta expects.

For the people of the Niger Delta, the treatment from successive federal governments ties in with the aforementioned theme of politics of revenue allocation in the country. This is viewed as being grossly unfair, since they produce the main commodity responsible for the majority of the country's external earnings. A look at the history of derivation and revenue allocation shows the diminishing returns to the oil-producing regions. In 1953, the derivation formula was 100 percent, as recommended by the Chucks Commission. This changed at independence, at which point the constitution stipulated 50 percent, later reduced to 45 percent under the Gowon administration. A retrogressive slide ensued after 1970, with the Murtala/Obasanjo administration reducing it to 20 percent and the Shagari administration dropping it to 2 percent (and later 3 percent after a court ruling). By 1984, it had been reduced to 1.5 percent by the Buhari administration, although this was later slightly increased to 3.5 percent by the Babangida administration. As of 2006, it was 13 percent. This pattern instills in the people of Nigeria's oil-producing regions the impression of unfair treatment. The reward being sought from the struggle is an increase in the derivation allocated to them.

A variance of this exists in Angola, where the oil-rich Cabinda province remains, even to date, a region complaining of neglect amid affluence. However, the situation in Cabinda is slightly different from that of Nigeria's Niger Delta province. According to the international NGO Christian Aid, while the living conditions in the region are not "noticeably worse than in other Angolan province . . . the contrast between its poverty and the more obvious wealth there has . . . sparked vocal dissent."[72] The organization also notes that the cost of living in Cabinda is higher because the region has no port facilities and the consumer goods have to be "flown from the capital or trucked in from neighboring countries."[73] The location of petroleum resources has not brought any visible benefits, whether in the form of social services or local employment opportunities to the local Dinka and Nuer population in the Sudan, and the support the group is giving to the armed groups opposed to the central government in Khartoum cannot be ignored.

The second way through which disagreements over the management of proceeds and allocation of privileges has been linked to conflict is where offices and positions, either in the government or in the management of the oil sector, do not benefit the indigenes of the oil-producing communities. The idea of an unfair distribution of political appointments and promotion is rooted in the complex nature of politics practiced in postindependence African societies. It is assumed that the interest of ethnic groups in the somewhat zero-sum nature of national politics can only be protected by indigenes of these groups. This is behind the calls of the population of the oil-producing communities in needing a voice in government, especially in those circles where oil-related decisions are made. The assumption here is that such a representative will have domestic ties to the environment and be well aware of the plight of the people and thus be better placed to present their cause than outsiders whose attachment is considered to be at best peripheral and at worst nonexistent. The government's refusal to grant this concession has been at the root of some of the problems in the ensuing oil-related conflicts. Another dimension of the presence of local representation comes in the argument of the people that oil multinational corporations do not even employ local indigenes.[74] Consequently, in the local population's calculation, both the government and the oil companies are trying from to deprive oil-producing communities of representation. Again, Nigeria presents the best example of where this has been a major cause of conflict.

The third link between management of proceeds and cause of conflicts comes where technological and administrative structures created for the management of the oil resources (which often bring attendant opportunities in jobs and social developments) are located outside these communities. This is a problem underlined by the assumption that the location of such structures would bring some economic and social advantages to the community. In the Nigerian example, communities in the oil-producing areas have found it incomprehensible that oil refineries are located in the north, often up to a thousand kilometers away from the oil exploration sites. The failure of the government to offer credible technological explanation for this ensures that people in the oil-producing communities see it as part of the wider attempt by the north to dominate the management of oil. Apart from refineries, boards and agencies managing Nigeria's oil resources have their offices situated either in the capital or in regions far away from the oil deposit. These, as would be expected, have fueled tension and aggravated conflicts in the country. A similar picture exists in Sudan, where oil resources are located in the south and the refinery situated in the north by the politically dominant northern administration. In both countries, the oil-producing communities have found ethnic considerations in explaining these actions.

Complications Arising from the Process of Exploration

This is a major cause of conflict, again brought to the fore by the crisis in the Nigeria's Niger Delta. For a long time, the destruction of the environment was considered to be one of the inevitable consequences of oil exploration. As a result, the people in the oil-producing regions were expected to understand and accept these conditions. However, the growth of arguments purporting the environmental implications of oil exploration only came as a result of the neglect of other socioeconomic aspects of oil exploration.

In Nigeria's oil-producing regions, the environmental implications of oil exploration have been at the forefront of conflicts. Broadly, these have come largely from oil spillage and its destruction of farmlands and water resources. The extent of the destruction in some cases is such that the land is no longer suitable for farming. Additionally, the resulting pollution of water means that fishing has become almost impossible in many of these communities. For a population living almost exclusively on farming and fishing, this has meant a massive reduction in their economic conditions. The local inhabitants are further incensed because the oil corporations have persistently ignored their call for a reduction in the destruction of the environment and to assist in resolving the effects of past and current shortcomings. In this defiance to the plight of the people, the local population believes that the oil companies are receiving encouragement and support from the government.

Oil spillages in Nigeria come mainly from two sources: sabotage and mechanical problems, often arising from old and rusty pipelines. The ratio of spillage between these causes has also underpinned the conflict in Nigeria's oil-producing communities. The local communities argue that a greater percentage of the oil spillage occurs as a result of the old and rusty pipelines of the multinational corporations. They argue that many of these companies were more interested in the financial benefits of the oil and less with repairing pipelines. The people claim evidence in the fact that most of the pipelines have not been upgraded or reinstalled since oil was discovered more than five decades earlier.[75] While it is true that there are deliberate acts of sabotage, the people's view is that this accounts for less than the problems accruing to the use of rusty pipes.

Although all the oil companies have been accused of environmental pollution, Shell has been at the forefront of the criticism and, as would be expected, the company has tried to deny the charge. While not denying that the process of oil exploration comes with some negative consequences for the environment, Shell insists that the effects in the Niger Delta have been inflated. The company also claims that most of the environmental problems in the region are caused by the sabotage of oil installations by the aggrieved population. Both the inhabitants of the Niger Delta and many external observers have, however, insisted that Shell has inflicted on the environment significant environmental damage. The decision by a Nigerian High Court in June 2000 ordering Shell to pay US$40 million to a community in the Niger Delta for compensation for the environmental problems caused by oil spillage thirty years ago opened a new dimension to the controversy. This was the first time any oil multinational corporation in Nigeria would be forced to compensate local communities for environmental pollution caused by oil exploration.

Although Shell appealed against the judgment on the grounds that the oil spillage occurred during the Nigeria civil war and that there was no way it could be proved that it was caused by Shell, the fact that the case was successfully prosecuted through the court is remarkable. It is also believed that a floodgate of prosecution could have been opened, not only against Shell but other companies that could have polluted the environment.

Also, the government conceded there were environmental problems emanating from oil exploration and a number of institutions were set up to meet these challenges, including the Federal Environmental Protection Agency (FEPA). However, these were largely ineffective and have been of no direct benefit to the population suffering from oil pollution. By the time the local inhabitants add the implications of these environmental degradations to other difficulties coming from hosting oil deposits, they believe there are sufficient grounds to take up acts of violence against the oil corporations and the government, whom they see as not protecting their interest.

Insensitivity to Indigenous Practices of Culture and Religion

Another issue linking oil to the causes of conflict is insensitivity to local culture This consideration alone has never directly caused conflict in oil-producing regions, however, it has formed an important consideration in reinforcing other issues identified above to ignite tension in oil-producing communities. Among others, tensions here often arise from non-respect for the local population's sacred institutions. Evidences abound in oil-producing communities that oil-prospecting companies have not respected lands identified as sacred institutions. It is indeed the case that many of the inhabitants of Nigeria's oil-producing communities have sentimental attachment to their culture and religion, and they have found some of the activities of the expatriate community prospecting for oil in their region most objectionable. Another activity of considerable concern to the people is the perceived defilement of young women, who, with the influx of foreign oil workers, are increasingly becoming participants of the commercial sex industry. While the local communities agree that the expatriate workers are not solely to blame, they also argue that the economic deprivation of the oil communities present the young ladies with little option. They thus view the expatriate staff as exploitative, especially as many of their victims are barely at the sexual age of consent, both in legal and customary terms.[76] Closely linked to this is the issue of irresponsible fathering by expatriate oil workers.

Secessionist Desires by Oil-Rich Provinces

Also important in linking oil to the causes of conflict is the secessionist tendencies that sometime emerge among oil-producing communities. At the root of the conflict in this context is the desire of the oil-rich provinces to attempt secession from the rest of the country. This problem has been recorded in Angola, Sudan, and Nigeria and has manifested in different ways. In Angola, the region attempting secession is the Cabinda Province. As noted earlier, this province accounts for more than half of Angolan oil exports, and it has been fighting against the MPLA government in Luanda. Whether the insurgent groups that have emerged in Cabinda are fighting because of the oil deposit or because of other political reasons is a matter of opinion, what is, however, beyond doubt is that natural resources, especially oil, have been a key issue in the conflict.

The war in Cabinda has been going on since independence, although the other war between the government and with UNITA has overshadowed the intense conflict and human rights abuses in the Cabinda enclave.[77] Cabinda's war for independence began in the early 1960s, when several movements advocating for Cabinda's separate existence sprang up. Many of these movements united in 1963 to form a common front, Front for the Liberation of the Enclave of Cabinda (FLEC). By January 1967, it had created a government in exile, which succeeded in gaining recognition from just a few countries, notably Gabon, Uganda, CAR, Zaire, and Congo Brazzaville.

Following Angola's independence, the extent of external interference was a crucial factor that shaped the Angolan government's policy toward Cabinda. For much of the 1970s and '80s, FLEC operated a low-intensity guerrilla-type insurgency in Cabinda, and the government responded by stationing troops in the region. The division that plagued the Cabinda separatist groups reemerged in the 1980s, when FLEC was divided into FLEC-FAC and FLEC-R. A glimmer of hope came when the leader of the original FLEC, Ranque Franque, opened up with a rapprochement with the government in 1992. The rejection of the 1992 election results by Savimbi and the reemergence of conflict further gave hope that the government would be willing to make a deal with FLEC-FAC. This did not materialize, making the years 1997 and 1998 those of increased military activities in Cabinda. With the end of the war against UNITA, conflict has further increased with oil at its helm. This has seen FLEC-FAC and FLEC-R persistently carry out abductions of oil expatriates. Indeed, an astute commentator on the events in the region, Alex Vines, has noted that the abduction of expatriate oil, construction, and timber workers makes Cabinda "one of the most hazardous working environments outside Colombia."[78]

A similar separatist tendency exists in Nigeria. As far back as 1966, an indigene of the Niger Delta, Isaac Adaka Boro, declared independence from the Nigerian state and engaged the federal government in a war with a rebel army he called the Niger Delta Volunteer Force. Although he failed in this quixotic experiment that bemused even his own people, the cause for which he fought continued on in many of the inhabitants of the area.[79] It was thus not surprising that in 2004, the country recorded another declared intention by groups in the Niger Delta to secede from the country. This was through the formation of the Niger Delta People Volunteer Force (NDPVF) under one Mujahid Dokubo-Asari. The actual strength of the latest rebel group is not known, but estimates puts it at about 2,000, and they live in Okoronta, a village hideout in the mangrove swamps of Bayelsa State.[80] Not much is known about Dokubo-Asari, who sees people of mixed predisposition such as Mandela and Osama bin Laden as his heroes, except that he is the son of a retired High Court judge and a university dropout, who later converted from Christianity to Islam. Before leading the NDPVF, he had been a leader of one of the prominent gangs in the Niger Delta and had been involved in an ongoing battle with another warlord, Tom Ateke.[81]

Until the early part of 2004, the Nigerian government saw the threats from this group to be of mere entertainment value. Indeed, the government sees Dokubo-Asari's activities as a cover for his criminal tendencies.[82] By September 2004, the situation assumed a more dangerous dimension, with the rebel force taking over most of the oil installations in the Niger Delta and forcing oil companies to withdraw all their staff from the region.[83] Shell, in particular, had to close its Santa Barbara flow station with a loss of 28,000 barrels a day.[84] Indeed, the situation in the region resulted in oil prices reaching an unprecedented $50 per barrel. On September 27, 2004, Dokubo-Asari issued an ultimatum to the international community to withdraw their nationals from the Niger Delta oilfields by October 1, which was Nigeria's 44th independence anniversary, or face dire consequences. Two days after the ultimatum, Nigeria's President Obasanjo astonished the nation by holding talks with Dokubo-Asari, which resulted in the October 2004 disarmament and destruction of his arms.[85]

There is, however, an aspect of the Dokubo-Asari saga that is often left undiscussed, and this aspect shows the link that often exists between power elites and irregular forces in the politics of resource control. It is widely believed that an informal link exists between main actors in the political machinery that won the election for President Obasanjo in 1999 and Dokubo-Asari. Indeed, Dokubo-Asari and Governor of River States Peter Odili were political friends who allegedly supported Obasanjo and assisted him during the 1999 election. However, Dokubo was said to have turned against Obasanjo after the president sent in soldiers to destroy Odi town, an Ijaw community, in 2001 (discussed later in this chapter). But just as Dokubo-Asari was making his exit from the Obasanjo support team, his main rival in the oil-bunkering business, Tom Ateke, shifted to the Obasanjo camp, and he turned his base Okrika, hitherto a stronghold of the rival All Nigeria's People's Party, into President Obasanjo's Peoples Democratic Party. The government eventually took the step of arresting and charging Dokubo-Asari in September 2005 for treason, a felony.

Crisis Emanating from Domestic Petroleum Needs

The final factor linking oil to the causes of conflict, and also one that has brought considerable fatalities, comes from civil protests that often attend government's inability to meet the local petroleum demands or government's decision to increase the prices of petroleum products used for local consumption. Again, Nigeria presents a good example in this respect. While on the surface the problems are related to the astronomical increase in the prices of fuel—which ultimately affects every other thing in the country—the root causes are often more complex, and they reflect the clash between expectation of the population and the image the government presents to the populace of its disability vis-à-vis the production of oil to the local population. The population's position, with which they justify violent protests against oil price increases is simple: Nigeria produces oil and even exports to outside world, sometimes at concessionary rates. They thus could not understand why the country should experience fuel shortage, and why the government should increase the price of petroleum products far above what the population can afford. Many also contend that the root cause of the shortage and the increase in prices is the endemic corruption that they argue has characterized the whole oil business in the country. By their own logic, the government can reduce the amount of oil it sells at concessionary rates to satisfy local demands.

The government sees the above argument as simplistic, claiming that the price of petroleum in Nigeria is one of the cheapest anywhere in the world, and that the only way to ensure constant supply of fuel is to increase the price. The government also contends that many of the refineries in the country are damaged, and this has made it more difficult to meet local demands. Indeed, the capacity utilization of refineries in Port-Harcourt, Kaduna, and Warri in the first quarter of 2002 were respectively 56.77, 37.78, and 54.45 percent; second quarter were 49.90, 37.34, and 62.07; and the third quarter were 60.37, 36.06, and 84.38.[86] In conclusion, the government contends that the population's demand for cheap fuel prices is unrealistic, and that the people should cooperate with the government to ensure a constant supply.

The process of announcing fuel price increase in Nigeria often has an interesting sequence, which shows the changing tides of governance in the country. While during the military rule the announcement is often preceded with the stationing of detachments of armed forces to strategic locations to quell riots that are expected to follow the announcement, during the civilian administration such announcement will come after temporary scarcity, sometimes orchestrated by the government. This would then lead the population to a situation where they were willing to accept buying petroleum products at any price. In both cases, however, reactions have been the same, with the population embarking on strike actions and violent protests, often organized by labor unions and students. One of the most recent in the series of violent protests over an increase in oil prices was in July 2003, when the government increased the price of fuel by 56 percent. Coming just about a month after President Obasanjo won election for a second term, many people considered it as a betrayal of public trust, and the country's labor union called for a strike. Eventually, this resulted in conflict that led to the death of ten protesters.

In concluding discussions on the link between oil and the causes of conflicts, it can be seen that many of the issues discussed above are invariably linked to governance, especially the inability of the governments of some of the oil-producing states to manage all the complex issues associated with the management and careful distribution of oil. Indeed, in some of the countries where other problems of governance have caused conflicts, oil, again, has been linked to the prolongation of conflicts.

Linking Oil to Prolongation of Conflict

Conflicts in oil-producing countries are known to have been prolonged by oil, mainly because the presence of oil has enabled governments to resist rebel activities. Although in a few cases rebels have seized oil fields and have prevented exploration activities, the nature of the global oil market is such that it is difficult for these rebel forces to export the resource. Three conflicts that bring home the validity of this point are those in Angola, Sudan, and to a much lesser extent, Chad. There now seems to be no doubt that one of the main reasons the Angolan conflict continued for so long was the fairly equal share of control of the country's mineral resources by each side. While UNITA controlled most of the diamond deposits and exploited them in its prosecution of the conflict, the MPLA government operated in the oil-rich areas, and it too has been accused of being reckless and corrupt in the handling of the resources.[87] Table 5.2 shows the position of oil in Angolan GDP between 1994 and 1999.

Similar to the ways through which solid minerals have been linked to the prolongation of conflict, four considerations have linked oil to the prolongation of conflicts in Africa. The first is through the provision of money used to procure weapons for conflicts. This has been most noticeable in all three cases. In Angola, the MPLA government controlled most of the oil installations during the course of the civil war and used the proceeds from oil to procure weapons used to fight the UNITA rebels. Because of the scale of the war and the sophisticated weapons used by the UNITA rebels as a result of their access to diamonds, most of the weapons the MPLA acquired were equally sophisticated, consequently implying greater use of oil revenue. In Sudan, it is believed that one of the main reasons the north needs the south is the enormous oil deposit in the latter. The recent discovery of a possible 12.5 billion barrels in the south of the country further implies that the stakes in the war are getting higher, and that the north will continue to fight to ensure the control of what is likely to be one of the world's largest oil fields. Indeed, the north used the oil revenue from the south to finance the war, with no attempt to shield this fact. Former Speaker of the National Assembly and Secretary General of the ruling National Congress, Hassan al-Turabi, declared in April

Table 5.2 Breakdown of Angolan GDP by sector percentage

	1996	1997	1998	1999	2000	2001
Agriculture, Forestry & Fishing	7.1	9.0	12.0	6.4	5.8	8.0
Oil and Gas	58.0	47.9	37.8	58.7	60.9	53.6
Diamonds	3.4	4.3	5.4	8.2	6.4	5.8
Manufacturing	3.5	4.4	6.3	3.5	2.9	3.8
Electricity & Water	0.0	0.1	0.1	0.0	0.0	0.0
Construction	3.1	4.1	6.2	3.1	2.8	3.5
Trade and Commerce	15.0	16.2	19.3	15.1	14.5	15.6
Non-Tradable Services	8.3	11.8	10.6	4.9	6.9	9.6
Import Duties	1.9	2.3	1.4	0.2	0.0	0.0

Source: Tony Hodges, *Angola: Anatomy of an Oil State*, London: James Currey, 2004, p. 212.

1999 that oil revenue would be used to finance factories the government was building to produce tanks and missiles. It was, indeed, not a coincidence that the day the first shipment of 600,000 barrels of oil left Port Sudan in September 1999, was the same day that twenty Russian T-55 tanks entered Sudan. It was alleged that Chad also has been using revenue from oil to finance the civil war in the country. Indeed, in 2000, the government admitted diverting US$4 million of the pipeline investment to buy weapons for its war against the northern rebels.[88] Only recently in October 2005, the agreement the country made with the World Bank on how to manage revenue coming from its oil has been altered in ways to allow the government more money to procure weapons.

The second way of linking oil to the prolongation of conflict is through the fierceness in the control of oil sites during the course of conflicts. Again, this tendency is present mainly in Sudan and Angola. To ensure the undisturbed flow of oil that could fuel the war, the Sudanese government protects the workers by encircling the sites with the fiercely loyal Mujahedeen units. Also operating in the oil-producing areas are the armed southern militias such as the Nuer forces. In some of its military campaigns, the government made use of "militias," which is a broad term for an array of people including government's People Defense Force, press-ganged youths and Islamic zealots, the southern forces of politicians co-opted by Khartoum, government-paid Murahileen, and Arab speakers from the north–south border areas out for booty and adventure.[89]

The third link is through the corruption of political elites benefiting from oil's links with conflicts. Indeed, oil and corruption have contributed to the prolongation of the war in Angola in a number of ways, most of which indict the activities of the MPLA government, which has held control of the majority of the sites for most of the war period. Key members of the government, who were allegedly exploiting the opportunity of the conflict to benefit from oil, wanted a prolonged duration of the war. Specifically there have been allegations linking the Angolan leadership, including key generals in the Angolan Army and powerful politicians, to arms deals.[90] Companies were allegedly set up to act as fronts to re-divert money from Angolan oil to private accounts.[91]

The final link is through intransigence to Peace Moves. Although it may be difficult to identify in concrete terms the ways through which the control of oil has encouraged warring factions to become intransigent to peace moves, there is anecdotal evidence to support the assertion that the control of oil reserves has made actors involved in wars neglect the path of peace. For example, between 1994 and 1997 the Angolan government was expending a minimum average of 34.1 percent on defense, while a dismal average of 0.5 percent was being expended on the peace process during the same period. In this process, there has also been the government's suppression of the civil society, especially those questioning the activities of individuals within the government and their operating with impunity. There have been cases of journalists arrested and detained without charges, through which the government is weakening the base on which durable peace can be established in the country.[92]

Also worth considering in the link between oil and the prolongation of conflict (this time around communal conflicts) is the role of bunkering. This has been a crucial issue in Nigeria, one in which government officials and individuals, with deep involvement of external actors, have been seizing the opportunity found in instability in the Niger Delta to engage in illegal bunkering. Some of these actors have continued to encourage political instability in the region to further maximize their profit from bunkering. Estimates from Shell allegedly claimed that the country was losing up to US$100 million per week.[93] The extent to which the scandal could have reached the upper echelon of the Nigeria security establishment became clear when three senior naval officers were court-martialed over the disappearance of a Russian ship that had earlier been detained for bunkering.

It is ironic that oil can play a crucial role in prolonging conflict even when the country at war does not have the resource. This happens when external countries intervening in the conflict have oil and can use its proceeds to sustain their involvement in an external country. This can, however, come about with varying intentions as the oil-endowed country can also aim at a quick resolution to the conflict if its involvement is in a peacekeeping operation. In Africa, the best example of this is Nigeria's involvement in Liberia. It is possible that individual Nigerian soldiers might have deliberately prolonged the Liberian war to make more money from the oil allocation being made by the Nigerian government to assist in bringing about durable peace. All this shows how intricately oil plays a crucial factor in national politics in Nigeria, Africa's foremost oil-producing country.

Oil, National Politics, and Communal Conflicts

Because of a link with national politics, and because management is often under exclusive government control, communal conflicts over oil inevitably have an impact on national politics. Nigeria presents perhaps a most complex example of where oil has been linked to communal clashes. The ramifications of the communal clashes are complex, and their effects on ethnic groups in the oil-producing communities of the country have been devastating. At the center of most of these conflicts are three main issues: the politics of ethnic identity, the role of youths, and the disagreements over land.

The politics of ethnic identity vis-à-vis oil politics and communal conflicts in Nigeria centers largely on the plight of the Ijaws. Perhaps some words about the Ijaws are necessary as an introduction. They are the most prominent of Nigeria's ethnic minorities, as they constitute the fourth largest ethnic group after the dominant Hausa/Fulani, Ibo, and Yoruba ethnic groups. Unlike these dominant groups, however, the geographical division of the country into states has not allocated any specific states for the Ijaws. The people are thus divided among many states, and in none of these are they in sufficient numbers to form a majority. Consequently, they suffer minority syndrome at all levels, both at the federal and various state levels. This is crucial in understanding some of the actions of the Ijaw in their protest against the Nigerian state and in their conflicts with other groups. However, the Ijaws are vital in Nigeria's oil politics, as their land produces more than 2 million barrels per day.

In terms of communal conflicts, the Ijaws have had conflicts with a number of other ethnic subgroups in the oil-producing states, especially the Ilajes, the Itsekiris, and the Binis, all of whom are accused of aligning themselves with successive governments to marginalize the interest of the Ijaws in the zero-sum politics of the country's oil-producing region. The Ijaws also accuse these communities of exploiting the disagreement between the government and the Ijaws over the latter's forceful agitation for better deals at the benefit of their (the Ijaws') expense. Specifically, they alleged that the federal government located major oil-related infrastructures and amenities in other communities outside Ijaw, which allegedly produce more oil. For example, the Ijaw people argued that major NNPC establishments, such as the Integrated Data Services Limited (IDSL), the Nigerian Petroleum Development Company Limited (NPDC), the NNPC zonal office, depot, and medical center, were all located in Benin City, after being previously listed for location in Warri. The violence has been more paramount in Bayelsa, Rivers, and Warri areas of Delta state.

In looking at the role of youths, any discussion of their role in the context of conflicts involving oil in the Niger Delta should address four interrelated questions: why the youths are restive; the targets of their anger; the manifestations of the protests; and the implications of their actions. In addressing the reasons for their being restive, answers may be obtained from the fact that they believe they should be at the vanguard of the call for a better Niger Delta. They believe that the older generations are either tied or badly compromised. They see themselves as the neglected majority in an unjust social order that transfers the wealth from their soil to develop other regions of the country, leaving them impoverished. This explanation, however, answers only one aspect of the problem. Also important in understanding the politics of youth activities in the Niger Delta is that the difficulties of survival in the environment and the hardship that had been inflicted on them by successive military administrations in the country have toughened them and made them utterly fearless and defiant.

Contrary to what is often assumed, the youths have not always directed their anger at oil multinational corporations and the government alone. Indeed, there are two other targets. First are their traditional rulers. For several years, the youths left their rulers unquestioned, and this gave the latter opportunities to strike different deals with the oil companies that were against the community. With the emergence of Ken Saro Wiwa came the first attempt to enlighten the youths about the dangers inherent in "internal sabotage." With this, the youths became empowered to challenge their traditional rulers. Consequently, the activities of their fellow indigenes became an issue in the youths' war against what they saw as injustice in the management of their oil resources. Second are other youths from other regions of the country. They are seen as coming into the Niger Delta to take up positions that should be given to local indigenes but which they could not take because of their lack of opportunity to have the requisite education. It is thus a usual practice for these youths, who have come from other parts of Nigeria to work in the oil installations in the Niger Delta, to pay "protection" fees to youth groups in the Niger Delta before they can work safely in the region.

In terms of manifestation, youth activities in the Niger Delta have come in different ways, including violent contacts with youths from rival ethnic groups, destruction of pipelines, kidnapping of foreign oil workers, and demonstrations against government targets. The somewhat disorganized nature of all these, however, changed during the second half of the 1990s, when youths across the Niger Delta made a number of declarations against the government (state and central) and against oil multinational corporations. These include the Ogbia Declaration, the Ikwerre Rescue Charter, and the Kaiama Declaration. Of these, perhaps the most important here is the Kaiama Declaration issued in December 1998 by Ijaw youths.[94] After reviewing the historical causes of the problem in the Niger Delta, the declaration came up with a string of demands, including the declaration that all land and natural resources in the Ijaw area belong to the people and not the Nigerian Federal Government; declaration of the nonrecognition of all undemocratic decrees that are considered antithetical to the Ijaw people, including the Land Use Decree; expulsion of all military personnel in Ijawland; and a warning to all oil companies using military personnel to do away with them or expect to be treated as an enemy; clear instruction to all oil companies to stop exploration and exploitation activities and to withdraw from Ijaw territory by December 30, 1998; the declaration of intention to cooperate with other nationalist groups in the Niger Delta, and with other groups struggling for self determination; the rejection of the transition program that was then underway in the country because it was not preceded by the restructuring of the country and a Sovereign National Conference; and a reaffirmation that the Ijaw would remain within Nigeria to demand and work for self-government and resource control.[95]

A look at the declaration by the Ijaw youths above would show how disillusioned they are about the Nigerian state. Not long after the declaration, the situation in the Niger Delta took a turn for the worse.[96] After the transition to civilian administration in 1999, the youths continued their struggle. Apart from reaffirming their commitment to the Kaiama Declaration, they asked the new Obasanjo administration to address the problem of local government creation crisis, especially the relocation of the headquarters of Warri North Council Area to Ogbe-Ijoh.[97] Also included in their demands is the withdrawal of the 13 percent derivation proposed by the president to the National Assembly and the disbandment of the special project division of the presidency. Obasanjo rejected the proposals of the youths, criticizing them as bordering on defiance and rudeness.

Although the activities of the Ijaw youths are the most pronounced, there are other groups in the Niger Delta that are involved in struggles against the Nigerian government over its management of oil. Also important are the activities of the Isoko National Youth Movements (INYM). The organization made its demands known in its publication "Why We Struck." On the whole, there were seven main demands: the creation of two additional local government areas for the Isoko people; the appointment of an Isoko indigenes into the constituted OMPADEC for equitable representation of all oil-producing areas; payment by Shell of a N50 billion development fund for Isoko to mitigate the decades of oil exploration and exploitation; immediate employment of qualified Isoko youth by Shell and the absorption of all its contract workers in Isokoland; immediate registration of qualified Isoko people as contractors to Shell; reopening of the Ozoro Polytechnic by the Delta State Government; and tarring of all untarred roads in Isokoland.[98]

A new dimension that has been added to the layers of conflict in the Niger Delta is the threat now being issued by the local population against their own indigenes working with Shell. Local militias have issued warnings to these people that they would face the wrath of the local population. For example, the leader of one of these militia groups, the Ijaw Monitoring Group, Joseph Evah, warns that his group would attack family members of Ijaw people who work with Shell. This, according to him, will make "their sons and daughters who work with Shell be forced to look out for our interest."[99] The main implication of youth's revolt in the Niger Delta is the reduction in the amount of oil produced in the country, a situation that has not been made better by the incessant conflicts among the various ethnic units in the region over land.

On the issue of disagreements over land, it has to be pointed out, as noted in chapter 3, that lands bearing natural resources are often sources of major

Table 5.3. Ethnic community conflicts in the Niger Delta Region

Date	Combatants	Observation
1993	Urhobo–Itsekiri (Delta State)	2 killed, 7 injured; Delta State Government accused of complicity.
1993	Okrika–Ogoni (Rivers State) Andoni–Ogoni (Rivers State)	Destruction of property worth about N38 million; the Ogoni alone lost about 438 people; forced migrations.
1994	Ogoni (Rivers State)	Riot; 4 prominent Ogoni sons were killed; culminated in execution of activist Ken Saro Wiwa in November 1995.
1995	Ijaw–Urhobo (Delta State)	100 people feared dead; land tussle.
1996	Ogoni (Rivers State)	Clash between Ogoni youths and security agencies sent to stop the first anniversary of the hanging of Ken Saro Wiwa; 2 killed; more than 70 injured.
1997	Ijaw–Ilaje (Ondo State)	More than 100 people feared dead; land tussle; forced relocation.
1998	Itsekiri–Ijaw (Delta State)	Destruction of property; people killed; thousands forced to relocate.
1999 (January 1)	Ijaw Youths–Soldiers (Yenagoa, Bayelsa State)	Expiration of deadline to oil companies to leave the area; 4 persons killed; 12 arrested.
1999 (June 2)	Ijaw Youths–Soldiers (Warri, Delta State)	4 soldiers killed; 200 youths feared dead; youths burnt down an entire village.
1999 (June 6)	Ijaw–Itsekiri (Warri, Delta State)	Unannounced attacks by youths; counterattacks over 3 days; commercial town of Aruton razed; nearly 200 people killed; affected community deserted.

Table 5.3 (*continued*)

Date	Combatants	Observation
1999 (June 7)	Itsekiri–Urhobo (Delta State)	Violent clash; more than 200 houses set ablaze; lives lost; quick intervention of police saves situation from further degeneration.
1999 (August 2)	Ijaw Youths–Police/Navy (Warri, Delta State)	500 Ijaw youths attack Divisional Police Headquarters (Sapele); seize arms; militant youths in army uniform attack naval base.
1999 (August 11)	Ilaje–Arogbo Ijaw (Ondo State)	Several people, mostly children and the elderly, killed, apparently with sophisticated weapons and war boats; bodies float in the rivers; many people displaced as refugees to places such as Aiyetoro, Lagos, and parts of Edo State.
1999 (November 12)	Youths–Police (Odi, Bayelsa State)	Militant youths killed 12 policemen.
1999 (December 6)	Youths–Soldiers (Warri, Delta State)	Attempt to retrieve rifles from youths in Pessu Market area; 3 youths killed.
2000 (January 10)	Itsekiri–Urhobo (Warri, Delta State)	Property destroyed.
2000 (January 24)	Evwereni–Police (Delta State)	Four youths killed, after alleged murder of Evwereni Town's monarch by police.
2000 (March 17)	Eleme–Okrika (Rivers State)	Land tussle; 1 person killed, 6 injured.
2000 (May 23)	Warri Youths–soldiers (Amukpe, Delta State)	Roadblocks mounted: movement of motorists obstructed; 3 people killed.
2000	Diema Community–Okpoama (Bayelsa State)	Dispute over ownership of land; attacks and reprisal attacks; loss of lives and destruction of property, including buildings; Forced migration: refugee problem.

Source: Nyemutu Roberts, *The State, Accumulation and Violence: The Politics of Environmental Security in Nigeria's Oil Producing Areas*, NISER Monograph Series, No. 17, 42; and newspaper reports.

intergroup conflicts among communities in Africa. This is particularly the case in all oil-producing communities of Nigeria, where ownership of land has caused conflicts among different communities, such as the Itsekiris, Isokos, and Ijaws. Closely linked to this are disputes over chieftaincies issues and the citing of local government headquarters. Table 5.3 shows some of the communal conflicts in oil-producing countries in Nigeria.

The general instability in Nigeria's oil-producing communities continues to affect the country's oil production. For example, the March 2003 conflict in Warri resulted in the loss of about US$631.8 million. At the height of the crisis, which took the form of sporadic violence involving rival ethnic groups and the government security forces, the oil firms closed their facilities, resulting in the country losing 815,000 barrels of crude oil—about 40 percent of its production. Of this, Chevron lost 440,000 barrels per day, which translated into about 5,280,000 barrels over the period in which the crisis lasted. Shell lost 320,000 barrels daily, resulting in the total loss of 3,840,000 barrels during the crisis, while Elf lost 7,500 barrels per day.[100] Even as of June 2003, the country was still losing about 300,000 barrels per day.

On the whole, communal clashes in oil-producing communities are a clear indication of the political situation in the country. Indeed, there are clear indications that some of the conflicts were sponsored and encouraged by the government, both as diversionary tactics as well as a means to ensure divide-and-rule tactics in subduing opposition in the oil-producing region. Indeed, communal conflicts in Nigeria's oil-producing regions have been a crucial factor in understanding how oil comes into the interface between local claims and the politics of international control in the country.

Local Claims, National Interest, and International Involvement in Oil Politics

Of all the conflicts caused by oil in recent years, Nigeria's case shows the complex mix of power and politics. The web here is difficult to untangle, but the key actors are the leadership of the Nigerian state, the oil-producing communities of the Niger Delta, and the oil multinational companies. As noted earlier, the bulk of the complexities of oil and conflict politics in Nigeria center on the Niger Delta. This geopolitical entity inhabited by about twenty ethnic groups has a land mass of about 70,000 square kilometers. Although the preponderance of oil in the Niger Delta became pronounced in the last decade, the roots of the problem date far back, such that most of the recent problems only feed on historical issues.

The story that has brought the relationship among the state, local community, and oil multinational corporations to the fore of international attention is from the Ogoni community in Nigeria's Niger Delta. In its summary, the

Ogoni story demonstrated a string of fundamental issues including the links (hidden and open) between the state and oil multinational corporations against oil-producing communities; the interjection between power and politics in resource control; the role of the international community, including NGOs and multilateral organizations, in mounting pressure on authoritarian states; the deprivation in oil-producing communities; the role of enigmatic leadership in the struggle for recognition of minority right; and the role of intra-ethnic division in the pursuit of a common goal.

A lot has been written about the Ogoni crisis, such that a summary will suffice here. The population of Ogoniland is about 500,000, most of whom are fishermen and farmers, and consists of three groups: Khana, Gokana, and Eleme. The region is endowed with a significant amount of oil deposit, with Shell Petroleum Development Corporation (SPDC) being the main multinational corporation operating in the region, and Chevron being the lesser actor. At the beginning of its struggle, the main objective of the Ogoni people was to attract the attention of the federal government and Shell to the destruction of their environment and the impoverishment of their people.[101] Armed with a determined population and an enlightened leadership, the Ogoni people were unable to get any positive response from Shell and the Nigerian government, which led to the declaration of what they called the Ogoni Bill of Rights. The bill catalogued the problems that had come to their society because of the oil deposit and accused the federal government and the state government of ignoring the plight of the people. It demanded that the Ogonis be considered as "a separate and distinct ethnic nationality," with political autonomy to participate in the affairs of the country as a "distinct and separate unit." Furthermore, the bill asserted that the people should be allowed to control their political affairs and use a fair share of the economic resources derived from their land to advance their culture and language.[102] In monetary terms, the Ogonis demanded payment of US$6 billion in rent and royalties and a compensation of US$4 billion for environmental devastation caused by Shell.[103] From this moment, the line was drawn between the Nigerian government, which saw this as a subtle form of secession attempt, and the leadership of the Ogoni people, then under a well-known author and playwright, Kenule Saro Wiwa, or Ken Saro Wiwa, for short. In this situation, Shell was aligned with the government, as the corporation saw in the Ogoni demand a precedence which, if successful, could lead to a similar demand in other parts of the country.

Events took a major turn in 1990, when the Ogoni people formed the Movement for the Survival of the Ogoni People (MOSOP). A year after the formation, MOSOP wrote a letter to Shell and the federal government to complain about gas flaring, oil spillages, and other environmental damages resulting from oil exploration. The organization attached a copy of the Bill of Rights to the letter and asked for compensation and royalties for oil extracted from Ogoniland. Nothing came of this, and in November 1992, MOSOP gave a thirty-one-day ultimatum to Shell and Chevron to either pay up royalties and damages or move out of the region. This expired on December 31, 1993, and on January 4, 1994, a crowd of about 200,000 protesters assembled in Bori, one of the Ogoni towns, and declared Shell a persona non grata in Ogoniland.[104] From this moment, Ogoniland became the theater of conflicts between agents of Nigerian security forces and the Ogoni people, with the former inflicting extreme brutality on the Ogoni population. Names of military officers who inflicted untold hardship on the Ogoni people still remain engrained in the minds of the Ogoni people, with Paul Okutimo of the Internal Security Task Force, and the military administrator of the state, Lieutenant Colonel Dauda Komo, being the most prominent in what the Ogonis consider the role of dishonor.[105] Apart from the direct military attack, the Ogonis also believed that the government gave arms and ammunitions to their neighbors, the Andonis, who were then engaged in communal conflicts with them.[106]

But just as the struggle became intensified, division emerged among the Ogoni. As Akpandem James has noted, as the division grew, the focus of the struggle became blurred and divided.[107] Some key members of MOSOP disagreed with Ken Saro Wiwa and some of them, including the first president of the organization, Gary Leton, left the organization. All this played well for the strategy of the Nigerian government and the oil corporations who further encouraged the division with the sole intention of ostracizing the radical leadership of the organization believed to be under the leadership of Ken Saro Wiwa. At the roots of the division was the allegation that some of the leadership of MOSOP had sold out to the government and the oil companies. These people were thus derisively tagged as the "Vulture." On the other side, too, those accused of betraying the Ogoni cause accused Ken Saro Wiwa of encouraging violence and of making unrealistic promises in order to spur the population to violence.

The division among the Ogonis reached its peak in May 1994, when four Ogoni chiefs—Edward Kobani, Albert Badeyi, Samuel Orage, and Theophilus Orage—were killed by rioting Ogoni mobs for alleged betrayal of the Ogoni cause. Although it was not contested that Ken Saro Wiwa was not at the scene of the killing, he and eight other MOSOP leaders were arraigned before a tribunal and, in a process that has been widely criticized, were found guilty and condemned to death by hanging.[108] On November 10, 1995, despite international appeals, the Abacha administration carried out the death sentence.[109] The fact that the execution took place during the Commonwealth Conference in Auckland, New Zealand, where special appeal had been made to the Nigerian leadership to commute the sentences passed on these people, was seen as an act of demonstrative defiance of the Nigerian leadership to international opinion. In the end, Nigeria was suspended from the Commonwealth, although there were those who considered the punishment too little, too late.[110]

The international reactions to the hanging of the "Ogoni Nine" embarrassed Shell, and the company came up with a number of explanations to convince a largely skeptical global audience that it had nothing to do with the hanging of Saro Wiwa and others, and that it had, in fact, done its best to save the lives of the nine men. Not many were, however, convinced. Indeed, societies and organizations that are not known to be political in their activities protested against the oil multinational company. For example, the Royal Geographical Society decided in January 1996 to remove Shell as its patron on the grounds that "the activities of Shell in Nigeria are appalling."[111] The Nigerian government for its part continued its intransigence and high-handedness in Ogoniland, and it was only after the death of Abacha in June 1998 that a new shift emerged in the relationship between the Nigerian government and the Ogoni people.

The dawn of the political change that marked the death of Abacha did not, however, resolve the differences among the Ogoni elites. Ledum Mitee, who had led the group from exile after the death of Saro Wiwa soon had problems with other members of MOSOP abroad, especially those in the United States. In October 1998, the MOSOP (USA), which included Dr. Owens Wiwa, Ken Saro Wiwa's brother, suspended Mitee as the interim president of MOSOP, a suspension that was treated with derision by the MOSOP at home. Allegations of financial mismanagement soon started flying against Mitee. These, in fact, surfaced, when one of MOSOP's strongest supporters, Bodyshop's Anita Roddick, visited Saro Wiwa's hometown of Bane, and Ken's brother Owens, and his father, the late Benson Wiwa, asked her to help recover money on behalf of the Ogoni struggle. In a somewhat subtle way, Mrs. Roddick debunked this allegation and told the complainants that money wasn't given to any individual but tied to specific projects and that the possibility of individual embezzlement did not arise. Although there are now attempts to conceal the differences, it is clear that elite differences had undermined the activities and strength of MOSOP.

Another major conflict that received international mention, albeit on a comparatively lower scale, was the Umuechem massacre of 1990. Here, youths demonstrating against Shell had their protest violently put down. As in most violent protests, there are different versions of what happened. The police's version, also supported by Shell, was that there was a violent protest during which hostages were held and a policeman was killed. The police also claimed that the uniform and the helmet of the police were hung in the chief's house to taunt policemen. Consequently, the police invaded the town and killed the chief and his two sons. At the end of the clampdown, eighty people had been killed. The local population of the town disputed this version and claimed that it was a peaceful protest that was met with brutal force. The government set up a Commission of Inquiry to investigate the case.[112] In its findings, the commission declared the police version of the story as being untrue and that the protest was largely peaceful. It also recommended various compensatory measures, which as at the end of 2004 had not been implemented.[113]

The repression of Nigeria's oil-producing communities continued even after the dawn of democratic rule. Perhaps the most profound manifestation of this was the attack on Odi by members of the Nigerian security forces in February 2000. The Nigerian government claimed that the attack was motivated by the government's determination to get the indigenes of the community who had kidnapped and killed twelve mobile policemen. The local community, however, complained of remarkable high-handedness on the part of the policemen, who killed hundreds of defenseless citizens. The attack on Odi dented the democratic credentials of President Obasanjo, and those who argued that the former military ruler had not completely abandoned his autocratic tendencies got more strength for their position.

In their protest against the companies, groups in the Niger Delta adopted three major tactics. The first was to embark on acts of sabotage against oil installations. It is impossible to obtain accurate figures on the sabotage, most of which are targeted against Shell, as there are sometimes disputes over the figures. However, between 1988 and 1997, the Shell Petroleum Development Company's Manager for Community Affairs, Environment, Safety and Security, Mr. Chukwudozie Okonkwo, said that the organization recorded 180 disruptions to its oil installation by the aggrieved youths of the Niger Delta.[114] The objective behind this strategy is to disrupt the flow of oil and to make the project frustrating for the companies by disputing the economic lifeline of their investment.

The second way through which the people of the Niger Delta have signified their protest is through the kidnap of oil workers. Three points are worthy of note about this policy. First, it was often target-specific, and on no occasion have any of the victims been killed. Apart from trying to draw international attention to their situation, they sometimes want specific demands from the oil companies, including ransom for their victims. Second, unlike oil sabotage, which took place over a very long period, hostage-taking took place only for a brief period. Indeed, most of these took place around 1999. Third, and again unlike the sabotaging of oil installations, it was not a policy that was accepted by all the varying groups fighting in the Niger Delta.

But perhaps the most difficult aspect of the oil management politics in Nigeria is the way accusations have been traded among all the major actors— the federal government, the oil multinational corporations, and the local population. The local population accuses the federal government of three things: the passing of laws the population considers obnoxious, especially the Land Use Decree and the Terminal Tax; the forceful repression of protests the local population consider legitimate; and the refusal of the government to produce basic amenities for the population. Their accusations against their respective state governments is that the states are often so anxious to carry out laws passed by the federal government, despite knowing that such laws are unpopular.

Against the oil companies, the criticisms again come under three headings: refusal to contribute sufficiently to the socioeconomic development of the areas where they are prospecting for oil; the environmental degradation that comes as a result of the exploration; and the implicit endorsement the companies are giving to the Nigerian state in the forceful suppression of what they consider to be legitimate protest.

The politics of resource governance in the Niger Delta assumed another dimension when a state governor of one of the oil-producing states in Nigeria, Diepreye Alamieyeseigha of Bayelsa State, was arrested in London for money laundering. Although the details of the story are discussed in chapter 7, suffice it to point out here that he jumped bail and escaped to Nigeria where his position as a state governor offers him immunity from prosecution. He was later impeached as a governor and was arrested.

The Nigerian Federal Government accuses the local population of being unreasonable with their demands and of trying to blackmail the government because they live on the land endowed with the resource that forms the mainstay of the country's economy. Against the oil multinational corporation, the federal government also has a number of accusations. First, companies are not taking sufficient care of the communities where they are extracting oil, especially as the government claims there are informal agreements between it and these oil companies. Second, the government accuses the oil companies of falsifying production figures. This, according to the government, is being done through a variety of ways, one of which is for the oil companies to claim they are prospecting for oil in some areas, whereas exploitation has actually started. In a veiled accusation of the multinational companies, the finance minister under the Abacha administration, Anthony Ani, noted in a public display of frustration:

> We don't even know how much it costs to explore and exploit; all that is happening is that we get bills which we have to settle. . . . Nigerians have not been actively involved in the whole business.[115]

For their part, too, the foreign oil companies have made allegations against the local population and against the federal government. Their problem with the local population is that they are unreasonable with their demands, and that some of the things the local people are expecting from the companies are the duties of the government. Consequently, the whole attitude of taking hostages, destruction of pipelines, locking of flow stations, and others, are just misplaced aggressions. They argue that the little being done by the oil companies in terms of infrastructural provisions should be appreciated. The companies' disagreement with the federal government is that it is not using the money derived from oil to cater for its population. On the whole, I have identified sixteen layers of conflict involving oil and its management in the Niger Delta as represented by table 5.4

Table 5.4 Layers of conflicts and controversies in the Niger Delta

Layer of conflict	Causes of conflict	Manifestation
1. Among different oil-producing communities in the Niger Delta	(i) Controversies over land (ii) Unresolved chieftaincy disputes (iii) Location of Local Government Headquarters	Armed clashes by indigenes, especially youths
2. Between the federal government and oil-producing communities	(i) Unacceptable method of revenue allocation (ii) Divide-and-rule strategies often employed by the government, especially through the citing of amenities and local government headquarters (iii) Lack of sympathy over the environmental abuse being suffered during the course of oil exploration	Armed clashes between the youths of the Niger Delta and the government security apparatus
3. Between the federal government and the state government	(i) Disagreement over offshore–onshore dichotomy (ii) Irregular disbursement of allocation	Court cases
4. Between the state government and oil-producing communities within the state	(i) Nondisbursement of allocation from the federal government (ii) Hidden and sometimes blatant support given to the federal government's repressive policies (iii) Links with oil multinational corporations	Armed resistance, especially by the youths
5. Between oil multinational companies and oil-producing communities in the Niger Delta	(i) Environmental pollution involved in the process of oil exploration (ii) Endorsement given to government's repressive methods (iii) Lack of respect for indigenous customs and practices (iv) Failure in the promise to carry out promised developmental projects	Kidnap of foreign oil workers; sabotage of oil pipelines

Table 5.4 (*continued*)

Layer of conflict	Causes of conflict	Manifestation
6. Between federal government and oil companies	(i) Lack of transparency in the amount of oil extracted Nonpayment of all necessary tax (iii) Allegation of "sharp" practices, especially over the 2005 Bid Round for the award of oil blocks	Formal and informal complaints
7. Between youths from the Niger Delta and youths from other parts of the country working with oil companies in the Niger Delta	(i) Anger by the youths in the Niger Delta that youths from other parts of the country have come to take up employment that should have been given to them	Payment of fees to the Niger Delta youths by non-indigenes to maintain their position
8. Among ideologically opposed groups within the same ethnic group of the oil-producing communities	(i) Differences over method to be adopted in fighting recognized common enemy (ii) Allegations of sell-out by one group against the other (iii) Method of distributing international assistance given to fight the minority cause	Armed conflicts among different segments of the ethnic group as in the case of the Ogoni
9. Between youths and the traditional rulers	(i) Allegations of corruption against their traditional leaders, especially for collecting money from the government and the oil companies to betray ethnic cause	Direct attacks on the residence of the traditional rulers and physical assault on them and their family
10. Between militant youths and older leaders of the Niger Delta struggle	(i) Disagreement over the hardened attitude adopted by the militant youths against the government,	Open condemnation of the policies adopted by the militant youths

Table 5.4 (*continued*)

Layer of conflict	Causes of conflict	Manifestation
	especially the direct confrontation that became prominent during the second half of 2006	
11. Between local employees and their foreign counterparts	(i) Allegation of unfair treatment of local staff by the management	Strikes and holding foreign staff hostage
12. Between state governments and oil multinational corporations	(i) Complaints by state governments that claims by oil multinational corporations of their public-relations activities are not accurate	Formal and informal complaints
13. Between militia groups in the Niger Delta and other Niger Delta indigenes working for Shell and other oil multinational companies	(i) Complaints that the workers are "sell-outs," and that they are not looking out for their people's interests	Threats of attacks on their family members
14. Among different oil multinational companies	(i) Accusation that some oil multinational companies are deliberately playing low-key roles to ensure that rival oil companies receive all the negative criticisms from the press and the local communities	Informal complaints
15. Between foreign MNC and indigenous companies going into oil exploration	(i) Accusation that big oil companies are trying to frustrate and drive out the local companies and accusation of staff poaching	Informal complaints

Table 5.4 (*continued*)

Layer of conflict	Causes of conflict	Manifestation
16. Between militant youths and elected politicians of Niger Delta origin	(i) Complaints by militants that some of the elected representatives, especially those in the federal Parliament, are supporting the federal government on key controversial issues such as the alleged third term for President Obasanjo	Threatening letters to the members and to their families

It is indeed the case that many oil multinational corporations operating in Africa have been involved in conflicts over oil. In some cases, their activities have been linked to conflicts, while in others they have been alleged to have fueled conflicts, both communal and those between the state and regional entities challenging the state in its management of oil reserves.

In appreciating the nature of the activities of these oil companies, the extent of their involvement needs to be noted. In Nigeria, the continent's largest oil-producing country, there are a number of oil multinational companies. The Shell Petroleum Development Company (SPDC), which is the Nigerian subsidiary of the Anglo-Dutch Shell Company, is the main oil multinational operating in Nigeria, and it produces about 40 percent of the country's crude oil output. It operates the largest joint venture in the country, operating in conjunction with the state-owned National Petroleum Company (NNPC) (55 percent), Shell (30 percent), Elf, a French company (10 percent), and the Italian Agip (5 percent). The SPDC contributes 14 percent of the Royal Dutch/Shell's global oil production. But apart from these companies, there are other multinational companies involved in offshore production. These include Mobil and Chevron, both of which are North American companies.

The complex ways through which oil multinationals have been connected with oil-related conflicts in Nigeria can be brought under two major headings. The first and relatively straightforward one is through their creation of environmental pollution and their failure, for a long time, to rectify the environmental implications of their activities. The process of oil exploration has left damages to the largely fishing and agricultural communities in the Nigerian Niger Delta. Indeed, the environmental pollution created by the process of oil exploration is one of the main causes of conflict in the oil-producing communities. Although some of these companies are now embarking on public relation exercises to give the impression that the extent of the damage is limited and that sabotage activities are more responsible for the environmental problems, not many observers are convinced. Another public relation exercise being utilized in recent years is that of attempting to take special interest in the environment of the communities from where they prospect oil. For example, they built schools, hospitals, and other social amenities in the surroundings where they operate. They also have scholarship schemes, which are publicized on national televisions. These are, however, considered by many as coming too late, as the years of neglect have left damages from which the communities cannot easily recover.

Closely related to this is the allegation often leveled against the multinationals that they are not taking any interest in the socioeconomic development of the societies from where they prospect for oil. The abject poverty in these societies belies the enormous amount of money that the corporations extract from these areas.

What many of the corporations would, however, find most uncomfortable to be connected with is the allegations of having been associated with corruption. One company that has allegedly been involved in this kind of act is France's Elf. The company has been accused of bribing African heads of state to maximize the company's profit.[116] For example, the president of Gabon, Omar Bongo, has been accused of channeling payments through the accounts of senior Elf Officials.[117] The company's ex-Africa's supremo, Andre Tarallo, confirmed this further in an interview he granted to *Le Monde*:

> In the petroleum field we talk of bonuses. There are official bonuses, which are anticipated in the contracts . . .; the petroleum company which wants an exploration permit agrees, for example to finance the construction of an hospital, a school, or a road, or to pay a sum of money, which may be a considerable amount if the interest in an area is justified. . . . This practice has always been used by Elf as well as other numerous companies.[118]

In early 2004, claims also began to emerge that Shell had been exaggerating the extent of its oil reserve in Nigeria. In a development that resulted in the ousting of its chairman, Sir Philip Watts, and Walter van de Vijuer, the head of exploration and production in February 2004, it was revealed that Shell executives were encouraged to inflate the level of oil reserve in Nigeria by the prospect of huge bonuses for its staff.[119] Under a complex arrangement, Shell's reporting systems provided an incentive for overstating reserves in order to get the tax breaks the Nigerian government offered to companies that declared they had uncovered oil reserves.[120] Based on these inflated results, bonuses for local employees soared between 1996 and 1999. By January 2004, Shell admitted overstating proven oil and gas reserves by 3.9 billion barrels, about 60 percent of which is believed to have been in Nigeria. Much more damaging for the company's public relation image, however, was the report that the company was also exaggerating the claims of its charitable works in Nigeria. The London *Financial Mail*, quoting a memo from the company's auditor, KPMG, notes that Shell's report of its charitable activities contained a "litany of overstatement and inaccuracies" and that it contains "over-reporting of project activity and assertions that appear to be unsupported, inaccurate or unbalanced."[121] For example, the *Financial Mail* reported that while Shell claims to have rehabilitated twenty-two town halls, four socioeconomic centers, and eighteen civil centers, evidence on the ground showed that only two town halls had been rehabilitated. Furthermore, the auditing company noted that Shell had further slashed its community project by more than 50 percent in 2003.[122] To crown the problem for Shell, its own conflict consultants confirmed to the company that it had been part of the conflict in the Niger Delta. The consultants further noted that the company's community development work had been allocated to shady contractors.[123] Possibly in its attempt to ensure greater credibility and closer relations with Nigeria, Shell appointed a Nigerian, Basil Omiyi, as its first Nigerian managing director of SPDC in July 2004.[124]

Events in the Niger Delta took on a more violent dimension from the beginning of 2006, and by the end of March 2006, the multiple problems had resulted in the loss of US$1 billion in revenue for the Nigerian state.[125] A new armed faction, the Movement for the Emancipation of the Niger Delta (MEND), emerged to raise the stakes in the Niger Delta with renewed attacks on oil installations and the taking of foreign oil workers as hostages. The group asked for the release of Dokubo-Asari, who had been arrested and charged for treason, and the payment of US$1.5 billion compensation. The taking of foreign workers as hostages embarrassed the Nigerian government, who was torn between engaging the insurgents in a military attack or embarking on negotiation. Eventually negotiation prevailed and the foreign hostages were released in two batches. The MEND attack forced Shell to evacuate more than three hundred workers and forced shut down of about 10 percent of Nigeria's crude oil production.[126] Shortly after this there was an attack on Port Harcourt office of Agip, resulting in the death of eleven people, including seven mobile policemen, and the carting away of a significant amount of money. The taking of foreign hostages continues throughout most of 2006, forcing senior officials of the government to concede there is really very little that can be done to prevent hostages from being taken.[127]

The last quarter of 2006 witnessed more violent clashes in the Niger Delta, with the militant groups taking a more determined stand against the government security forces. The spate of kidnapping of foreign oil workers also increased dramatically, with many countries warning their nationals against traveling to the region. By the first week of October 2006, the government had begun admitting high casualty figures in the Niger Delta, forcing the

Nigerian president to call an urgent meeting of the military chiefs. But what was also of considerable concern for the government was the new dimension the conflict seemed to be taking. One of the militant groups, MEND, gave a warning that it would begin "strategic attacks on targets of relevance" and that it would "lift the embargo" it had placed on hostage taking. All these, the organization warned, would "increase in severity depending on the response from the Nigerian military." There was particular concern that the militants may want to target Bonny Island, a major oil and gas export hub.

The renewed violence that began during the last quarter of 2006 was particularly worrying for at least two reasons. First, some of the hostages taken by the militants, especially the ExxonMobil contractors arrested in Eket in Akwa Ibom State, were arrested from their residential compound after the militants had killed two Nigerian security guards looking after the compound. This was the first time that militants had kidnapped expatriates from within a residential compound. Second, the state where many of kidnapping took place, Akwa Ibom, was considered one of the relatively safe states in the Nigerian oil-producing states. The spreading of violence to this state was thus seen as a new development that should attract concern from the government and oil multinational corporations.

The role of multinational corporations in the Sudan is slightly different. This is because of the ethno-religious undertone of the war, which added a flavor not found in any other oil conflict in Africa. First, oil companies are cautious about rushing into the country. It is worth noting that after the war began, one of the first acts of the SPLA was to attack the oil installations in the south, a step that resulted in the death of three Chevron workers. This sent a clear message to oil multinationals that the location of the oil in Sudan is not one of the places that are undisputed parts of the country. The French oil giant, Total, also abandoned its activities in 1984. Presently, four companies are involved in the Sudan. These are the China National Petroleum Company, which controls 40 percent; the Malaysian Petronas Cargali with 30 percent; the Canadian Talisman Energy with 25 percent; and the Sudan National Oil Company with 5 percent. The Chinese dimension is particularly interesting, as it is the only place in Africa where China has come in as a key player in the oil business. This has been mutually beneficial for the Chinese and the government in Khartoum. Apart from providing a source of oil for China, it has also provided employment opportunities for several thousands of Chinese workers working on Sudanese oil fields. For its part, the Sudanese government has benefited from the protection China has offered in the international community.[128] The Malaysian government too has tried to assist the Sudanese government, paying, for example, the sum of US$500 million to the IMF in 1997 to cover Sudan's debt repayment.

Illegal Bunkering, National Security, and International Interest

Defined very broadly, illegal bunkering is the process whereby individuals or companies engage in illegal trading in oil. This simple definition, however, conceals a complex web of activities entailed in the process. Before going into the details of illegal bunkering in Africa, it needs to be clarified that the process reflects an interesting paradox: while it is not a problem that is common across the continent, the few countries where it does exist is sufficient to ignite international concern. This is largely because the affected region holds, to a large extent at least, the key to global interest in African oil supply. This is the West African coast.

Continuing in broad generalizations, illegal bunkering on the West African coast occurs mainly in Nigeria, and this takes place through four main methods, although the actors in most cases are interwoven. The first is through the overloading of vessels. Here, payment is made but the vessel is unofficially overloaded beyond the payment made to the government. The main actors here are businessmen involved in international marketing of oil, international criminal gangs, officials of oil multinational corporations, and staff of the NNPC. The second method, which is more complex, involves interfering with oil pipelines to siphon oil into barges, from which they are then transferred to large vessels berthing offshore. Because most of the pipelines pass through creeks and areas with shallow waters where big vessels cannot berth, barges are used to siphon and transfer the oil to waiting vessels. Those involved in this are streetwise youths of the Niger Delta, owners of foreign vessels, local businessmen, and members of the Nigerian security apparatus, especially the navy and the police. The third method is a process in which oil is given to an individual to sell and make profit. Such an individual in this case is not paying any money into official coffers, and neither does the individual have permission to trade in oil. The actors operating here are often senior officials of the NNPC, and the objective is to grant oil concession to individuals as an expression of affection or as an assistance package for those who hitherto had been at the corridors of power but had fallen on hard times.[129] The fourth method is the illegal bunkering across the border from Nigeria to other West African countries. In this case, refined petroleum products are bought at previously subsidized prices in Nigeria and smuggled across the border to Niger, Cameroon, Benin, and Chad, only to be sold at international price.

Illegal bunkering is not limited to crude oil alone. There is also the illegal bunkering of refined petroleum products, especially of Premium Motor Spirit (PMS), also known as petrol; Automobile Gas Oil (AGO), also known as diesel; and the Low Pour Fuel Oil (LPFO). AGO and LPFO are illegally bunkered for exports, as they are used as heating and industrial oil. A lot of this illegal bunkering is done in the Atlas Cove.[130]

While the main implications of illegal bunkering remain largely in the loss of revenue, there are also a number of security implications. First, it often results in further damage to the environment. As the process is usually not well-managed or handled, oil spills have further added to the destruction of the ecosystem. Indeed, the claims by oil multinational corporations that illegal bunkering has contributed to damage to the environment is true, even if the extent is significantly lower than often claimed by the corporations. There have been several cases of explosion, which have resulted in loss of lives. Second, illegal bunkering provides a good source of funding for all the ethnic militias in the Niger Delta region. Indeed, many of those involved in the activities are often heavily armed—arms that are also used for other crimes, such as armed robbery. Third, illegal bunkering has created a new class of criminally minded noveau riche, who eventually hijack the political process in some parts of the country using proceeds from their illegal bunkering activities to fix themselves and their cronies in important political offices. The thwarting of the political will of the people using such ill-gotten wealth has grave political, social, and eventually security implications for the larger society. Finally, the activities of this group have had a consequential effect on transborder crime around the Nigerian border with her neighbors, especially Benin Republic and Chad.

But perhaps the most important security implication of illegal bunkering on the West African coast is the extent of involvement of members of security forces. The level of involvement came to national attention in October 2003, when a vessel, *African Pride*, and its thirteen Russian sailors were arrested aboard with some 11,000 tons of crude oil stolen from Nigeria.[131] Not long after the arrest, the ship disappeared with the contents. The embarrassment this caused the Nigerian government resulted in the three senior officers of the Nigerian Navy being court-martialed.[132]

The extent of illegal bunkering and the growing international interest in the oil deposits in the Gulf of Guinea have resulted in a situation where foreign countries, especially the United States, have signified interest in monitoring the affairs of the region. This, however, has its own potential problems, as it is likely to put intervening foreign countries in serious collision course with local warlords who have been intricately linked with politicians, both at the state and national levels, security agents operating in the Niger Delta, and oil multinational corporations. Indeed, the general belief in the Niger Delta is that despite the occasional open confrontation among the Nigerian state, the insurgent movements in the Niger Delta, and oil multinational companies, there remains a network of understanding and alliances among all of them, and these have allegedly centered on illegal oil bunkering and the changing nature of state and national politics. But just as oil has caused and prolonged conflicts, the resource can also be a factor in the resolution of conflicts.

The resultant importance of Africa in global oil supplies has resulted in the continent becoming targets for military intervention by the United States,

France, and China. This is particularly pronounced in the case of the United States, where they seem to have a deep involvement in the affairs of oil-producing countries in the continent. In recent years, the expansion of North American military programs in Africa and the provision of U.S. arms, military equipment, and technical assistance has been remarkable. Specifically, this aid is intended to strengthen the security of these states. Particular attention has been given to Nigeria and Angola. Apart from aid to these countries, the United States is also supporting a number of multilateral or regional-based initiatives aimed at enhancing internal security capacities of oil-producing African countries, especially through the International Military Education and Training (IMET).

Oil and the Resolution of Conflict

In all the countries where oil has been linked to the cause of conflicts, efforts to resolve them have always taken the resource into consideration. This has been most evident in two countries, Nigeria and Sudan. In the case of Nigeria, where oil has brought diverse issues such as ownership, pollution, and the non-consideration of the interests of the producing communities into focus, the role oil has played in the resolution of the attendant multidimensional conflicts has been wide. First, there have been attempts by the government to use proceeds from oil to bring about the development of the oil-producing communities and in the process, address some of the causes of conflict. As mentioned earlier, there were a number of institutions created by the Nigerian government to address the development of the Nigerian oil-producing communities, including OMPADEC and the NDDC. Although the principles behind the formation of these bodies are laudable, there have been many operational difficulties that have made them unable to meet the objective of their formation. To address some of the issues associated with pollution, the Nigerian government has also come up with a number of laws, including the Federal Environmental Protection Law. Although these laws have not achieved the desired results, they are indicative that the government is aware of the problem if not yet the solution to it.

In terms of a direct attempt to use oil to resolve a dispute, the recent situation in Sudan seems to present the best example. Under the umbrella of the Machakos Protocol signed in 2002 between the Sudanese government and the SPLA rebels, a highly contentious issue has been the management of oil revenue. By January 2004, an agreement had been reached between the government and the SPLA over wealth sharing. Under the agreement, there will be a roughly equal division of revenue coming from oil. The country's central bank will have two laws. In the north, there will be Islamic banking laws, while the south will have western banking regulations. There will also be two currencies, for the north and the south, respectively.[133]

Oil has been known also to soften the resolve of governments that had hitherto taken a resolute stand against an oil-producing state once the latter has taken a basic step toward reconciliation. Although the official position may pronounce otherwise, the decision by the Blair government to easily accept the olive branch offered by Libya's President Ghadaffi was no doubt because of the country's importance as a rich oil country. The moment the Lockerbie court case was resolved,[134] and Libya officially denied supporting groups associated with terrorism, Britain immediately showed indications of welcoming Libya back into the international community, even before the official resolution of the Fletcher murder case.[135]

Conclusion

In this chapter I have argued that the nature of the politics surrounding oil conflicts is inextricably linked to the management of the resources. As noted earlier, oil has been linked to major conflicts in three African countries—Angola, Nigeria, and Sudan. In two of these countries, Angola and Sudan, there are major civil conflicts, which threaten the continued existence of the countries, with organized armed groups fighting against the central governments. Although the conflicts are political, oil has become the crucial factor determining the developments surrounding them. Here, the themes evoked are quite different from Nigeria, where it remains at the core of governance and politics without, at least as yet, resulting in a sustained armed opposition against the central government.

In Angola and Sudan, the themes evoked are basically three. First, the faction in control has always tried to defend it at all cost. This though is more pronounced in the Sudan, as the deposit is in the territory of the southern rebel force. Despite this, the government in the north, which controls the territory, has employed all means to hold control. Second, the sides controlling the resources have exploited it to prosecute the war. This again is expected, however, there are slight differences in the manifestations in these countries. Whereas in Sudan it is the main resource sustaining the government, the Angolan government has access to other resources, thus reducing the burden on oil. Finally, in both countries, the complexities of oil conflicts altered the strategic pattern of global politics. Despite the antipathy that existed between the United States and the governments in Angola and the Sudan, links still existed over the crucial oil resource. This, perhaps, underlined the dictum that vital economic interest might put religious and ideological differences aside.

But by far the country that brings out the complexities in the manifestation of oil conflict is Nigeria. This is due largely to the governance problem in the country, where dominant ethnic groups have suppressed the minority, and the socioeconomic and political deprivation of the community has set the people against themselves and against all those believed to have any link with the exploration of the oil from their land. Apart from the problems the oil-producing communities have against the government, many of these communities have problems among themselves, such that a significant percentage of lives have been lost as a result of these intra-ethnic conflicts.

6

WATER AND CONFLICT

Rivers have no respect for political frontiers. They are the common property for many people and, if they are to be harnessed to the service of mankind, it is essential that we should continue to consult together, to exchange information and to discuss our problems.

Abubakar Tafawa Balewa, Nigeria's first prime minister

Water conflicts are inevitable if we continue to do nothing to prevent them from occurring. While this response may appear simplistic, it is guided and framed by the key insight that the continent's finite fresh water resources cannot continue indefinitely to support the escalating demands that we make on them.

Peter Ashton

Like land, water's link with conflict lies deep in history, as over the centuries societies have fought to protect access to, and sources of, water supply.[1] In modern times, the increasing diversification in its uses has further increased the ways through which water has been linked to politics, conflict, and diplomacy. For Africans, the importance of the resource is further reinforced by its sociocultural and religious significance, as the sources of major rivers have been known to serve as deities through which people engage in communion with the supreme being.[2] There are, however, ways in which water differs from other natural resources discussed in this book, and these serve to underlie the peculiarities of the resource's linkage with conflict. First, unlike other resources, water offers very limited opportunity for individual ownership or control. Although in recent years the issue of water privatization has become a subject of discussion, more often than not, water still offers low opportunities for elite greed, as the predominance of the community's role in ensuring necessary regulations for its management is greater than any other natural resource. Second, as Anthony Turton has noted, water is crucial to a string of ecological, social, economic, and political issues in ways other resources are not, especially as its availability determines the nature and extent of development,

the level of food, security, and the health of populations.[3] This further rein-
forces the necessity of the resource to human existence. Third, water can be
a means of identity, as countries and regions across the continent have been
named after major rivers.[4] In recent times, too, a number of politico-
economic "unions" are being formed around rivers, as in the cases of the Mano
River Union and Volta River Union. Finally, most of the killer diseases in the
continent are waterborne, as in the case of malaria, river blindness, and diar-
rhea. Pesticides and other chemicals can also become waterborne, affecting
the availability and quality of water; their use is a potential cause of conflict.

Although the controversies surrounding water in some parts of Africa have
attracted interest and attention, as is the case with the Nile riparian states and
countries in southern Africa, this did not, at least for a long time, translate
into any concerted attention at a continental level to take water issues seriously. Public and academic interests in water in Africa have, however, changed
in the last two decades, with scholars within and outside the continent taking
a detailed look at potential conflicts surrounding water and water resources.[5]
At least five reasons may have accounted for this change in attitude. First, a
fear being entertained in many circles is that population explosion and the
increasing pace of industrialization might result in water scarcity or the reduction in the quality of water, which, in turn could result in political instability.
Second, there is expanding global interest in the environment, which has
resulted in the emergence of many environmentalist groups and international
organizations with specific interest in water and water resources.[6] Third, there
is growing concern for the numerous problems associated with the management of international waters and their possible links with interstate conflicts.
Fourth, ongoing controversies surrounding water privatization are taking
place in some African countries. Fifth, water is coming up in discussions over
the controversies surrounding other natural resources, especially pollution of
water resources through oil spillage and the tension in the relationship
between pastoralists and agriculturists. The outcome of all the above is the
emergence of scholars, especially in southern Africa and in the Nile riparian
states, who are drawing attention to the growing water problems in their
respective regions and their potential security implications.[7]

In this chapter I look at some of the ways through which water has been associated with recent conflicts in Africa. The main argument here is that because
water has historically offered minimal opportunities for elite greed, its link
with actual conflicts has been reduced, and many of such conflicts are more
anticipatory than manifest. I contend, however, that this historical assumption
is quickly changing, and that key issues such as the management of international water basins; the politics and environmental implications of some of the
developmental projects that may come with water, especially dam construction
and disputes over fishing; and the increasing tendency to privatize water and
energy supply are key considerations that can widen the scope of water's link
with real conflict. Consequently, I argue that, like other natural resources

discussed in this book, the future of Africa without conflict over water is rooted in the effective governance of water and water resources in the continent.

Approaches and Themes in the Linkage between Water and Conflict in Africa

With the growing interest in water politics, different approaches have emerged in the academic study of the subject. Anthony Turton has grouped existing approaches to the study of water into five categories.[8] First are those adopting the Malthusian discourse, which, in the principle of Thomas Malthus, link water availability to population growth, and at the root of this thinking is the argument that with population growth there will be scarcity in the water available for use. Perhaps the best-known proponent of this approach is Malin Falkenmark, who developed the Water Stress Index that has now gained global recognition. This indicator is based on an approximate minimum level of water required per capita to maintain an adequate quality of life in a moderately developed country in an arid zone, and the conclusion is that population growth in many areas would result in water scarcity, which in turn, would lead to conflict.

The second approach is the "Virtual Water Discourse," developed by Tony Allen. *Virtual Water* is defined as the quantity of water required for essential food imports needed by an economy. This approach is, in a way, a direct response to the Malthusian discourse, and it argues that there is an almost total lack of evidence of any water war in areas that are known to be highly water stressed.[9] To a large extent, this approach is a modernized version of David Ricardo's theory of "comparative advantage." In Allen's position, there are options that governments of countries facing a water crisis can take to prevent the conflict confidently predicted by the proponents of the Malthusian school of thought. Allen has used the process involved in producing grain as the empirical tool to challenge the Malthusian discourse mentioned above. Empirically, he argues that it requires 1,000 tons of water to provide a ton of grain. He further argues that an individual needs approximately the equivalent of a ton of grain per year and concludes, "water trade in food staples is the means by which water-deficit economies balance their water budgets."[10]

The third approach in Anthony Turton's categorization is the "Structural Inequality Discourse," which focuses attention on conflicts that can arise when there is unequal access to water and water resources. One important feature of the discourse here is that it has political ramifications, as it focuses on the societies often neglected in the scheme of the political management of water resources. Here, conflict arises when the inequality coming from positions of hydro-political privileges are contested. This may appear in different forms, for example, when water is used to the advantage of a particular ethnic or racial group, as was the case in apartheid South Africa, or when the resource is used to the advantage of a particular group of professionals (e.g., exporters of specific agricultural products). Inevitably involved in this equation are attempts to protect this unequal and unjust arrangement and a simultaneous attempt to challenge it. In many of its ramifications, this discourse focuses on water scarcity and some of the ways it can be linked to conflict.

In the fourth group is the "Environmental Scarcity Discourse." At the center of the thesis is the culmination of resource scarcity that can come from the activities of a dominant group against a weaker segment of the population. In a way, the argument is similar to the Structural Inequality Discourse highlighted above. The ripple effect that can result from broader marginalization of a group of people over the management of natural resources is at the core of discussion of this discourse. Also like the Structural Inequality Discourse, the role of politics is profound, with issues such as ethnic and racial marginalization being key issues in the analysis of possible water conflict. One other feature this discourse has in common with the Structural Inequality Discourse is that it is applicable to other natural resources in addition to water.

The final discourse as identified by Turton is the "Social Scarcity Discourse," which was recently advanced by Leif Ohlsson. In this argument is the position that attention has often been placed on how scarcity can affect society without much consideration for how societies have changed their lifestyle to suit the complication brought about by scarcity. In this context, Ohlsson calls for a distinction between a "natural resource" and a "social resource," and concludes that it is possible for a social entity that is being confronted by resource scarcity to adapt to these conditions, provided that a level of social adaptive capacity is available.[11] In recent years, Ohlsson has been joined by other water scholars, such as Turton, to explore other ramifications of this discourse, and some of their conclusions have further served to explain why many countries have defied some of the predictions made by the Malthusian Discourse.

Drawing examples from across the world, Peter Gleick has identified major links between water and conflict.[12] First, conflict is possible when water is seen as a military and political goal. This evokes four important variables: the degree of water scarcity; the extent to which the supply is shared by more than one group; the relative power of those groups; and the ease of access to an alternative source of water. Second, conflict is possible when water is seen as an instrument or tool of conflict, with the sources of its supply becoming legitimate targets in periods of war;[13] third, is when water and hydraulic installations are seen as targets of war;[14] and finally, when inequalities in water distribution, use, and development have served as causes of internal and interstate wars.[15] One perspective that seems to be missing from the above list is the role of water resources during conflict, which in recent years has been a crucial issue in conflict consideration.

Generalizing broadly, it can be said that water serves about nine overlapping functions in Africa: (1) consumption and other domestic use; (2) agricultural purposes; (3) habitation for aquatic creations; (4) religious purposes; (5) means of transportation; (6) recreational activities; (7) energy supply; (8) industrial use; and (9) military purposes. Although on the surface this might indicate a level of minimal pressure on the region's water demands, the geographical attributes of the region, the disparity in the water demands of individual countries, the political relationship among many of the countries who have to share rivers and water resources, and the pressures coming as a result of the depression in the economy of many of these countries, have all heightened potential conflicts over water in Africa.

Potential conflicts over water have focused largely on the regions where peculiar geographical attributes, especially vulnerability to drought and the extent of use, have introduced complexities to water politics. Here, two regions, the Horn of Africa and southern Africa, have come out distinctly. For the Horn of Africa, the potential conflicts over water are rooted mainly in an interesting paradox: while the region is abundantly endowed with water resources, these are not evenly distributed. Also, as Yacob Arsano has rightly noted, although the water resources are "inexhaustibly replenished by nature, these resources are finite in their annual quantities."[16] Furthermore, in discussing water or other natural resource politics in the Horn of Africa, the complex characteristics of the region have to be taken into consideration, as a string of competing interests dominate its affairs: the "sub-Saharan and Supra-Saharan, the Africa and the Arab, the Middle Eastern and the Africa, the Islamic and non-Islamic, and the national and the inter state."[17] On the part of southern Africa, the high number of rivers that cut across national frontiers, the blurred demarcation between land and maritime boundaries, and the disparity in the amount of water needed by the states and the extent of access to it, are the key issues underlying potential conflicts. Again, as the years of apartheid, minority regimes, and civil wars have served to underline uncoordinated water policies among the countries, now having to strike a balance to suit present political realities has given rise to sources of subtle tension between some of the countries. Also important in appreciating the peculiarities of the Horn of Africa and southern Africa is the nature and extent of the water demands of individual countries in the regions and the military might of dominant countries in these regions (Egypt and South Africa, respectively) vis-à-vis other countries they have to relate to in the politics of water resources.

Water: Possibility of Scarcity and Conflict

In the last decade or two, concerns have grown over how shortages in the supply of water for domestic and agricultural uses can lead to conflict in Africa. The possibility of conflict here has two main characteristics. First, many have linked it to the management and control of international rivers (to be discussed later in this chapter), and the argument being put forward by nations is that the inconsiderate use of international waters by others can affect their own domestic requirements. Second, fear of water scarcity is more profound in some countries than others, with those where industrial demands increased the need for water and those where ecological considerations such as drought limit the water available for use, being considered more vulnerable.

As noted earlier, most analysis on water needed for domestic use is based on the Water Stress Index designed by Malin Falkenmark. This index is based on the minimum water requirement for an individual to sustain an adequate quality of life. Under the calculation, an allowance of 100 liters per day per person is made for drinking and personal needs, while an additional 500 to 2,000 liters is made per individual for agriculture, industry, and energy production. There is also an allowance made to cover dry season.[18] On the whole, the index provides 4,660 liters per day per person. If this drops to less than 2,740 liters per day, a country is said to be having chronic water scarcity, while a further drop to 1,370 liters means that the country has fallen into an "absolute water scarcity" situation.

In discussing how water quantity can be linked to conflict in Africa, the Water Stress Index raises three interrelated questions: How many African countries fall under the stress level, or can come under the stress level in the immediate future? How has the situation resulted in conflict or can result in conflict? How has, or can such conflict(s) manifest? In answering the first question, the number of African countries believed to be under water stress has varied from between three and six. For example, Lomborg argues that three African countries are under stress,[19] while a Johns Hopkins University study puts the figure at six.[20] Each, however, maintains that the figures will increase in the years ahead, with Lomborg putting it to thirteen by 2025 and the Johns Hopkins University team putting it at eighteen by the same time. Drawing conclusions from a variety of other data, Ian Woodman concludes that two countries, Kenya and South Africa, had reached a water stress level by 2000, with six more, Somalia, Niger, Eritrea, Mauritania, Sudan, and Chad, likely to join by 2050. Tables 6.1 and 6.2 show these figures.

Table 6.1 Water stress level in 2000

Country	Per capital m3 (cubic meters) 2000	Precipitation
Kenya	985	572
South Africa	1,154	451

Source: Ian Woodman, "War of Scarcity: Myth or Reality? An Examination of Resource Scarcities as a Cause of Conflict in Africa," in *Seaford House Papers*, ed. J. E. Spence (London: Royal College of Defense Studies, 2002), p. 9.

Table 6.2 Envisaged water stress level in 2050

Country	Per Capital m3 (cubic meters) 2050 Medium variant population estimates	Precipitation
Somalia	384	253
Kenya	545	572
Niger	627	180
Eritrea	878	329
South Africa	1,057	451
Mauritania	1,349	99
Sudan	193	436
Chad	551	388

Source: Ian Woodman, "War of Scarcity: Myth or Reality? An Examination of Resource Scarcities as a Cause of Conflict in Africa," in *Seaford House Papers*, ed. J. E. Spence (London: Royal College of Defense Studies, 2002), p. 9.

Ian Woodman has identified another way through which future water scarcity can be measured. This is through the concentration on the position in key water basins and wetlands. Apart from reducing the risk of broad generalization of data, looking at the position of water basins offers a sufficient yardstick for measuring stress, as the eighteen major watersheds in Africa account for around 50 percent of total renewable water supplies and, as such, a sufficient yardstick for measuring stress.

In his conclusion, Woodman argued that three of the eighteen principal water basins had, by 2000, begun undergoing stress. These are the Limpopo, Orange, and Jubba; whereas no reliable data exists for three others, Zambezi, Shaballe, and Okavango. This is shown in table 6.3. The three confirmed cases will likely be increased to nine by 2050, as the figures in table 6.4 show.

On the whole, while it is widely assumed that the possibility of water scarcity turning into a cause of conflict in Africa is still futuristic, what appears more certain is that the possibility of such conflict occurring depends, to a large extent, on how future political developments in the identified countries unfold. Also crucial in the equation between water scarcity and conflict is how the picture painted above can lead to conflict. Three issues are likely to determine this: the domestic political situation in those countries where there already exists acute water scarcity; the wider regional politics that may incorporate water considerations as part of wider security problems; and the politics governing the management of international river basins. Where the domestic political situation is unstable, water scarcity is likely to further heighten tension,

Table 6.3 River basins experiencing water stress in 2000

Water basin	Principal countries within river basin	Estimated population (000s)	Water per person m³/year 2000
Limpopo	Mozambique, Zimbabwe, South Africa, Botswana	13,476	716
Orange	South Africa, Namibia	10,355	1,050
Jubba	Ethiopia, Somalia, Kenya	5,972	1,076
Zambezi	Zambia, Zimbabwe, Angola, Mozambique	23,983	No data
Shaballe	Ethiopia, Somalia	10,098	No data
Okavango	Angola, Namibia, Botswana	1,443	No data

Source: Ian Woodman, "War of Scarcity: Myth or Reality? An Examination of Resource Scarcities as a Cause of Conflict in Africa," in *Seaford House Papers*, ed. J. E. Spence (London: Royal College of Defense Studies, 2002), p. 10.

Table 6.4 Likely river basins experiencing water stress in 2050

Basin	Principal countries within river basins	Estimated population (000s)	Water per person m³/year 2050
Orange	South Africa, Namibia	42,000	259
Jubba	Ethiopia, Somalia, Kenya	27,883	230
Limpopo	Mozambique, Zimbabwe, South Africa, Botswana	28,651	337
Nile	Sudan, Ethiopia, Egypt	425,137	743
Niger	Nigeria, Mali, Niger	346,233	852
Volta	Burkina Faso, Ghana	68,679	511
Lake Turkana	Kenya, Ethiopia, Sudan, Uganda	54,733	1,020
Lake Chad	Chad, Niger	143,385	1,656
Senegal	Mauritania, Mali, Senegal	15,440	1,569
Zambezi	Zambia, Zimbabwe, Angola, Mozambique	97,278	No data
Shaballe	Ethiopia, Somalia	47,151	No data
Okavango	Angola, Namibia, Botswana	5,851	No data

Source: Ian Woodman, "War of Scarcity: Myth or Reality? An Examination of Resource Scarcities as a Cause of Conflict in Africa," in *Seaford House Papers*, ed. J. E. Spence (London: Royal College of Defense Studies, 2002), p. 10.

a tendency that becomes all the more probable where there is regional instability to fuel internal conflicts in volatile societies.

Using the principles postulated by Falkenmark, two countries, Kenya and South Africa, are facing possible water stress. While there are cases of political difficulties in both countries, as indeed, all other countries in the continent, there is no indication as yet that there is likely to be any water-based conflict in either of the countries. Furthermore, looking into the future, there are no serious compelling domestic or regional considerations that are likely to result in serious water conflicts in either of the countries. The main natural resource that is likely to create tension in either of the countries is land, with Kenya's situation coming in the form of rivalry between differing ethnic groups and between agriculturist and pastoralists and in South Africa coming in the form of the imbalance between racial groups' access to land. For the latter, however, the picture can change to include a water conflict if adequate considerations are not given to the management of the international river basins in the southern African subregion.

Management and Control of International Rivers and Basins

This is the aspect of water conflict that has attracted the interest and attention of scholars, due largely to the diversity of the national interests that have to be taken into consideration in any of its discussions. The problem here arises from the difficulties and strains that one riparian state shifts onto others sharing the same international waters. Although variants of the problem exist in different parts of the world, the implications for Africa are quite profound because some of the international agreements governing the management of these rivers were made by erstwhile colonial masters, and as such, are not often acceptable to the countries after their independence. Consequently, many of them have found reasons to repudiate the treaties governing the management and control of these rivers.

Before going into specific cases, some general observations may be necessary. There are about eighty international rivers and lake basins in Africa, and more than a quarter of these "have catchments greater than 100,000 square kilometers."[21] Table 6.5 shows some of the major international rivers in the continent.

Inevitably, the access to and management of some of these rivers have been major causes of tension in the continent. In this section, there is a discussion of some of the main rivers and basins over which there have been tensions and conflict, and the themes evoked by the conflicts and potential conflicts are later discussed.

The Nile

The Nile is undoubtedly one of the most politicized rivers in the world, and many of the potential conflicts surrounding it are well documented in academic literature.[22] With a length of 6,485 kilometers, the Nile is the world's longest

Table 6.5 River basins and the riparian states

River	Major riparian	Other riparian states
Nile	Egypt Sudan	Burundi, Ethiopia, Rwanda, Tanzania, Uganda DRC, Eritrea, Kenya
Senegal	Mauritania Senegal	Guinea Mali
Limpopo	Botswana Mozambique	South Africa, Zimbabwe
Gambia	Gambia	Guinea, Senegal
Congo	Congo	Cameroon, CAR, DRC
Niger	Niger Mali	Côte d'Ivoire, Guinea, Nigeria
Lake Chad	Chad	Cameroon, CAR, Niger, Nigeria, Sudan
Zambezi	Mozambique	Angola, Botswana, Malawi, Namibia, Tanzania, Zambia, Zimbabwe
Orange	Namibia	Botswana, Lesotho, South Africa
Djuba Webi Shebeli	Somalia	Ethiopia, Kenya

river. The source of the river was not discovered until the middle of the twentieth century, when it was traced to the mountains of Burundi.[23] The Nile is made up of three tributaries: the White Nile, the Blue Nile, and the Atbara. The White Nile rises from its source in Burundi, passes through Lake Victoria and flows into Sudan, where it meets up with the Blue Nile, which commences from Ethiopian highlands. The two flow together to the north of Khartoum, where they join the waters of Atbara, whose flow is also located in the Ethiopian highlands. The river passes through ten countries, with Egypt and Sudan constituting the upper riparian states, and Burundi, the Democratic Republic of Congo (DRC), Eritrea, Ethiopia, Kenya, Rwanda, Tanzania, and Uganda making up the lower riparian countries.

The potential conflicts surrounding the river Nile are rooted in at least five factors. First, the location of the river could be a factor, passing through ten African countries, some of which are strategically placed to influence politics and trade in the continent and even as far as the Middle East. Second, the economic weakness of most of the Nile riparian states is a factor that forces many of them to have an increasing dependence on the river. It should be noted at this point that many of the countries sharing the Nile River, though strategically important, are also among the poorest in the world. Third, there are political differences that sometimes characterize the relationship between some of the Nile riparian states. Although these differences may have nothing to do with the Nile directly, the ripple effects have reflected in the politics surrounding the management of the river. Fourth, the varying nature of the military strength of the countries could become a factor. While some of the countries have considerable military strength, such that they can protect their interest in the Nile no matter how unfair to other riparian states, others are so weak that they cannot defend their claim to the river, even if legitimate. Fifth, there is a huge disparity in the extent of these countries dependence on the Nile, and the inverse relation this may have to their contribution to the river.

Egypt is the dominant country in the Nile politics. The importance of the river to the country has been recorded by many.[24] More than 90 percent of the Egyptian population dwell along the Nile banks, and the river comprises the sole water resource of the country. Agriculture, which takes about 90 percent of available water, could not dispense with the Nile. Also, electricity generation, which covers 27 percent of national demands with energy generated from Aswan dam, depends on the river. All this has made Egypt pay considerable interest to developments in other riparian states, especially Ethiopia, where 85 percent of the water flow originates. Egypt has always desired ambitious projects for the Nile, and these are perceived by the other riparian states as being against their own interests. Two projects underline this. First is the El Salam Canal, which leaves the Nile twenty kilometers south of Damietta on the Mediterranean, passing under the Suez Canal and heading eastward for 242 kilometers to East Arish. This was to irrigate 242,800 hectares of the Sinai Desert. Second is the Sheiekh Zayed Canal, which is to irrigate 168,420 hectares to be established in the Nubian Desert. To supply these schemes, Egypt would need to increase its annual quota of Nile water by 15.5 billion cubic meters to 71 billion cubic meters. A second country that is strategic in any equation of the Nile is the Sudan. The river's two great branches, the Blue Nile, coming from the Ethiopian highlands, and the White Nile from Central Africa, meet in the country. Like Egypt, the country has wide ambitions for the Nile, as evidenced in the desire to construct the Jonglei Canal.

Contrary to what is often assumed, diplomatic initiatives to manage water resources in the Horn of Africa preceded the 1929 agreement between Britain and Egypt to manage the Nile resources. For example, in 1881, Britain signed a protocol with Italy (which was acting on behalf of Ethiopia) forbidding the construction of any project that would affect the flow of water in the Atbara River, which discharges into the Blue Nile. In 1902, another agreement was signed demarcating the borders between Ethiopia, Eritrea, and Anglo-Egyptian Sudan. This was signed in Addis Ababa, and it gave Britain and Egypt a veto over the construction of any project on the Blue Nile, Lake Tana, or Sobat River that would affect the discharge of water to the Nile.

The November 1929 agreement is often regarded as the first major agreement on the Nile. The agreement was signed between the Egyptian prime minister and the British high commissioner in Egypt, and it allocated 48 billion cubic meters per year to Egypt as its acquired right and 4 billion cubic meters to Sudan. Under the agreement, no work would be undertaken on the Nile, its tributaries, and the Lake Basin. Egypt also had the right to "inspect and investigate" the whole length of the Nile River. In 1959, another agreement was signed between Egypt and Sudan. Under this, Egypt's allocation was increased to 55.5 billion cubic meters and 18.5 billion cubic meters to Sudan. Apart from Ethiopia, which at this time was a sovereign nation, all other countries were under colonial rule.

Controversies surrounding the Nile River come under two broad categories. The first is mainly between the two upper riparian states—Egypt and Sudan— while the other is between the upper states, especially Egypt, and the lower states. The tensions between Egypt and Sudan over the management of the Nile is often subsumed under the wider conflicts between the upper and lower riparian states, but it is a problem that is likely to increase in the years ahead and, as such, worthy of greater attention. Another reason why the conflict here has been reduced to the background is that both countries have to come up with a united front, even if with difficulty, to ensure that the lower riparian states do not exploit the possible division between them to acquire greater control of the Nile.

The conflict between Sudan and Egypt over the Nile is rooted in a 1929 agreement between the two countries, but with Sudan then under British colonial rule. Under this agreement, Sudan was obliged not to undertake any construction that would interfere with the run-off to Egypt. After independence, Sudan saw no reason to respect an agreement that was entered into on its behalf by its erstwhile colonial master, especially as the agreement was seen as being antithetical to its interest. Consequently, the country initiated construction work on the Roseires Dam along the Blue Nile. This was also the time Egypt wanted to continue plans for the Aswan Dam, a project that would leave 165 square kilometers of Sudanese territory flooded, and a dislocation of 70,000 people. Egypt saw no need in pursuing a militant line, and subsequently entered into an agreement with Sudan, under which the latter dropped its own plan on the promise of financial compensation and a revision of the treaty. This was the origin of the aforementioned 1959 agreement between the two countries.[25]

There are now concerns, however, that Sudan no longer feels comfortable with its agreement with Egypt, as there are calls from within Sudan advocating for the repudiation of the agreement. The politics of the Nile has now come to underline other political differences between the two countries. Issues such as Islamic fundamentalism, alleged links with international terrorism, domestic instability, all of which were hallmarks of the government of Sudan, are all issues the Mubarak government in Cairo considered disturbing, and President Mubarak has never hidden his conviction that the government in Sudan was determined to assassinate him. Indeed, when there was an attempt on his life in Addis Ababa during a 1995 OAU Conference, Mubarak specifically mentioned Sudan as the country behind the plot. Indeed, there are those who attribute Sudanese government support for Egyptian Islamic fundamentalists to the politics surrounding the management of the Nile River.[26]

Also important in understanding the politics of the Nile is the civil war in the Sudan, where the role played by Sudan's neighbors has been determined, at least to an extent, by their interest in the river. Egypt is playing a double-sided strategy of maintaining workable relations with all those involved on both sides of the Sudanese conflict. For example, in November 1997, President Mubarak met with the former SPLA leader, the late John Garang, during which the latter promised the Egyptian president that his movement would not seek the dissolution of Sudan. Sudanese ex-premier El Sadek El Mahdi also went to Egypt shortly afterward, while in June 1998, Egypt's deputy prime minister, Youssef Wali, met Democratic Unionist Party leader, Mohamed Osman e Mirghani. The Sudanese president, Omar Hassan Ahmed el Bashir, also visited Egypt in 1998. Furthermore, the Egyptian government has assisted in remodeling the Sudanese government's international image, with Cairo voting against UN sanction against Khartoum and going as far as to accuse the United States of supporting Sudanese opposition.

The Nile water has been a crucial factor in the Sudanese Civil War, although this is sometimes reduced to the background because of the dominant position of oil in the conflict. Water has become a factor in two ways. First, southerners see many of the actions of the northern-dominated government on the Nile as signifying utter disregard for southern interest. For example, the decision of the Nimeiri government in the early 1980s to build the Jonglei Canal, which would have drained the vast Sudd swamp, was seen as being insensitive to the plight of the southerners who lived in the area. This, in fact, explained the 1983 attack on the rig digging the canal by the SPLA. It is possibly against this background that there has been no further attempt to revive the project. The second way is the role of the Nile in the support the Egyptian government gives to the Sudanese government. As noted earlier, Egypt is always apprehensive of the intention of its neighbors over the Nile. Although Egypt and Sudan have their own differences over the Nile, the former still prefers to deal with the government in Sudan rather than the SPLA, who has made it clear that it would not tolerate the previous arrangement in which sharing the Nile implied depriving the inhabitants of the Sudd swamp of their livelihood without compensation.

The second category of tension concerning the Nile brings the lower riparian states in collusion with the upper riparian states of Egypt and Sudan. The ramifications of the potential conflicts here are more complex, and they have been going on for several years, with recent years heightening tension sometimes to the level of violent confrontation. Although there has been no actual conflict over the Nile, there have been significant tensions between many of the states, with Egypt making it clear to all the other riparian states its determination to go to war to protect its access to the Nile River, and other lower riparian states arguing that they are not having adequate reward for their contribution to the river.

The upper riparian states have never hidden their disapproval of the unfair nature of the agreement that gives Egypt and Sudan dominance over the Nile. However, because the problem is felt more by some states than others, and because of the political differences among some of the upper riparian states, they have not been able to come up with a coherent position against the obvious domination of Egypt and Sudan over the Nile management. The fact, too, that even the combined military strength of all the upper riparian states cannot match those of Egypt and Sudan has meant that the states have not gone beyond the platitudinous repudiation of the agreements. Increasingly, however, many of the states are becoming more forceful in their complaints and some have in fact begun making subtle challenges to Egyptian domination.

Of the upper riparian states, Ethiopia has been one of the most vocal against the arrangement that gave domination of the Nile to both Sudan and Egypt. This is because the country is the worst affected by the present arrangement. Ethiopia contributes about 86 percent of all the water that eventually becomes the Nile stream flow. Indeed, the country believes that it had no reason to have water scarcity. First, being a mountainous country, it enjoys a reasonable amount of rainfall. But this aside, many of the main rivers in the region pass through its territory. These include the Blue Nile, Sobat, and Atbara rivers, which flow into Sudan to add to the flow of the White Nile, and the Wabi Shebelle, Genalle, and Omo rivers, which go into Somalia and Kenya, respectively. Ethiopia has always argued that the 1959 agreement impedes development in the country, and they have called for its nullification. Recently, the Ethiopian minister of water resources announced his intentions to develop irrigation projects and construct two dams on the Blue Nile subbasins.

As early as the beginning of the 1990s, Ethiopia had made known its determination to take more from the Nile. For example, the head of the Ethiopian Development Studies in Addis Ababa, Zawole Abate, has signaled a protest on behalf of his country:

> To date, the level of utilization of Nile waters by the co-basin states varies with their respective socio-economic advancement. Egypt stands high in this regards, utilizing 55.5 billion cu.m. of the Nile waters to irrigate 28 million ha. Next to Egypt, Sudan has developed 1.8 million ha. of irrigated agriculture consuming 18.3 billion cu.m of water annually . . . while Ethiopia, contributing about 86% of the Nile water utilizes a mere 1.6 billion cu. M. annually. This huge gap of water resources development between the downstream and upstream would not remain for long in light.[27]

Egypt has always seen Ethiopia as the only country among the upper riparian states that has the kind of determination that needs to be taken very seriously. Indeed, it is likely that the late President Sadat of Egypt had Ethiopia in mind when he noted that the next war in northeast Africa would be over water. It is also likely that Egypt's support for the Eritrean liberation activities against Ethiopia and the assistance Egypt has given to Somalia during its invasion of Ethiopia's Ogaden region in 1977 were all geared toward ensuring that Ethiopia did not have sufficient opportunity to develop the Nile waters passing through its territory. When in 1977 Ethiopia announced its desire to exploit hydrological opportunities in the Nile basin, Egypt immediately threatened the use of military action against the authorities in Addis Ababa. In November 1989, the Ethiopian ambassador was called to the Foreign Office in Cairo to provide an explanation for the presence of Israeli hydrologists and surveyors studying the areas on the Blue Nile with the possibility of dam construction. In the same day, Egyptian Members of Parliament lined up to support military action against Ethiopia. While Ethiopia was under Marxist rule, there was little cause for concern, as it had little chance of getting finance to build dams. But with the end of Marxism and the increasing access to international finance, Egypt thinks it now has to take the matter more seriously.

Other countries are also becoming more assertive. For example, Kenya has noted that it was considering withdrawing from the Nile Basin Agreement, a threat the Egyptian Minister of Irrigation and Water Resources Mahmoud Abu Zeid has said would be considered as an official declaration of war. In February 2004, Tanzania, another upper riparian state, launched a project to draw water from Lake Victoria to supply the Shinyanga region. The project calls for the construction of about one hundred miles of inland pipeline. To mitigate the anticipated Egyptian reaction, Tanzania announced that the pipeline was designed to provide drinking water to its thirsty population rather than to irrigate land. Nevertheless, Egypt expressed its irritation with the Tanzanian project, arguing that under the 1929 agreement, it has the right to veto any project—agricultural, industrial, or power. Egypt is handling the issue diplomatically, however, Egyptian officials stressed that the diplomatic dialogue does not mean that Cairo will not consider any number of other options, if necessary. This has not weakened Tanzania's resolve, and the country's deputy permanent secretary in the Ministry of Water and Livestock Development, Dr. C. Nyamurunda, has made this clear.[28]

Another region where fresh water could cause tension is the Horn of Africa, mainly between Somalia and Ethiopia. Somalia's access to surface water is limited to only two rivers—Shebelle and Juba. These two rivers originate from Ethiopia. The Shebelle flows only during the raining season and does not reach the Indian Ocean, disappearing instead in a swamp in central Somalia. It is the area between these two rivers that forms Somalia's agricultural zone.[29] Almost all the water utilized for agriculture in Somalia originates from Ethiopia. Ethiopia has enormous water reserves. Its fourteen major river basins carry only an estimated 116 billion cubic meters surface run off. However, over the years, because of political instability in the country, a coherent policy on the country's water resources was never formed. With some form of stability now present, Ethiopia began taking an assertive position on its water resources, with the possibility of clash with some of its neighbors.

On the whole, the Nile River and the entire Horn of Africa continue to evoke bitter controversies among states in northeast and central Africa. But another region where international rivers have been at the center of interstate tension is southern Africa.

Rivers in Southern Africa

In discussing international rivers, special attention needs to be devoted to the southern African subregion, mainly because of the number of international rivers in the region and the water scarcity problem sometimes anticipated in certain circles among the SADC countries. Before going into the politics surrounding some of the rivers, the interconnections are worth noting as pointed out in table 6.6. Of all the rivers in southern Africa, five have featured very prominently in discussions about conflicts and potential conflicts. These are the Orange, Okavango, Zambezi, Chobe, and Kunene.

Orange River

Three countries—Lesotho, Namibia, and South Africa—are the dominant countries in the management of the Orange River, with a fourth country, Botswana, operating on the periphery. The potential conflict over the management of the river centers mainly around the creation of the Lesotho Highway Water Project (LHWP), which relies heavily on the river. Although the Orange Basin involves four countries, only two of these, South Africa and Namibia, are involved in the LHWP.[30] South Africa's military intervention in the 1998 Lesotho unrest underlined the importance of water politics in Pretoria's calculations. South Africa made two military deployments to Lesotho: one to the capital, Maseru, and the other to the Katse Dam Complex.

Table 6.6 Major river basins and flow in southern Africa

River	Country
Chobe	Botswana, Nigeria
Congo	Angola, DRC, Zambia
Zambezi	Angola, Botswana, Malawi, Mozambique, Namibia, Tanzania, Zambia, Zimbabwe
Buzi	Mozambique, Zimbabwe
Cuvelai	Angola, Namibia
Nata	Botswana, Zimbabwe
Orange	Lesotho, Namibia, South Africa
Punge	Mozambique, Zimbabwe
Inkomati	Mozambique, South Africa, Swaziland
Shire	Malawi, Mozambique
Luangwa	Mozambique, Zambia
Okavango	Angola, Botswana, Namibia
Kunene	Angola, Namibia
Limpopo	Botswana, Mozambique, South Africa, Zimbabwe
Save	Mozambique, Zimbabwe

Okavango River

As noted above, the Okavango River is shared by Angola, Namibia, and Botswana.[31] Potential conflicts surrounding this river can be divided into two: international and local. The international dimension of the possible conflicts is rooted in the different pressing needs that each of these countries has and the demands the countries are placing on the river. As Anthony Turton has noted, the hydro-political power configuration is complex because the two downstream states, Namibia and Botswana, have water scarcity and have only perennial rivers located on their borders—neither has permanent rivers on its sovereign territory except Okavango. At the center of the conflict is scarcity, especially for Namibia, which desperately needs water from Okavango. Tension indeed arose between Namibia and Botswana when Namibia announced its intention to build a pipeline to abstract water from the Okavango River near Rundu. Turton has identified three issues that underline the present and future power relations over the Okavango River.[32]

- Namibian economic growth and prosperity is being severely limited by water scarcity, thus raising the issue to a level of strategic concern.
- Botswana too is facing water scarcity and if the economy continues to grow as it is currently doing, then existing water supplies will be insufficient to sustain that growth, thus raising water to a national security issue.
- Both Namibia and Botswana are dependent on the whims of Angola, the upper riparian state. In the eventuality of postwar Angola needing more water for development, relations with the two lower riparian states can change.

A number of contentious problems have surrounded the Okavango basin. The basin is one of the world's largest inland deltas, covering more than 4,500 square kilometers. It is also unique as an untouched sanctuary for flora and fauna. Looking at the three countries, attempts to meet domestic water needs have been crucial to expanding the potential conflicts. Botswana was the first country in recent years to demonstrate the desire to extract from the river. This intention, which was mooted in 1987, was later shelved after international pressure from environmental groups warned about the effects this could have on the ecosystem. A few years afterward, Namibia, faced with a severe drought, also wanted to abstract water from the Okavango, a move that was strongly opposed by Botswana. The potential conflict was eventually averted when heavy rainfall enabled Namibia to make do with water from its existing sources. However, although the Botswana Minister of Natural Resources and Water Affairs Mr. D. N. Magang was hopeful that there would be no conflict, he, at the same time, confirmed that it is a "possibility."[33]

Namibia's situation vis-à-vis the Okavango or other international rivers in the region needs to be put in context. The country is the driest in Africa,[34] and there are constant pressures on the government to address the perennial shortage of water. One way through which Namibia has tried to address this problem is to abstract from the Okavango River at Rundu. This has raised a lot of concern in Botswana, especially as it is believed that such an extraction would have environmental impacts on the country. However, what seems to have added to the potential tension in the management of the river is the conflict between two countries—Namibia and Botswana—over the Kasikili/Sedudu Island on the Chobe River.[35]

Also important in the understanding of potential interstate conflicts over the river is Botswana's determination to preserve the Okavango Delta status as a tourist center. Indeed, in 1996, the country unilaterally registered the delta as a Ramsar Wetland of International Importance, without informing its upstream neighbors. This gives the site protection, but it also makes future development on the site subject to the approval of international role-players who are outside the region. While Angola was, for most of the 1980s, quiet over its claims to the river, mainly because the river was under UNITA control during the war, the country is now trying to exercise its right as a major actor. With the end of its civil war, the country is becoming more involved in the subregional hydro-political developments, and the Okavango River is particularly prominent in its calculation.

Zambezi River

The Zambezi River is one of the most prominent rivers in southern Africa. It is the largest shared river basin in the region and the third in Africa after the rivers Congo and Nile. The river's importance can also be seen in that almost 40 million of SADC's estimated 208 million live within its basin.[36] The links the Zambezi River has with conflicts center largely on the number of countries connected by the river and the divergent and often conflicting uses they want, need, and plan for the river.

Jo-Ansie van Wyk has identified some of the ways in which the Zambezi River has been potentially linked to conflict. First, the river drains eight members of the SADC, but the Zambezi River Authority (ZRA) involves only two of the states, Zimbabwe and Zambia. Second, two of the countries, Angola and Zambia, did not sign the SADC protocol on Shared Watercourse System, which means they are not obliged to follow the stipulations of the protocol. Third, there is a potential political confrontation, with South Africa planning to solve its water demands by obtaining supplies from the Zambezi River. Fourth, three consecutive years of drought have forced the Tanzanian government to investigate alternative water resources, and Zambezi is a prime target.[37]

Chobe River

What has brought Chobe River to the focus of attention is the conflict over the ownership of the disputed island between Botswana and Namibia. As noted in chapter 3, this island is known as Sedudu in Botswana and Kasikili in Namibia, and it has an area of approximately 3.5 kilometers. The roots of the dispute can be traced to the Berlin Treaty of 1875, which partitioned Africa among the colonial powers, and the governments in both countries have contested the ownership. Botswana's arguments at the court were: (1) that the northern and western channel of the Chobe River in the vicinity of Kasikili/Sedudu Island constitutes the main channel of the Chobe River in accordance with the provisions of Article III (2) of the Anglo-German Agreement of 1890; and (2) consequently, sovereignty in respect of Kasikili/Sedudu Island vests exclusively in the Republic of Botswana.

Namibia's arguments were that (1) the channel that lies to the south of Kasikili/Sedudu Island is the main channel of the Chobe River; (2) the channel that lies to the north of Kasikili/Sedudu Island is not the main channel of the Chobe River; (3) Namibia and its predecessors have occupied and used Kasikili Island and exercised sovereign jurisdiction over it, with the knowledge and acquiescence of Botswana and its predecessors since at least 1890; (4) the boundary between Namibia and Botswana around Kasikili/Sedudu Island lies in the center (that is to say, the *thalweg*) of the southern channel of the Chobe River; and (5) the legal status of Kasikili/Sedudu Island is that it is a part of the territory under the sovereignty of Namibia.

There were efforts to resolve the dispute at the SADC level but this failed. The dispute has the unpleasant distinction of being the only water-related conflict that has brought two countries to the brink of war, with both countries threatening military action and Botswana actually making military occupation of the island. Local residents of both countries residing on the island also impressed it on their respective governments to ensure that the island was not lost. Eventually, both countries subjected their claims to the adjudication of the International Court of Justice at The Hague in May 1996. The court delivered its judgment in 1999, upholding Botswana's claim to the island. It, however, needs to be pointed out as Peter Ashton has done, that at the core of this conflict is "sovereignty," and not water or water resources per se, and it would probably have happened even if the Chobe River had not been involved.

Kunene River Basin

The river has been at the focus of controversy for quite some time and here again the potential conflicts have centered on the different uses to which the countries sharing the river want to put it. As noted in chapter 2, three countries, Angola, Namibia, and Botswana, are the main countries connected with the Kunene River. However, and as noted earlier, Namibia is one of the driest countries in the continent, a characteristic that leaves the country desperately searching for water sources. The first major controversy over the Kunene River has to do with Namibia's decision to construct a dam, the Epupa Dam, on the river. This has generated reactions from several sources, three of which are important. The first is from other riparian countries. While initially both Angola and Namibia agreed on the need to have a dam constructed along the river, disagreements soon ensued on a site for the dam. The feasibility study sponsored by the two countries recommended two possible sites: the Baynes site and the Epupa site. The Angolan government supported the Baynes site, which would be dependent on Angola's Gove Dam. The country was even willing to secure funding for repairing the damage that its civil war had caused on the Gove Dam. Namibia, for its part, supported the Epupa site. Both countries still hold divergent views on the construction of this dam and it adds to other rivalries that exist between them over the management of international waters they share.

The second, and perhaps most important reaction to the construction of the dam, is coming from the Himba people, who are going to be affected by the construction of the dam. The opposition of the Himba people to Namibia's decision is that the construction would flood more than 380 square kilometers of their land and resources, resulting in loss of homes and grazing lands on which the people have depended for centuries. Also of concern to the people is the loss of ancestral gravesites that form the nexus of their cultural, social, and economic structure. Being largely pastoralists, the Himba people see no way the construction would not affect their livelihood. On another level, the people fear that the construction of the dam would inevitably lead to the influx of foreign workers into their community. Indeed, it is estimated that as many as 4,000 workers could be involved in the construction, with the attendant implications of HIV/AIDS and the defilement of their society.

The third source of opposition to the construction of the Epupa Dam has come mainly from international environmental bodies who are largely against the construction because of what they see as inimical environmental implications. Many of these organizations argue that the whole initiative is a so-called white elephant project, whose short- and long-term implications are not in Namibia's interest. They argue that Namibia cannot afford the project, which they claim is likely to cost about US$550 million, without factoring into this other hidden costs. They claim that Namibia's dryness would mean that up to 630 cubic meters of water would be lost annually through evaporation. Consequently, it would take approximately twenty-nine months for the dam to be 70 percent full. There is also the attendant carbon gas emitted, which according to these organizations would be more than the international standards. Finally, the organizations argue that the construction would affect tourism, as it would submerge the impressive Epupa Falls and the unique ecological zones that surround them. They have thus come up with a string of alternatives, which they argue are cheaper with far less significant side effects.[38]

All these lead to some political undertones of the project, which centers on the allegation that the main objective of the dam is to bring jobs to the majority Ovambo ethnic group and thus cement political support for the ruling party. The Namibian government appreciates that the politics surrounding the construction of the dam has brought it in collusion with a string of local and international actors but has insisted that the construction is in its national interest. In a statement to a government minister, President Nujoma made it clear that the construction of the dam was a foregone conclusion.[39]

Lake Chad

The potential conflicts surrounding Lake Chad have been ignored for a long time. In recent years, however, some of these have started to come to the fore of attention. There are two reasons for this. First, because of the shrinking nature of the lake, it has drawn the attention of scholars and policymakers to the problems that may ensue among those who depend on the lake as a means for their livelihood.[40] Second, there is legal conflict between Nigeria and Cameroon over the Bakassi. Also connected with the legal dispute is the ownership of a number of villages along Lake Chad. The location of the lake—on the edge of the Sahara Desert—makes it of vital strategic importance to five countries: Cameroon, Chad, Nigeria, Niger, and the Central African Republic (CAR).[41] Of these five countries, three, Nigeria, Chad, and Cameroon, are very close to the politics of the lake. Although it is extremely shallow, just about seven meters in depth, it holds one of the largest areas of wetlands in the Sahelian region.

The recent controversies surrounding Lake Chad can be brought under two headings: between the three countries sharing the lake and between local communities around the basin. The conflicts between the three countries differ in intensity. Cameroon and Nigeria have disputes over the ownership of parts of Lake Chad, and this, indeed, was part of the case that was taken for adjudication at the International Court of Justice. Unfortunately, the dominance of oil and the Bakassi overshadowed the Lake Chad dimension of the conflict. Cameroon argued that this portion of Lake Chad was part of its territory. The country's claim of sovereignty was based on colonial agreements, while Nigeria, again as in the case of the Bakassi Peninsula, argued that colonial powers lacked the power to make such a treaty on behalf of the colonized state. Nigeria also contended that it administered the villages without any protest from Cameroon before 1994, and this, in Nigeria's contention, amounts to acquiescence. In the judgment made in October 2002, Nigeria lost and, the following month, the country handed over thirty-three villages around Lake Chad to Cameroon.[42] Nigeria and Chad also had major disagreements over the ownership of portions of the lake. This reached a dangerous phase in 1980, when Nigeria dispatched troops to the basin to meet challenges poised by the Chadian gendarmes. This has, however, rescinded in recent years and both countries have found more amicable ways of managing their differences over the basin. Indeed, despite occasional hiccups in their relationship, all the countries sharing the Lake Chad basin have formed close relationships and have developed joint projects on the management of the basin.[43]

The conflicts between the local communities have centered largely on the relationship between nomads and farmers, and the main cause has been the shortage of water for livestock and the inadequacy of agricultural land that often leads to the encroachment of farmers into pasture lands and vice versa. Some of the farmers and nomads have been forced to migrate from the basin and have gone into cities to swell the ranks of the unemployed, thereby adding to social crises in the cities. Another country where the legacy of colonial agreement has threatened conflict over maritime boundaries is between Guinea-Bissau and Senegal. The agreement was signed between France and Portugal. Again, this went to court for adjudication and it was given to Senegal.[44]

On the whole, while it is impossible to discuss all international rivers, the samples selected for discussion here have shown that disagreements surrounding the management of international waters have been rooted in at least five factors. These are

- the numerous and often conflicting uses into which the states want to put the rivers in question;
- the controversial legal agreements governing the management of the river;
- the disproportionate allocation of the river(s), vis-à-vis the contribution made by the states to the basin;
- the geographical characteristics of the region and the impact these have on the resource management; and
- the political instability that characterizes the internal affairs of some of the states and the tension in the interstate relations of some of the states.

It is most likely that the management of international rivers will continue to attract concern as a potential cause of conflict. Already, countries in Western Europe are preparing their armed forces to meet the increasing threats on wars over water,[45] a tendency that has not been made easier by other natural resources embedded in these rivers.

Clashes Associated with Fishing and other Marine Resources

It has to be admitted from the outset that conflicts relating to water resources are considerably few when compared with land, although the few conflicts here have wider international ramifications. Simon Fairle has provided an explanation for the relatively peaceful coexistence in marine resource relations.[46] The relatively weak technology used to exploit river resources makes the possibility of easy exhaustion of the resources a distant possibility. Consequently, the tension that often comes with the imminent depletion of natural resources is not common with marine resources. But Fairle also notes there is an extent of camaraderie among those involved in the fishing profession, which can also explain the reduction in tension among them. According to him, "every fisherman on the sea, whether skipper of a Spanish freezer-trawler or crewman on an African pirogue, is a simple mortal trying to gain a living by pitting his wits both with and against the elements, with and against the fishing bureaucracy, and with and against his fellow fishermen."[47] All this introduced considerable humor into their relationship, even amid the competition that underlies their profession.

Several considerations have brought fishing to the focus of attention vis-à-vis conflict.[48] These include complications arising from industrial harvesting and over-fishing, disagreements arising from the use of wrong fishing methods, problems associated with population growth, and the effects of rapid urbanization. In different ways, each of these have been associated with conflicts across fishing communities in Africa. The conflicts associated with industrial fishing have been linked largely, though not exclusively, to the activities of large fishing trawlers, often owned by foreign fishing companies, but operating in African fishing waters, especially their alleged intimidation of the weaker and smaller fishing vessels of local fishermen. Indeed, the activities of European and Asian fishing companies and how this threatens local fishermen's livelihood and government's income are now becoming issues of great concern. The consequences have been profound in Senegal and the Gambia, two of the countries where fishing constitutes one of the most vital sources of revenue. It was, in fact, recorded that about seven hundred foreign trawlers were operating illegally in the Gambia alone in 2000.[49] Most of the huge trawlers came from Europe and Japan. In some cases, too, these trawlers depleted even the close inshore stocks that are the only barriers to famine for many coastal villages. The process of fishing adopted by these companies—hauling huge trawl nets, sometimes twenty miles long—also threatens the lives of local fishermen operating with local wooden canoes. The helplessness of many of these countries was reflected by David Graham, manager of the Gambian Fish Surveillance Organization, when he notes "they are certainly fishing illegally, and while we have evidence against them we are powerless to stop them."[50] Indeed, only two countries, South Africa and Nigeria, have patrol vessels that can monitor their waters.[51] Another country in the region, Somalia, seems to have addressed this problem in another way. Heavily armed militiamen operating from motorized speedboats have been seizing foreign trawlers for ransom. This has kept poaching fleets at bay.

Closely related to this is the nature of agreement between western nations and African coastal countries over fishing. Many African countries consider the agreements as not being favorable, and some of them are now seeking better deals for their marine resources. Morocco for a long time refused to renew a US$800 million four-year agreement covering the waters of western Sahara without at least a 100 percent increase in yearly fees.[52]

Industrial prawn is another marine resource whose monopolization by foreign interests has serious potential for causing conflicts in some of the affected countries. In Tanzania, for example, the African Fishing Company, has been at the center of a major criticism from local villagers and many international NGOs, especially the Environmental Law Alliance Worldwide. The cause of controversy here is the envisaged destruction of nineteen villages and the dislocation of more than 30,000 people in the Rufiji River Delta for the process of constructing a 10,000 hectares prawn farm that the company claims would fetch the country between US$200 and $300 million foreign exchange earnings and employment for about 2,000 Tanzanians. Those who oppose the project, however, claim that these figures are questionable, and that the number of people to be affected makes it potentially inadvisable. But there is another factor that makes the project even more controversial. The desperate intention of the Tanzanian government to attract foreign investment resulted in its allocating land to the African Fishing Company without following the proper procedure. Under the Tanzanian Statute, any land held under the customary law has to be first acquired by the president for "public purpose" before it can be transferred to another occupant. But before the president can do this, there has to be a series of public hearings, at which objections, if any, can be raised.[53] This was not done before the government gave the Rufiji to the African Fishing Company.

Disagreements arising from access to fishing rivers and wrong fishing methods have caused conflicts in a number of countries. For example, Mozambique and Malawi have been having an uneasy relationship over fishery resources on Lake Chiuta. Communities from the two countries have been at war over issues related to who has access to fish and when should requirements for closing season for fishing activities be enforced. The fishing industry in the two countries is vital to the economy, creating employment and contributing to poverty alleviation. A major cause of conflict here is the use of inappropriate fishing methods. For example, the practice of lining nets with mosquito netting has been a common practice, which results in the catching of juveniles and prevents natural recruitment. Noncompliance with the off-season regulations is also a problem, and it often means that fish in breeding stages are removed.

Another region where fishing has caused considerable controversy is Lake Victoria, and here, fishermen from Kenya, Uganda, and Tanzania have historically operated. As of August 2003, it was estimated there were 120,000 fishermen in the region operating on the lake, with about 10,000 families believed to be benefiting directly from its resources.[54] Furthermore, there were about 40,000 boats operating in the lake with about 10,000 engines on about 2,000 landing beaches.[55] Among the causes of conflict in the lake have been piracy, weak enforcement of laws and regulations, smuggling of fish, protection of fishing interest by hired gangs, and exploitation by middlemen.

What, however, seems to be of more immediate concern for fishermen in the region is the controversy over boundary crossing, with fishermen from one country unknowingly trespassing into the fishing territories of others.

This tendency has increased because most of the fishermen are illiterates and are often unaware of the boundaries and their limitations as fishermen operating in international waters. Kenyan fishermen have been the most vulnerable in this respect. For example, in August 2003, some Kenyan fishermen were arrested for trespassing on the Tanzania part of Lake Victoria. Although they were released after government intervention, fishing equipment, including twenty-seven boats and several nets, was forfeited to the Tanzanian authorities. The losses incurred by the seizing of these vehicles have heightened tension between fishermen from both countries, with the fishermen in the Kenyan towns of Migori and Suba threatening revenge.

The involvement of Western European countries has added another dimension to the politics of fishing in Africa, especially as they often undertake fishing with far more advanced technology that puts local fishermen at a disadvantage. Indeed, the European Commission has been trying to negotiate with Mauritania to allow EU fleets to operate in the country's fishing territories, especially the Island of Agadir, lying inside Mauritania's Banc d'Arguin National Park. However, Mauritania's fishing boat owners are applying pressure on their government to relax the rules that keep them out of Banc d'Arguin. Many of Mauritania's fishing boats are crewed by Senegalese fishermen, and they are based in the north port of Nouadhibou, barely thirty kilometers from Banc d'Arguin. These fishermen complained that they were being intimidated by foreign trawlers. As of 2001, money generated by selling fishing rights to foreign fleets in waters except the Banc d'Arguin provided the country with 20 to 25 percent of budget receipt. Fishing also generated 36,000 jobs in the country. At the same time, 173 trawlers from EU countries and 161 from other foreign countries had permits to fish in Mauritanian waters, and in the four years that ended on July 31, 2001, agreement with EU on fishing was worth US$233 billion.

Conflict has also been known to affect fishing, with fishermen not being able to embark on their trade or having their fishing implements stolen or destroyed. For example, the May 2001 coup attempt to overthrow the government of CAR by the former President Andre Kolingba, had effects on fishing in the country, especially the fishing community living along river Oubangui. The uprising drove fishermen away from their bases, and their equipment and canoes were looted by rebels from DRC who came to CAR to support the government.[56]

Fishing conflicts have been more complex in places where oil politics intermingle with fishing. A number of recent conflicts have demonstrated this. In Nigeria's Niger Delta, one of the main problems underlining conflicts is the disruption that oil exploration has caused to fishing. Indeed, one of the main protests of the people in many riverine areas of Nigeria's oil-producing communities is the destruction of fishing opportunities.

A conflict that is often forgotten in this category is the one in the Bakassi Peninsula, where the conflicts associated with fishing have been subsumed under the general controversy surrounding the ownership of the oil-rich area. There are four major rivers that drain into Nigeria's Cross River estuary. These are the Cross River itself, the Calabar River, the Kwa River, and the Akwa Yafe River. The estuary gives access to Calabar, a large Nigerian city, where the country also has one of its major naval bases. This has affected fishing in the region. A similar problem may be in the pipeline for Uganda, especially as Lake Victoria is envisaged to play a major role for the transportation of Uganda's oil. On the whole, among the key issues that are likely to affect fishing in the near future are overgrowth of hyacinth, pollution, industrial harvesting and over-fishing, wrong fishing methods, population growth, and rapid urbanization. Some of these are also issues that have come to the fore of concern in the politics of dam construction.

With the economic hardship being experienced in many local communities across the continent, it is likely that water resources will be a major cause of conflict in the years ahead. The established dominance of internal fishing companies is likely to attract opposition from local fishermen, while unintentional trespassing will continue to affect relations between countries where local fishermen do not appreciate their limits in international boundaries. But as countries across the continent continue to brace themselves for the diverse implications of these, also important are the affairs of states in the politics surrounding dam constructions.

Dam Construction, Dam Management, and Conflict

Across Africa, dam construction has been linked to conflict in three major ways. First, there are consequences arising from people displaced in the process of construction; second, there are environmental problems that come with the construction; and third, there are politics involved in the management of dams after their construction. Table 6.7 shows the displaced population in the construction of some of Africa's dams. Although most of the dams in Africa were completed shortly after independence, there were also cases in which dam construction created tensions and conflicts during the last decade of the twentieth century. In these cases, the disputes have centered mainly on the displacement of people for the projects and, in some cases, conflict between states over the management of the rivers to be dammed and disagreements over the management of the dams. The internal disputes arising from dislocation have complex ramifications. Before the construction of these dams, the rivers were often the lifelines of the people living within the river plains, with culture, tradition, and occupation woven around them. Many of the people have lived their lives as fishermen and farmers. With the construction of the dams, however, this natural order was shattered, with the alteration to the natural flow of the rivers affecting the inhabitants, animals, and fishes.

Table 6.7 Displaced population from dam construction

Dam	Countries	Number of displaced people
Aswan	Egypt and Sudan	120,000
Akosombo	Ghana	80,000
Kossou	Côte d'Ivoire	75,000
Kariba	Zambia, Zimbabwe	50–57,000
Kainji	Nigeria	42–50, 000
Ruzizi	DRC, Rwanda	12,000
Manantali	Mali	10,000

Source: Extracted from Peter Gleick, ed., *Water in Crisis: A Guide to the World's Fresh Water Resources* (New York: Oxford University Press, 1993).

An example of this is the Shiroro Dam, commissioned in Nigeria in May 1990. This dam was located at the confluence of rivers Niger and Dinya, and it has four generating units and an installed capacity of 600 megawatts. Since the beginning of its operation, the irregular discharges from the station have caused its downstream channels to experience flooding during the rainy season. The upstream location, too, is threatened with impounded water, which invariably accumulates, causing backwash and spill over the farms and homesteads in the surrounding areas. Other complications that have been identified include sedimentation problems. The sediments, rich in plant nutrients, have led to the proliferation of water hyacinth, which, in turn, is known to provide habitats for poisonous water snakes. What has further compounded the problems for the communities here is that the other two dams in the country (Kainji and Jebba) are in the immediate vicinity. The victims are all the riverine areas of Niger, Kwara, Kogi, and Kebbi states of the country. It is difficult to get the exact figures for the problems suffered by the communities, but in 1999 alone, about two hundred villages in Niger State were submerged when excess water was released from the three hydro stations. In the same year, Kwara State recorded the submerging of 152 communities. A number of potential conflicts have been avoided in the management of dam construction along Lake Chad. A major dam, Kafin Zaki, under construction on the basin had to be suspended when it became clear that the negative impact far outweighed the possible benefits.

While these have not led to conflict, there are simmering tensions within these communities, such that the governors of all the affected states have come together to form the Hydroelectric Power Producing Areas Development Commission (HYPPADEC). In their maiden meeting in July 2000, the governors called on the Nigerian government to find an immediate and long-term solution to the problem and to release a significant amount of money as an initial sum for the resettlement of the affected communities. They also demanded 13 percent of total revenue of the National Electric Power Authority (NEPA) to enable them to cater for the need of the communities whose lands have been degraded, demanding also that the principle of derivation enshrined in the constitution be applied to hydroelectric power generation.

Conflict can also halt the construction of canals, as evidenced in the ways the activities of the SPLA in Sudan halted the construction of the Jonglei Canal in 1984. Indeed, the construction of the canal itself shows some of the ways by which the construction of dams and canals can be associated with conflict. The idea of the canal was conceived during the colonial era, but it became a practical reality in the early 1970s after Sudan had exhausted its allocation of the Nile River. Although an investigation team was created to look into the implications of the construction, not much respect was given to its findings. As it turned out, the construction fell into the politics of the country's north–south conflict, as the southern population objected to the construction on a number of grounds: first, the canal would affect livestock and wildlife activities in the region; second, the flooding that could come from the construction would necessitate the evacuation of many villages, especially during the raining season; third, it was speculated that the process of construction could result in the influx of hundreds of thousands of Egyptians, resulting in an "occupation" of the south by Egyptians.[57]

Also important in any discussion of dams and conflict are the ways in which dams have been destroyed or polluted in the course of conflict. While this experience may be a fairly common practice in many parts of the world, it is a relatively recent experience in Africa. Indeed, one of the earliest recorded cases was in the 1980s, when apartheid South Africa engaged in regular destruction of the Caborra Bassa Dam in Mozambique. RENAMO, the Mozambican dissident force, also made the dam a target of constant destruction. The only recorded case in the 1990s was in 1998, when there was an attack on Inga Dam during the effort to overthrow the late President Laurent Kabila of the DRC. But while the continent is getting used to some of the problems associated with dam construction, a somewhat new challenge is emerging in the continent, which has arisen as a result of water privatization.

Water Privatization and Conflict

While in theory the idea of water privatization is not an altogether new phenomenon in Africa,[58] the practice only began attracting attention in the last few years when there arose an increase in the number of countries moving in this direction. Also intertwined with the whole practice is the issue of energy privatization. Countries where water privatization has been undertaken include Cameroon, Chad, Djibouti, Egypt, Ghana, Kenya, Morocco, Mozambique, and South Africa. Other countries that are in the process of undertaking some form of privatization include Niger, Tanzania, Congo, and

Nigeria. Table 6.8 lists some of the countries that have undertaken water privatization in the continent. Although the primary motivation for this practice may vary from country to country, the pattern is the same: a private company is awarded a contract for a specific period of time to provide water for the

Table 6.8 Water privatization in Africa

Country started	Multinational corporation(s)	Contract type	Year
Côte d'Ivoire	SAUR (France)	Concession renewed every 15 years on negotiated basis	1960
Guinea	SAUR, EDF	Private company (SEEG) signed 10-year leasing contract	1989
CAR	SAUR	15-year leasing contract from 1991	1991
Mali	SAUR, EDF, HQI	4-year overall management contract	1994
Senegal	SAUR	SAUR has 51 percent of Senegalaise Des Eaux	1995
Guinea-Bissau	Suez-Lyonnaise, EDF	Management contract	1995
South Africa	Suez-Lyonnaise	Queenstown and Fort Belfort	1995
Gabon	Vivendi, ESBI	20-year concession	1997
Morocco	Electricidade de Portuga, Pleida, Dragados, and Construcciones (Spain)	30-year distribution concession	1998
South Africa	SAUR	30-year concession, Dolphin Coast	1999
South Africa	Biwater/Nuon	30-year service contract, Nelspruit	1999
Mozambique	SAUR	15 years for Maputo and Matola and 5 years for other cities	1999
Kenya	Vivendi	10-year contract for Nairobi for water billing and revenue management	1999
Chad	Vivendi	30-year management contract	2000
Cameroon	Suez Lyonnaise	20-year concession national	2000

Source: Extracted from Kate Bayliss, "Water Privatisation in Africa: Lessons from Three Case Studies," http://www.psiru.org/reports/2002-05-W-Africases.doc.

population, with the latter being asked to pay for the service rendered. What has been used to justify this is that for services to be effective, they have to be privatized. But what seems to be common in almost all cases is the encouragement that has come for such practice from the World Bank and other financial institutions. For the purpose of any discussion of the linkage between natural resources and conflict, this tendency has brought water in line with other natural resources. Before the issue of water privatization, what distinguished water from other resources in terms of the linkage with conflict was that it gave the most minimal opportunity for elite ownership as water was, hitherto, often owned and controlled by governments and/or communities. With the emergence of water privatization, this resource too entered, even if in a less significant way as yet, the whole arena of elite manipulation.

Indications have linked the practice of water privatization to conflict along several lines, three of which are particularly important. The first is the widely held assumption of its non-compatibility with African traditional belief about water, which is that water is one natural resource that is free. The efforts to control waterborne diseases and a number of other considerations have made governments across the continent deeply involved in provision of water for the population. It has thus become difficult for governments to turn around and say that water has become a service for which payment will be extracted from the population. The perception of the majority of the population that has already been deeply affected by the effects of the Structural Adjustment Program will be that water, which is crucial to existence, is again to be made the exclusive preserve of the rich. For example, under the privatization exercise in Kenya, the inhabitants of Nairobi will have to pay a total of US$25.3 million in ten years for water under the scheme to transfer water billing and revenue collection from the city council to Sereuca Space of France. This represents a 40 percent increase over the current tariffs.[59] Some companies have withdrawn from the project because they realized that the cost will be difficult for the population to afford.[60]

The second concern is the prospect of job loss. Populations across Africa have associated the process of water privatization to the prospect of job loss. For example, the exercise in Nairobi mentioned above will lead to a loss of about 3,500 jobs. Other countries have varying figures of expected job losses as a result of the privatization process. Populations are also worried that the loss of jobs is not likely to be marked by any efficiency in the services to be delivered.

Third, there are allegations of corruption that now seem to cover the process across the continent. It has been alleged that in many of the cases that there were no tenders, and companies were selected after questionable financial transactions allegedly took place between the companies and the political elites in affected African states. To cite some specific examples, it was reported that the water contracts awarded to Vivendi in Chad and Kenya were made without any financial details of the agreement. Also in Uganda, the energy

minister, Richard Kaijuka, was forced to resign after he was accused of accept-
ing a bribe in a water privatization arrangement that would have made the
country give priority to a business interest.[61] Again, in Lesotho, a number of
water and energy multinational corporations were prosecuted for bribery.[62]
Attendant on this are the criticisms across the continent that the process of
water privatization was often done without consultation with the population.

Two countries where there are coordinated responses to the efforts to
privatize water are Ghana and South Africa. In Ghana, a Coalition against
Privatization of Water (CAP) was formed in 2001. This is a broad-based coalition of individuals and civil society organizations, and it has five objectives: (1)
create a mass civil society campaign to stop the transfer of water supply to foreign multination corporations; (2) direct mass involvement in decisions about
water sector reform alternatives; (3) inclusion of public sector opinions in
water supply and overall restructuring of the water sector; (4) full public disclosure of all documents and details of transfer proposals, bids, and negotia-
tions; and (5) access to water for all Ghanaians, backed by statutory rights to
water by 2008. The organization also accused Britain of holding back aid
money meant for Ghana until the process of privatization in complete.[63] In
the organization's struggle for the above objectives, it has received the support of a number of international NGOs, including Christian Aid, which has
been quite vocal in its condemnation of the World Bank, IMF, and the UK's
Department for International Development (DFID) for using a carrot-and-
stick policy to browbeat the Ghanaian government into conformity.

South Africa, coming out of the apartheid experience and ever so sensitive
to any form of discrimination, has also taken active steps to ensure that water
privatization is not allowed in the country. In this country, too, a coalition
against water privatization was formed in 2003, demanding a reversal of the
government's policy of privatizing water.

The United Nations, Regional Organizations, and the Management of Conflicts over Water

Largely because the main actors involved in possible water conflicts are nation-
states, attempts to address many of the complications involved in the natural
resource have been spearheaded by international organizations. For Africa,
most of the issues surrounding water have been managed by the United
Nations and subregional organizations. The United Nations has recognized
the vital importance of the linkage between water and conflict. Specifically, the
organization has shown keen interest in managing conflicts and potential conflicts among states sharing river borders. It has, however, been difficult to have
enforceable laws to govern shared watercourses. Indeed, the existing international
laws are of very limited use. Key concepts in the law are implicitly contradictory.

For example, while the law recognizes what it calls "prior appropriation," which technically gives recognition to the state that mobilizes the water previously, it also calls for the respect of riparian rights, which respect the rights of other sovereign nations through which a river passes.[64]

In 1970, the United Nations General Assembly passed a resolution calling for the clarification of the laws applicable to non-navigable uses of international waterways. This led the United Nations International Law Commission (ILC) to come up with a set of "Rules on the Non-Navigational Use of International Watercourse." These rules are intended to provide clear principles that can be applied to specific river basins, and they give clear priority to the principle of equitable and reasonable use. Other actions were to follow. In 1977, there was the Mar del Plata Action Plan, which served as a guiding policy document for more than two decades. In 1992, there was an international conference on water and the environment, organized by the World Meteorological Organization in Dublin, Ireland, while water issues were also raised at the UN Conference on the Environment and Development in Rio de Janeiro, Brazil, in the same year.

Apart from resolutions and conferences, agencies of the United Nations have provided support in the area of scientific research. For example, as early as 1965 UNESCO had started undertaking research into the management of international freshwater systems. Further scientific research undertaken by UNESCO's International Hydrological Decade (IHD) has "helped to improve knowledge about the world's major river systems."[65] Another UN agency that has taken prominent interest in Africa's water conflict is the United Nations Environmental Program (UNEP), which assisted in the formulation of an action plan for the Zambezi River. This plan was subsequently adopted by all the riparian states in 1987.

The UN's activities have been complemented by a number of regional organizations in the continent. Without doubt, the organization that has played the most important role in the management of water within its borders is the Southern African Development Community (SADC). In 1995, the SADC signed the Protocol on Shared Watercourses.[66] This was revised and signed by SADC leaders in 2000. The goals of the protocol include:

- harmonization of national water plans in order to develop a basin-wide plan;
- standardization of water-pricing policies to enable the implementation that water is an economic good;
- standardization of water-related legislation throughout the basin (water rights/permit issues, environmental protection, pollution and water quality standards according to the Helsinki Rules, the SADC Treaty, and Protocols);
- establishing procedures for the resolution of conflicts between riparian states;
- establishment of an inventory and database on the basin's resources and water utilization patterns from national databases;

- basin-wide unified monitoring and data collection system from the basin's database;
- reviewing strategies for the development of shared watercourse systems; and
- stimulating public awareness and participation in the development of the environment.

But apart from the protocol that governs all shared water resources among its members, specific rivers have attracted the interest of the SADC, and on these rivers, there have been special agreements to govern the management and reduce propensity for conflicts. Possibly because of the high number of SADC member states involved in its management, the river that has attracted the organization's greatest interest is the Zambezi. In 1987, the SADC adopted an action plan for the Zambezi River Basin (ZACPLAN), with the sole purpose of ensuring environmentally sound planning and management of the water and water-related resources.

Later in 2004, the eight countries formed the Zambezi River Commission (ZAMCOM). According to the SADC executive secretary, Prega Ramsamy, ZAMCOM will play a "critical role in ensuring balanced and harmonious development of the Zambezi Basin Water resources, with a view to preventing potential conflicts and ensuring adequate and effective benefit-sharing among all riparian states."[67] The functions of ZAMCOM include:

- collection, evaluation, and dissemination of data and information on the Zambezi watercourse for implementation of the agreement;
- promotion, coordination, and harmonization of the management and development of the water resources of the Zambezi watercourse;
- advise member states of the planning, management, utilization, development, protection, and conservation of the Zambezi River watercourse as well as on the role and position of the public with regard to such activities and the possible impact on social and cultural heritage matters;
- advise member states on necessary measures to avoid dispute and assist in the resolution of conflicts among members states with regards to the planning, management, utilization, development, protection, and conservation of the watercourse; and
- foster greater awareness among the inhabitants of the Zambezi watercourse of the equitable and reasonable utilization and the efficient management and sustainable development of the resource of the watercourse.[68]

But apart from these international organizations, other international agencies have been involved in the management of some of these rivers. For example, the Nile Basin Initiative has received considerable international support, especially from agencies such as the World Wildlife Foundation (WWF), World Bank, Rockefeller Foundation, Canadian CIDA, OECD, and a host of others.[69] However, as the *African Economist* has rightly observed, the effectiveness of the organizations' effort in resolving conflicts depends on the creation of institutions and procedures that allow for joint integrated management of water that crosses political boundaries. Other important components include the willingness of parties to cooperate, the involvement of high level decision makers, and the assured neutrality of a third-party with the capacity to offer financial assistance.

But apart from steps specifically directed to managing water-related conflicts, there are also several initiatives being undertaken to ensure better management of water resources. Most of these have focused on raising awareness on the importance of water for sustainable development and on raising additional resources for investment in the water sector. Three of these are particularly important. First, there is the African Water Vision and Framework for Actions, which envisages "an Africa where there is an equitable and sustainable use and management of water resources for poverty alleviation, socio-economic development, regional cooperation and environment."[70] To achieve this, the framework calls for strengthening governance of water resources, improving water knowledge, meeting urgent water needs, and strengthening the financial base for the desired water future.[71] The second initiative is the NEPAD Water Program, which stresses the importance of effective management of shared water river basins and meeting basic needs in water supply and sanitation. The third initiative is the African Water Facility. This effort aims to reduce poverty and promote sustainable development by expanding the capacity to access existing and future sources for the development of water resources.[72] Other initiatives include the African Ministerial Council on Water (AMCOW), the African Water Facility, and the UN Water African Forum. Many of these initiatives have received assistance from international development agencies working on water-related issues, including the USAID, Global Water Partnership, the Global Environmental Facility, and the UN Habitat.

Conclusion

While water may not have caused as many controversies as other natural resources discussed in this book, it is clearly certain that the years ahead will witness far more concern for the resource and, increasingly, the politics of its management is likely to dominate governance issues in Africa. Already, a number of countries in the continent have made clear their intention to go to war to protect their access to water supply; while in many others, key issues such as the privatization of water, the management of water resources, and displacement and other environmental considerations associated with dam construction are likely to be potential sources of conflict. The main argument advanced in this chapter is that the assumption that water conflicts are likely to remain "potential" rather than "real" is becoming a weak argument, and that like other natural resources, the role of governance and the influence of globalization, especially as this relates to the activities of multinational corporations and the international financial institutions, are quickly becoming crucial determinants of how water can be linked to conflict in Africa. I also argue that as many African countries are being forced by international financial institutions to privatize water, domestic and international opposition against the initiative is likely to increase the propensity for violence in many African countries, with sympathies coming from antiglobalization forces across the world. Consequently, the future stability in the management of conflicts surrounding water, as indeed, in the case of other natural resources, depends on how local and international efforts are made in the governance of the resource. It is thus against this background that the next chapter looks at the link between governance and conflicts over natural resources in Africa.

7

GOVERNANCE AND NATURAL RESOURCE CONFLICTS

When at creation God blessed Angola with abundant mineral wealth, other nations of the world complained at the favorable disposition towards the country; in response God told them: wait till you see their leaders.

An Angolan Anecdote

For a Commercial Company trying to make investment, you need a stable government. Dictatorship can give you that.

Emeka Achebe

Discussions in the preceding chapters have shown that recent conflicts over natural resources in Africa have raised a number of questions, two of which are particularly important. First, why has there been a prevalence of such a category of conflicts in Africa, as compared with other continents of the world? Second, why are some natural resources linked to conflicts in some countries and not in others; or put differently, what are the circumstances and/or political dispensation that can predispose a particular natural resource to become an issue of conflict? In seeking to provide answers to these questions, one is inevitably drawn into matters relating to governance. In this context, *governance* is defined very broadly as the socioeconomic and political management of state affairs, especially as this relates to the determination of who gets what, when, and through what process. It also involves the interplay of relationships among the different actors concerned with the politics of natural resource management.

The primary objective of this chapter is to situate discussions in the preceding chapters within the framework of governance. The central argument here is that most of the conflicts over natural resources in Africa are rooted in the absence, or considerable weakness, of the structures designed to manage natural resources, especially as they relate to the distribution of opportunities, privileges, fiscal management, revenue allocation, protection of minority rights, guaranteeing of property rights, and other considerations linked to resource management, and those parties that can adjudicate impartially in the disagreements emanating therefrom.

The State and the Citizens in Resource Management: The Changing Attitude in the Demand for Accountability

In Africa, the relationship between the state and the citizens on the issue of accountability in the management of natural resources has changed over time. Broadly, three phases can be identified. First, the period between independence and the 1970s, an era that can be described as that of "passive and understandable tolerance"; second, the period between 1980 and 1990, which can be described as the era of "violent accountability"; while the third was the post-1990 era, which can be labeled that of "civil accountability."

During the first era, the combination of euphoria of independence and the hangover from the colonial experience resulted in a situation where the citizens did not ask critical questions from the new leaders about the management of natural resources. Coming from a colonial experience in which governance was outside the direct scrutiny of the populace, and in which those in government were not accountable to the population in the management of natural resources, the broad section of the population was not so keen to scrutinize the activities of those in power. Arguments that the newly elected leaders needed time to settle in before their activities are critically examined by the populace were also advanced by the ruling elite to further reduce the oversight functions the population might want to exercise in the management of natural resources. By the time this argument began to wear thin, military dictatorship and autocratic one-party rule had emerged in many of the countries to stifle any form of criticisms that the populace would have wanted to muster against the mismanagement of their natural resources by the ruling elite. The initial passivity on the part of the populace may also have roots in the traditional African belief that demands respect to those holding leadership positions. In short, not much demand was placed on those holding leadership positions as to how natural resources were managed. The response of the ruling class to the lack of oversight interest of the populace was to exploit the opportunity to acquire a greater grip on the natural resources, such that by the end of the first decade of independence, the management of natural resources in many countries in Africa had become intertwined with corruption and lack of accountability. The political elite were able to equate governance with the control and exploitation of natural resources of the state. Key agricultural and mineral resources were brought under government control, through state-established "boards" and "corporations" that were established for the management of these resources. Although the background for this was laid during the colonial rule, the strings were tightened in the period immediately after independence. With these, all the structures for corruption were accomplished with the connivance of civil servants, whose role in the destruction of governance in many African countries is often ignored.[1]

The second phase commenced in the beginning of the 1980s, when segments of the population began to ask crucial questions about the political management of state affairs. Those who championed this call for genuine accountability in governance included academics, journalists, and other professionals. These critics also opposed the incursion of the military into political governance of some states. It was, however, not possible for this set of actors to change the attitude to governance for at least two reasons. First, the wider population did not see them as being representative enough, especially as some of their members were also parts of the governments they were opposing. Consequently, they could not carry a large proportion of the population along with them in their quest for a new order in resource management. Second, the wider international environment was still in support of the political order in many of the countries, with western countries propping up leaders such as the late President Mobutu Sese Seko of former Zaire.

It was during this phase, too, that attempts began to emerge to hold the governing elite directly responsible for the mismanagement of the natural resource endowment of the state. This came mainly from members of the armed forces, who, in forcefully overthrowing governments, cited natural resource mismanagement as one of the justifications for their action. The first such example was in Ghana, where former Flight Lieutenant Jerry Rawlings overthrew General Fred Akuffo in 1978. In this case, his government killed the immediate-past president and went further to kill most of the leaders who had ruled the country since independence for offenses allegedly committed against the state. Again, at the center of this allegation was the mismanagement of proceeds coming from the country's natural resource endowment. Also in 1981, the late Samuel Doe's coup in Liberia resulted in the public execution of all the key members of the ruling government of William Tolbert. Regardless of the justification for this course of action, one outcome of it was that it demystified political leadership in Africa in a somewhat negative way. Although leaders had been killed before in military coups, there had not been a mass execution of public officeholders in any part of the continent. Ghana was able to escape some of the most gruesome consequences of this action, largely because the military regime that carried out the mass killing was not late in handing over power to another elected administration, even if the leader eventually came back into power. Liberia, however, suffered the consequences, as the military coup was to be a major signpost in the events that resulted in its cataclysmic civil war.

While Liberia and Ghana represented cases in which erstwhile leaders were made to violently account for the mismanagement of the natural resource endowments of their countries, Nigeria presented a slightly different case.

After the December 1983 military coup against the Shagari administration, Special Military Tribunals were established to try members of the former civilian administration for corruption, and in most of their verdicts, long jail terms were handed down to those found guilty. In a number of other countries, organized rebellion against the leadership resulted in the forceful removal of leaders who were alleged to have corruptly managed their country's natural resources. This was the case in countries such as Uganda and Ethiopia, where popular rebellion drove out leaders considered to be corrupt.

With the coming of the 1990 decade, the attitude of the population as to what is expected from those in charge of governance entered what may be described as a third phase. This phase is interlinked with the concept of "good-governance" that subsequently became the dominant theme in Africa during the period. An amalgam of actors, often working at cross-purposes, was responsible for this shift in the attitude to governance. These include those neglected in the political order who had prevailed since independence, international financial institutions, civil society, and others. The outcome was the emergence of a new political order that gave room for greater participation of the general population in the process of governance.

The emergence of this order has at least two major implications for accountability in the management of natural resources. First, it resulted in the rise of groups raising questions about the management and control of natural resources. Second, a new approach emerged in the attempt to hold past leaders accountable for their management of the country's natural resources. Under this new phase, some countries recalled previous political officeholders to explain the mismanagement of the country's natural resources. This, for example, was the case in Zambia, where the former president Frederick Chiluba was charged in court for mismanaging proceeds from the country's natural resource endowment. Attempts to recover money from deposed political leaders became issues for an international legal tussle, as in the case of the efforts by the Obasanjo administration in Nigeria to recover money kept in foreign banks by the late head of state, Sanni Abacha. This phase also witnessed outside efforts to exert pressures on African leaders, with pressures coming from sources such as the Commonwealth and other organizations demanding accountability from elected leaders.

Thus, by the end of the 1990s, attempts to classify governance and conflicts over natural resources in Africa would bring the countries into three broad groups. First are those in which the structures of governance collapsed completely as a result of conflicts having a major bearing on natural resources, such as Sierra Leone, Liberia, and DRC. These are states often categorized as "failed states." Second are the conflicts, with a bearing on natural resources, that have dominated the attention of the states, and where a significant attention of the state had to be devoted to managing protests and revolts coming from restive sections of the population. These could be categorized as "wounded states," and under this broad heading is a country such as Sudan. Third are those cases in which conflicts over natural resources are merely between different ethnic groups, with minimal or no threat to the authority of the central government. These states can be described as relatively "stable states." Regardless of the category to which a state belongs, however, "governance" has been a key factor in the precipitation of conflicts over natural resources.

Governance and the Precipitation of Conflicts over Natural Resources

Drawing from the discussions in the preceding chapters, two issues link governance to the causes of conflicts involving natural resources: first is the role of national constitutions, which, at least in theory, is meant to guide governance activities; and second is the activity of the ruling political elites, whose responsibility it is to administer the proceeds from these natural resources according to the provisions of the constitution. A discussion of how these two have separately and jointly accounted for the precipitation of conflicts over natural resources in Africa is presented below.

Role of National Constitutions

In broad terms, there are two ways through which constitutions can be linked to the causes of conflict over natural resources. The first is the process through which the constitution came into existence in the first instance, especially the extent of popular participation in the process of constitution making. This will determine the extent of its recognition and acceptance, including the respect the judiciary will command in its effort to correctly interpret the law and in adjudicating on disputes relating to natural resource management. The general impression across the continent is that the independence constitutions of African countries were a coexistence of compromises between the desire of the outgoing colonialists and the incoming political elite. Consequently, in the last decade or so, many African countries have had reasons to review their postindependent constitutions to reflect changing realities. The processes of constitutional review in recent years have, however, been diverse, leading to the identification of eight different ways through which the process of constitutional reform has manifested.[2]

- Constitutional conferences, with full sovereign powers, as in Benin Republic
- Constitutional conferences sponsored by, and packed with, agents of the state, as in Mobutu's Zaire
- Constituent assemblies packed with nominated representatives and persons elected under questionable circumstances, as in Abacha's Nigeria

- Constitutional review commissions with terms of reference designed and determined by the state and aimed at reaching conclusions favorable to the state, as in Tanzania
- Constitutional commissions with clear efforts to tinker with the constitutions in a way designed to deal with specific problems and political "enemies" of the president, as in Chiluba's Zambia
- Constitutional amendments that seek to re-establish state legitimacy while actually strengthening it vis-à-vis civil society, as in the case of Algeria
- Tentative but carefully programmed and very slow concessions to constitutional reforms aimed at making no concrete changes in the constitutional compacts, as in Moi's Kenya
- Constitutional processes designed to bring about a new constitutional contract between the state and the people based on past experiences and aimed at a new political environment to promote democracy and democratic values as in Eritrea, Ethiopia, Uganda, Ghana, and South Africa

When constitution making is linked to conflicts over natural resources in Africa, it would be discerned that in situations where the constitution-making process is not sufficiently representative, the tendency for conflicts over natural resources is significantly increased. It is indeed no coincidence that all the countries where natural resource conflicts have been at the roots of "state collapse" are those with no popularly compacted constitutions. For example, Liberia's constitution was modified under the administration of President Doe, but despite the efforts of the review team to put in place people-oriented structures, the government ensured that certain clauses that guaranteed elite domination were included.[3] That constitution remained in force throughout the reign of office of former President Charles Taylor. The fact that Taylor retained the constitution he had spent almost a decade fighting, confirms that ruling elite would retain any constitution that offered them opportunity to make the most personal benefit of the natural resource endowment of their country, regardless of their objections during the course of a popular struggle. The Zairian constitution under Mobutu was one that clearly covered despotic powers of the leader. Even in cases in which controversies over natural resources have been at the forefront of national politics in such countries as Nigeria, Sudan, and Zimbabwe, the pattern has been the same. In Nigeria, with the exception of the 1963 constitution, all other constitutions are creations of the military, and the persistent calls for a Sovereign National Conference (SNC) to discuss, among other things, a workable constitution for the country, have been ignored.[4] Until the recent peace agreement, Sudan's constitution was only recognized by a section of the country, while that of Zimbabwe has been criticized as being manipulated in ways that have given the incumbent leadership near-autocratic powers.

The other way through which national constitutions become a factor in natural resource conflicts relates to what the constitution says (or does not say) on key issues relevant to the control and management of natural resources, especially as this relates to the ownership, management, and control of natural resources. There are some key subject areas on which there is need for constitutional clarity, if conflicts are to be avoided over natural resources; five of these are particularly important. The first is on the crucial issue of revenue allocation. As shown in the preceding chapters, constitutional stipulations on revenue allocation have become crucial in natural resource conflicts, especially in those countries where the particular natural resource that is vital to the national economy comes mainly from a particular section of the country. The natural resources that are particularly crucial here are mineral resources, such as oil, diamonds, and gold. Often at the root of the conflict is what percentage of the accruing revenue should go to the producing communities. While most constitutions stipulate a particular percentage, controversies have often emerged over three issues: complaints from resource-producing communities that the percentage allocated under the constitution is small and unacceptable; claims that there is a wide disparity between the percentage provided for in the constitution and the amount that actually gets to the producing communities; and allegations of corruption against the officials of the different administrative organs set up by the government to manage the disbursement of the revenue. The ultimate outcome is the creation of a disenchanted and aggrieved population that is prepared to take up arms against the central government. This has been at the roots of the conflicts relating to oil in Nigeria and Sudan.[5] It is also a crucial factor in explaining aspects of the conflict in Sierra Leone.

The treatment meted to minority groups constitutes the second way through which the stipulations of the constitution become linked with conflict. Again, while constitutions across Africa have clauses that recognize the rights of minority groups, these are often frustrated by other constitutional stipulations or ad hoc policies of the government. Consequently, even though constitutions make claim to equality of all groups, the reality is often different, and across the countries, there are numerous evidences of minority groups being oppressed and intimidated in the management of natural resources. This cuts across many issue areas, ranging from the ethnic communities in Niger Delta of Nigeria to white commercial farmers in Zimbabwe. A layer of minority group who is often ignored in most politics of resource management are those who can be described as a "professional minority." Their profession or the way they go about it places them into the category of minorities within their communities, as in the case of pastoralists. Again, constitutions across the continent recognize the equality of all citizens, regardless of professional affiliation. The reality has, however, been different. Indeed, beyond platitudinous promises that all minority groups are to be respected, there are no specific guarantees for those considered a professional minority. In the context of the conflicts surrounding natural resources, this explains the incessant conflicts involving pastoralist groups. As shown in chapter 3, governments across Africa have unfavorable impressions about pastoralist groups, a view that is motivated as much by the perception of the group to a number of social issues as their being a professional minority vis-à-vis the rival farming community.

The third subject area is the nature of the judiciary. The links among governance, judicial system, and conflicts over natural resources come in three main ways. The first way is the issue of the independence of the judiciary. Again, while constitutions across Africa recognize the independence of the judiciary, the reality is often different, as there have been many cases of interference from the executive. Consequently, the citizens' suspicion that they will not get fair hearings in disagreements involving natural resources has underlined many conflicts over these resources. The second way relates to the role of governments in establishing ad hoc mechanisms to address issues pertaining to natural resources. Across the continent, governments are known to have instituted ad hoc institutions, such as Commissions of Inquiry, Management Commissions, and Adjudication Panels, to manage issues relating to natural resources.[6] More often than not, these institutions do not have a constitutional basis and populations across many of the affected countries believe that the commissions are set up to sidetrack constitutions. Indeed, unpopular decisions that would be difficult to pass through the law courts have been known to pass through such ad hoc institutions, such as in the "trial" of Ken Saro Wiwa and other activists in Nigeria.[7] The final way is the deliberate act of some governments to intimidate the judiciary, especially on issues relating to natural resource governance. Perhaps a most recent example of this tendency is in Zimbabwe, where the judiciary is alleging interference from the government. The resignation of the former chief justice, Anthony Gubbay, and four of his five colleagues in 2001 is indicative of the downward plunge of governance in the country and the helplessness of the judiciary to resolve conflicts that have much bearing on resource management. Referring to the legal challenges to his seizure of farms, Mugabe declared: "Courts can do whatever they want but no judicial decision will stand in our way. They are not courts for our people and we shall not be defending ourselves in these courts."[8] The Legal Reform Foundation of Zimbabwe was to confirm later that "the professionalism and independence of all the legal system have been severely compromised."[9] With the weakness of the judiciary, a main pillar in ensuring harmony in resource management seems to have been destroyed.

The fourth subject area is the role and use of the armed forces. Like the judiciary, there are differences in statutory role and the actual use of the armed forces across Africa. While all constitutions declare that armed forces are to protect the territorial integrity of the nation, realities in many of the countries show that armed forces are being used to suppress dissent, especially on issues relating to the exploitation of natural resources. The incessant use of the Nigerian Army to suppress protests in the Niger Delta is an example.

Also worth mentioning is the politics that often surrounds the use of national armies in external engagement, and the constitutional implications this raises. As highlighted in chapter 4, this has been a crucial issue in explaining the complexities of the conflicts in the Democratic Republic of Congo. The issues that come to the fore here include: Who determines the decision to dispatch the force? Who determines the terms of engagement, especially in cases where there are gross violations of human rights or the illegal transactions involving natural resources? Who determines the extent of involvement within the international community? Even in cases in which there seems to be a quasi-legal endorsement of the intervention, as in the case of ECO-MOG activities in Liberia and Sierra Leone, these issues still arose, especially because there were often major gaps between the mandate issued and the actual activities of the military forces.

Another consideration under the broad discussion on the role of national armies is the constitutional provisions on irregular and ad hoc military forces, and what should be their relationship with the state. Viewed from the perspective of natural resource politics, other armed "forces" whose activities have received the implicit endorsement of the state can be grouped into four: irregular forces, such as in the case of Kamajors in Sierra Leone; ethno-political militias, such as the Odua People's Congress (OPC) and Egbesu Boys in Nigeria; mercenary groups, such as the Executive Outcome and Sandlines in Sierra Leone; and the security wings of multinational corporations. While countries across the continent have related with and sometimes exchanged security details with all these security outfits, there are no constitutional provisions for the existence of the forces. Thus, the fact that governments have related and cooperated with them indicates the apparent weakness of the security apparatus of the country to meet national security demands and has further underlined the complexities of the issues involving the management of natural resources in the continent.

The final subject area focuses on the crucial topic of citizenship. Virtually all constitutions have a definition of who is a "citizen," and broadly, all constitutions have provisions for the acquisition of citizenship by non-nationals. Indeed, with the exception of Liberia where the constitution states clearly that only people of Negro descent can be citizens of the country, all other African countries are flexible on the issue of citizenship, with some countries also permitting dual nationality. However, a number of issues have brought citizenship to the fore of resource conflicts. The first is that attainment of citizenship status often comes without the claims to local resources. Consequently, it is possible to be a legal citizen of a country without deep-rooted local claims to operate as such. Another issue is the overriding effect of charters of regional organizations on national constitutions over the rights of citizens of other countries. While the charter of regional organizations cannot force the definition of citizenship on any nation, there have been cases in which freedom of movement and settlement across regional boundaries have allowed foreigners to partake in enterprises that have been linked to conflicts over natural resources. This has been a major issue in explaining conflicts in Côte d'Ivoire. Apart from the citizenship question involving Alassanne Quattara,[10] many other West Africans who have been involved in cocoa plantations in the country were affected when labor considerations became key factors in the country's civil war.

Role of Power Elites

How power elites have managed natural resources has always been a major issue in most discussions over natural resource governance in Africa. It is what underlines, to a large extent, the "greed" thesis in the evaluation of the cause of conflicts over natural resources in Africa. Although the desire by political leaders to personally benefit from natural resources seems to be the most important and most publicized consideration, there are also a number of ways in which power elites have, sometimes unwittingly taken steps that have resulted in conflicts over natural resources.

A feature that is common in Africa is that the control of natural resources is almost exclusively under the government, with the exception of agricultural production at the subsistence level. Because of this tight control, the population has realized that the only way through which they can benefit directly from natural resources is through activities such as illegal oil bunkering and illegal artisanal trading in mineral resources. While average citizens do not engage in bunkering, as it requires considerable financial capital, they have made themselves available to those who have used them for such illegal activities. This is to be of crucial consideration in the politics of local claim and national interest discussed later in this chapter.

From the discussions in the preceding chapters, it will not be too difficult to conclude that the elites in power across Africa have been dishonest in their management of the natural resources of their countries. While for a long time evidences of fiscal recklessness and corrupt management of natural resources by the political elite have been largely anecdotal, there is now evidence to back up many of these claims. The arrest of an elected governor of one of Nigeria's oil-producing states, Diepreye Alamieyeseigha, for money laundering shows that there are clear cases of fraud and mismanagement of revenues coming from natural resources.

Manifestations of Governance Issues in Specific Natural Resources

Different natural resources raise different governance issues, and each highlights different weaknesses in the structures of governance in Africa. In this section, there is a discussion of the key issues each of the natural resource categorizations in this book (land, solid minerals, oil, and water) raise for governance.

In sub-Saharan Africa, land is a natural resource that has the most exhibited links with governance. This is because of the importance of the resource to the socioeconomic and political life of the people. Broadly, the management of land has four major implications for governance issues. First, the general nature of land tenure systems in Africa, which, as noted earlier in chapter 3, involves the coexistence of three different systems—traditional, western, and sometimes religious—without a clear structure of how these systems can coexist in societies that have different levels of appreciation for each of these systems, and the determination of the ruling elite to maintain grip over land in their bid to hold on to power and ensure the control of land and other resources embedded in it. The confusing system of land tenure has sometimes resulted in situations where people may have "legal" claim to land without having the "social" claim to work on it. This, as shown in chapter 3, has been at the roots of many conflicts in the continent.

The second implication is the weakness often demonstrated by the judiciary in many of these countries in arbitrating cases relating to land, both between communities and between communities and governments. The population no longer believes in the independence of the judiciary on matters relating to land, especially as judges have been known to be corrupt and often suffer intimidation by the executives. Indeed, the corruption of the judiciary has been a key issue that has been widely discussed in many African countries. For example, in a national survey conducted by the inspectorate of government in Uganda in 1998, the judiciary was ranked the second most corrupt institution in the country. While 63 percent of the 18,412 households surveyed claimed they had paid bribes to the police, 50 percent of respondents confirmed they had bribed the courts.[11] In Kenya, too, corruption in the judiciary has been a major concern and there are efforts now to remove corruption from the institution.[12] But apart from corruption, the attempts by governments to establish ad hoc mechanisms for handling conflicts over land, especially through institutions such as Land Review Commissions, have weakened the ability of the judiciary to handle the problems and further given room for elite interference in land management.

The third implication is the way through which governments of African countries have related with foreign multinational companies on land matters. At the heart of the consideration is the way in which land is often allocated to these companies without due consideration to local claims. Although the constitutions of many of the countries provide conditions under which land can be acquired by governments, namely, overriding public interests, there are still procedures that should be followed. However, efforts to encourage multinational companies to come to Africa and "assist" in development initiatives have, especially in recent times, made governments across the continent ignore these procedures. As noted from examples in chapter 3, this has been at the root of many conflicts across the continent.

The fourth implication is the peculiar "governance" issues raised by countries that inherited specific land problems, particularly Zimbabwe, Namibia, and South Africa. It is the case that the extent to which these countries considered the implications of the compromise they reached for their independence on land is limited. While land was an issue during the wars of liberation, it became a slightly lesser factor in the negotiation for independence. The nature of transition in these countries was such that political independence was considered the ultimate desire, with other attendant issues delayed for subsequent years. It was inevitable that not long after independence, land came to the fore of controversy. However, it is also worthy of note that the extent to which land played a major role in these countries has been determined by the local political situation and the extent to which political elites were willing to use it as a diversionary tactic from other contentious domestic issues. This, to a large extent at least, explains why land was such a major issue in Zimbabwe and not in other countries such as Namibia and South Africa. With relevant structures in place to address issues such as property rights and indigenization policy, it would have been possible to handle key issues such as the amount of land to be taken from the minority whites; the process through which the land is to be taken; how it is to be distributed; and who is to pay necessary compensation for the acquisition.

The link between solid minerals and conflict has also shown clear indications in the problem of governance in Africa. Again, at least four of these are particularly important. The first indication is the weakness or, in some cases, the refusal, of governments to exercise oversight abilities on the numerous interest groups involved in solid mineral extraction. This has manifested both in the financial activities of these interest groups and even in the technical processes of the extraction. Specifically, foreign multinational companies and foreign nationals have exploited this opportunity to further erode the powers of governments across the solid minerals producing countries. In several cases, political elites have connived with foreigners to cheat the state out of proceeds from mineral extraction. Second, the emergence of some of the actors in the conflicts surrounding solid minerals, especially actors such as warlords and mercenaries, shows extreme weakness in the governance structures in the affected countries. The fact, too, that some of these actors are sometimes invited by the government or have had to operate as near-equal partners with governments shows that the capacity of the government to discharge some of the basic duties of governance has been eroded. Third, there are often no policies to cater for the interests of the local communities from where these resources are extracted. Furthermore, there are often no specific policies to address the environmental concerns of these communities and where this exists they are not respected. Fourth, the policy of management of the resources in many of the countries appears confused, especially as this relates to issues such as management of proceeds and the activities of artisan operators. Again, while efforts are being made to address these, there are also groups that are determined to frustrate the minimal efforts being made by governments.

Oil conflicts have shown some of the same indications of governance failure as solid minerals show. As highlighted in chapter 5, oil is crucial to governance because of its dominating effect on the economy of the state. Indeed, there is almost an unwritten rule that where there is a total dependence on a particular natural resource, the ability of the government to relate on equal footing with the multinational corporation involved in the extraction is weakened. This is because the future of the government and that of the company is linked, and everything is done to ensure the strengthening of the mutually beneficial nature of the relationship. The victims in this case are often the local producing communities. The determination to make as much profit as possible underlies why many oil companies, despite serious security problems, continue exploration in these communities. In the case of Nigeria, for example, it explains why Shell, despite the advice from its own consultants to leave the country, has remained rooted in the country.[13]

Perhaps the most pronounced governance issue raised by oil is the level of graft in the management of the resource, which is present in varying degrees in most of the oil-producing countries. The corruption has been possible because of the convergence of interests of the three main actors in the oil extraction business: the government, the oil multinational corporations, and the local power elite. Increasingly, the protests from the oil-producing communities are making the alliance between these groups of actors difficult to sustain, and divisions between them are becoming more glaring.

Also important in any discussion on how oil and governance intertwine in the conflict equation is the near-autonomous status that oil multinational companies enjoy in some African oil-producing states and the potential impact of this in some of these oil-producing communities. Unlike other natural resources, multinational corporations involved in oil exploration have a "more permanent" concept of their stay in the host nations. Many of these companies live in communities that are constructed to provide facilities that are comparable with life in Western European capitals, with special schools for their children and a constant supply of electricity, water, and other services. Although initially planned for expatriate staff, many Africans have joined this elite class and have become some of the most vociferous supporters of the activities of these companies. One unintended consequence of this is that it shows the deprived population in the oil-producing communities that oil resources can provide this level of impressive comfort for them too if the resource is well managed.

Nigeria dominates most discussion linking oil, governance, and conflict in Africa, especially as these relate to corruption, the nature of fiscal federalism, the absence of clear environmental standards for exploration, acrimonious intergroup relations, disregard for minority interest, and the lack of oversight on the activities of foreign multinational corporations. What is at the root of the problem with Nigeria's oil management is the presence of many people intent on benefiting illegally from the system at various ministries, national and state assemblies, the refineries, and in the sprawling parastatals of government. While there is definitely corruption in the management of the oil in other African countries, especially Equatorial Guinea, Angola, Gabon, and Sudan, the scale is nothing comparable with Nigeria's.

Conflicts surrounding water are of a very different classification vis-à-vis governance. As noted in chapter 6, the politics of water control raises minimal consideration for elite greed, as water has offered little or no consideration for individual ownership, although this seems to be changing with ongoing exercises in some of the countries to privatize water services. This explains why there have been very few conflicts over water, despite the celebrated claims that the next round of conflicts would be over water. The relative ease with which governments have been able to address the multiple issues associated with the management of international rivers has shown that on issues in which the personal interests of elites are not at stake, reaching some form of understanding in conflicts involving natural resources can be easier. The underlining implications of some of the issues raised by this argument will be further illuminated in the discussion of the role of warlords in conflicts involving natural resources.

The Politics of Warlord Governance

Warlords have introduced complexities into governance, and most of these have been linked to the politics of natural resource management. Without going into the wide array of studies on warlord politics, this section examines aspects of their activities as they relate to governance and natural resource management in recent African conflicts. Perhaps some conceptual considerations may be necessary in the form of a preface. It is almost certain that Mark Duffield has natural resource consideration in mind when he defines the warlord phenomenon as

the appearance of local strongmen able to control an area and exploit its resource and people while, at the same time, keeping a weak central authority at bay. Apart from the control of the territory, which is often of a fluid character, a factor to emphasize about modern warlords is the linkage that they forge with international economy. Today, successful warlords act locally but think globally.

Central to the activities of warlords in periods of national emergencies are three basic factors: the management of human and natural resources in ways that will further entrench the disorder of the central government while simultaneously strengthening their own power base and ensuring cohesion among their members; the establishment of strong subregional connections to ensure the marketing of natural resources that sometimes need the official "state" label to sell in the international market; and the creation of administrative structures that are just strong enough to ensure continued loyalty of the troops and offer some form of stability.

Perhaps more important than all this, however, is the specific focus on which the warlords intend to put their strategies. Indeed, it is not all warlords who aspire to put in place structures to ensure political or economic governance. This, for example, is the case of all the warlords who have managed the rebellion in northern Uganda. What seems to be the most important factor that has to be attained before structures of governance can be put in place is a clear control of specific geographical territory within the country. Unlike other warlords in Africa, successive warlords in northern Uganda never held control of any part of the territory, even if they were able to intimidate sections of the country. In this circumstance, the establishment of structures of governance that can ensure the management of natural resources is difficult. Perhaps a second reason, too, is the absence of key natural resources in northern Uganda that can fetch any rebel group significant financial return.

Warlords who have tried to establish structures for economic governance have also realized that the nature of the international system still places limitations on their operations, and all of them have had to operate through sovereign countries that serve as conduit pipes, especially to sell certain categories of natural resources and procure weapons for prosecuting their respective wars. These countries also assist in putting in place paraphernalia of government for some of these warlords. While the most convenient practice for the warlords has been to use neighboring countries, as Charles Taylor of Liberia and Foday Sankoh of Sierra Leone did in Côte d'Ivoire and Liberia, respectively, Jonas Savimbi of Angola's UNITA usage of far away countries such as Togo and Burkina Faso showed that the importance of the natural resource in question takes precedence over geographical proximity. During the conflicts in these countries, the warlords established structures to manage these resources in ways that maximum benefits would come from the resources. For example, Savimbi had a "ministry" that handled the sales of mineral resources in the portion of Angola that was under his control, while during the 1989–92 civil war in Liberia, Charles Taylor had administrative structures that managed these natural resources.

Recent experiences have, however, shown there are difficulties that can confront warlords-turned-presidents, especially those relating to the manipulation of initial populism that sustained the rebellion. Charles Taylor's experience reflects this. While he exploited the tyranny of the late Samuel Doe to launch a popular rebellion, he failed to realize that this could only be sustained if he met the expectation of the population and managed their natural resource endowments properly. Indeed, the story of Taylor confirms all that is wrong with African elite in the management of natural resource endowment. He made his initial wealth from misappropriating funds from the country's procurement agency, of which he was manager under Doe. In pursuing the war, he exploited the natural resources under his control and was, in the process, able to establish a network of subregional links that exploited and marketed natural resources for the rebel groups. The wealth and prestige this brought him, to a large extent, made it possible for him to win the election. However, after he became the president he realized that, while he was able to go beyond legal boundaries as a rebel leader, the options open to him as a president were limited. Consequently, his efforts to ensure the continued supply of money from the managing of regional natural resources, brought him into conflict with international law, resulting in his indictment by the International Court in Sierra Leone, while his inability to meet domestic needs and to provide a system of governance that would heal wounds resulted in the organization and successful launching of a rebellion against him.

Also related to the discussion is the irony that comes in warlords' pursuit of political power through the control of resources. Many of them realize after assuming political power that this long sought-after position has severe limitations, and that some of the acts and practices they hitherto engaged in are no longer possible. This is due to the existence of at least a minimal level of accountability that comes with elective political power that is absent in warlord politics. Furthermore, elected officeholders have to consider international opinion in decisionmaking. They also have to consider ways of supporting state institutions and fulfilling domestic obligations. With the resources of the state now under this kind of strain and control, the ability of warlords-turned-presidents to maneuver is often reduced. This explains why former President Taylor of Liberia had to strike a balance between these conflicting tendencies. In the end, one of the reasons his authority was challenged by other rebel forces was his inability to officially manage the transition from a warlord to an elected leader.

Governance, Local Claims, National Interest, and International Enterprise

At the center of most conflicts over natural resources in Africa are the divergent views of the local "owners" of the resources, that is, the inhabitants of the resource-bearing land, the elite in government who determine what constitutes national interest, and the multinational corporations exploiting these resources. Discussions in this section cover two aspects: first, the dichotomy between local claim and national interest; and second, between local claim and international enterprise. The clash between local claim and national interest is rooted in the absence of clearly defined procedures of meeting local demands and the lack of input by the local population into what constitutes national interest. Before examining the ramifications of these conflicts, it is perhaps necessary to consider the divergence of views. Local populations base their claim first and foremost on the fact that the resource(s) in question are embedded in their soil and, as such, they have the right to be the main beneficiary on account of nativity. Often linked to this is the African traditional attachment to land, which perceives land and the resources underneath as endowment from God for the benefit of the society. While the people may be willing to share some of the benefits of these resources with other ethnic groups within the national boundaries, they are unequivocal in their demand for higher returns and privileges from these resources. A second basis of claim by a local population for better treatment is the argument that they suffered from the environmental and ecological damages resulting from the extraction of these resources. Because most of the resources at the base of the controversy are extractive, there are often environmental problems associated with the exploitation, and the local population thus claims they should be given better treatment in the benefit of the resources.

National interest is a more nebulous term, especially when considered in the context of resource politics in Africa. This is because of the centrality of resources to governance and elite survival. Defined broadly, however, *national interest* is often taken as all issues considered central to the survival and well-being of a nation and the steps that are to be taken to protect these goals. In Africa, where there are fragile institutions, these goals are often those set by the elite, and consequently they serve the purposes of the ruling elites in perpetuating themselves in power and in the handling of the resource base that is needed to ensure the control of political power. The fluidity of what constitutes national interest has given the ruling elite the power to monopolize the control of natural resources under the guise of protecting them for national interest.

In discussing the tension between local claims and national interest vis-à-vis resource politics, a number of variables come into play as determining factors. These include the ethnic composition of the state in relation to access to political and economic power, the environmental consequences of resource extraction, the historical rivalries between segments of the state, the cohesiveness and effectiveness of the civil society, and the extent to which the resource(s) in question is (are) vital to the national economy. The ethnic composition of the state in relation to access to political and economic power relates to how dominant ethnic groups interact with minority groups when vital natural resources are domicile within the geographical boundaries of the minority. Politics is as much a question of number as it is of power, and when ethnic groups that are numerically inferior have vital natural resources, the struggle to ensure that they are not completely marginalized becomes a key consideration in resource politics.

Environmental consideration has become a key issue that is easily linked to the above discussion on the tendency of dominant ethnic groups to marginalize the interest of the minority groups. Indeed, the ease with which the interests of minority groups are marginalized on the issues of environmental consequences of resource extraction has become a major topic in the politics of local claim and national interest, and it has increased the "we" versus "them" dichotomy between the people and the government. Sierra Leone, Sudan, and Nigeria present good examples in this respect.

Historical rivalries between segments of the state come into play here as they determine the possible pattern of alignment between those who support the claims of the local population and those who pitch their tents with the argument of the government, for the protection of national interest. In many of the countries where there are problems between local claims and national interest, support for the government against resource-producing communities often comes from groups that have long-standing disagreements with the resource-producing regions. Consequently, their support for the government is not motivated by their conviction of the validity of the government's argument but more by their historical opposition to the resource-producing communities. This is clearly evident in the cases of Nigeria, where many of the communities aligned with the government in its military activities against the Ogoni people.

In recent years, civil society groups and NGOs have come in as major actors in the politics of local claims and national interest vis-à-vis conflicts over natural resources. The relevance of these organizations has come through the support they give to local communities having an unfair deal in their relationship with the government over natural resources embedded in their soil. In recent times, the local and international dimensions of the activities of NGOs have been crucial in curtailing the excesses of governments. However, for conflicts that have not assumed a level where there is significant support and assistance coming from local and international civil society groups, there is the likelihood that the dichotomy between local claims and national interest will continue to underlie relations between the groups.

The importance of the natural resource in question in relation to national economy presents the last vital issue in the link between local claims and national interest. Cases in which the natural resource is vital to national economy have local claims that are often met with violent reaction from the government. On their part, too, local claimants have often fought more fiercely because of their conviction that they are entitled to better deals. This again has been the case of oil in Nigeria and Sudan.

A new beginning now seems to be emerging on the dichotomy between local claims and national interest, as demonstrated in the Chadian–Cameroon oil project. Consultations on the project lasted up to ten years, and the entire 1,070 kilometer course of the pipeline was assessed by experts traveling on foot. There were almost 1,000 village-level meetings and 165 consultations with the Pygmies of Cameroon. The original route was altered twenty times.[14] Another example of where the interest of the local population has been taken into consideration in construction is the Katse Dam in Lesotho, which under its phase 1A completed in 1997, was producing 505.7 million cubic meters of water to South Africa.[15] However, under phase 1B, the interest of the local population to be affected by the dam construction was factored into the contract. There was a conscious determination to ensure that the construction results in improvements in the quality of their lives. At each site, there was a human-relations representative and a community liaison officer, both employed to ensure that all the conditions were fulfilled and that local people were employed in the project, thus ensuring the delivery of employment. Construction engineers were required to take responsibility for people being aware of project developments and how they may affect community life. A technology transfer program allows the advancement of local staff to management positions as expatriate staff is gradually eased out of the project. Throughout the project, multidisciplinary teams worked to deal with a range of issues including public health, resettlement, community participation in project activity, compensation, and the generation of alternative income to compensate for any loss of livelihood due to its impact. The picture becomes clearer when the politics of local claims is further considered alongside foreign control.

On the dichotomy between local claims and international enterprise, it should be noted that this comes as a result of two considerations: the underdeveloped mode of production in many African countries and the lack of technical expertise to process some of the natural resources found in many African countries; and the historical links that had been developed during the colonial era in many African countries with individuals and multinational corporations in the colonial capitals. The underdeveloped nature of Africa's mode of production makes it inevitable that many of the countries rely on foreign expertise to exploit these resources. Since the incorporation of the countries into global capitalism and the capitalist mode of production gave some natural resources the importance they never had historically, it also became inevitable that foreign expertise would be required to handle them. For the local population, the disadvantages are in the fact that the process and nature of exploitation, the quantity exploited, and the prices fixed for the resources are all outside their control. They are often thus left with the meager returns given to them by the multinational corporation and the state, which in their perception, are often united in the bid to maximize benefit of their resources to the locals' disadvantage.

The historical links developed during the colonial era explain why many of the major multinational corporations in the countries are those from the erstwhile colonial rulers. As Faysal Yachir notes, while

European colonization of South America was, from the beginning linked to the exploitation of precious metals . . . in Africa, mercantilist capitalism was for centuries based on human resources through slave trade, and wealth underground was neglected.[16]

When it thus began, large-scale mining in Africa coincided with the early Leninist stage of imperialism, based on banking and industrial monopolies. With the coming of the first diamond rush in 1870 in southern Africa, the main mining companies that were to dominate local scenes for more than a century were established, including Rio Tinto-Zinc, De Beers, and Consolidated Goldfields. By the end of the nineteenth century, Cecil Rhodes, who owned De Beers Diamond Company and Consolidated Goldfields, had formed the South African Company, which ruled most of Central Africa until the British Crown took over in the mid-1920s. With the imperial control came the influx of many major multinational corporations into Africa, and other mineral resources, including oil, became vital attractions to these companies. Among the first set of laws established by the colonial powers over mineral rights, dispossessed the local populations of their rights over these resources and placed the resources under the control of the colonial authorities.

Recent controversies over foreign control in local resources often come in two different forms: the activities of multinational corporations and those of individual foreign nationals operating in African countries. In both cases, the home governments of the individuals and corporations have often had to intervene to protect their interests when this becomes necessary. This tendency is, however, less visible in the cases of multinational corporations who have often devised ways of managing their problems with the local community and the governments. The clash between the local interest and foreign individuals over resources in Africa has often centered on land. Perhaps the conflict that brings these issues to the fore is the Zimbabwe land controversy, where land has been at the center of local claims and foreign control. Foreign control in this context, however, needs qualification. While both sides contesting for land in the country are Zimbabweans, the historical circumstances of the country make for distinction between black and white Zimbabweans. The claims of the black Zimbabweans are that the land arrangements agreed to at the Lancaster House Agreement are not in their favor, and that land has to be rearranged to ensure a more equitable distribution. The white Zimbabweans do not dispute this claim and would appear to be ready for some form of concession, provided, of course, there is compensation for the land repossessed for redistribution. Thus, at the center of the Zimbabwean land controversy is, at least to an extent, the issue of compensation.

The activities of multinational corporations have clashed with local claims in three different ways: when the local population feels that the multinational corporations are getting more than they are giving back to the society; when the local people believe they are getting less than they are entitled to; and when the local community considers itself a victim of unacceptable environmental consequences. Increasingly, one of the ways through which local claims are being addressed is through the activities of civil society.

A noticeable trend in some African countries, and one that should be discussed under the broader theme of local claims, national interest, and international enterprise, is the practice of getting multinational corporations involved in resource extraction to be invested in the production of social amenities for the communities where they extract the resources. This is a particularly important trend in Nigeria, where oil multinational corporations are providing amenities such as hospitals, good roads, and schools for the population. This trend is indicative of the complex nature of the relationship between the local population, the government, and the multinational corporations, and it is indicative of the defective nature of the natural resource governance in many countries practicing this system. In actuality, the provision of social amenities is the responsibility of governments and not that of multinational corporations. But simple as this argument may seem on the surface, a number of considerations make issues along these lines somewhat complicated in Africa, since all the key actors in this equation—the government, the multinational corporations, and the local population—are engaged in a complex web of intrigues. The government realizes that the multinational corporations are not completely faithful in their activities, either because they are engaged in illegal exploitations or they are not respecting environmental laws. However, since the government is often not in a position to completely monitor the activities of these multinational corporations, it is thought that getting them to pay more in terms of provision of infrastructure for the local communities would, at least, mean getting more from them to pay for the illegal and fraudulent things they could be doing.

On their part, the multinational corporations have accepted to provide infrastructure because, first, it suits their public relations image, as it portrays them as putting something back into the societies from which they are extracting resources, and second, the companies know that what they are evading in terms of overexploitation, the irregular payment of royalties, and the evasion of normal environmental standards for resource extraction, are far more than they are expending on the provision of social infrastructure. In all this, the producing communities see themselves as victims of a ring of dishonesty, and this has supported their determined effort to extract benefits from both the government and the multinational corporations. Ordinarily, the process of asking these companies to invest in providing social amenities would not have been necessary if all the structures had been in place to ensure that what was due to the countries in the form of royalties and other taxes was obtained and that the companies did not violate the basic environmental concerns of the population in the process of extracting natural resources. Other issues relating to this will be appreciated when one considers the role of civil society in the conflicts over natural resources.

Governance and Civil Society

The term *civil society* has attracted a variety of thoughts and attention. Because of the wide interest in post-Cold War civil society, the subject has been defined in different ways, but most of these see the term as representing the connectivity between the individual and the state. Included under this broad category are institutions and private groups, such as voluntary associations, professional groups, trade unions, youth organizations, the media, religious associations, nongovernmental and community-based organizations, and other similar groups. There is also the international civil society, which includes global finance and business forums, such as the Institute of International Finance; development NGOs, such as Oxfam; environmental NGOs, such as Friends of the Earth; trade unions, such as International Confederation of Free Trade Unions; Policy Research Institutes, such as the Overseas Development Council; and faith-based groups, such as those connected to Christianity, Islamic, and other religions.[17] This section discusses the role of local and international civil society in the politics of natural resource conflict.

The level of involvement of local civil society organizations in the management of resource-based conflicts in post-Cold War Africa has depended on the nature of conflicts and the extent of destruction brought on the structures of governance. In the cases in which conflicts have resulted in the complete collapse of the institution of governance, as in the cases of Liberia and Sierra Leone, the emergence of civil society organizations has been remarkable, and civil society has found itself playing a complex diversity of roles that have included issues such as the provision of basic infrastructures, such as water, and taking care of orphan children, in addition to the search for peace. However, in cases where the nature of conflict has been more localized, the extent of involvement has been understandably less intense.

It has to be pointed out that civil society does not always speak in one voice. Indeed, a noticeable trend in some of the countries where natural resources have been at the root of conflict is the divergence of opinion among civil society. This tendency has further increased with the realization by the elite of the importance of civil society and their attendant determination to exploit it to their advantage. For example, in Liberia, the civil society was divided at the beginning of the war. The media, for instance, was divided between those who supported the old order and those in support of Charles Taylor's order. The same applied to Sierra Leone, where a segment of the civil society actively supported the government and the other pitched their tent with the rebels. However, the best example was in Rwanda, where the Church, historically part of the ruling party, actively supported the genocide. It was, however, not long after the beginning of conflicts in all these countries, when the extent of the devastation became pronounced, that a "people-conscious" civil society emerged to challenge the elite monopolization of the civil society. This has been assisted by two factors: the formation of nongovernmental organizations geared toward the activation of the civil society and the foreign sponsorship of the organization, and other forms of mass participation in governance.

One resource-related conflict in which civil society has played a major role was in Sierra Leone. It should be noted, however, that the effort here was to end the war and not necessarily to address the natural resource aspect of it. Although the civil society had started making efforts to get the Momoh government and the rebel group RUF to find a way of ending the war, the efforts became more pronounced after the military took over from Momoh in 1992. Indeed, by the time Valentine Strasser was overthrown and Julius Maada Bio assumed power, civil society had become strong enough to force the government to hold elections, despite the government's desire to the contrary. From this period onward, civil society became stronger and has been active in the attempt to end the war. As a civil society spokesperson in the country noted, civil society decided to hijack the initiative and thus prevent a situation where the RUF and the government "give the people peace when they (RUF and government) want and take it back when they like."[18]

Initially, civil society was reluctant to talk to the RUF so as not to give them what was considered undeserved recognition. However, after the January 1999 crisis, the civil society realized that the government or even the Economic Community of West African States (ECOWAS) could not provide the necessary protection, and thus decided to talk directly with the RUF but insisted it must be on its own terms. Civil society formulated the principles that would guide discussion. Among these are

• provision of direct dialogue with the RUF,
• provision of a Truth and Reconciliation Committee,
• provision of a conditional but not a general amnesty,
• the RUF to withdraw from Kono and other resource-rich areas,
• no provision for power sharing, and
• unconditional release of all abducted children.

One particular NGO that has played a formidable role in organizing the civil society is the Campaign for Good Governance (CGG), led by Zainab Bangura. Civil society tried to put its views across before the Lomé Peace Agreement was signed but was ignored. In response the civil society organized a successful one-day protest. The success of this made the government and the RUF realize the new resolve of civil society.

In Liberia, too, the effort was more to end the war than look at the natural resource dimension. Unlike Sierra Leone, however, this involvement came much later. The subsequent proliferation of armed factions in the war further meant that several segments of civil society that could have stood up to protest inevitably found themselves involved in partisan alliance with one of the numerous armed factions that emerged in the course of the war. When eventually the civil society took the initiative, they made little impact. After the

Akosombo Agreement, when it appeared that the factions were not willing to make peace, there was a demonstration across Monrovia that they should not come back home unless an agreement had been reached.

Also worthy of consideration in the role of local civil society are the activities of youth. A major issue in natural resource conflicts across Africa is the involvement of youth. In DRC, Liberia, Nigeria, Sierra Leone, and Zimbabwe, youth have played a prominent role in the expression of conflicts related to natural resources. Even in communal conflicts over land, such as those in southwest Nigeria between the Ife and Modakeke people, and in northern Ghana between the Nanumbas and the Kokumbas, youths have been at the forefront of attention.

Three patterns can be identified in the involvement of youth in natural resource conflicts. First, there are those youths who believe that their identity and group interests are threatened and, as such, feel the urge to fight and protect what is seen as group interest. Examples include communal clashes over land, such as in northern Ghana, southwest Nigeria, and in Nigeria's Niger Delta Province. A common feature is that the actions are often not colored by any expectations of personal advantage, and, in some cases, there are often cultural constraints that make the youth put ethnic interest before personal gains. Second, youth have embraced conflicts mainly for personal gains. Here, the intention is often clear from the beginning—or shortly after the outbreak of the conflict—that the interest is selfish. One characteristic of conflicts here is that they are often very brutal, as there is often zero-sum dimension to the pursuit of personal acquisition. Perhaps the best example of this is the involvement of youths in Sierra Leone's diamonds, especially the so-called *San-San* boys. Third, there are cases in which youths operate in ways that satisfy a warlord, while, at the same time, protect their own personal interest. A resource-centered conflict that provides a good example of this was the Liberian Civil War, where youths in all the different armed factions were engaged in dual desire to satisfy their respective warlord, while at the same time, to acquire substantial personal resources. Although there are distinctions between the last two, these are sometimes blurred.

There are three explanations of youth involvement in resource conflicts. First, in most countries, youth see themselves as the neglected majority in an unjust social setup. Consequently, they believe that they owe no allegiance to the state and would not hesitate to bring it down. The problem is compounded by the fact that youth witnessed a period of boom in their country's economies and waited anxiously for the time they would be in positions to benefit from their country's natural resource. Hence, a collapse of their national economies was accompanied in most cases by frustration on the part of youths, a situation that explains some of their violent reactions. Second, the impact of globalization, which, among other things, brought down boundaries, gave the youth access to information about developments in other places. Third, the demonstrated arrogance and unsympathetic display of wealth by the ruling elites ignited complete aversion in youth, which ultimately resulted in their resorting to violence.

The activities of youth over resource conflicts raise a number of issues for governance. First, why have youth opted for violence to seek redress for what they could, at least in theory, address through peaceful ways? The answer is found in the weak level of confidence in the institutions of governance, including the judiciary. Second, the responses of governments to the activities of the youths in natural resource related conflicts have sometimes been highhanded. Perhaps the worst example of this is the Nigerian government's brutal repression in Odi, in the southeastern part of the country. Here, the civilian government of President Olusegun Obasanjo dispatched a military force that razed the town completely and killed several hundreds of people. To this day, Odi remains a major stain on Obasanjo's administration.

With respect to global civil society, it needs to be noted that a major consequence of globalization is the proliferation of nongovernmental organizations with activities crisscrossing international boundaries. Many of these organizations have formed strong interest groups in the politics of natural resource management in developing countries and many have, indeed, become strong actors in the management of conflicts over natural resources in developing societies. In a way, the nature of the emergence of these organizations, the methods they have adopted in the pursuit of their objective, and their determination have made them clash with other actors involved in resource exploitation in those societies—namely, nation-states and foreign multinational corporations, which are the two groups that are known to be involved in an unholy alliance to deprive indigenous communities of their resources to satisfy local political elites and international capitalism. In some cases, too, these organizations have targeted foreign governments for criticism for alleged involvement in unethical business deals in developing countries.

International NGOs involved in African natural resource politics can be divided into four broad categories: those concerned with conflicts in the Third World but tangentially interested in resource conflicts; those concerned with democracy, democratization, and good governance; those concerned with global environmental issues; and diaspora organizations, that is, abroad-based citizens of regions where there are conflicts over natural resources.

Because of the mutually reinforcing nature of these programs in Africa, the activities of these organizations have been interwoven. Most of the international NGOs pursuing the above mentioned, focused their attention in two major directions: the destruction of the environment through the activities of multinational corporations involved in the extraction of oil and solid mineral resources and the preservation of wildlife and struggle against illegal appropriation of land from indigenous communities. Of these two, however, the groups agitating against the activities of multinational corporations have attracted more attention. There are at least three reasons for this: first, natural resources in this category have brought some of the most devastating consequences on the environment; second, the resources are seen as those on which governments across Africa hold as key to oppressing their people, and consequently, they are the resources whose management should be brought under closer monitoring; and third, many of the companies involved in the extraction of these resources are based in the home countries of many of these international NGOs. This makes it possible for the organizations to effectively counter any of the propaganda strategies of these multinational corporations. There have also been organizations that focused on the management of specific natural resources, especially solid minerals, oil, and land, and in recent years the issue of water privatization has been added to the group of natural resources around which international environmental NGOs have focused interest and attention.

Many of the NGOs focused attention on multinational corporations and have adopted a name-and-shame policy. At the fore of international NGOs that have adopted this policy is the Global Witness, which had identified and named many multinational companies at the forefront of alleged illegal exploitation in the Third World. Contrary to the impression, however, it is not all the time that the NGO has criticized foreign companies. For example, Global Witness commended the British Oil Company (BP) for its role in the Angolan oil management. The BP disclosed signature bonus payment of approximately US$150 million to the Angolan government, a step that allegedly earned the company warning in form of reprisal by Sonagol (the Angolan government company managing oil). The BP also noted in a letter dated February 6, 2001, by BP's Group Managing Director Richard Oliver that the company has maintained regular dialogue with the World Bank and IMF over Angola. The company promised to publish annual information on their Angolan operations containing details of its total net production figures by block, its aggregate payment to Sonagol, and total taxes and levies paid by BP to the Angolan government as a result of their Angolan operation. Global Witness commended this more, which it argues is a step toward ending "corporate complicity in state corruption."[19]

In recent years, ex-environmental activists have been joining the corporate sectors they have spent years opposing. For example, Tom Burke, whose protest against Rio Tinto in the early 1970s as a Friends of the Earth activist stopped the company from mining copper in a national park in Wales, joined Rio Tinto in 1996.[20] In an ironic twist, in 2004, Tom Burke was championing the cause that would extract 750,000 tons per year of ilmenite, a whitening substance used in paint and toothpaste, for the next sixty years in Madagascar on the grounds that it would bring economic growth. His former allies in the environmental world, however, argue that it would destroy the "subsistence lifestyle of largely illiterate villages who live off the forest and ocean."[21] Soon after hiring Tom Burke, Rio Tinto asked him to organize meetings for company managers, environmental activists, and local officials. He has put together a list of local concerns, including large inflow of people from the countryside looking for work could increase prostitution and HIV infections, destruction of the forest could choke off hopes for an ecotourism industry, and port traffic could destroy whale migrations. Since then, Rio Tinto has modified its plans, moving the port to an unpopulated spot away from Fort Dauphir. It also changed the port specifications to allow for tourist vessels. Furthermore, it has brought in academics to catalog flora and fauna in the area, producing a survey that even opponents recognize as the most extensive ever done in the country. It can be argued that the willingness of some of the multinational corporations to hire former activists reflects a growing trend among big industrial companies to deal with environmental groups rather than dismissing their concerns. Earlier in 2004, Exxon Mobil agreed to hold regular meetings with Amnesty International to monitor the oil company's human rights performance, and Home Depot Inc has worked with environmentalists to ensure that the wood imported from Chile, Indonesia, and elsewhere is responsibly logged.

On their part, the international NGOs focusing on human rights have been concerned with how governments and international business interests have violated the interests of local populations in the management of natural resources. Specifically, these organizations have focused attention on cases in which governments have clamped down on populations clamoring for better deals in the management of natural resources. An example of where these organizations have played an important role is in the Nigerian Niger Delta, where the concern of the plight of the Ogonis, especially after the hanging of Ken Saro Wiwa, attracted considerable international interest.

Another category of international NGOs with some form of interest in the management of natural resources in Africa are those looking at governance issues. These organizations have identified the centrality of natural resources to governance in developing countries, and among the issues they have brought into their concept of "good governance" is to ensure there is proper accountability in the management of natural resources. Sometimes these organizations have come together to exert pressure on specific countries in the effort to bring about desired results. A recent example is the pressure mounted on the government of Chad in ensuring there is proper accounting procedures in the management of the country's oil revenue.

The activities of these organizations have been both positive and negative. From the positive side, they have been able to curb some of the excesses of governments in many developing countries and of the multinational corporations that have cooperated with them in unfair business tactics. They have also been able to champion the causes of the oppressed in these societies. On the other hand, these organizations have also contributed to the weakness of the state, especially through their mustering of international support against domestic policies of some of the states. Since many of the organizations have propaganda machineries that are stronger and more extensive than many of African states, the states have often found it difficult to compete with them.

The use of other tools of globalization, such as the Internet, has made it easier for these organizations to get their messages across the world. There are times, however, when the activities of these organizations have served as a caution against the states, especially in the countries' pursuit of policies that are detrimental to their population. But also adding to the external pressure being exerted on states in Africa is the increasing role of global governance in the management of natural resources in the continent.

Governance and Globalization

A number of issues link globalization to conflicts over natural resources, however, this section examines how these are connected to governance. In this respect, two main issues are identified for discussion. The first focuses on how economic liberalization and market deregulation affect the ways in which governance intertwines with natural resource conflicts, while the second looks at all the ramifications of global governance in the management of conflicts over natural resources.

While it is widely accepted that globalization has many facets, it is the economic component, characterized by economic liberalization and market deregulation, that forms its core. For African countries, perhaps the most important link between economic globalization and the conflicts over natural resources comes through the activities of the International Financial Institutions (IFI) and their economic liberalization policies. This has manifested in a number of ways, the most prominent being the policy of economic liberalization and market deregulation introduced through the Structural Adjustment Policy (SAP).

The impact of SAP on African countries has been so well-documented in the literature that it serves little purpose discussing it again here,[22] leaving us to discuss specifically the link between SAP, governance, and natural resource conflicts. Going into specifics, the policies of economic liberalization and market deregulation have made an impact on conflicts over natural resources in a number of ways. First, as Mark Duffield has noted, the whole idea of market deregulation has made it easier for warring parties to develop the parallel international linkages that are necessary for their survival, with many of these actors exploring unconventional ways to get connected to the international market. Indeed, in many of the conflicts that have occurred in the last few decades, there have been instances in which warlords have become key actors in international business. Savimbi in Angola and Taylor in Liberia are good examples of how this tendency can be exploited by warlords. Savimbi became a key actor in the international diamond business, with contacts with presidents across Africa serving as his outlet to the international market, while, as Reno has noted, at one time Charles Taylor was supplying one-third of

France's hardwood requirements.[23] In the DRC, warlords developed a string of activities with the international market to trade in natural resources. Apart from the fact that these are warlords exploiting natural resources to further selfish political and economic goals, the entire practice has served to prolong conflicts and to create long-term instability in these societies. It is thus not surprising that these conflicts have taken a long time to resolve.

Second, market deregulation has resulted in situations in which states have become major actors in illegal business, often involving natural resources. Although many states participating in international trade have never really adhered to strict codes of conducts, the instances of involvement in illegal enterprises had not been common occurrences before the market deregulation that came in the aftermath of SAP. Furthermore, states are no longer concerned with the implications of acquiring pariah status because of their practices involving natural resources. The desire to get revenue to sustain the state and satisfy the greed of elites has made many countries abandon time-honored principles. As shown in chapter 4, Uganda and Rwanda threw caution to the wind in their involvement in the illegal exploitation of natural resources in the DRC. Also, Congo Brazzaville and Liberia became deeply involved in the illegal diamond business in DRC and Sierra Leone, respectively, resulting in situations where these two countries, not known to be key diamond producers, officially submitted to the international markets figures that are deliberately forged. Apart from the impacts this practice has on conflicts involving natural resources, the participation of the state in illegal activities involving natural resources have served to further weaken the state.

Third, in widening cross-border trade, market deregulation has served to increase the propensity of cross-border conflicts involving natural resources. In many of the subregions, especially West Africa, the routes that have been used for many of these trades have also served as passages for small arms and light weapons. Indeed, the whole issue of mobile dissident activities in the region, especially in the Mano River Union countries of Liberia, Sierra Leone, and Guinea, can be traced, even if only to an extent, to the whole issue of cross-border implications of market deregulation. However, while this has significant negative effect, there are also positive sides to it. The attempt to address some of the problems have resulted in situations in which there is greater collaboration between states on how to address some of the problems and to ensure that the positive side effects that can come from cross-border trade are not affected by an illegal flow of weapons. This is particularly the case with West Africa, where there are concrete attempts by the subregional organization ECOWAS to address the problems raised by proliferation of small arms.[24]

Fourth, the urge to portray economic liberalization policy as a success has made International Financial Institutions, and sometimes western governments, shut their eyes to those countries where various forms of dictatorship are still being practiced. An example that can be cited here is Uganda, regarded in many quarters as a success for liberalization, but one which, to all intents and purposes, is still seen in several quarters as running a dictatorial one-party state, even if this is sometimes disguised under a different façade.

Fifth, market deregulation and economic liberalization have resulted in a situation in which there now emerges unhealthy relationships among African states. Efforts to maximize the gains from globalization now make African states see themselves more as rivals in the race for attention, especially in the management of natural resources. For example, immediately after white farmers were expelled from Zimbabwe, other African countries scrambled to have them in their countries, with many of the new recipient states not taking sufficient care of some of the attendant implications of the decision. As noted in chapter 3, some of the land the Kwara State government in Nigeria allocated to the white Zimbabwean farmers belongs to local populations who have already begun to express their anger against the government's decision. However, the desperate desire to seize the opportunities coming from the departure of the farmers from Zimbabwe has made the government ignore the short- and long-term implications of this decision.

Sixth, attempts to benefit from globalization have made African countries relax their laws, especially those that can attract foreign investors, without the attendant clauses to ensure that the relaxation of these laws does not result in blanket opportunities for these companies. The urge to make the best out of inroads into global markets has not encouraged the countries to scrutinize the activities of these companies who have exploited this opportunity to their own advantage. There have been cases of where allegations of fraud and improper business practices have been leveled against some of the companies involved in natural resources, as in the case of Halliburton activities in Nigeria.[25] Even after African countries have discovered fraudulent activities in these companies, caution has been exercised in taking any punitive actions against them.

This brings in discussion on the role of multinational corporations. Increasingly, the activities of multinational corporations are being included in most of the recent discussions on globalization. There are at least three reasons for this. The first is the increasing role of these corporations in global economy; second is the effects brought about by globalizations, which have introduced significant changes to the activities of these corporations vis-à-vis their roles in developing societies; and third, many of the organizations have served as avenues through which their respective home countries have attempted to maximize their benefits in a global economy. Indeed, China, not known to be a traditional actor, now has its multinational corporations actively involved in Africa, with more than seven hundred companies operating in forty-nine African countries in businesses from oil to hotel management. The deep involvement of China has resulted in a situation where Chinese diplomacy has undergone a significant turnaround, with China shielding Sudan from possible UN Security Council sanction for its human rights activities.

Two issues are worthy of note about the link between globalization, multinational corporations, and natural resource conflicts in Africa. First, some of these companies have been allegedly involved in unethical practices in some of the countries where there are ongoing conflicts over natural resources. For example, the U.S. company Halliburton was allegedly involved in a number of illegal oil deals in Nigeria. Apart from this, there have been other alleged cases, as in the BG Plc. (formerly British Gas state company) and Britain's HSBC Bank in Equatorial Guinea;[26] Standard Chartered Bank in Angola,[27] and numerous Chinese companies engaging in oil extraction in Sudan. Second, a string of backstabbing often belies their apparent display of camaraderie among multinational corporations operating in regions of conflicts. For example, it is believed that while Shell and Mobil often tried to ensure a coherent position on the situation in the Niger Delta, Mobil enjoyed the position of condemnation that is often given to its rival, Shell. Indeed, a senior public relation official of the company was quoted to have said that Mobil intends to keep a low profile while Shell remained "the target of international outrage and protest."[28]

The activities of the World Bank and the IMF in encouraging African countries to privatize their water and energy sector is a consideration that is worth noting, especially as its links with potential conflicts (noted in chapter 6) is likely to be a crucial issue in the years ahead. A World Bank Policy Paper on privatization of the energy sector in Africa was unambiguous in its stance.

> The importance of attracting private investment into the energy sector cannot be overstated. . . . The Bank will focus on countries which demonstrate—through actions—a credible intent to privatize and liberalize. The team's objective is to have as much of the sector as possible transferred into private ownership through open, transparent procedures and in a manner, which mobilizes significant investment.

For African states already heavily indebted to international financial institutions, the implicit blackmail in the above policy statement cannot be more glaring. Indeed, the bank made privatization of the water sector conditionality for future financial assistance. To further encourage the move toward privatization of this sector, the World Bank has overlooked some of the corruption and other unethical practices that have characterized the process of water and energy privatization in the continent. For example, there are many cases where tender was not undertaken and the bid had been given to sole bidders,[29] while in several other cases corruption and bribery of African officials by foreign companies that came to the attention of the World Bank were ignored.[30] For example, the Public Services International Research Unit (PSIRU) identified a number of cases of in which World Bank employed subtle blackmail to get some African countries to embark on water and energy privatization, despite clear opposition from the domestic population to the exercise.

The role of the World Trade Organization (WTO) in the politics of global trade in agricultural resources has come under recent attention through the amount wealthy countries spend on farm subsidies. It is now estimated that developed countries spend about US$300 billion per year on farm subsidies, which is six times the amount of money spent on aid. In the World Bank's estimate, the removal of subsidies would cause a 17 percent rise in global agricultural production, adding US$60 billion per year to the rural income of low- and middle-income states.

The activities of individual countries in further tightening the screws on agricultural produce of developing countries in developing countries have also been a subject of concern. For example, the more than US$3 billion annual subsidies on cotton by the U.S. government have been noted by the World Bank as depressing "world cotton prices and crowd[ing] out poor but efficient farmers in West Africa." The European Union Agricultural Commissioner Franz Fischler was somewhat undiplomatic in the ways he rebuffed African nations who were calling for an end to subsidies, when he said: "if they want to do business, they should come back to mother earth. If they choose to continue their space odyssey, they will not get the stars, they will not get the moon, they will simply end up with empty hands."[31] African countries have continued with their protests against the WTO and are particularly disappointed that the organization has not been forthcoming in announcing the time frame for the abolition of agricultural subsidies in Europe and the United States.

Global governance is a process whereby external institutions attempt to develop broad policies on governance and try to impose these on countries, especially developing ones. In a way, the idea of global governance came as a means of instituting some moral codes to the activities of nations without fundamentally altering the structures governing international relations or the sovereign status of states. In this process, organizations and institutions developed codes of conduct for countries to comply with in order to safeguard the citizens of these countries.

The whole issue of global governance comes into the debate of natural resource conflict in three broad ways. These are through the clamoring for the establishment of democracy and good governance in developing countries, through the call for the introduction of an international code of practices to govern trade in natural resources in developing countries, and through the imposition of minimum standards of performance that are expected from states in many of these countries. Since the beginning of the 1990 decade, there have been attempts to ensure that democratic values are established in developing countries. For Africa, pressures have come from organizations such as the African Union (AU), which, even before its transition from the Organization of African Unity (OAU), had begun imposing conditions for its members on the whole issue of good governance. Indeed, the organization later instituted clauses calling for a modification in its time-honored policy of noninterference in the affairs of other states, and military coups in some states were later rescinded by military intervention from powerful neighbors. In the last few years, the African Union has also come up with a mechanism to monitor the activities of African countries and to ensure that they conform to certain minimum standards. This is through the Peer Review Mechanisms of the New Partnership for African Development (NEPAD).

Other subregional organizations such as ECOWAS and Southern African Development Community (SADC) also came up with policies that attempt to establish good governance codes. These include the abolition of coups and illegal political transitions. The determination of one of these organizations (ECOWAS) was tested with the illegal transfer of power in Togo after the death of the long-serving President Gnasingbe Eyadema. The organization stood up to the challenge of ensuring that the illegal transfer of power to the son of the late leader was not allowed to stand. However, the organization that most gave publicity to its policies is the Commonwealth, which through its famous Harare Declaration of 1990 gave broad principles of what is expected from its members on the whole issue of good governance. While in all these cases there are major lapses, the decision by the organization to impose some clauses of good governance on their members had some effects on the management of natural resources. The attendant recognition given to the activities of civil society also imposed limitations to the activities of nation-states to mismanage these resources.

Global efforts to create principles for the management of natural resources have now become a major aspect of global governance, bringing together different actors in the politics of natural resource management. Perhaps the most important of these is the Kimberley Process on conflict diamonds, discussed in chapter 4.

Another regulatory initiative is the Extractive Industries Transparency Initiative (EITI), advanced by the British government, and the sole purpose was to ensure transparency through full publication and verification of company payment and government revenues from oil, gas, and mining. The initiative was formed from the assumption that transparent management of resources, backed by strong government, can prevent the situation whereby resource-rich countries are facing serious security challenges as a result of their natural resource endowment. At the center of the EITI is the effort to ensure that multinational corporations involved in extractive business are transparent in their activities, and in the process, prevent graft that has bedeviled a number of resource-producing countries.

Although considerable success seems to be attending the efforts of the EITI, with a high number of countries signing on to the initiative, the whole exercise has a number of limitations. First, it is limited in its focus, as it deals mostly with "extractive" natural resources. It has no consideration for nonextractive natural resources, especially land and international waters. Second, the success depends, to a large extent, on the willingness of multinational corporations to open all the relevant files for public scrutiny. Third, it aspires to put only extractive industries under close monitoring, without putting such a high level of accountability on governments in the management of natural resources of their respective countries.

Equally controversial among recent initiatives at governing the management of natural resources is the Governance and Economic Management Assistance Program (GEMAP) in Liberia. This is a framework designed to assist in the reformation of economic and natural resource management in postwar Liberia. Unlike the Chadian–Cameroon Pipeline, which was created to prevent fraud, the GEMAP was specifically suggested to address suspected fraud and other unsatisfactory practices of the National Transitional Government of Liberia (NTLG). At the center of the initiative are key donor countries and agencies including the African Union, ECOWAS, European Commission, IMF, Ghana, Nigeria, United States, and the World Bank. The objective was to put in place structures to ensure proper management of economic affairs of the country. In its operation, the GEMAP has six components: financial management and accountability, improving budgeting and expenditure management, improving procurement practices and granting of concessions, establishing effective processes to control corruption, supporting key institutions, and capacity building. Under the arrangement, all state-owned enterprises will be reformed, and financial experts, with signatory powers, will be recruited from abroad to supervise and assist their government counterparts. Much more important, an external supervisor with binding cosignatory authority will be brought into key governmental institutions such as the Bureau of Custom and Excise, Ministry of Land, Mines, and Energy to assist transparency and accountability. The program was signed into law in September 2005, and it was to last for thirty-six months At her inauguration, President Ellen Johnson Sirleaf said her government "accepts and enforces" the terms of GEMAP.

Opinions in Liberia have been divided on the issue of GEMAP, sometimes with strange bedfellows coming together to accept or condemn the program. Those who support the program argue that some form of externally monitored initiative has been needed to prevent graft in governance. Furthermore, an initiative that brought together the caliber of groups within the GEMAP was the only way to caution the government. Those who oppose the GEMAP are concerned about the loss of sovereignty that comes with the external vetting of Liberian financial accounts. But regardless of where one stands in the controversy, there are some issues that call for concern in the GEMAP initiative. First, the level of civil society involvement in it was almost nonexistent. It was just a package presented to the interim by the donor community. Second, it was signed by an interim government that had less than six months left in office. Consequently, the extent to which the government took into consideration the possible interest of the incoming government was questionable. Third, the interim government that signed the agreement had already been implicitly indicted of corruption. Against this background, it could have signed the agreement to satisfy the donor community and portray the impression that it was willing to turn a new leaf, as opposed to the conviction that the package was in the best interest of the country.

Conclusion

The core argument in this chapter is that the institutions designed to manage natural resources in Africa have not measured up to the expectations of the population. I also argue that while most of the problems associated with natural resources are associated with the issue of governance at national-based levels, there are aspects of them that are linked to the nature of global governance of natural and economic resources. I contend that people go to war over natural resources when the structures to manage these resources and the people to supervise the management of these structures fall below expectation and need. Specifically indicted in this regard are political elites who are charged with the administration of these countries and the constitutions that are to provide guidelines for the management. Indeed, most of the conflicts over natural resources in Africa have shown major links to these interwoven issues. While many of the countries are trying to address the gaps created by the weakness of governance institutions in the continent, interests continue to focus on the management of natural resources, with component units of the states trying to wrestle more control from the center in the management of these resources.

CONCLUSION

Advanced countries have long-ago discovered a strong correlation between a good system of government and striking developmental strides so much that even those of them with hardly any natural endowment and other economic potentials are at the top of the ladder. Our problem [in Nigeria] is not just that we are unlucky to be saddled with leaders without vision most of the time, but that majority of the citizens have no idea as to what they really want out of governance except the basic necessities like food, drinkable water, shelter and good roads. You therefore have people praising to high heavens corrupt and incompetent leaders for merely patching few kilometers of road . . . really what people in other lands takes for granted. Once in a while, the people grumble, dare to openly protest and get clobbered on the head. And all is soon forgotten and forgiven as people got used to their suffering and become the "happiest people on earth."

Bimpe Aboyade

The political and economic history of Sierra Leone provides many lessons in the perils of denying a large percentage of the citizenry the noble desire of equal access to opportunities and rewards and the fruit of an endless striving for liberty, justice and material well-being.

Olutayo Adesina

In this book I have advanced a number of major arguments. The first is that the tendency to see natural resources either as a "curse" or a "blessing," or the conflicts emanating from them as being rooted in "scarcity" or "abundance," is inherently flawed. I have argued that what natural resources are, the role they can play in the socioeconomic and political affairs of a particular country, and their vulnerability to causing conflicts, are mainly functions of the laws, structures, and practices guiding the management of such resources—especially the distribution of privileges and opportunities from them—and not the circumstances or nature of their physical existence. Indeed, a close look at the conflicts over natural resources in Africa will show that neither scarcity nor abundance has been a consistent factor as a cause of conflict. For example, scarcity of land was a major cause of conflict in Rwanda, but the same phenomenon has not occasioned any countrywide conflict in a country such as the Gambia. The same applies to abundance of natural resources, which, in the case of diamonds, was at the root of the prolongation of conflict in Sierra Leone but has been the major source of Botswana's relative political stability and economic growth. Again, oil has, to a large extent at least, been a blessing to Libya while many Nigerians consider the same resource as a curse, largely because of the hardship and controversies brought about by its mismanagement. All this shows there is really no direct correlation between natural resources and conflict beyond the structures, processes, and actors associated with the management and control of these resources. Also implicit in this argument is that regardless of geographical location, human idiosyncrasies, or the level of socioeconomic and political development, human beings all across the world are most likely to fight over natural resources if there are no proper ways of distributing the privileges and benefit emanating from them. The prevalence of violent conflicts over natural resources in Africa is due largely to the management of these resources.

Second, I have advanced the position that, despite the euphoria surrounding the ongoing calls for transparency and good governance in Africa, these efforts, though commendable in themselves, will not put an end to conflicts over natural resources in the continent. Although some of the conflicts are rooted in corruption and lack of democracy, a far greater percentage of these conflicts have emerged because these resources are not distributed and managed in ways that benefit the population, especially the resource-producing communities, even in so-called democratic countries. In short, conflicts over natural resources in Africa have emerged because citizens across countries in the continent do not have any control over their country's natural resource endowment, and they cannot see a way of seeking redress through existing structures—democratic or authoritarian. In other words, even if, for example, there is far greater accountability in Nigeria's oil production but the money from these resources is not able to have an impact on the population of the oil-producing region, conflicts in these areas would most likely continue. While concentrating attention on transparency and accountability, there is also the need to remove clauses under existing democratic structures that, although they may be legal and constitutional, are unfair to segments of the population. In short, the issue is not necessarily "democracy" but rather the "fairness" of clauses even in the so-called democratic structures.

All the above thus leads to the third and perhaps most important argument of this book, which is that virtually all conflicts over natural resources in Africa can be linked to the governance of the natural resources sector. Looking across the continent, it is evident that African countries do not have structures to manage natural resources in ways that can prevent conflicts. Crucial issues such as ensuring equity and fairness in the allocation of benefits and opportunities coming from natural resources, prevention of environmental hazards coming from the process of resource extraction, striking an acceptable balance between local claim and national interest, proper definition of the limits of the activities of foreign multinational corporations, institutionalization of credible property rights, and a host of other considerations that can ensure harmonious intergroup relations in the management of natural resources, are either completely absent in most African countries or are merely selectively efficient. In many of the countries, too, the laws governing natural resources are contradictory and confusing, while the processes and the sources of many of the laws are, at best, contestable. Even the greed of the political elites, which seems to underline the "greed" factor in the "greed *versus* grievance" thesis popularized by Paul Collier, has manifested because there are no credible administrative structures in place to prevent "greed" and to address "grievance."

But apart from the causes of conflicts, even the link between natural resources and the prolongation or fueling of conflicts is also connected to governance. As shown in the preceding chapters, one of the reasons warlords and rebel groups have been able to use natural resources to fuel their conflicts against the state is because of the absence of credible and fair structures to manage these resources. In some cases, the disenchanted base that the mismanagement of natural resources has created in the resource-producing communities has been the key issue that rebel groups have exploited in the prolongation of conflicts, as in the cases, for example, of Liberia and Sierra Leone. Furthermore, if there had been acceptable procedures for managing the exploitation and sale of these resources, illegal exploitation would have been far more difficult, just as external assistance to stem the illegal flow of these resources would have been easier to implement. Indeed, the Kimberley Process has shown how accountability and proper governance can reduce, even if it cannot completely stop, the illegal use of natural resources. It is ironic that rebel groups and warlords appreciate the importance of "governance" of natural resources more than sovereign states do, as evidenced in the complex structures that warlords such as Jonas Savimbi and Charles Taylor put in place to derive maximum, even if selfish, benefit from the natural resources under their control.

The important role of governance in explaining conflicts over natural resources raises three important questions, answers to which will form the basis of this concluding chapter. The first question relates to why African countries have not been able to develop the kind of structure that can prevent conflict in the management of their natural resources. Answers to this will of course remain a matter of opinion, but I offer three possible explanations. The first answer lies in the inherited constraints bequeathed by colonialism. As argued in the last chapter, there is a historical link between colonialism, governance, and conflicts over natural resources in Africa, and there are ways in which many of the issues linking recent natural resource conflicts to governance in Africa have roots far entrenched in the nature of colonial rule. Indeed, resource exploitation was at the center of colonialism, and one of the first sets of laws passed by colonial governments was over mineral rights. These laws saw the rights over these resources taken away from the natives and placed under colonial offices in Europe. There were also several instances in which foreign multinational companies played important roles in political governance. Consequently, the postindependence dispossession of natives of their rights over natural resources, and the whole advantage foreign multinational corporations have in the management of natural resources in Africa, two of the key issues now linking natural resources to conflict in Africa, have their antecedence deeply rooted in colonialism.

Another link between colonially-bequeathed constraints and conflicts over natural resources in Africa emanates from the diversity in the ethnic and social entities brought together to constitute nation-states. This makes the establishment of harmonious intergroup relations difficult. Although there is the tendency in some circles to dismiss any discussion about the consequences of colonialism as "flogging a dead horse," it is, indeed, the case that some of the legacies are still prevalent across the continent, and they have engendered conflicts over natural resources. For example, comparing Africa with Europe, Richard Dowden draws out some considerations that underline conflicts in intergroup relations and how this can be linked to the politics of natural resource management when he notes:

Nigeria, . . . like Europe, . . . has three big tribes and several other ethnic groups, 25 in the case of Europe, more than 400 in the case of Nigeria. Imagine a united European state—united by force not by referendum—which has to elect one President [and] one government. Europe in which the French are Muslims, the German, Catholic, the British, Protestants, and there is only one source of income, oil, and it is under the Germans.[1]

Evolving credible structures to manage affairs under situations such as depicted above is somewhat difficult, and many African countries, especially those where a particular natural resource dominates the national economy, have had to face daunting challenges.

The second explanation for the lack of credible structures with which to manage natural resources can be traced to the activities of the elites, who, in trying to maximize personal benefits from these resources, have prevented the establishment of credible structures that can prevent graft. Since independence, most African countries have been managed by elites who have defined national interest in selfish and narrow ways. While in some countries the inheritance elites, who took over at the time of independence, tried to put in place structures, in most others, greed and irresponsible management of natural resources began almost immediately after independence. Many of the wars that were later to bedevil some of these countries had their antecedents in immediate postindependence mismanagement of natural resources. The situation did not improve in subsequent years, as military dictatorship and autocratic one-party-rule made strides across the continent. Not even the current trend of having "new-breed" politicians has effectively removed this problem. Indeed, across the continent, the expectation that this crop of younger generation politicians would be bringing in vigor and patriotism seems not to have materialized, as many of the new-breed politicians are more corrupt than the "old-brigade" they replaced. In many of the countries, new-generation politicians who were former "socialists" have subsequently become "socialites," and those who accused old politicians of corruption and resource mismanagement began to follow the same line on their assumption of political offices. Indeed, so extensive was graft that a new "profession," known as "govementing" (the art of making a living from government resources), became a widely known phenomenon.

To a large extent, the graft in the management of natural resources in Africa has arisen because of the perception of political elites to governance. Indeed, it is the case that many of them do not have any confidence in the perpetual survival of the state, and as such would want to amass as much as they could before what they see as the inevitable collapse. But, although the tendency has always been to look at the political elites in the corrupt management of proceeds from natural resources, a class of elites that is often neglected is the civil servants, especially those working in finance ministries and departments of government relevant to natural resources. Indeed, civil service technocrats have been crucial to the ease with which political elites have looted resources of their respective countries. Ironically, because they are often out of public gaze, they have escaped on the few occasions when attempts have been made to hold political leaders accountable for resource mismanagement. The fact too that they stay longer in office than elected officials has offered them the opportunity to maximize their corrupt practices over successive administrations. In the years ahead, it is likely that the neglected role of this set of actors in natural resource management and how this has been linked to conflict will be subjects of interest to academics.

The final explanation for the lack of credible structures for governing natural resources in Africa is the nature of the international system and how this has exploited the two issues discussed above. It is widely known that the nature of international trade is still largely skewed against developing countries, and despite persistent cries for better and more equitable management, the situation has not improved in any significant way. In situations where the nature of global management of natural resources is seen to be against the continent, the extent to which credible structures can be established at the national level has been greatly hampered. Furthermore, multinational corporations operating in the continent have further exploited the existing weak structures and the greed of elites to further prevent the establishment of credible structures that can hold them accountable. Many of the companies have also realized their indispensability to the government and the elite class, and they have further exploited this to ensure the continued perpetration of weak and unaccountable order.

The second concluding question on the importance of natural resource governance and conflicts over natural resources focuses on the effectiveness of recent global initiatives aimed at ensuring that natural resources do not cause or inflame conflicts, especially the Kimberley Process. While there can be no doubt that the Kimberley Process has achieved considerable success, it should not naively launch the world on any feeling of euphoria, and neither can it serve as an alternative to the establishment of credible natural resource governance in individual countries. In the first instance, to attempt using the Kimberley Process as a model is to imply that every single natural resource will need its own framework or "Process" to prevent illegal trade. It is inconceivable to expect each natural resource—gold, oil, water, uranium, coffee, cocoa, and others—to have separate structures in place to address conflicts associated with them, just as the Kimberley Process has done for conflict diamonds. Apart from this, arrangements like the Kimberley Process can only address natural resources that have global markets and not those with only local relevance. There is, for example, no way that an international mechanism can be made to address land conflicts, which as noted earlier, have the greatest implications for security in Africa. Finally, the contents of agreements such as the Kimberley Process are understandably narrow, as they cannot address the fundamental problem of political governance at the resource production level, and neither can they impose on the state mechanisms for distributing opportunities and privileges coming from these resources.

But, while there might be difficulties in the wider applicability of mechanisms such as the Kimberly Process, the developments that led to its establishment, especially the coming together of key actors in the diamond trade, is a major achievement, and in this, international NGOs deserve considerable commendation. The "name-and-shame" policy adopted by many of these NGOs has also been successful, but how far this can go in the threats of possible libel suits remains to be seen, especially as many of the multinational companies have the financial muscles to browbeat small NGOs into submission. Multinational companies are also trying to be politically correct in their policies, even if this is only to satisfy international demand and to meet the ethical standards of some of their shareholders. The general verdict across the continent, however, is that many of these companies are still falling far short of expectation, and that they are taking far more from the continent than they are prepared to give back.

The final question on the link between natural resources, governance, and conflict asks how to ensure that conflicts surrounding these resources are prevented and the endowment made to benefit Africa's teeming population. Because the economy of all African states depends on their natural resource endowment, this is a question of pertinent political and socioeconomic concern. For Africa to derive maximum benefit from its natural resource endowment, two interrelated steps are imperative. The first step needs countries in the continent to recognize the importance of natural resource governance, and the second step undertakes a comprehensive reform of natural resource sectors. The content and strategy to be adopted in addressing both steps may vary from country to country, but the basic principles involved are similar. Recognizing the importance of natural resource governance will include identifying all the "sources" of laws that are relevant to governing natural resources. These sources include cultural practices and norms, national constitutions, regional peculiarities, international obligations and treaties, and more. It will also require the identification of the level of importance to be accorded to each of these sources and which one takes precedence over another.

Once the sources have been recognized, the contents would need to be properly identified. Among the key issues to be taken into consideration here include the role of the country's constitution in natural resource management; the politics of revenue allocation; indigenization policies and the politics of expatriate involvement in the ownership, management, and control of natural resources; property rights; human rights concerns; the relationship with global market demands; and the complexities of managing environmental issues relating to resource extraction. Apart from all these, the crucial sectors of the economy that can assist in ensuring that maximum benefits are derived from natural resources, such as the banking, insurance, custom, and excise, should be harmonized with the natural resource sector. For African countries, the need for the establishment of credible natural resource governance mechanism becomes all the more paramount because the resources forming the backbone of the economy of most of the countries are nonrenewable, and it is believed that some of these resources are dwindling in their deposits. Consequently, unless the wasteful management that comes with the absence of credible natural resource governance is immediately arrested, African countries will be denied the opportunity of using the resources now to build a diversified economic base that will prevent future conflicts over natural resources.

The second step will be to embark on a comprehensive reformation of this sector, just in the same way there are now global interests in security sector reform. Again, while the contents of the reformation will vary from country to country, among the key issues to address include how to align natural resource governance with strong and credible democratic institutions. This will ensure the effective participation of all stakeholders in the politics of resource management.

The approach of this book to discuss natural resources across the board has made it possible to take a holistic look at natural resource conflicts and to compare the issues generated by one natural resource with another and from one country to another. It has been shown here that natural resources exhibit different patterns in their links with conflict and these have again sometimes varied from country to country. However, what seems to have proved to be the primary determinant in the linkage between these resources and conflict is the importance of the resource in question to the state and its ruling elites. As argued in this book, land seems to be the most important natural resource in

Africa, especially because its importance transcends economics to an array of political, spiritual, and social considerations, and also because it is the abode of most other natural resources. Indeed, contrary to the general assumption, land, and not mineral resources, has been most central to conflict over natural resources in Africa. It is also the case that most of the conflicts (mis)labeled as conflicts over diamonds or oil, are actually over the land on which these resources are situated. As yet, water remains the natural resource whose linkage to actual conflicts has been most minimal, even if the potential for violent outburst is equally profound. Solid minerals and oil have been more associated with prolongation of conflicts, even though, in many cases, the unjust management of their proceeds has caused violent conflicts. But the prevalence of conflicts over natural resources should not becloud a number of positive developments going on in the areas of natural resource management in the continent, especially through the activities of civil society groups and the general anticorruption exercises in the continent.

On the whole, it is certain that Africa has enough resources to meet the demands of its population. The reasons the continent has not been able to maximize the opportunities from these endowments are because structures are not in place to ensure fair and equitable distribution, and a string of external influences have emerged to exploit these weaknesses to their advantage. As Africa faces the challenges of the future, ensuring that its natural resources serve the needs of its teeming population will continue to engage national and international attention. But Africa's primary natural resource is its people, and the resilience they have shown amid formidable odds is the asset the continent can draw from in its bid to activate the African renaissance. Investment in its people will offer the greatest benefit for the continent and will prevent the cycle of conflict that has brought Africa to the focus of international concern.

In conclusion, natural resource conflicts in Africa have many ramifications, which cannot be covered in any single book. What I have done here is to identify one of the key issues that threads through many of these conflicts and to situate it within the context of continental discussion. It is my hope that this book will add to the growing literature on the subject while also stimulating others to look at other themes that link natural resources to conflict in Africa, many of which, for now at least, still await their own scholars.

NOTES

Introduction

Epigraph One. A resident of Koidu, the diamond-rich town of Sierra Leone, in a private discussion held in September 1998.
Epigraph Two. "Africa's War Business," *International Herald Tribune*, August 9, 1999.

1. Land seems to be the main natural resource that has led to the rise and fall of ancient kingdoms and empires. For example, the defeat of Ai by Biblical Israel led to the fall of the latter, hitherto a dominant player in the affairs of the ancient Middle East, and the further consolidation of Biblical Israel.

2. For example, the book of Joshua in the Bible (written between 1046–616 BC) records how King Ahaz of Judah aligned with King Tiglath-pilear of Assyria to fight against the alliance formed by King Rezin of Syria and King Pekah of Israel. King Ahaz appeased the Assyrian king with resources such as silver and gold. In the ensuing battle, the Assyrians attacked Damascus, the Syrian capital, took the land and resettled the population in Kir.

3. Water is a crucial example here. For example, in AD 1091, the Egyptian ruler, Calipha Fatimid al-Mustashir, sent the Patriarch of Alexandra, Michael IV, to the Ethiopian Court with gifts in an attempt to have the Nile water return to its bank. See Yacob Arsano, "Sharing Water Resources for Economic Co-operation in the Horn of Africa," in *Trading Places: Alternative Models of Economic Cooperation in the Horn of Africa*, ed. Belay Gessesse et al. (Uppsala: Life and Peace Institute, 1996), p. 29.

4. SIPRI Yearbook 2000, *Armament, Disarmament and International Security* (Oxford University Press, 2000).

5. Martin W. Holdgate, *A Perspective of Environmental Pollution* (Cambridge: Cambridge University Press, 1979), p. ix.

6. Judith Rees, *Natural Resources: Allocation, Economics and Policy* (London: Routledge, 1990), p. 3.

7. Ibid.

8. This also caught the attention of politicians. See, for example, the position of the former American Vice President Al Gore in *Earth in the Balance: Forging a New Common Purpose* (London: Earthscan Publications, 1992).

9. The meeting was attended by more than 30,000 participants, including 103 heads of states, monarchs, and prime ministers. Its purpose was to set a series of agendas and establish a number of conventions and treaties to control the deterioration of the global environment.

10. The developing countries argued that the agenda of the conference showed a clear bias in favor of the developed world who, having exploited their own environment for development, wanted to hinder the Third World's advancement by imposing unfavorable environmental restrictions. For more discussion on the summit, see Derek Osborn and Tom Bigg, *Earth Summit 11: Outcome and Analysis* (London: Earthscan, 1998).

11. For more on this, see Abiodun Alao, "The Environment and the Future of African Security: The Security Implications of Continued Neglect," in *Africa after the Cold War: The Changing Perspective on Security*, ed. Adebayo Oyebade and Abiodun Alao (Trenton, NJ: Africa World Press, 1997), pp. 63–90.

12. This has been the focus of many studies. See, among others, Elise Boulding, ed., *New Agenda for Peace Research: Conflict and Security Re-examined* (Boulder, CO: Lynne Rienner, 1992); Chester Crocker, ed., *Managing Global Chaos* (Washington, DC: USIP Press, 1996); John Baylis and Steve Smith, eds., *The Globalisation of World Peace* (Oxford: Oxford University Press, 1997); Sola Akinrinade and Amadu Sesay, eds., *Africa in the Post–Cold War International System* (London: Cassell, 1997); Michael Hogan, ed., *The End of the Cold War: Its Meaning and Implications* (Cambridge: Cambridge University Press, 1992); Hans-Henrik and George Sorensen, *Whose World Order? Uneven Globalisation and the End of the Cold War* (Boulder, CO: Westview, 1995); Jason Ralph, "Security Dilemmas and the End of the Cold War," *Review of International Studies* 25, no. 4 (October 1999).

13. An earlier example of this can be found in the attempts at secession by Biafra (from Nigeria) in 1967.

14. One recent publication on this is Glen Oosthuysen, *Small Arms Proliferation and Control in Southern Africa* (Johannesburg: South African Institute of International Affairs, 1996).

15. This is particularly the case with De Beers, the company that controls most of the world's diamonds trade. In recent years, the company has participated in many incentives to stem the flow of conflict diamonds.

16. It is worth pointing out that the hiring of mercenaries and local militias has its own implications, especially as those hiring them do not consider their human rights records. For example, in 2004, the Austrian-based Anvil Mining Company hired members of the Congolese Armed Forces (FARDC) to protect the Diklushi Copper Mines in Kilwa, Katanga Province. They were engaged in the killing of about one hundred people.

17. In a response to the article written by Jedrzet George Frynas, "Political Instability and Business: Focus on Shell in Nigeria," *Third World Quarterly* 19, no. 3 (1998): 457–78, staff of the Shell Public Relations Department, Alan Dethridge and Noble Pepple, admitted that Shell owned 107 pistols in Nigeria. See "A Response to Frynas," *Third World Quarterly* 19, no. 3 (1998): 479–86.

18. William Reno, "Shadow States and the Political Economy of Civil Wars," in *Greed and Grievance: Economic Agendas in Civil Wars*, eds. Mats Berdal and David Malone (Boulder, CO: Lynne Rienner, 2000), pp. 43–68.

19. See Musifiky Mwanasali, "The View from Bellow," in *Greed and Grievance: Economic Agendas in Civil Wars*, ed. Mats Berdal and David Malone (Boulder, CO: Lynne Rienner, 2000), pp. 147–48.

20. Both the National Resistance Movement government in Uganda and the Rwandan Patriotic Front government in Rwanda have a history of relationships that saw both sides fighting together to remove three governments in the region (Obote in

Uganda, Habyarimana of Rwanda, and Mobutu of Zaire). The soldiers of both sides lived and fought together and a complex network of friendship and boisterous camaraderie between them existed before the DRC debacles.

21. The Kimberley Process involved the coming together of the key actors involved in the diamond trade: international NGOs, diamond processing companies, and the diamond producing countries.

22. Roger Blench studies include *Resource Conflict in Semi Arid Africa: An Essay with Annotated Bibliography* (London: ODI Working Paper, 1997); *Conflict in Protected Areas of Africa: Livestock and Conservation of the Rwenya Wildlife Management Area, North East Zimbabwe* (London: ODI, 1998); and *Hunter-gatherers, Conservation and Development: From Policy Institute to Policy Reform* (London: ODI, Resource Briefing Paper 43, 1999).

23. Mamadou B. Gueye, "Conflicts and Alliances Between Farmers and Herders: A Case Study of the Goll of Fandene Village, Senegal," Drylands Programmes, Issues Paper No. 49 (London: International Institute for Environment and Development, 1994).

24. Peter Gleick, "Water and Conflict: Fresh Water Resources and International Security," *International Security* 18, no. 1 (Summer 1993).

25. Mark Bradbury, Simon Fisher, and Charles Lane, *Working with Pastoralists NGOs and Land Conflicts in Tanzania*, Pastoral Land Tenure Series No. 7 (London: International Institute for Environment and Development), 1995.

26. Most of Global Witness' early publications were on Cambodia. These include *Forest, Farming and War: The Key to Cambodia's Future* (March 1995); *Thai-Khmer Rouge Links and the Illegal Trade in Cambodia's Timber* (July 1995); *Corruption, War and Forest Policy: The Unsustainable Exploitation of Cambodia's Forest* (February 1996); *Cambodia, Where Money Grows on Trees: Continuing Abuses of Cambodia's Forest Policy* (October 1996); *A Tug of War: The Struggle to Protect Cambodia's Forest* (March 1997). In recent years, interest has focused on Angola, with the publication of *A Rough Trade: The Role of Companies and Governments in the Angolan Conflict* (December 1998).

27. This has featured in many of Human Rights Watch publications and among the conflicts they have discussed are those in Nigeria (over oil in the Niger Delta), Sierra Leone (diamonds), Liberia.

28. Conciliation Resources' main contribution in this regard is the organization's short publications in 1997 on diamonds and the conflict in Sierra Leone.

29. ICG's interest here can be seen in their publications on the civil conflicts in Sierra Leone and in their book, *God, Oil and Country: Changing the Logic of War in Sudan* (Brussels: ICG Publication, 2002).

30. This project has produced a number of useful reports on the link between diamonds and conflicts in Africa, including *Destabilizing Guinea: Diamonds, Charles Taylor and the Potentials for Wider Humanitarian Catastrophe; Diamonds: Forever or For Good: The Economic Impacts of Diamonds in Southern Africa; Hard Currency: The Criminalized Diamonds Economy of the DRC and its Neighbors; War and Peace in Sierra Leone: Diamonds, Corruption and the Lebanese Connection; and Diamonds in the Central African Republic: Trading Valuing and Laundering*. Partnership Africa also publishes the *Diamond Industry Annual Review*, which has been a source of useful information on global diamond trade.

31. UN publications include "Reversing the Curse: Successes and Failures in Non-Renewable Natural Resources, Revenue Management from an Economic Development and Political stability Perspective"; and "Meeting the Challenge of the 'Resource Curse': International Experiences in managing the Risks and Realising the Opportunities of Non-Renewable Natural Resources Revenues," January 2006.

32. John Markakis, *Resource Conflict in the Horn of Africa* (London: Sage Publication, 1998).

33. Of all the resource conflicts in Nigeria, perhaps the most reported is the crisis in the oil-rich Niger Delta province. See, among others, Eghosa Osaghae, "The Ogoni Uprising: Oil Politics, Minority Agitation and the Future of the Nigerian state," *African Affairs* 94 (1995); Wumi Raji, Ayodele Ale, and Eni Akinsola, *Boiling Point: A CDHR Publication on the Crisis in the Oil Producing Communities in Nigeria* (Lagos: CDHR, 2000).

34. See Jakkie Cilliers and Christian Dietrich, *Angola's War Economy: The Role of Oil and Diamonds* (Pretoria: Institute for Security Studies, 2000); Tony Hodges, *Angola: Anatomy of an Oil State* (London: James Curry, 2003).

35. Studies here include William Reno, "The Business of War in Liberia," *Current History* 95, no. 601 (May 1996).

36. See, for example, Abiodun Alao, "Diamonds Are Forever . . . But So Also Are Controversies: Diamonds and the Actors in the Sierra Leone Civil War," *Journal of Civil Wars* (Autumn 1999); Gregory Copley, "Diamonds Are Not Forever," *Strategic Studies: The Journal of the International Strategic Studies Association*, no. 19 (1999).

37. See Sam Moyo, *The Land Question in Zimbabwe* (Harare: SAPES, 1995).

38. Ben Cousins, "Conflict Management for Multiple Resource Uses in Pastoralists and Agro-Pastoralists Contexts," *IDS Bulletin* 27, no. 3 (1996).

39. Most of these were undertaken directly by the World Bank or were sponsored by some of its programs, especially the Post-Conflict Fund. Perhaps the most prominent of these studies, even if equally controversial, is that by Paul Collier and Andre Hoeffler, "*Greed and Grievance in Civil War*," World Bank Policy Research Working Paper No. 2355, October 2001.

40. Studies here include William Reno, *Warlord Politics in Africa* (Boulder, CO: Lynne Rienner, 1998); John Mackinlay, "Warlords," *RUSI Journal* 143, no. 2 (1998); William Shawcross, *Deliver Us From Evil: Warlords and Peacekeepers in a World of Endless Conflicts* (London: Bloomsbury, 2000); Abdel-Fatau Musah and J. Kayode Fayemi, *Mercenaries: An African Security Dilemma* (London: Pluto Press, 1999); David Shearer, *Private Armies and Military Intervention*, Adelphi Papers 316 (London: IISS, 1997); Jakkie Cilliers and Peggy Mason, eds., *Peace, Profit or Plunder: The Privatisation of Security in War-Torn African Societies* (Half-Way House: Institute for Strategic Studies, 1999); Abdullai Ibrahim, "Bush Path to Destruction: The Origin and Character of the RUF," *Journal of Modern African Studies* 36, no. 2 (1998): 203–35; Paul Richards, *Fighting for the Rain Forest: War, Youth and Resources in Sierra Leone* (Oxford: James Curry, 1996); Jeff Herbst, "Economic Incentives, Natural Resources and Conflict in Africa," *Journal of African Economies* 9, no. 3 (2000); and David Keen, *The Economic Functions of Violence in Civil Wars.*, Adelphi Papers 320 (London: IISS, 1998).

Chapter 1

Epigraph One. Nicholas Hildyard, "Blood, Babies and the Social Roots of Conflicts," in *Ecology, Politics and Violent Conflicts*, ed. Mohamed Suliman (London: Zed Books, 1999), p. 21.

Epigraph Two. Alex de Waal, *Who Fights? Who Cares? War and Humanitarian Action in Africa* (Trenton, NJ: African World Press, 2000), p. xv.

1. Malthus' main thesis was of natural laws governing the relationship between population and resources. If population increase exceeds resource availability, starvation and disease were inevitable to restore the balance. See Thomas Malthus, *An Essay on the Principle of Population* (London: Dent and Sons, 1966).

2. Vandama Shima, "Resources," in *The Development Dictionary*, ed. Wolfgang Sachs (London: Zed Books Ltd., 1995), p. 206.

3. Ibid.

4. Ian G. Simmons, *The Ecology of Natural Resources* (London: Edward Arnold, 1974), p. 3.

5. Judith Rees, *Natural Resources: Allocation, Economics and Policy* (London: Routledge, 1994), p. 14.

6. Richard Lecomber, *The Economics of Natural Resources* (London: Macmillan, 1979), p. 3.

7. Simmons, *Ecology of Natural Resources*, p. 3.

8. John Stuart Mill, *Three Essays* (London: OUP, 1912).

9. Geoffrey Kay, *Development and Underdevelopment: A Marxist Analysis* (London: Macmillan, 1975), pp. 4–6.

10. This is centered on the whole debate of "People–Nature" relations in Marxist principle. Some scholars have argued that Marxism is incompatible with an ecological perspective and effective protection of the environment. These scholars include M. Bookchin, *Rethinking Society* (Montreal: Black Rose, 1989); J. Clarke, "Marx Inorganic Body" *Environmental Ethics*, vol. II (1989), pp. 243–58; and R. Morrison, "Two Questions for Theory and Practice: Can You be Marxist and Green? Can Marxism be Green?" *Rethinking Marxism* 7, no. 3 (1994): 128–36. Others, however, argue that Marxism offers a satisfactory basis for the development of a sociophilosophical approach to understanding ecological problems. One of the scholars here is Paul Burkett, "Value, Capital and Nature: Some Ecological Implications of Marx's Critique of Political Economy," *Science and Society* 60, no. 3 (1996): 32–59.

11. George Liodakis, "The People-Nature Relations and the Historical Significance of the Labor Theory of Value," *Capital and Class*, no. 73 (Spring 2001): 114.

12. Quoted from Rees, *Natural Resources*, p. 12.

13. Ibid.

14. Erich Zimmermann, *World's Resources and Industries* (New York: Harper and Brothers, 1933), pp. 3–9.

15. Francis Deng, "Anatomy of Conflict in Africa" in *Between Development and Destruction: An Enquiry in the Causes of Conflict in Post Colonial State*, ed. Luc Van de Goor, Kumar Rupesinghe, and Paul Sciarone (The Hague: The Netherlands Ministry of Foreign Affairs, 1996), p. 219.

16. Michael Nicholson, *Conflict Analysis* (London: English University Press, 1971), p. 2.

17. Quoted from Van de Goor, Rupesinghe, and Sciarone, eds., *Between Development and Destruction*, p. 2.

18. Ibid.

19. Mark Duffield, "Post-Modern Conflict: Warlords, Post Adjustment States and Private Protection," *Journal of Civil Wars* 1, no. 1 (Spring 1998): 66.

20. David Keen, "The Economic Functions of Violence in Civil Wars," Adelphi Papers 320 (London: IISS, 1998).

21. Nick Lewer, Jonathan Goodhand, and David Hulme, "Social Capital and Political Economy of Violence: A Case Study of Sri Lanka," *Disasters* 24, no. 4 (2000): 390–406.

22. I have used this to describe a broad range of studies that adopt a distinctive approach to the study of resource conflict, different from those linking it to the environment and security. I have coined this from the title of one of the main studies in this range, David Keen's "The Economic Functions of Violence in Civil Wars." I have, however, dropped "civil" to enable a wider discussion of conflicts that are not internal.

23. Robert McNamara, *The Essence of Security: Reflections in Office* (London: Hodder and Stoughton, 1968).

24. Richard Falk, *This Endangered Planet* (New York: Random House, 1970).

25. Arthur Westing, ed., *Global Resources and International Conflict* (Oxford and New York: SIPRI/OUP, 1986).

26. Barry Buzan, *People, State and Fear: The National Security Problem in International Relations* (Brighton: Wheatsheaf Books, 1983).

27. Barry Buzan, *People, State and Fear: An Agenda for International Security Studies in Post Cold War Era* (Boulder, CO: Lynne Rienner, 1991).

28. Caroline Thomas, *The Environment in International Relations* (London: Royal Institute of International Affairs, 1992).

29. Susan Carpenter and W. J. D. Kennedy, *Managing Public Disputes: A Practical Guide to Handling Conflict and Reaching Agreements* (London: Jossey-Bass Publishers, 1988).

30. David Wirth, "Climatic Chaos," *Foreign Policy*, no. 74 (Spring 1989).

31. Peter Gleick, "Environment, Resources and International Security and Politics," in *Science and International Security*, ed. Eric Arnette (Washington, DC: American Association for the Advancement of Science, 1990), pp. 501–23.

32. Jodi Jacobson, *Environmental Refugees: A Yardstick of Habitability*, Worldwatch Paper No. 86 (Washington, DC: Worldwatch Institute, 1988).

33. Peter Wallensteen, "Food Crops as a Factor in Strategic Policy and Action," in Westing, *Global Resources*.

34. Ted Gurr, "On the Political Consequences of Scarcity and Economic Decline," *International Studies Quarterly* 29, no. 1 (1985): 51–75.

35. Ibid.

36. "Linkage Between Environmental Stress and Conflict," London: CSDG Occasional Paper No. 2, 2002.

37. The most prominent of these are Toronto/AAAS Project on Environment and Acute Conflict and the Environmental and Conflict Project (ENCOP) in Switzerland.

38. For more on this, see Jon Barnett, "Destabilizing the Environmental Conflict Thesis," *Review of International Studies* 26, no. 2 (April 2000).

39. Richard Kaplan, "The Coming Anarchy," *Atlantic Monthly*, February 1994.

40. Ibid.

41. Richard Kaplan, *The End of the Earth* (New York: Random House, 1996).

42. Paul Richards, *Fighting for the Rain Forest: War Youth and Resources in Sierra Leone* (Oxford: James Curry, 1996).

43. Keen, "The Economic Functions of Violence in Civil Wars."

44. Ibid., p. 11.

45. Jakkie Cilliers, "Resource Wars—A New Type of Insurgency," in *Angola's War Economy: The Role of Oil and Diamond*, ed. Jakkie Cilliers and Christian Dietrich (Pretoria: Institute for Strategic Studies, 2000).

46. Ibid., p. 3.

47. The four categorization of insurgencies made by Clapham are Liberation, Separatist, Reform, and Warlord. See Christopher Clapham, "Analyzing African

Insurgencies," in *African Guerrillas*, ed. Christopher Clapham (Oxford: James Curry, 1998).

48. Cilliers, "Resource Wars—A New Type of Insurgency," pp. 4–5.

49. Paul Collier, "Doing Well out of War: An Economic Perspective," in *Greed and Grievance, Economic Agendas In Civil Wars*, ed. Mat Berdal and David Mallone (Boulder, CO: Lynne Rienner, 2000).

50. Ibid.

51. For a critique of Collier's position, see Abiodun Alao and Funmi Olonisakin, "Economic Fragility and Political Fluidity: Explaining Natural Resources and Conflict," *Journal of International Peacekeeping* 7, no. 4 (Winter 2000).

52. It is noteworthy that many have found the term *warlords to* be somewhat problematic, especially as it presupposes, even if subtly, a sort of contempt for the people for whom it is used to describe. The term is only used in connection with Africa and Eastern Europe, and hardly has the term been used to describe the activities of past Western European and American actors such as Oliver Cromwell and George Washington, even though their activities are similar to those who are being so tagged in recent African and Eastern European civil conflicts.

53. William Reno, "The Business of War in Liberia," *Current History*, no. 211 (1996), and *Humanitarian Emergencies and Warlord Economies in Liberian and Sierra Leone* (Helsinki: UNU World Institute for Development Economics Research, 1997).

54. William Reno, *Warlord Politics and African States* (Boulder, CO: Lynne Rienner, 1998).

55. Mark Duffield, "Post-Modern Conflict: Warlords, Post-Adjustment States and Private Protection," *Journal of Civil Wars* 1, no. 1 (Spring 1998): 65–103.

56. Ibid., p. 65.

57. William G. Thom, "Congo-Zaire's 1996–97 Civil War in the Context of Evolving Pattern of Military Conflicts in Africa in the Era of Independence," *Journal of Conflict Studies* 19, no. 2 (1999): 93–123.

58. David Shearer, *Private Armies and Military Intervention*, Adelphi Papers 316 (London: IISS, 1998).

59. The activities of these organization evoked considerable controversy, especially the Sandlines where a parliamentary committee had to be set up to investigate the extent of the government's involvement in the activities.

60. Kevin O'Brien, "Private Military Companies and African Security, 1990–98," in *Mercenaries: An African Security Dilemma*, ed. Abdel-Fatau Musa and J. Kayode Fayemi (London: Pluto, 1999), pp. 43–75.

61. Herbert Howe, "Private Security Forces and African Stability: The Case of Executive Outcome," *Journal of Modern African Studies* 36, no. 2 (1998).

62. Funmi Olonisakin, "Arresting the Tide of Mercenaries," in *Mercenaries: An African Security Dilemma*, ed. Musa and Fayemi, pp. 233–56.

63. Laurie Nathan, "Trust Me, I am a Mercenary: The Lethal Danger of Mercenaries in Africa," *African World Review*, November 1997–March 1998.

64. Ibid., p. 4.

65. Gerald Garvey and Lou Ann Garvey, eds., *International Resource Flow* (Lexington, MA: Lexington Books, 1977), p. ix.

66. Kisangani is the third largest city in the DRC and the site of considerable mineral deposits. The battle for the control of the town is discussed in chapter 4.

67. See Tony Hodges, *Angola: Anatomy of an Oil State* (London: James Curry, 2004), p. 170.

68. In Angola, there were several efforts at peace, all of which were frustrated by Savimbi. There were thirteen peace agreements to end the Liberian Civil War, and it is believed that Charles Taylor's intransigence, and the implicit encouragement he received from his subregional allies, especially Côte d'Ivoire and Burkina Faso, were key issues in his attitude toward the peace agreements. See Abiodun Alao, John Mackinlay, and Funmi Olonisakin, *Peacekeepers, Politicians and Warlords: The Liberian Peace Process* (Tokyo: United Nations University Press, 1999). In Sierra Leone, there were the Abidjan and the Lomé accords, signed in November 1996 and July 1999, respectively.

69. The British position during the discussions leading to the agreement was that the interest of the whites over the land they occupy must be protected. Although the liberation fighters, especially those in Mugabe's Zimbabwean African National Union (ZANU), were determined to ensure the repossession of land, subtle diplomacy was to prevail. As will be shown later in this book, this was to become a crucial issue in post-independence politics.

70. This is under Article 7, sub-section 12 of the Lomé Peace Accord. Under the agreement, the elected president could not remove him from this position.

71. See, for example, Abiodun Alao and Comfort Ero, "Cut Short for Taking Short Cuts: The Lomé Peace Agreement in Sierra Leone," *Journal of Civil Wars* 4, no. 3 (Autumn 2001).

72. See, among others, Donald Rothchild's studies, including "Structuring State-Society in Africa: Towards and Enabling Political Environment," in *Economic Change and Political Liberalization in Sub-Saharan Africa*, ed. Jennifer Widner (Baltimore: The Johns Hopkins University Press, 1994); "Ethnic Bargaining and State Breakdown in Africa," *Nationalism and Ethnic Politics* 1 (1995); Donald Rothchild and Naomi Chazan, eds., *The Precarious Balance: State and Society in Africa* (Boulder, CO: Westview, 1988).

73. Nakanyike Musisi, "Development Cost of Conflict: A General Overview" (paper presented at the Conference on Engendering the Peace Process, Kampala, Uganda, February 9–11, 2000).

74. Adebayo Adedeji, ed., *Comprehending and Mastering African Conflicts* (London: Zed Books, 1999), p. 364.

75. Quoted from Sola Akinrinade, "Proceeding from the ECOMOG Experiment" (unpublished mimeo).

76. Figures provided by the representative of the UNHCR put Africa's refugee population at eight million as of May 1999. See *Conflict Trends*, no. 3 (1999): 3.

77. These are the excuses reeled out in every annual report by agencies such as the IMF and the World Bank.

78. Quoted from Jide Owoeye and P. S. Airewele, "Economic Underpinnings of Security in Africa" (unpublished manuscript, p. 6).

79. Larry Diamond, *Prospect for Democratic Development in Africa* (Palo Alto: Hoover Institution, 1997), p. 2.

80. See Richard Joseph, "Africa, 1990–1997: From Abertura to Closure," *Journal of Democracy* 9, no. 2 (April 1998).

81. Sam Moyo and Daniel Tarera, "The Environmental Security Agenda in Southern Africa," *Southern Africa Political and Economic Monthly* (*SAPEM*), June 2000.

82. Ramesh Thakur has discussed this paradox at some length in his article "Peace Research," in *Work in Progress* (United Nations University Bulletin) 15, no. 3 (Summer 1999).

83. Boutrous Boutrous Ghali "Supplement to Agenda for Peace: Position Paper of the UN Secretary General on the Occasion of the Fiftieth Anniversary of the United Nations," A/50/60-S/1995/1, January 3, 1995, in *An Agenda for Peace* (1995), p. 9.

84. This was formally adopted at the Assembly of Heads of States and Government's meeting in Maputo, Mozambique, in July 2003.

85. This resulted from the merging of different initiatives designed to equip Africa for the challenges of the future. The two prominent initiatives were Millennium Partnership for the African Recovery (MAP) initiated by presidents Mbeki, Obasanjo, and Bouteflika, respectively of South Africa, Nigeria, and Algeria, and the Omega Plan, championed by President Abdulaye Wade of Senegal.

86. Those in this group derisively describe the initiative as "Kneel-pad," derogatively coined to reflect Africa's submissive position to the West in the search of economic assistance.

87. As of June 2006, twenty-five countries have acceded to the APRM, with five others seeking ascension.

Chapter 2

Epigraph One. A Liberian Civil Society Activist, in a private discussion held September 2001.

Epigraph Two. Fred Pearce, *Climate and Man: From the Ice Age to the Global Green House* (London: Vision Books, 1989), p. 70.

1. Michael Tovar, *Economic Development in the Third World* (New York and London: Longman, 1989), p. 27.

2. Successive World Bank Reports continue to indicate the enormity of the socio-economic situation in Africa. While the deploring situations in other developing societies are also mentioned, the reports have been unequivocal that Africa is relatively worse-off than other regions.

3. L. Lewis and L. Berry, *African Environment and Resources* (Boston: Unwin Hyman, 1988), p. 1.

4. Ibid.

5. E. A. Boateng, *A Political Geography of Africa* (Cambridge: Cambridge University Press, 1978), p. 36.

6. The Cambrian period is the oldest time in the division of the Paleozoic Era, believed to have begun some 600 million years ago and lasting between 80 and 100 million years.

7. Alan Mountjoy and David Hilling, *Africa: Geography and Development* (London: Hutchinson, 1988).

8. Reuben K. Udo, "Environment and the Peoples of Nigeria: A Geographical Introduction to the History of Nigeria," in *Groundwork of Nigerian History,* ed. Obaro Ikime (Ibadan: Heinemann, 1999), p. 10.

9. William Hance, *The Geography of Modern Africa* (New York: Colombia University Press, 1969), p. 15.

10. These are major regions in which distinctive plant and animal groups usually live in harmony with each other and are well adapted to the external conditions of the environment.

11. A. M. O'Connor, *An Economic Geography of East Africa* (New York, Frederick A. Praeger, 1966), p. 73.

12. For example, David Livingstone was surprised to find that the Mozambican blacksmiths considered British iron to be of poor quality as compared with local iron.

13. The link between population and natural resource consideration is discussed at some length in Gareth Jones and Graham Hollier, *Resources, Society and Environmental Management* (London: Paul Chapman Publishing, 1997). The entire second chapter of the book discusses Resources and Resources Future.

14. Pieter Esterhuysen, ed., *South Africa in Sub-Equatorial Africa: Economic Interaction* (Pretoria: Africa Institute of South Africa, 1994), p. 9.

15. See World Bank/IMF AGM Daily, October 2, 2004, p. 15.

16. Ian Woodman, "War of Scarcity: Myth or Reality? An Examination of Resource Scarcities as a Cause of Conflict in Africa," in *Seaford House Papers*, edited by J. E. Spence (London: Royal College of Defense Studies, 2002).

17. Ibid.

18. Ibid.

19. Steven Metz, "A Strategic Approach to African Security: Challenges and Prospects," *African Security Review* 9, no. 3 (2000).

20. Ibid.

21. Ibid. Indeed, the Ugandan President Museveni confirmed that it is frustrating to spend money training military officers that may die of AIDS shortly after training.

Chapter 3

Epigraph One. A peasant farmer in Modakeke, southwest Nigeria, in a private discussion held in August 2003.

Epigraph Two. Robert Mugabe, *Sunday Times* (Johannesburg), September 10, 2000.

1. One consequence of this is the increasing number of external interests in land politics in Africa. Most of these, though, have focused on land reform exercises across the region. Development agencies of western countries, World Bank, and international NGOs have taken active interests in funding reports and organizing meetings on the topic. For example, the British Department for International Development (DFID) funded land reform projects and meetings on Uganda, while an international NGO, such as Oxfam, has a Land Policy Adviser for Africa. Universities in Europe and America have also undertaken a number of collaborative projects with African universities on the politics of land reform.

2. For more on land scarcity in Rwanda, see Jean Bigagaza, Carolyne Abong, and Cecile Mukarubuga, "Land Scarcity, Distribution and Conflict in Rwanda," in *Scarcity and Surfeit: The Ecology of African Conflicts*, ed. Jeremy Lind and Kathryn Sturman (Pretoria: ISS, 2002), pp. 51–84.

3. Ibid., p. 52.

4. Ibid., p. 68.

5. Ibid., p. 69.

6. Ian Woodman, "War of Scarcity: Myth or Reality? An Examination of Resource Scarcities as a Cause of Conflict in Africa," in *Seaford House Papers*, ed. J. E. Spence (London: Royal College of Defense Studies, 2002), p. 6.

7. Discussion with Suleiman Rahal of the "Nuba Survival," a London-based NGO working on the political situation in the Nuba Mountains of the Sudan, March 2001.

8. Discussions and interview in Cotonou, December 2002.

9. The areas most affected by this are Gbede Kekere and Gbede Nla in Oke Ira Nla communities of Badore, Ajah. See *This Day* (Lagos), April 14, 2004, p. 5.

10. There are different opinions as to what the Islamic system says about the treatment of women over ownership and control of land. While in operation it seems to discriminate against women, some Islamic scholars have challenged this tendency as not being in conformity with Islam. Indeed, the *Hadith* (the saying of the Prophet) notes that people are partners in three elements: water, grass, and fire, with grass here being interpreted as land.

11. There are exceptions in the case of Nigeria, where, although the country as a whole has not adopted Islamic laws, some states within the country have declared Sharia law. In this situation, Islamic law may govern land tenure at the state level, while western law applies at the federal level. In theory the federal law supersedes state laws, but the reality is often more difficult and in situations like this, the propensity for conflict becomes heightened.

12. Okechukwu Ibeanu conducted a comprehensive study on the Aguleri–Umuleri conflict. See Okechukwu Ibeanu, "Aguleri-Umuleri Conflict in Anambra State," in *Civil Society and Ethnic Conflict Management in Nigeria*, ed. Thomas Imobigbe (Ibadan: Spectrum Books, 2003), pp. 164–222.

13. For more on this, see "The Tiv Crises," *News* (Lagos), November 12, 2001.

14. *African Research Bulletin* (Political), July 1992, p. 10658.

15. This is the *Zaramos* (coastal African groups and Arab Swahili). Although this has taken religious dimensions (Christians versus Muslims) it is, in origin, a resource-based problem.

16. *African Research Bulletin* (Political), May 1992, p. 10583.

17. *African Research Bulletin* (Political), March 1993, p. 10935.

18. See *UN News Service* for August 10, 2004.

19. Emizet Kisangani, "Legacies of the War Economy," in *The Democratic Republic of Congo: Economic Dimensions of War and Peace*, Michael Nest, François Grignon, and Emizet Kisangani (Boulder, CO: Lynne Riennes, 2006). I thank the author for giving me an advance copy of this paper.

20. While it may not be recognized in western societies, local charms play an important role in local conflicts, especially those over land. Indeed, researchers now looking at African conflicts recognize that a different order of knowledge exists in these societies, and this order is sometimes such that the western scientific precision tools may not be able to understand.

21. For example, the judicial commission set up by the Nigerian government to handle the Aguleri–Umuleri land conflict recommended that government should declare the area in dispute as a "no-man's-land." When the government released the white paper on the findings, however, it directed that further development on the land should concentrate on the Umuleri held areas "to compensate for their loss." This gave many people the impression that "powerful" people from the Umuleri clan have influenced the findings in their favor. In a country where powerful individuals have altered the course of justice, many are apt to believe such allegations. While not disproving the claims of the Umuleris, public availability of the judicial report is believed to be more in line with justice and fair play. As expected, the Aguleris rejected government's decision, and tension over the disputed territory continues.

22. Indeed, there were allegations that under President Moi, the Kalenjin people were brought "food" by government agencies while they were in the process of forcefully

acquiring land from the Luos. See *African Research Bulletin* (Political), March 1992, pp. 10508–9.

23. The Kalenjins in particular were believed to have suffered considerably in this respect as they lost land around the Rift Valley to the Kikuyus.

24. The Chambas have always denied the Danjuma connection, but the Kutebs insist on this claim, and many of the neighboring communities believe in the hidden involvement of General Danjuma.

25. See Omon Julius Onabu, "Edo, Kogi Deputy Governors Meet over Land Dispute," *This Day* (Lagos), July 15, 2003.

26. See *This Day* (Lagos), October 31, 2004.

27. *African Research Bulletin* (Political), June 2002, p. 14899.

28. The decision to take the case to the ICJ was made in February 1995 at a summit meeting in Zimbabwe. Both countries also agreed at the summit that they would accept the judgment of the ICJ as binding.

29. This position was made clear by the Ethiopian president. See "A Closed Chapter," *African Economy*, October 2004, p. 18.

30. Ethiopia has met with the special envoy, even through Eritrea has refused any meeting, insisting first that Ethiopia should respect the ruling of the boundary commission.

31. This aspect of the Nigerian–Cameroon dispute is not often discussed, as it seems to have been overshadowed by the dispute between the two countries over the oil-rich Bakassi Peninsula.

32. As at the end of 2004, a new round of conflicts seems to be brewing as the inhabitants of some of the villages refuse to see themselves as part of Cameroon. A Nigerian official told me that all the country can do is to hand them over in line with the judgment of the International Court of Justice. Whether the people see themselves as part of Cameroon or not is, according to him, outside the concern of Nigeria.

33. For example, the domestic opinion in Nigeria was against handing over the villages to Cameroon. There were even protests in London by Nigerians whose territories were caught up in the exchange.

34. Conflict did arise earlier in the experience of British rule over Ghana (Gold Coast). After the annexation of Fante land, the elites, led by J. E. Casely-Hayford, protested; this was to lead to the formation of the National Council of British West Africa. After this, the British no longer tried to annex tribal Ghana land.

35. This explains the deep involvement of the Catholic Church in the efforts to resolve the conflict.

36. For more on this conflict, see *African Research Bulletin* (Political), February 1994, p. 11342.

37. "Ghana: North versus South," *African Confidential* 36, no. 14 (July 7, 1995): 4.

38. For more on the relationship between the Ife and the Modakeke people before the recent rounds of conflict, see Oyeleye Oyediran, "Modakeke in Ife: Historical Background to an Aspect of Contemporary Ife Politics, *Odu*, no. 10 (July 1974): 63–78.

39. Samuel Johson, *The History of the Yorubas* (Lagos: CMS, 1921) and I. A. Akinjogbin, "Ife: The Years of Travail, 1793–1893," in *The Cradle of a Race: Ife from the Beginning to 1980*, ed. I. A. Akinjogbin (Port Harcourt: Sunray Publications, 1992).

40. Sir Adesoji Aderemi was the last governor of the western Region and the longest reigning *Ooni* in recent history.

41. This was a decree promulgated by the Federal Military Government in Nigeria in 1979. This is discussed later in this chapter.

42. The first of these conflicts came as a shock to the government, and the government set up the Justice Ibidapo Obe Commission of Inquiry.

43. For a more detailed discussion of the Ife–Modakeke conflict, see I. O. Albert, "Ife Modakeke Crisis," in *Community Conflict in Nigeria: Management, Resolution and Transformation*, ed. O. Otite and I. O. Albert (Ibadan: Spectrum Books, 1999).

44. The first manifestation of the tension between the two was over who was to be the chairman of the Oyo State Council of traditional rulers. It is believed by many that one of the reasons the state was broken into two (Oyo and Oshun) was to separate the two traditional rulers.

45. Interviews conducted during visits to Ife and Modakeke between 1998 and 2002.

46. It would appear that the resolution of the conflict depends largely on coercion, and its success depends on the expectation that the heavy force the government threatened to use in the eventuality of another uprising would prevent the occurrence of conflict. The government has decided to, among other things, build a police college, to demarcate the two communities, with the hope that policemen in the college would forcefully suppress any uprising conflict.

47. I thank Tajudeen Abdul Raheem for drawing my attention to this point.

48. Angola and Mozambique, the two other countries that could have been affected, were left largely unaffected for three reasons: first, the nature of the Portuguese imperialism was not predisposed to the ownership of large farm plantations; second, there was a policy of land nationalization by the immediate postindependence governments in these former Lusophone countries, especially Mozambique. This put the land ownership problems in the country under a different context. Third, the civil wars that ultimately engulfed the countries diverted national attention to problems considered more fundamental than land ownership controversies.

49. Donna Pankhurst, *A Resolvable Conflict? The Politics of Land in Namibia* (Bradford, UK: University of Bradford Department of Peace Studies, 1996), p. 1.

50. During the war of liberation, Mugabe was the black nationalist most hated by the whites. The popular saying among white Zimbabweans was "ABM" meaning "Anybody but Mugabe."

51. For more on the land dispute in Zimbabwe, see Steve Kibble, *Land, Power and Poverty: Farm Workers and the Crisis in Zimbabwe* (London: Catholic Institute of International Relations, 2001); Marongwe Nelson, *Conflict over Land and other Natural Resources in Zimbabwe* (Harare: Greenwood Park, 2003); Emerson Zhou, *Socio-economic Implications of the Current Farm Invasion in Zimbabwe* (Harare: Friedrich-Stiflung, 2002).

52. Evidences to support the fact that many of the guerrilla fighters saw the war in land terms could be seen in many of the *Chimurenga* (Liberation) songs. They were also encouraged in this belief by the leaders of the liberation movements.

53. Sam Moyo, *The Land Question in Zimbabwe* (Harare: SAPES Books, 1995), p. 3.

54. An anecdote in Zimbabwe shows the extent of alleged corruption and irregularities in the land-reallocation exercise. A key cabinet minister was said to have spotted a huge expanse of land during a drive through the suburb of Harare and immediately told his driver that he must acquire the land, to which the driver allegedly responded that he only just acquired it the previous week.

55. The referendum has its roots in the constitutional commission set up by the government in May 1999 to gather people's views on a new constitution and to submit a report to the president within six months. The draft was submitted on November 29, 1999, and was gazetted on December 2, 1999.

56. On the first day of the two-day referendum, the state-owned *Herald* newspaper wrote a front-page editorial comment titled "Let Us All Vote for Land, Peace and a Democratic Future," see *Herald* (Harare), February 12, 2000. Indeed, the issue divided the newspapers in the country, with the *Herald* supporting the government and other newspapers such as the *Zimbabwe Independent* and the *Standard* supporting the opposition.

57. Discussions held with Zimbabwe's opposition members, April 2000.

58. Editorial of *Zimbabwe Independent* (Harare), "Let us Vote 'No' to Dictatorship," February 11, 2000.

59. I was in Zimbabwe during the period and this sentiment was clearly noticeable.

60. There seems to be a disagreement within the ZANU-PF over land occupation. For example, the Home Affairs Minister declared on March 10, 2000, that farm occupation had served its purpose and should end. Mugabe, however, contradicted him by declaring that the occupation must continue.

61. BBC News, April 6, 2001.

62. *New Vision* (Kampala), June 3, 2000, p. 12.

63. In an interview he granted to Sky Television on May 24, 2004, Mugabe conceded that some mistakes were made, but these, according to him, did not affect the principle behind the action and that he had no regrets.

64. *Guardian* (Lagos), September 9, 2003.

65. *Punch* (Lagos), July 28, 2004, p. 10.

66. Curiously, the land the Kwara State government allocated to the Zimbabwean farmers is currently occupied, with about 20,000 people who consider themselves as traditional occupants. As expected, the Zimbabweans were concerned that their arrival would result in land being seized from local people. According to the leader of the team, "we know what it feels like to be kicked off farms. If the same happens to the local population in Nigeria, the project will fail because we will get a bad name locally and internationally." See Stephan Hofstter, "Zimbabwe Farmers Get 200,000 Hectares in Kwara," *This Day* (Lagos), May 5, 2004.

67. For example, although the farmers indicated preference for title deed ownership, they were offered leases of ninety-nine years. They were also offered signed guarantees prohibiting the state from expropriating their land in future dates. See *This Day* (Lagos), May 10, 2004.

68. Martin Meredith, *Mugabe: Power and Plunder in Zimbabwe* (Oxford: Public Affairs Limited, 2002), p. 167.

69. I am, of course, aware of the *Mujibars*, the young intelligence gatherers who took active part in the war of liberation, but most of those who took part in the land-invasion exercise were even too young to have been *Mujibars* during the war.

70. Although his estranged wife, Wieslawa Humzi, made this allegation, nothing has been done to deny that the Chenjerai Humzi was a medical student in Yugoslavia during Zimbabwe's war of liberation. Humzi died of cerebral malaria shortly after the land occupation crisis had assisted him to secure a seat in the parliament.

71. A list of those who benefited from the forceful acquisition of land shows a number of people hitherto known for their radical socioeconomic and political views.

72. *Chimurenga* is the *Shona* word for struggle, and it has been used in Zimbabwean history to describe the war against foreign control. The *Chimurenga* 1 was the war fought to resist the establishment of imperial control. *Chimurenga* 2 was the main war of liberation that resulted in the political independence of the country in April 1980.

73. See *African Confidential* 44, no. 4 (February 21, 2003).

74. *Independent* (London), May 1, 2001.

75. Ibid.

76. The relationship later degenerated with Prime Minister Tony Blair and President Mugabe trading personal insults, and Britain championed the imposition of EU sanction on Zimbabwe in February 2002.

77. There was a distinct division within the organization over the issue of Zimbabwe. While most African members of the organization, especially Nigeria and South Africa, wanted Zimbabwe back, Britain was unambiguous in the position that Zimbabwe should remain suspended.

78. See Meredith, *Mugabe*, pp. 170–71.

79. This, for example, was the position of some of those who attended a discussion meeting organized by the African Security Unit, Centre for Defense Studies, King's College London, in January 2001. A participant was particularly enraged, calling British policy "ridiculous and hypocritical."

80. The timing was also strategic, as the government wanted to give the land before seed-bed preparation at the end of June.

81. Christopher Thompson, "Return to Hell," *London Line* (London), June 2, 2005, p. 9.

82. "South Africa: Space Invaders," *Economist*, July 14, 2001, p. 62.

83. *Daily Telegraph* (London), April 25, 2000, p. 16.

84. *Democracy and Land Reform in Zimbabwe* (New York: International Peace Academy [IPA] Workshop Report), February 2002, p. 6.

85. Ibid., p. 6.

86. Ibid.

87. *Newsweek*, July 13, 2001.

88. Of all the South African movements during the war of liberation, the PAC was the most militant in its position against the whites. Its slogan was "one-settler, one bullet." Its decision to make land an issue was predicated, to a large extent, on the importance of land to the settler community. It, however, did not have a wide appeal and no military might to pursue any radical anti-white policies even during the apartheid regime.

89. *African Research Bulletin* (Political), July 2001, p. 14494.

90. Mrs. Mandela had a widely publicized meeting with Chenjerai Humzi, the leader of the War Veterans, during the peak of the occupation of farms in Zimbabwe.

91. "Zimbabwe Land Grabs are a Wake-up Call for South Africa," *Monitor* (Kampala), May 17, 2000.

92. *South African Times* (London), August 28, 2002.

93. In 2005, there was an infamous case of a white farmer who threw the body of one of his workers to hungry lions.

94. *Guardian* (Lagos), February 15, 2001.

95. *South Africa* (London), August 15, 2006, Issue 172, p. 4.

96. Ibid.

97. *New Vision* (Kampala), June 15, 2000.

98. During the September 2002 World Development Summit in Johannesburg, South Africa, where once again Prime Minister Blair and President Mugabe demonstrated their aversion for one another, the Namibian President, Sam Nujoma, gave an open endorsement of Mugabe's land policy.

99. *African Research Bulletin* (Economic), October/November 2000, p. 14534.

100. Ibid.

101. This is the process through which land would only get into the market if the owners were willing to sell. It is also for the landowner to determine the price for the land.

102. The camp was created in 1990, after Liberian refugees began to arrive in Nigeria. By the time the Sierra Leonean civil war started, more refugees came from the country to the camp.

103. Interview with the Chief Refugee Officer for Oru Refugee Camp, November 1999.

104. Interviews and discussions in Ghana, October 2003.

105. This became the Land Use Act, under Section 315 (d) of the country's 1999 constitution.

106. This has been at the root of many conflicts in Nigeria, especially in the oil-producing regions of the country where the population has tied the activities of oil MNC to the somewhat blanket permission they have received from the government to prospect for oil and what they see as the injustice in acquiring their land. This is discussed in chapter 5.

107. *East African Chronicle* (Nairobi), May 12, 1995.

108. *African Research Bulletin* (Economic), September 16–October 15, 2003, p. 15800.

109. *East African Chronicle* (Nairobi), May 12, 1995.

110. Quoted from *Land, Oil and Human Rights in Nigeria's Delta Region* (Lagos: Constitutional Rights Project, 1999), pp. 1–2.

111. Ambreema Manji has conducted a study on Land Reform in Africa. Although the study focuses on three countries, Uganda, Tanzania, and South Africa, some of the comments have applicability to other countries in Africa. See Ambreema Manji, "Land Reform in the Shadow of the State: The Implementation of New Land Laws in Africa," *Third World Quarterly* 22, no. 3 (1991): 327–42.

112. See *Sunday Nation* (Nairobi), May 25, 2003.

113. Discussions with staff of Ghana Land Commission, Accra, Ghana, November 2003.

114. These communities include Kpah-wra Town, Garnawoloins Town, Gbor Town, Bonding Camp Town, Chanbakon Town, Budyuagar Town, Monfleen Town, Nonpue Town, Bording Camp Village, Garpue Town, and New Wonuru Town.

115. Quoted from a letter written by Cllr. Alexander G. Attia Sn, the administrative manager of the Liberian Agricultural Company on August 25, 2004.

116. The Foundation for International Dignity (FIND), an NGO taking care of human welfare in the Mano River Union countries of Liberia, Sierra Leone, and Guinea, is planning to take up the case of the affected groups.

117. The government created two settlements, Kaudwane and New Xade, where it wanted the Bushmen to resettle.

118. Rodrick Mukumbira, "We Will Not Be Moved," *NewAfrica* (London) February 2005, p. 24.

119. See, for example, "Social and Economic Impact of Large Refugee Populations on Host Developing Countries," EC/47/SC/CRP.7 6, UNHCR Document, January 1997.

120. Discussion with UNHCR staff in Uganda, August 2003.

121. *African Research Bulletin* (Political), January 1991, p. 9715.

122. For more, see Jinmi Adisa, *The Comfort of Stranger: The Impact of Rwandan Refugees on Neighbouring Countries* (Ibadan: UNHS, 1996).

123. Discussions in Gulu, Northern Uganda, July 2003.

124. I gathered this from the discussions I had in Rwanda during my visit to the country. See also Jean Bigagaza, Carolyne Abong, and Cecile Mukarubuga, "Land Scarcity, Distribution and Conflict in Rwanda," p. 73.

125. For example, the UNHCR now tries as much as possible to settle refugees in ways that will not allow for deeper penetration into host countries. This has, however, not gone far and many of the existing settlements still remain as they are.

126. Scott-Crossley was sentenced to life in jail in September 2005, while his co-accused, Simon Mathebuka, was jailed for fifteen years.

127. Private discussions with Zimbabweans, March 2000.

128. "Kenya's Coffee Crunch," *Business Africa*, February 2000, p. 65.

129. Ibid.

130. Githuku Mwangi and David Ndili, "Centralized Marketing Will Give the Coffee Farmers a Better Deal," *Sunday Standard* (Nairobi), May 25, 2003.

131. *African Research Bulletin* (Economic), September 16–October 15, 1991, pp. 10471–72.

132. The conveners of the meeting were kidnapped at dawn but were rescued five hours later by armed policemen. See *African Research Bulletin* (Economic), October/November 2000, p. 14554.

133. Ibid.

134. For example, residents of the Casamance region say that the roads are bad and that a journey of thirty kilometers would take about six hours, while the communication network in the north is among the best in the continent.

135. Geography is playing a part in this, as does religion. Casamance is separated from the rest of the country and since it is bigger than Gambia, the people feel they have a justifiable case to be a viable state.

136. *African Research Bulletin* (Economic), December 16, 2001–January 15, 2002, pp. 15035–36.

137. The conflict in Côte d'Ivoire reached another dangerous level in November 2004 when French soldiers who had come into the country were killed by troops loyal to President Gbagbo. In retaliation, the French force in the country attacked and almost completely destroyed the entire Ivorian Air Force.

138. The conflict has pushed cocoa prices to a seventeen-year high. Future contracts touched 1,600 pounds sterling per ton, while prices rose by 2.25 percent to $2,317 per ton on the New York market, the highest since September 1985. See Jon Offei-Ansah, "Violence Hits Where It Hurts—The Economy," *New Africa*, November 11, 2002, p. 13.

139. It should be pointed out too that one of the key issues in the conflict is "citizenship." Many people from the neighboring countries who have lived in the Côte d'Ivoire for a long time and have been regarded as Ivorian citizens suddenly had their access to some privileges withdrawn.

140. Two-thirds of the timber comes from the Sangha and Likouala region in the north, which are unaffected by the war.

141. Emizet Kisangani, "Legacies of War Economy."

142. Discussion held in Ile Ife, July 2004.

143. Tony Hodges, *Angola: From Afro-Stalinism to Petro-Diamond Capitalism* (London: James Curry, 2001), p. 152.

144. This is in a letter dated April 26, 1989, written by the South West London Company to Mr. Shad G. Kaydea, the Managing Director, Forestry Development Authority of Liberia.

145. Letter written by late President Doe on February 15, 1985, to the export marketing manager of the South West London Company.

146. This was the 1988 figure. See Philippa Atkinson, *The War Economy in Liberia: A Political Analysis* (London: ODI, 1997).

147. For example, logging concessions were granted to Israel in Sinoe and Grand Gedeh counties. William Reno, *Warlord Politics and African States* (Boulder, CO: Lynne Rienner, 1998), p. 90.

148. This movement draws its support from the Krahn ethnic group, the ethnic group of the late President Samuel Doe. It entered the conflict in early 2003 and it is believed to be supported by Côte d'Ivoire.

149. I was in Liberia in April 2004 and was able to see the destruction of some of these agricultural bases.

150. The sanction was imposed because of President Taylor's support for regional destabilization. The initial sanction had been an arms embargo and a ban on exports of diamonds smuggled in from neighboring countries.

151. In private discussions with officials from Rwanda and Uganda, they are quick to point out the contradiction on the part of the DRC government. They also believe that the international community is handling other countries with soft gloves.

152. *Daily Telegraph* (London), October 6, 2002.

153. The animal is a national symbol, and its head graces almost everything Angolan, from postage stamps and passports, to bank notes and tailfins of national airlines. So important too is the animal that even UNITA uses it as its resistance symbol.

154. *African Research Bulletin* (Political), March 1993, p. 10947.

155. The two other countries that share the global population of the less than 700 gorillas believed to be existing in Uganda and the DRC are also involved in conflicts. Both countries are, however, trying to ensure the survival of the animals. See *African Economy*, October 2004, p. 57.

156. Leif Manger, "East African Pastoralism and Underdevelopment: An Introduction," in *Pastoralism and Environment: Experiences from the Greater Horn of Africa*, ed. Leif Manger and Abdel Ghaffar M. Ahmed (Addis Ababa, Ethiopia: OSSREA, 2000), p. 1.

157. Belay Gessesse et al., *Trading Places: Alternate Models of Economic Co-operation in the Horn of Africa* (Upsalla: Life and Peace Initiative, 1996).

158. Ibid., p. 18.

159. Ibid.

160. Ibid.

161. Ibid.

162. Dylan Hendrickson, Jeremy Armon, and Robin Mearns, "Conflict and Vulnerability to Famine: Livestock Raiding in Turkana, Kenya," *Dryland Issues Paper*, no. 80 (1998): 1.

163. The Centre for Basic Research (CBR) in Kampala has done a lot of detailed study on the subject. See, among others, Charles Ocan Emunyu, *Pastoralism and Crisis in North East Uganda: Factors That Determined Social Change in Karamoja* (Kampala: CBR Publication, Working Paper No. 2, June 1992).

164. The policy of creating national parks has created tension in pastoralist-related conflicts. Apart from the Karimojong, the establishment of the Awash National Park in

Ethiopia in 1966 in the Middle Valley and the construction of the Koka dam in the Upper Valley also represented major changes in natural resource use in the Awash Valley. See Ali Said, "Resource-use Conflict between Pastoralism and Irrigation Development in the Middle Awash Valley of Ethiopia," *Eastern Africa Social Science Research Review* 10, no. 2 (1994).

165. Indeed, there was a colonial law that two Karimojong people standing together must be arrested, because they must have either finished cattle raiding, or are about to raid, or are planning raiding.

166. *Monitor* (Kampala), September 14, 1999, pp. 1, 2.

167. Martins Aiko, "Understanding the Problem of Karamoja," in *Neither War Nor Peace: Perspectives on the Karamoja Problem and Its Effects on Neighbouring Communities,"* ed. Abiodun Onadipe (London: Conciliation Resources, 2002), p. 29.

168. *New Vision* (Kampala), February 7, 2000, p. 12.

169. R. Kabushenga, "Karamoja: Uganda's Ticking Time Bomb," *Sunday Vision* (Kampala), June 25, 2000, p. 9.

170. Moses Byaruhanga, "Cattle Rustling Problem Explained," *New Vision* (Kampala), July 1, 1993, p. 20.

171. *New Vision* (Kampala), May 31, 2000, p. 3.

172. *New Vision* (Kampala), January 7, 2002.

173. Ibid. These figures were given by the Commander of 3rd Division of the UPDF, Col. Sula Semakula.

174. Discussion with a former Ugandan parliamentarian, February 2000.

175. Melakou Tegegn, "Political Marginalization vs. Good Governance: The Case of Pastoralists in Ethiopia," in *Breaking Barriers, Creating New Hopes: Democracy, Civil Society and Good Governance in Africa,* ed. Abdalla Bujra and Said Adejumobi (Addis Ababa, Ethiopia: DPMF, 2003), pp. 319–35.

176. Ibid., p. 319.

177. Ibid.

178. Idrissa Maiga and Gouro Diallo, *Land Tenure Conflicts and their Management in the 5th Region of Mali,* Issue Paper No. 76, International Institute for Environmental Development, Dryland Programs, April 1998, p. 2.

179. Ibid., p. 11.

180. The tension between the two is rooted in history and a bloody conflict had broken out between them in January 1936.

181. *This Day* (Lagos), May 19, 2004.

182. Ahmed Wakili, "Herdsmen Invade Taraba," *Today Newspaper* (Lagos), July 11–17, 1999.

183. A. G. Adebayo, "Fulani and Yoruba Farmers in Iwo," *Journal of Asian and African Studies* 32 (1997), pp. 93–109.

184. For example, Cabinet Minister Francis Lotodo is alleged to have given his fellow Pokot tacit political backing. See Gitau Warigi, "Who's Fuelling Cattle Rustling by the Pokot," *East Africa Chronicle* (Nairobi), February 14–20, 2000, p. 7.

185. Statements made by Abdullahi Leloun, the district commissioner for West Pokot, *Monitor* (Kampala), January 29, 2003.

186. *Today Newspaper* (Lagos), July 11–17, 1999.

187. R. Copson, *Africa's Wars and Prospects for Peace* (New York: M. E. Sharpe, 1994), p. 98.

188. *African Research Bulletin* (Political), March 2001, p. 14325.

189. O. Bennett, *Greenway: Environment and Conflict* (London: Panos Institute, 1991), pp. 84–95.

190. These include the Lord's Resistance Army (LRA) in the northern part of the country, mainly in the Acholi land, and the (ADF) operating in the west and the north. Other armed groups such as the West Nile Bank and the UNRF are either ineffective or have stopped fighting the government.

191. For more on this, see Mobolaji Ogunsanya and S. O. Popoola, "Intervention in the Conflict Between the Yoruba Farmers and Fulani Herdsmen in Oke-Ogun, Oyo State," in *Building Peace, Advancing Democracy: Experience with Third-Party Interventions in Nigeria's Conflict,* ed. Isaac Olawale Albert (Ibadan: John Archers, 2001), pp. 86–100.

192. The OPC was one of the militant ethno-nationalist groups that emerged during the final years of the Abacha dictatorship in Nigeria. It agitates for the cause of the Yorubas against the perceived northern domination that was seen as underlining the Abacha dictatorship. It is named after Oduduwa or Oduaa, believed to be the ancestral father of the Yorubas. Other militant groups that emerged included the Arewa Congress among the northerners and the Egbesu boys among the Ibos. In the context here, the OPC came in to "protect" the interest of the Yorubas against the perceived Hausa/Fulani herdsmen.

193. Managing disputes over land tenure in Burkina Faso has a history of its own. As Christian Lund has noted, before the 1983 election, land tenure disputes that were not settled at village level were dealt with at the Tribunal de ler ou Zeme degree de juridiction de Droit Coutumier. This was presided over by the government representative of the department. During the revolutionary period (1983–91), this was replaced by the Tribunaux Populaire de la Revolution (TPR). See Christian Lund, *Land Tenure Dispute and State, Community and Local Law in Burkina Faso,* Issue Paper No. 70, International Institute for Environment and Development, May 1997.

194. In October 1998, the ECOWAS Heads of State and Government had already taken decisions on transhumance in the region.

195. *This Day* (Lagos), May 5, 2004.

Chapter 4

Epigraph One. Tajudeen Abdulraheem in a private discussion with the author held in July 2001.

Epigraph Two. Lansana Gberie, West Africa: Rock in a Hard Place, The Political Economy of Diamonds and Regional Destabilization, Occasional Paper No. 9, The Diamonds and Human Security Project, 2003.

1. As will be shown in the case of oil in Nigeria's Niger Delta, discussed in the next chapter, these expectations are sometimes misplaced. This, however, has not stopped local communities from expecting a form of windfall from their endowment, which they think would come, even if not for their sake, for the benefit of government agents, including expatriates, who would be coming to extract these resources.

2. This is at the dichotomy between local claims and national interest discussed in chapter 7.

3. *Tell Magazine* (Lagos), February 11, 2002.

4. I visited the two communities in July 2004. Although peace now prevails, remnants of the mutual suspicions still characterized their relationship.

5. The Highlanders are other Ethiopian groups such as the Amhara, Oromo, and Tigra, who had come to the region to settle but have now dominated the politics and economy of the region because of support from the government.

6. *Daily Monitor* (Addis Ababa), February 12, 2004.

7. The other country where solid minerals have come up as a factor in conflict is Angola. However, as the conflict began immediately after independence, the extent to which "mismanagement" policies of the MPLA was a cause of conflict is almost nonexistent. It seems to be a factor more in *prolonging* than *causing* conflict.

8. People in the country often say that the war has come in three phases. The first war was the one against Doe, while the war against Taylor has been divided into three. I find this potentially confusing for those who are not deeply knowledgeable about events in the country. Thus, for convenience, I have divided the war into two: against Doe and against Taylor.

9. Among the factions that emerged in the course of the conflict are the National Patriotic Front of Liberia (NPFL) under Charles Taylor; the Independent National Patriotic Front of Liberia (INPFL) of Prince Yomie Johnson; Liberian Peace Council (LPC) of George Boley; and United Liberation Movement for Democracy in Liberia, ULIMO-K of Alhaji Kromah and ULIMO-J of Roosevelt Johnson.

10. Liberians United for Reconciliation and Democracy (LURD) began its campaigns in September 1999. It later joined with another group, the Movement for Democracy in Liberia (MODEL). In June 2003, their action degenerated into a bloody civil war, and its attendant cataclysmic three phases referred to in the local Liberian parlance as World War I, II, and III.

11. See, for example, Krijn Peters and Paul Richards, "Why We Fight: Voices of Youth Combatants in Sierra Leone," *Africa: Journal of International African Institute* 68, no. 2 (1998); "Sierra Leone Prisoners of War?" *Children Detained in Barracks and Prisons, Index* (London: International Secretariat of Amnesty International, 1995); Paul Richards, "Rebellion in Liberia and Sierra Leone: A Crisis of Youth?" in *Conflict in Africa*, ed. O. Furley (London: I. B. Tauris, 1995); and Ibrahim Abdullahi, "The Lumpen Proletariat and the Sierra Leone Conflict," *Journal of Modern African Studies* 36, no. 2 (June 1998). These include David Shearer, *Private Armies and Military Intervention*, Adelphi Papers 316 (London: IISS, 1998); William Shawcross, "In Praise of Sandlines," *Spectator*, August 1998; Funmi Olonisakin, "Mercenaries Fill the Vacuum," *World Today*, June 1998. Examples of these include Funmi Olonisakin, "Nigeria and the Peacekeeping Mission in Sierra Leone," *Jane's Intelligence Review*, July 1998; Paul Conton, "The Battle for Freetown," *West Africa*, March 2–15, 1998; Desmond Davies, "Peacekeeping: African Style," *West Africa*, May 4–17, 1998. See, among others, E. Garcia, *A Time of Hope and Transformation: Sierra Leone Peace Process Report and Reflection* (London: International Alert, 1997).

12. Foday Sankoh was a member of the Sierra Leone armed forces. He was arrested and jailed for alleged involvement in a military coup against the government of the late President Siaka Stevens. After his jail term, he went on self-imposed exile and from there went on to plan his rebellion. He died in July 2003 from a stroke.

13. The number of those who died in the Sierra Leone civil conflict has been quoted as being between 75,000 and 200,000. It is, of course, impossible to get an accurate figure, but I think a figure of about 100,000 may not be too far away from the mark.

14. The word *Kamajor* is the Mende (one of the main ethnic groups in Sierra Leone) word for "hunter."

15. For a discussion on all these actors in the civil war, see Lanasana Gberie, *Sierra Leone: Destruction and Resurgence* (London: Hurst, 2005).

16. "Resources, Primary Industries and Conflict in Sierra Leone," The Conciliation Resources Special Report No. 3, September 1997.

17. A major characteristic of the alluvial type diamond is that it is closer to the surface, and therefore can be mined by any prospector.

18. This is the oldest and largest of the mines, and it is situated in the traditional homeland of the Kono people.

19. This spans eight Mende chiefdoms. The deposits are rich, offering a potential yield of up to 3 carats/ton.

20. This runs south of Zimmi town along the Mano River down to the Liberian border. The deposits are shallow and require minimal exploitation to guarantee returns. The location as a gateway to war-torn Liberia also made it strategic during Liberia's conflict.

21. Ibid.

22. The instability in the country dated back to the period immediately after independence, when conflicts between its leaders resulted in a bloody civil conflict that ultimately resulted in the dispatch of the United Nation's first international peacekeeping force in Africa in 1963.

23. These conflicts were: the Congolese government versus assorted rebel groups; the Rwandan government versus the Congolese government; the Rwandan government versus Rwandan insurgents; the Ugandan government versus Sudan-supported rebels; the Ugandan government versus the Congolese government; the Ugandan and Rwandan government versus the Zimbabwean and Angolan governments; Rwandan-backed Congolese rebels versus Ugandan-backed Congolese rebels; the Ugandan government versus the Rwandan government; the Burundian government versus the Burundian rebel factions; the Angolan government versus UNITA and anyone who supports UNITA; Mai Mai elements versus the Rwandan government and RCD; and the Sudanese government versus the Ugandan government.

24. Two of the vice presidents are from the rebel factions; one, from the political opposition; while the fourth is allied with President Kabila. All the cabinet ministries were also divided among the factions.

25. See Emmy Allio, "Why Everyone Is Fighting For Congo," *New Vision* (Kampala), September 10, 1999.

26. This was established in 1985 by the Momoh government. The GGDO itself replaced the Precious Mineral Mining Company. The GGDO again changed its name in 2004 to the Gold and Diamond Department. Before the war, the government collected a 2.5 percent duty on the value of diamonds exported from the country.

27. Victor A. B. Davies, "Sierra Leone: Ironic Tragedy," Ad Hoc Expert Group Meeting on the Economics of Civil Conflicts in Africa (Addis Ababa, Ethiopia: Economic Commission for Africa, 2000), p. 2.

28. A Swedish newspaper alleged that the head of the NPRC Government, Captain Valentine Strasser, was involved in diamond deals.

29. UNDP Reports for 1990 and 1992.

30. The anthem specifically demanded: "Where are our diamonds, Mr. President? Where are our gold? . . . All our minerals have gone to foreign lands."

31. "Zaire: Business at War," *African Confidential* 38, no. 9 (April 25, 1997): 1.

32. William Reno has discussed this at great detail in *Warlord Politics in Africa* (Boulder, CO: Lynne Rienner), pp. 84–91.

33. Ibid.

34. Ibid., p. 86.

35. President Taylor had direct involvement in the management of key natural resources, with close associates and trusted loyalists placed in strategic positions. Many of these people are under direct indictment by the International Court.

36. During my visit to this part of Sierra Leone in 2000, there were free comments by the inhabitants that diamonds have been more of a curse to the province than a blessing.

37. In Africa, due largely to the link between ethnicity and politics, leaders of insurgent movements often found it convenient to commence rebellion from their ethnic base.

38. I thank Max Ahmadu Sesay for drawing my attention to this point.

39. The late President Doe targeted the inhabitants of Nimba County for repression after a failed coup attempt by an indigine of the county, General Qwonkpa.

40. *Diamond Industry Annual Review*, Sierra Leone, 2004, p. 2.

41. *African Business*, June 2004, p. 54.

42. At the peak of conflicts in these countries, when foreign nations left for their safety, many Lebanese families remained. A Lebanese businessman in Liberia who remained in the country throughout the war told me that those who stayed when the bullets were flying would clear the fortune when the situation settles.

43. See *Sentinel* (Zwedru), May 2006, p. 4.

44. I visited this town in February 2006 and was able to see the activities of these illegal miners, many of whom were ex-combatants. Indeed, many of those interviewed during the visit argued that it was their right to extract these resources, especially as they alleged that the government was not showing any specific interest in their plight.

45. There are physical distinctions between the diamonds from the two regions. The diamonds from Cuango Valley are typically yellow and roundish while those from Lucapa tend to be grayish white and more angular. This has made it easier for experienced traders to distinguish.

46. Tony Hodges, *Angola: Anatomy of an Oil State* (Oxford: James Curry, 2001), p. 171.

47. Even before the death of Savimbi, the battle tides had begun to turn against him; prominent members of the MPLA government, including the president, had begun to alert even external observers that the defeat of UNITA was in sight.

48. Tony Hodges, *Angola From Afro-Stalinism to Petrol-Diamond Capitalism* (Oxford: James Curry, 2001), p. 152.

49. Paul Richards, "Understanding Insurgencies in Liberia and Sierra Leone." Unpublished paper.

50. *Africa Confidential* 37, no. 7 (March 29, 1996): 3.

51. John L. Hirsh, *Sierra Leone: Diamonds and the Struggle for Democracy* (Boulder, CO: Lynne Rienner, 2007), 15.

52. *Africa Analysis*, no. 344, April 7, 2000.

53. Assis Malaquias, "Diamonds Are a Guerrilla's Best Friend: The Impact of Illicit Wealth on Insurgency Strategy," *Third World Quarterly* 22, no. 3 (June 2001): 321.

54. There have been three peace agreements signed on Sierra Leone, but the RUF has been a direct signatory to two of these. The first was the Abidjan Accord signed

between the RUF and the Kabbah government in November 1996; the second was the Conakry Agreement signed between the ECOWAS and the military administration of Major Koroma; while the third was the Lomé Agreement signed in July 1999 between the government and rebels.

55. Discussions with DRC officials, March 2002.

56. "Diamond, Dollars and Democracy," *African Confidential* 37, no. 7 (March 29, 1996): 3.

57. "Angola: Mining and Undermining," *African Confidential* 39, no. 3 (October 9, 1998).

58. Mark Duffield, quoted in Paul Jackson, "Warlord as Alternative Form of Governance," *Small Wars and Insurgencies* 14, no. 2 (Summer 2003): 132.

59. Sankoh was imprisoned in Nigeria for alleged gunrunning during the Abacha administration. The detention had a controversy of its own, as there were rumors, even though ultimately unfounded, that Sankoh was jailed for backing out of diamond deals he had made with Nigeria's former dictator, Sani Abacha.

60. Sam Bockarie was killed in Liberia in April 2003.

61. Johnny Paul Koroma is believed to be dead, but no one is sure.

62. Among the groups allegedly formed with the encouragement of ECOMOG are the ULIMO factions of Alhaji Kromah and Roosevelt Johnson. It needs to be mentioned though that the motivation for this action was mainly to dilute the strength of Charles Taylor and thus prevent him from launching military attacks against the peace-keeping force.

63. See *Sentinel* (Zwedru), May 2006, p. 4.

64. David Keen, *The Economic Functions of Violence in Civil Wars*, Adelphi Papers 320 (London: IISS, 1998), p. 30.

65. Discussion with a former senior member of the RUF in London, June 2003.

66. This was the claim by Savimbi's biographer, Fred Bridgland, *Jonas Savimbi: A Key to Africa* (London: Hodder and Stoughton, 1988).

67. All these came out in the findings of the UN Special Commission on Angola. This is discussed later in this chapter.

68. *Diamond Industry Annual Review*, Special Edition on Congo, 2004, p. 8.

69. This, for example, is the position of Tajudeen Abdulraheem of the Pan-African Movement in Kampala in a private discussion.

70. Emizet Kisangani, "The Conflict in the DRC: A Mosaic of Insurgent Groups in a Web of State Constraints." Forthcoming. I am grateful to the author for giving me an advance copy of this publication and for permitting me to cite it.

71. These are the militias of the former National Republican Movement for Democracy and Development (MRND) government in Rwanda who took part in the 1994 genocide and later fled the country into the DRC. The word *Interahamwe* in Kiyarwanda means "those who come together to kill."

72. These reasons were provided by the Ugandan President, Yoweri Museveni, in addresses to the Ugandan Parliament on May 28 and June 5, 2000.

73. Discussion with Rwandan officials.

74. This, for example, is the position of Dr. Tajudeen Abdulraheem of the Pan African Movement in Kampala, Uganda.

75. Around the early 1990s, there were comments in several circles that a new crop of leadership was unfolding in Africa with the emergence into power of younger leaders in countries such as Uganda, Ethiopia, and Eritrea. It was the expectation that

these younger generations would succeed where their predecessors had failed. In some circles, therefore, there was a subtle rivalry between the old order and the younger generation, with the latter considering the former to be too conservative and the former seeing the latter as being too ambitious.

76. Despite the extent of the Kisangani conflict and the international interests it received, it is ironic that the leaders of both Uganda and Rwanda tried to reduce the extent of the conflict. Uganda President Museveni went so far as to write a letter to a local newspaper that there was no battle in Kisangani. See *New Vision* (Kampala), August 24, 1995.

77. In my discussions with officers from the armed forces of both countries, the role of natural resources is always played down significantly, and the key issue of national interest and threats to national security are given prominence.

78. President Museveni said this in his speech to the Parliament. See *New Vision*, June 16, 2000.

79. Discussion with Rwandan officials in Kigali, June 2000.

80. Discussions with senior members of the Ugandan Army.

81. Quite expectedly, both countries have different versions of the role Bamaliya played in the conflicts between them. Uganda claims that Rwanda had always wanted Bamaliya diamond mines after the country had allegedly reached an agreement with a South African–based Anglo-American company. In my discussions with Rwandan officials, this was emphatically denied and dismissed as one of Ugandan's lies to gain popularity.

82. These include the Joint Political Committee and the Army Commander Committee.

83. To date, Kisangani remains a crucial reference point in the relationship between the two countries.

84. *Sunday Vision* (Kampala), October 18, 1998.

85. See Martin Meredith, *Mugabe: Power and Plunder in Zimbabwe* (Oxford: Public Affairs Limited, 2002).

86. Report of the Security Commission to the Great Lakes, May 15–16, 2001.

87. Ibid.

88. Zimbabwe was actively involved in the war between the FRELIMO government and the RENAMO rebels in Mozambique. For most of the first decade, commitment to the war in Mozambique was President Robert Mugabe's main foreign policy agenda, especially as the war was seen as part of the wider efforts by apartheid South Africa to destabilize the region. For more on Zimbabwe's involvement in Mozambique's civil war, see Abiodun Alao, *Brothers at War: Dissidence and Rebellion in South Africa* (London: British Academic Press, 1994).

89. Report of the Security Commission of the Great Lakes.

90. Michael Nest, "Ambions, Profit and Loss: Zimbabwe's Economic Involvement in the DRC," *African Affairs*, 2001, pp. 469–90.

91. See Meredith, *Mugabe*, p. 149.

92. Ibid.

93. Tajudeen Abdul Raheem, "Enough For Our Need, Not Enough For Our Greed," *New Vision*, October 26, 1998.

94. See *African Confidential* 43, no. 5 (April 19, 2002): 1.

95. It is worth noting that there is a close friendship between President Benjamin Mkapa and Robert Mugabe and indeed the former declared the 2005 election in Zimbabwe free and fair, despite the criticism from different quarters.

96. I visited the two countries several times during the conflicts, and there were evidences that members of the Nigerian contingents took part in illegal activities.

97. For more on this see Abiodun Alao, *The Burden of Collective Goodwill: International Involvement in the Liberian Civil War* (Aldershot: Ashgate Publishers, 1996).

98. The desire to regain power for Kabbah was motivated by the desire to regain honor, as could be seen in the code name of the operation "Operation Death before Dishonor."

99. Garba was Jetley's deputy, Kpamber was the former ECOMOG commander, and Khobe was also a former commander. Adeniji was the UN Secretary General's Special Representative.

100. Quoted from Dena Montague, "The Business of War and the Prospect of Peace in Sierra Leone," *The Brown Journal of World Affairs* 9, no. 1 (Spring 2002): 236.

101. *News* (Lagos), October 9, 2000.

102. Discussions with UN officials in Sierra Leone, October 2004.

103. Isaac Olawale Albert, "The Impact of Blood Diamond on the Protractedness of African Conflicts," in *Rethinking Peace and Security in Africa*, ed. M. Ozonnia Ojielo (Lagos: CPA Books, 2002), p. 34.

104. Abdel-Fatau Musah, "A Country under Siege: State Decay and Corporate Military Intervention in Sierra Leone," in *Mercenaries: An African Security Dilemma*, ed. Abdel-Fatau Musa and J. Kayode Fayemi (London: Pluto Publishers, 1999), p. 87.

105. Ibid., pp. 87–88.

106. Ibid., p. 91.

107. David Shearer, "Explaining the Limit of Consent: Conflict Resolution in Sierra Leone," *Millennium: Journal of International Studies* 26, no. 3 (1997): 853.

108. For more on this, see Sean Dorney, *The Sandline Affair: Politics and Mercenaries and the Bougainville Crisis* (Sydney: ABC Books, 1999); Mary-Louise O'Callanghan, *Enemies Within: Papua New Guinea, Australia and the Sandline Crisis: The Inside Story* (Netley: Doubleday, 1999).

109. See Musa, "A Country under Siege."

110. This was actually the declaration of both the Executive Outcome and the Sandlines.

111. *African Research Bulletin*, August/September 1996, p. 12710.

112. James Rupert, "Diamond Hunters Fuel Africa's Brutal Wars," *Washington Post*, October 16, 1999.

113. *African Confidential* 40, no. 13 (June 25, 1999): 8.

114. *African Confidential* 40, no. 14 (July 9, 1999): 4.

115. See Partnership Africa, *The Heart of the Matter, Sierra Leone Diamonds and Human Security*, January 2000.

116. De Beers is the world's oldest and largest corporation involved in the diamonds sector. The company was established in Kimberley, South Africa, in 1888.

117. It has an equal partnership with the government of Namibia in Namdeb; the Namibian Diamond Company; the government of Botswana, in Debswana, which is the largest producer of gem diamonds in the world; and with the government of Tanzania in the Williamson diamond mine.

118. "Diamonds and Conflict: Strategies for Control," IISS Strategic Comments, Pretoria, 2000.

119. See "Angola: Rocks That Kill," *Economist*, May 29, 1999, p. 72.

120. Ibid.

121. George Franck, "Diamonds: No Stone Unturned," *Business Africa*, February 2000, pp. 16–17.

122. These were the figures provided by the chairman of De Beers during his speech to the Commonwealth.

123. Anietie Usen, "No to Blood Diamond," *This Day* (Lagos), September 6, 2000.

124. Written testimony before the U.S. Congress House Committee on International Relations, Sub-Committee on Africa, Hearing into the Issue of Conflict Diamonds.

125. BBC News, June 1, 2005.

126. This was contained in his memorandum to the House of Representatives Document 107–75, 107th Congress, 1st Session of May 24, 2001.

127. It must be noted here that the links between Osama bin Laden and diamonds are still controversial. During the trial of those convicted for bombing the United States embassies in Tanzania and Kenya in 1998, some of the witnesses claimed that Osama bin Laden was involved in diamonds and other minerals with key individuals in Africa.

128. The Diamond High Council is in Antwerp, Belgium, and it handles between 70 and 80 percent of all the rough diamonds going into the world market.

129. *Other Facets: News and Views on the International Effort to End Conflict Diamonds*, no. 13 (Ottawa, Canada: Partnership Africa-Canada), March 2004, p. 3.

130. Ibid.

131. Ibid. Smilie says that the United Nations was still spending $1.7 billion annually on peacekeeping missions in conflicts rooted to diamonds.

132. The UN Security Council had passed Resolution 865 (1993) and 1237 (1999) imposing a set of sanctions against UNITA. These include, among others, preventing free movement of UNITA officials and their families; freezing accounts of UNITA members, and prohibiting direct or indirect imports of all Angolan diamonds without certificate of origin.

133. UN Report.

134. This is specifically believed to be targeting Bulgaria, one of the countries indicted in the report.

135. *African Research Bulletin*, March 2001, p. 13908.

136. The Angolan Deputy Foreign Affairs Minister, Mr. Toko Diakenga Serao, initially dropped this hint during the first OAU Ministerial Conference on Security, Stability, Development, and Cooperation in Africa (CSSDCA) in Abuja, in May 2000. See *Comet*, May 14, 2000.

137. See Ivor Powell, "Dirty Truth Behind Clean Gems," *Mail and Guardian* (South Africa), September 1–7, 2000, p. 6.

138. UN Security Council Resolution 1343, March 7, 2001.

139. There were controversies on the asylum given to Charles Taylor. The Nigerian government argued that it took the decision to give peace a chance in Liberia, as his continued presence in the country would aggravate tension. But even in this, there were condemnations at home, with two Nigerians who each had one of their hands hacked off during the conflict challenging their government's asylum. At the UN level, the opinion seems to be that the Nigerian government should hand Taylor over to the court, as the head of the fourteen-member UNSC delegation visiting West Africa in June 2004, Emyr Parry, noted. Later, the AU Executive Council congratulated Nigeria for granting Taylor asylum, a move that was condemned by Amnesty International. In September 2004, the former UN Secretary General's Special Representative in Liberia,

Jacques Klein, noted that bringing Taylor to justice was crucial to ending the "impunity that has marked the last 25 years and turmoil in Liberia," *Other Facets: News and Views on the International Effort to End Conflict Diamonds,* no. 15, October 2004.

140. *Analyst* (Monrovia) July 27, 2004.

141. There are controversies as to what exactly happened. While the official position of the Nigerian government was that Taylor made a bid to escape and was caught, there were also many who believed that the whole "escape drama" was a setup to justify the Nigerian government's decision to hand over Taylor to the international court and, by so doing, win American favor.

142. See *Newswatch* (Lagos), April 10, 2006.

143. Paragraph 117 of the Ba-N'Daw report.

144. Oladiran Bello, "Post Cold War Conflict in Africa and the Politics of Revenue Control with Reference to the Democratic Republic of Congo" (Unpublished M.Phil. dissertation, Cambridge University, 2002).

145. *Daily Monitor* (Kampala), October 24, 2002.

146. This was the Justice David Porter Pane. The panel's report was released in May 2003.

147. *East African,* October 28–November 3, 2002.

148. The UN peacekeepers were killed during an ambush near the town of Kafe. It is believed they were patrolling a camp of those displaced from the fighting between Hema and Lendu militia forces.

149. *Other Facets: News and Views on the International Effort to End Conflict Diamonds,* no. 17, May 2005.

150. One of the offices the RUF also received was that of Minister for Energy and Power, another position strategic to mineral resources in the country. This position was occupied by a prominent member of the movement, Mr. Alimany Pallo Bangura.

151. Discussion with King's College London Research Team, August 2004.

152. *New Broom* (Monrovia), May 7, 2004.

153. *News* (Monrovia), May 7, 2004.

154. See *Other Facets: News and Views on the International Effort to End Conflict Diamonds,* no. 17, May 2005.

155. *Africa Confidential* 46, no. 9 (April 2005): 1.

156. See "U.S. Threatens Sanctions Over Congo," *East African,* June 19–25, 2000, p. 1.

157. Ibid., p. 32.

158. William Wallis, "Kimberley Process: Africa's Conflict Diamonds: Is the UN-backed Certification Scheme Failing to Bring Transparency to the Trade," *Financial Times* (London), October 29, 2003.

159. Ibid.

160. The Kimberley Process Review Mission had visited the country between May 31 and June 4, 2004, to conduct a review process. The mission was headed by Abbey Chikane of South Africa and was accompanied by experts representing Canada, Israel, the World Diamond Council, and the Ottawa-based Partnership Africa-Canada.

161. *World Bank/IMF Annual General Meeting Daily,* October 2, 2004, p. 25.

162. *Other Facets: News and Views on the International Efforts to End Conflict Diamonds,* no. 12, December 2003.

163. For example, there are agreements with Angola and a tripartite agreement between Angola, DRC, and Congo Brazzaville. DRC and Congo Brazzaville also signed

an agreement that by 2004 the exports of both countries must be of the magnitude that is verifiable.

164. This call was made by a journalist, Rafael Marques and a civil rights campaigner, Rui Falco de Campos, in their latest report, *Lundas: The Stones of Death: Angola's Deadly Diamonds.* See http://www.niza.nl/docs/200503141357095990.pdf

Chapter 5

Epigraph One. Joseph Fiennes, actor, "Oil: Blessing or Curse," *International Development Magazine,* no. 27 (Second Quarter, 2003): 23.
Epigraph Two. Hope Harriman, a community leader from the Niger Delta. Quoted from Tunde Babalola, "Niger Delta: The Pawn of Domination," *Sunday Tribune* (Ibadan), November 8, 1998.

1. As noted earlier, the United States has declared that up to 25 percent of its oil supply would come from Africa with effect from 2015. For more on this, see Paul Wihbey, "The Oil Power behind New US African Policy," *Africa Analysis,* no. 357, October 6, 2000.

2. The dominant position of these foreign oil companies is almost unchallenged in many of the countries. Indeed, the only country that has a fairly significant involvement of local oil companies in oil prospecting is Nigeria.

3. The name of the company was changed from ChevronTexaco to Texaco in May 2005.

4. For a discussion of the overall activities and strategies of these companies, see William N. Greene, *Strategies of the Major Oil Companies* (Ann Arbor: UMI Research Press, 1986).

5. *African Confidential* 43, no. 6 (March 22, 2002): 6.

6. For more on this, see Terry Lynn Karl, *The Paradox of Plenty: Oil Booms and Petrostates* (Berkeley: University of California Press, 1997).

7. The organization was created in September 1960 in Baghdad, and ironically among the founding members were Iran, Iraq, and Kuwait, three countries whose subsequent relations were to affect the role of oil in global politics. Other founding members were Saudi Arabia and Venezuela.

8. Michael O. Feyide, *Oil in World's Politics* (Lagos: University of Lagos Press, 1986), p. 52.

9. For more, Adrian Hamilton, ed., *Oil: The Price of Power* (London: Michael Joseph Limited, 1986).

10. Algeria, Libya, and Nigeria are full members while Sudan has observer status. Gabon withdrew from the organization in 1996 after the discovery of oil deposits in Rabi-Kounga made it difficult to keep to the quota set for it by the organization.

11. For example, members have been overgrowing their output target by as much as 10 percent. Also contributing to the loosening of the grip is the emergence to prominence of nonmember producers such as Angola and Russia.

12. Again, this is being disputed with the increasing unilateralism of Saudi Arabia as a result of its relation with the United States.

13. The continued membership of the organization has been a key political issue in Nigeria, especially during the country's Second Republic (1979–84), when the leader

of one of the political parties, the late Chief Obafemi Awolowo of the Unity Party of Nigeria, argued that the continued membership of the organization had no long-term interest for Nigeria, and that he would pull out of OPEC if he won the election. Although his party did not win, Awolowo's comment could not be dismissed because of the avowed respect people across the political spectrum had for him on economic matters.

14. This, for example, was the position of the 11th Nigeria Economic Summit during their June 2005 meeting. See *This Day* (London), June 6, 2005.

15. The visit by President George W. Bush to Africa in July 2003 is believed to have strong consideration for the impending role Africa would be playing in America's economic interest. Indeed, it is believed that his main discussion with the Nigerian leader, Olusegun Obasanjo, was on oil and the then ongoing crisis in Liberia.

16. In fact, unless other contending natural resources are equally high-income generating, as in the case of diamonds in Angola, all major oil-producing countries in Africa have allowed oil to dominate national economy.

17. For more on oil politics in Nigeria, see S. Tomori, ed., *Oil and Gas Sector in the Nigerian Economy* (Lagos: Faculty of Social Sciences, University of Lagos, 1991); K. Panter-Brick, ed., *Soldiers and Oil: The Political Transformation of Nigeria* (London: Frank Cass, 1978); Augustine Ikein, *The Impact of Oil on a Developing Economy: The Case of Nigeria* (New York: Praeger, 1990).

18. Prospecting for oil continued between these dates. For example, after the failure of the first effort, exploration activities resumed again in 1937, but it was forced to end because of World War I. Activities, however, resumed again in 1946, and by September 1951, the Shell BP Development Company of Nigeria was formed.

19. The Shell Petroleum Development Company of Nigerian Ltd., *Nigeria Brief*, London, January 25, 1995, p. 2.

20. This is set to increase to four million by 2010. Figures do fluctuate, and it is possible for other sources to quote different figures. This, to an extent at least, is indicative of the problems associated with oil exploration in Nigeria, as there are often disputes of how much oil is being extracted in the county.

21. Christy Butt, "Nigeria Has the Highest Volume of Discoveries," *Business Day* (Lagos), June 23, 2003.

22. This is about 3 percent of the world's natural gas reserve. Lack of infrastructure needed to liquidify and store natural gas has, however, meant that more than 75 percent of associated gas provided in the course of oil exploration is flared.

23. This was the view of Einar Holmefjord, the special adviser to INTSOK, the Norwegian Oil and Gas Partners. See Butt, "Nigeria Has the Highest Volume of Discoveries."

24. The Niger Delta Development contribution is the money being paid by oil multinational corporations for the development of oil-producing communities in Nigeria.

25. It is believed that as of 2001, there were 606 oil fields in the Niger Delta, 360 of which were onshore and 246 were offshore. See Wale Adebanwi, "Nigeria: Shell of a State," *Dollars and Sense Magazine*, July/August 2001.

26. D. S. P. Alamieyeseigha, "The Niger Delta Crises, Yesterday, Today and Tomorrow," *Tell* (Lagos), Discourse section, April 4, 2005, p. 2.

27. These are oil blocks that may not be cost-effective for major oil companies to handle. Consequently, they are licensed out to smaller companies with the technical know-how to exploit.

28. The 1955 discovery was made by Petrofina, while the Cabinda discovery was made by the Cabinda Gulf Oil Company (CABCOG), which became a subsidiary of Chevron in 1984.

29. Joao Gomes Porto, *Cabinda: Notes on a Soon-to-be-forgotten War*, Occasional Paper No. 77 (Pretoria: Institute for Strategic Studies, August 2003), p. 3.

30. Quoted from *A Crude Awakening: The Role of the Oil and Banking Industries in Angola's Civil War and the Plunder of State Assets* (London: Global Witness Publication, 1999).

31. Tony Hodges, *Angola: From Afro-Stalinism to Petro-diamond Capitalism* (London: James Curry, 2001), p. 125.

32. *Business in Africa*, February 2000, p. 62.

33. But the conflict also indicates the general dichotomy of the country, as the actors also reflect the racial and religious divisions of the country, with the central government being largely dominated by the Arab segment of the country and pursuing Islamic regime, while the SPLA are largely Christians and are of the black African stock. Although this is the main conflict in the country, there are other lesser conflicts, whose politics are inextricably tied to oil-related conflicts.

34. This was the position of Nimeri's Minister of Energy and Mining Dr. Sheriff el Tuhami.

35. The southerners have further evidences of the north's desire to dominate the oil reserve. Even the changes in the names of oil-producing fields were seen as a cause of objection. For example, the first oil-producing field was named Heglig, instead of its Dinka name, *Wunthau.*

36. *Business in Africa*, February 2000, p. 62.

37. Ateer Ejahi, "Will Oil Take the Center Stage in Sudanese Political Conflict," *New Vision* (Kampala), January 19, 2000.

38. This was the largest discovery since 1989, and it is expected to produce up to 50,000 barrels per day at the peak of its production capacity.

39. See http://www.era.doc.gov/emeu/cabs/eqguinea.html.

40. *African Research Bulletin*, September–October 2003, p. 15829.

41. See *World Bank/IMF AGM News*, October 2, 2004, p. 25.

42. *Africa South of the Sahara*, 2002, p. 392.

43. This is under the assumption that oil price does not fall below $15 per barrel.

44. *African Research Bulletin*, September 16–October 15, 2003, p. 15799. This, however, did not materialize.

45. An agreement was signed on January 31, 1995, providing for a 1,000-km buried pipeline to Kribi. This was to be laid and operated by a new joint company, the Cameroon Oil Transport Company (Cotco).

46. The estimate was made in September 2002. See *African Research Bulletin*, September 2002, p. 15010.

47. Problems over the management of the JDZ was to result in ministerial resignations and dismissal in Sao Tome.

48. See Lansana Fotana, "It Is All about Oil," *West Africa*, July 28–August 3, 2003, p. 29.

49. See Samuel Ibiyemi, "US Wants Nigeria out of Sao Tome," *Financial Standard* (Lagos), December 26, 2005.

50. Ibid.

51. There has been significant commercial interest in West African oil deposits. For example, Henton Oil and Gas, a North American company, has shown interest in

Senegal. Planet Oil (UK) and West Oil (Australia) are interested in Gambia; Monument (UK) and Petrobank (Canada) are looking at prospects in Guinea Bissau while Ranger (Canada) is investing interest in Côte d'Ivoire.

52. The plan is to ensure that the pipeline moves 160 m cubic feet of natural gas every day from Nigeria to Benin, Togo, and Ghana. There are, however, oppositions from global environmental groups against this project.

53. Stephen Boit, "Oil, Africa and the US: The Dangers," *West Africa*, December 2–8, 2002, p. 11.

54. Quoted from Olawale Ismail, "The United States and Security Management in West Africa: A Case of Cooperative Intervention." Forthcoming. I thank the author for giving me an advance copy of this paper.

55. Ibid.

56. Ike Okonta, "Genocide in Darfur," *This Day* (Lagos), July 11, 2004.

57. The increasing importance of the Gulf of Guinea in global oil politics needs further explanation here. Geographically, Gulf of Guinea is a somewhat loose term, but it is widely believed to encompass coastal states in the Gulf of Guinea. This includes West African states and other non-West African countries of Angola, DRC, Congo Brazzaville, Gabon, and Cameroon. While geographically the expanse is extensive, it is widely believed that Nigeria, because of its population and the extent of its reserve, will be the key actor in the region.

58. A community leader in Yenagoa, Bayelsa State, Nigeria, expressed this succinctly in an interview with me that such benefit would come because at least the government would want to make life comfortable for the staff posted to the region. It is thus the calculation of the people that they can tap from at least some of the benefit that would come as a result of staff that would be posted to their communities.

59. *African Research Bulletin*, September 16–October 15, 2003, p. 15800.

60. There were calls by Nigerians for the Shagari administration to take military action against Cameroon. Indeed, the leader of the key opposition party, Chief Obafemi Awolowo, noted that no country shoots down five soldiers without expecting a reaction.

61. Extracts of the submission at The Hague, reported in *News* (Lagos), October 14, 2002, p. 49.

62. There is, however, an aspect of the Bakassi Peninsula that is not widely known. This ties the complex legal arguments with a web of diplomatic intrigue. The southern part of Cameroon, with historical links with Nigeria and presently marginalized by the northern part of the country, sued the Nigerian government at the Nigerian High Court. The suit requested that the Nigerian government be compelled to support its claim for self-determination under the African Charter of People's Right. Southern Cameroon argued that since Nigeria is a signatory to the agreement, it is obliged to take its case for self-determination to the ICJ. Nigeria initially rejected this argument, but when it later viewed it as a way of extinguishing Cameroon's case over Bakassi, decided to settle with the south Cameroon out of court. It also agreed to pursue its self-determination claim at the ICJ. However, it is believed that the strategy here is to dismember Cameroon and thus weaken its case over the Bakassi.

63. Again, the war has fed on lesser conflicts over natural resources, as Nigerians living in the border towns engaging in fishing have complained of attacks from rival fishing communities on the Cameroon.

64. See "A Tale of Two Contenders: Equatorial Guinea and Gabon Search for Oil in Disputed Area," *African Economy*, October 2004, p. 13.

65. Although the memorandum was signed, there were still a number of issues over sovereignty of their maritime boundaries that are yet to be resolved between the two countries.

66. As of 2002, when I last visited one of the cities, Yenagoa, the capital of Bayelsa State, electricity to the city was still being rationed, with the population still relying on multinational corporations to provide them with electricity.

67. Tunde Babalola, "Niger Delta: the Pawn of Domination," *Sunday Tribune* (Ibadan), November 8, 1998.

68. This has remained a most contentious issue in the country, and the issues raised by the debate underline the complexities in ethnic politics in multiethnic societies. Those who argue in favor of northern domination of Nigerian politics argue that of the eight leaders that the country has had between independence and 2003, six have come from the north. However, those who disagree with this position claim that the simplicity in the argument comes from the fact that the definition of the "north" is ambiguous, as many of those categorized as "northerners" actually belong to the middle-belt and are, indeed, members of the minority ethnic groups. They further argue that even in cases where the northerners have ruled the country, back-up bureaucratic support that has provided the backbone for governance has always come from the south. Consequently, they argue that the concept of northern domination is a myth.

69. Discussions in the Niger Delta, April 2006.

70. These figures were given by the founding Executive Chairman of OMPADEC, Chief Albert Korobo, *This Day*, August 24, 1999.

71. The Petroleum (PTF) was the trust fund created by the Abacha administration to manage the revenue provided by the government for rural development. This, as will be discussed later, became another opportunity to divert oil money to private accounts.

72. "Fuelling Poverty: Oil, War and Corruption," *Christian Aid*, May 2003, p. 21 (see also http://www.christian-aid.org.uk).

73. Ibid.

74. Interviews held in the Niger Delta region, November 1999.

75. Interviews in Yenagoa, November 1999.

76. This is a problem that is often associated with societies where foreign expatriates are involved in the extraction of mineral resources. In other countries such as South Africa, Colombia, Venezuela, and Chile, there are similar cases. In Nigeria's oil-producing states, it is common to see commercial sex workers loitering around hotels where foreign oil workers reside, and it is a common sight to see them with these expatriates at the hotel bars.

77. Successive human right reports have indicted the Angolan government of human rights abuses in Cabinda. See, for example, the report by Amnesty International, 2003.

78. Quoted from Joao Gomes Porto, *Cabinda: Notes on a Soon-to-be-forgotten War*, Occasional Paper No. 77 (Pretoria: Institute for Strategic Studies, August 2003).

79. Boro and others were charged with treason, tried, convicted, and sentenced to death by the government of General Aguyi Ironsi. Less than two months after the conviction, the government of Ironsi was overthrown and the government of General Yakubu Gowon, which replaced it, commuted the death sentence to life imprisonment

before they were subsequently pardoned. Boro eventually joined the Nigerian Army to fight in the civil war. He was later killed in action.

80. Adibe Emenyonu, "Most Wanted," *This Week*, August 9, 2004, p. 25.

81. Asari calls these clashes "Operation Denis Fiberesima." But there is another dimension to the rivalry with Tom Ateke, as Dokubo-Asari claims that his own group is supported by the Rivers State governor, Peter Odili, while President Obasanjo supports the Tom Ateke group.

82. Specifically, the government accused him of involvement in oil smuggling along river routes in the Niger Delta.

83. For example, on August 29, 2004, the NDPVF attacked a marine base inside Port Harcourt and killed eleven people. This embarrassed the state governor, Peter Odili, who had earlier dismissed the force as petty oil criminals. He was to dismiss his entire cabinet for ineffectiveness.

84. Pini Jason, "Nigeria: The Rebel Who Outfoxed Obasanjo," *New African*, November 2004, p. 31.

85. The meeting between the Nigerian president and Dokubo-Asari was widely criticized. However, while the president was still explaining the reasons why he had a meeting with Dokubo-Asari, he issued another threat that the government was reneging from the agreement and threatened to go back to the mangroves and swamps to continue his guerrilla war against the government. See Roland Ogbonnaya, "Will Niger Delta Know Sustainable Peace?" *This Day* (Lagos), December 25, 2004.

86. Babs Ajayi, "Nigeria's Oil Wells: Fortune, Misfortune, Pillage and Poverty," *This Day* (Lagos), November 13, 2003.

87. A British NGO, Global Witness, has come out with a most damaging criticism of the Angolan government and the leadership of corruption or revenue coming from oil. See *All the Presidents Men: The Devastating Story of Oil and Banking in Angola's Privatized War* (London: Global Witness, March 2002).

88. See *This Day* (Lagos), July 22, 2003, p. 19, and *African Research Bulletin*, September 16–October 15, 2003, p. 15799.

89. *African Research Bulletin* (Economic), March 2001, p. 14324.

90. See *A Rough Trade: The Role of Companies and Governments in the Angolan Conflict* (London: Global Witness, December 1998).

91. Ibid.

92. Ibid.

93. The Nigerian naval boss, Samuel Afolayan, quoted this figure. See the interview with Afolayan in *Tell Magazine* (Lagos), December 13, 2004, p. 28.

94. The declaration took its name from the town where it was declared. Kaiama is the headquarters of the Kolokuma/Opokuma Council area, and it is the birthplace of the late Isaac Adaka Boro, who, as earlier noted, declared a separate autonomous nation of the Ijaws of the Niger Delta in 1966.

95. The Kaiama Declaration: Resolutions of the December 11, 1998, All Ijaw Youths Conference, held in the Niger Delta, Nigeria. Published for the Ijaw Youth Council by the Ijaw Council for Human Rights, Port Harcourt, March 1999.

96. Julius Ihonvbere, "A Recipe for Perpetual Crises: The Nigerian State and the Niger Delta Question," *Boiling Point* (Lagos: CDHR, 2000), p. 106.

97. Discussions in Warri, December 2005.

98. See Ehichioya Ezomon, "In the Niger Delta, the Wounds Run Deep," *Guardian* (Lagos), January 29, 1999.

99. Hector Igbikiowubo, "Ojobo Community, Shell and the Claims of Genocide," *Vanguard* (Lagos), December 7, 2004, p. 19.

100. See *Business Day,* June 23, 2003.

101. J. N. Nwankwo, "Problem of Environmental Pollution and Control in the Nigerian Oil Industry." Proceedings of the 1981 International Conference on the Petroleum Industry and the Nigerian Environment, Lagos, Nigeria, 1991.

102. For the full text of the Ogoni Bill of Rights, see Ken Saro Wiwa, *Genocide in Nigeria: The Ogoni Tragedy* (London: Saros International Publishers, 1992), pp. 93–96.

103. Chris Konkwo, "Discord At Niger Delta Conference," *Sunday Diet,* February 21, 1997.

104. From this day, January 4 has been celebrated as the Ogoni Day, and the day was subsequently adopted by the United Nations as the day to celebrate the International Year for the World's Indigenous People (IYWIP).

105. Interview in Ogoniland, December 2004.

106. Discussions in Eleme, December 2005.

107. See Akpandem James, "Ogoni: New Land New Struggle," *Sunday Punch* (Lagos), September 1999.

108. This was the Ogoni Civil Disturbances Tribunal (OCDT) under the leadership of Justice Ibrahim Auta.

109. Those hanged with Saro Wiwa include John Kpuinen, Dr. Barinem Kiobel, Baribo Bera, Daniel Gbokoo, Paul Levura, Nordu Eawo, Saturday Dobee, and Felix Nwate.

110. Many had called on the organization to exert more pressure on the Nigerian leadership. Indeed, the son of the late Saro Wiwa, Ken Saro Wiwa Jr. and the Nigeria playwright and Nobel Laureate, Wole Soyinka, traveled to the Commonwealth Conference to lobby leaders. After the hanging of the men, there were calls for the expulsion of Nigeria from the organization, and the mere suspension was seen by many as being too soft.

111. *African Expatriate,* June–July 1996, p. 17.

112. This Judicial Commission was headed by Justice Opubo Inko-Tariah.

113. At the Oputa Panel, set up by the Obasanjo government to investigate cases of human rights abuses, the lawyer who represented the victims of the Umuechen community disappeared mysteriously in the course of hearing the case.

114. This declaration was made before the Justice Idoko Commission of Inquiry on June 24, 1997.

115. Charles Ukeje (Unpublished PhD dissertation, "Oil Capital, Ethnic Nationalism, and Civil Conflict in the Niger Delta of Nigeria," Obafemi Awolowo University, Ile Ife, Nigeria, 2003), 188.

116. See John Henley, "Gigantic Sleaze Scandal Winds Up as Former Elf Oil Chiefs Are Jailed," *Guardian* (London), November 13, 2003.

117. This is the subject of an investigation conducted in France and Switzerland by a magistrate, Eva Joly. See *Le Monde,* October 25, 1999.

118. Quoted from *A Crude Awakening,* p. 10.

119. *Financial Mail* (London), March 7, 2004.

120. The tax break system was frozen in 1999 and the Nigerian government is now trying to recover about £200 million from oil multinational companies.

121. *Financial Mail* (London), March 7, 2004.

122. Ibid.

123. *African Confidential* 45, no. 13 (2004).

124. Philip Oladunjoye, "Historic Appointment at Shell," *Newswatch* (Lagos), August 9, 2004, p. 54.

125. This was the figure given by Minister of State for Petroleum Affairs Edmund Daukoru. See *This Day*, March 26, 2006.

126. Okey Epia, "Niger Delta: New Dimension to a Crisis," *This Day*, February 17, 2006.

127. Discussion with an official of the Nigerian National Petroleum Company. I need to add that discussions held with soldiers posted to the region conceded to the same level of helplessness as regards hostage taking.

128. For example, it has used its position in the Security Council to block any attempt to impose sanctions on the Sudanese government.

129. During the military administrations of Babangida and the late General Abacha, it was not uncommon for individuals, especially military officers to be given oil allocation. A former Minister for Petroleum in the country, Tam David West, once gave an implicit indictment of President Babangida that he sent notes to him to allocate oil to individuals.

130. This is a major reception facility where imported petroleum products are discharged before being pumped to Lagos satellite depot and the Mosimi depot in Shagamu.

131. *Nigerian Perspective* (London), March–April 2005, p. 5.

132. The officers were Rear Admirals Samuel Kolawole, Francis Agbiti, and Anthonio Bob Manuel. The court-martial found Kolawole and Agbiti guilty but released Bob Manuel.

133. Paul Morton, "Sudan Lurches towards Peace," *Federations* 14, no. 1 (March 2004): 15.

134. This was the bombing of the Pan Am Airline in Lockerbie, Scotland, in December 1988. Two Libyan officials were accused of the action, a claim the country immediately denied. The authorities in Tripoli, however, refused to hand the officials over to the British authorities because it was feared they would not receive a fair trial. After several international efforts, including the involvement of South African President Mandela, the officials were handed over to a special Scottish court that convened in The Hague. One of the officials was found guilty while the other was acquitted.

135. Ms. Fletcher was a British Police Constable who was allegedly shot from the Libyan Embassy in St. James Square in London.

Chapter 6

Epigraph One. Abubakar Tafawa Balewa, Nigeria's first prime minister. Quoted from Bertram Anyaoku, "Overview of Inland Waterways Transportation in West and Central Africa: The Nigerian Experience" (Paper presented at the International Conference on Navigation Activities within the River Basin in the West and Central African Sub-region, Abuja, Nigeria, June 2001).

Epigraph Two. Peter Ashton, "Are Water Wars Inevitable?" http://www.scienceinafrica.co.za.

1. For example, in the war between the Lagash and Umma around 2500 BC, Urlama, the King of Lagash, diverted water from the region to boundary canals, drying up the boundary ditches to deprive Umma of water. Again, around 720 and 703 BC, Sargon 11 of Assyria destroyed the irrigation network of Armenians and flooded their land.

2. This is more common in West Africa. For example, one of the most important deities among the Yorubas in southwest Nigeria is the Osun River, but there are also examples of this tendency among southern Africans. For example, the Bundu people in Zambia believe that the Zambezi River has spiritual significance, as it has a spirit called Nyami Nyami, which provides water and assists with fishing and growth of crops.

3. Anthony Turton, "Water and Conflict in an African Context," *Conflict Trends*, no. 4 (1999).

4. For example, Nigeria was named after River Niger, and some of the states in the country are named after major national rivers, including Benue, Niger, Ogun, Osun, and Yobe states. Another African country named after a river is Congo.

5. The initial crop of social science scholars who delved into water issues include Peter Gleick, Leif Ohlsson, Thomas Homer-Dixon, Okidi Odidi, Tony Allen, and others.

6. Examples of this included the European Economic Community (EEC) Study on the Nile River. Other organizations involved in similar projects include Inter-Africa Group and Saferworld.

7. The University of Pretoria in South Africa has an African Water Issues Research Unit (AWIRU) at its Centre for International Political Studies. In Addis Ababa, Ethiopia, there is the Inter-Africa Group and Saferworld conducting researches on the subject. Also at the School of Oriental and African Studies (SOAS), University of London, there is a Water Project that works closely with the South African Water Project.

8. Anthony Turton, "Water Wars in Southern Africa: Challenging Conventional Wisdom," in *Water Wars: Enduring Myth or Impending Reality*, ed. Hussein Solomon and Anthony Turton (Pretoria: Accord, 2000), pp. 35–64.

9. Tony Allen has advanced this position in a number of seminal studies, including "Virtual Water—the Water, Food and Trade Nexus: Useful Concept or Misleading Metaphor?" *Water International* 28 (2003): 4–11; "Water Resources in Semi-Arid Regions: Real Deficits and Economically Invisible and Politically Silent Solutions," in *Hydro-politics in the Developing World, a Southern African Perspective*, ed. A. Turton and R. Henwood (Pretoria: AWIRU, 2002), pp. 23–36; and *The Middle East Water Question: Hydro-politics and the Global Economy* (London: I. B. Tauris, 2001).

10. Anthony Allen, "Water Security Policies and Global System for Water-Scarce Regions," *The World Bank Group*, http://www.worldbank.org/mdf1/water.htm.

11. Turton, "Water Wars in Southern Africa," p. 44.

12. Peter Gleick, *The World's Water: The Biennial Report on Freshwater Resources, 1998–1999* (Washington, DC: Island Press, 1998).

13. This is a practice well rooted in history, with a recent example during the Gulf War when the allied coalition against Iraq considered the possibility of using the Ataturk Dam on the Euphrates River to shut off the flow of water to Iraq. Here, water is being used to force an opponent to succumb during a conflict situation.

14. This again is a factor that is deeply rooted in history, with the destruction of bridges and dams during warfare serving as one example.

15. See Turton, "Water Wars in Southern Africa," pp. 37–38.

16. Yacob Arsano, "Sharing Water Resources for Economic Co-operation in the Horn of Africa," in *Trading Places: Alternative Models of Economic Cooperation in the Horn of Africa*, ed. Belay Gessesse et al. (Uppsala: Life and Peace Institute, 1996), p. 29.

17. Ibid., 30.

18. Malin Falkenmark and C. Widstrand, "Population and Water Resources: A Delicate Issue," *Population Bulletin* 47, no. 3 (1992): 2–36.

19. B. Lomborg, *The Sceptical Environmentalist: Measuring the Real State of the World* (Cambridge: Cambridge University Press, 2001), p. 152.

20. See http:/www.jhccp.org/pr.m14. Quoted from Ian Woodman, Ibid., p. 9.

21. Turton, "Water Wars in Southern Africa," p. 35

22. For more on the politics surrounding the Nile River, see Terje Tvedt, *The Nile: An Annotated Bibliography* (London: I. B. Tauris, 2004).

23. For a long time, the writings of Herodotus, the Greek historian, were the most authoritative reference on the source of the Nile. He cited the source as being a deep spring between two tall mountains. John Speke thought he found the source when he reached Lake Victoria in 1862 but was later proved wrong. It was not until 1937 that the source was finally stumbled upon by the little-known German explorer, Bruckhart Waldekker.

24. See Robert Collins, *The Waters of the Nile* (Oxford: Clarendon Press, 1990).

25. This concentrated upon Jonglei Canal, which was meant to divert the water of the Sudd swamps in southern Sudan.

26. Stephan Libiszewski, "International Conflicts over Freshwater Resources," in *Ecology, Politics and Violent Conflict*, ed. Mohamed Suliman (London: Zed Books, 1999), p. 131

27. Quoted from Naigzy Gebremedhin, "The Environmental Dimension of Security in the Horn of Africa: The Case of Somalia," *Life and Peace Research* 5, no. 1 (1991): 13.

28. Nimrod Raphaeli, "Rising Tensions over the Nile River Basin," The Middle East Media Research Institute (MEMRI), February 2004.

29. Gebremedhin, "The Environmental Dimension of Security."

30. Jo-Ansie van Wyk, "River Dry Mountain High: Water Security in Southern Africa," *Conflict Trend*, no. 1 (October 1998).

31. A fourth country, Zimbabwe, is at the peripheral level and as such is not deeply involved in the Okavango politics.

32. See Turton at http://www.accord.org.za/web.nsf.open.

33. Carl Myers, "Water Co-operation in Southern Africa," *World Water and Environmental Engineering*, August 1997, p. 15.

34. The mean annual rainfall is approximately 284 mm and the total surface water reserve is about 4.1 billion cubic meters per year. See Richard Meissner, "Hydropolitical Hotspots in Southern Africa," in Solomon and Turton, *Water Wars*, p. 107.

35. Aspects of this conflict have been discussed in chapter 3.

36. *Southern African News Feature*, July 2004.

37. Jo-Ansie van Wyk, "River Dry Mountain High."

38. For example, one of the suggestions that has been made is the use of solar and wind power, which they argue the country can share with neighboring countries.

39. Nujoma quoted in a press release by the International Rivers Network, October 3, 1997.

40. It is estimated that the lake has shrunk from 30,000 square kilometers to 3,000 square kilometers in forty years and from 25,000 square kilometers to 1,500 square kilometers between 1966 and 1997.

41. These five countries form the Lake Chad Basin Commission (LCBC).

42. The villages are Aisa Kura, Bashakka, Chik'a, Darak, Darak Gana, Doron Liman, Doran Mallam (Doro Kirta) Dororoya, Fagge, Garin Wanzam, Gorea Changi, Gorea Gutum, Jribrillaram, Kafuram, Kanumburi, Karakaya, Kasuram Mareya, Katti Kime, Kirta Wulgo, Koloram, Kumunna, Logon Labi, Loko Naira, Mukdala, Murdas, Naga'a, Naira, Nimeri, Njia Buniba, Ramin Dorinna, Sabon Tumbu, Sagir, and Sokotoram.

43. One of such is the Lake Chad Replenishing Project, which would entail damming the Oubangui River at Palambo in Central African Republic and channeling some of its water through a navigable canal to Lake Chad.

44. *African Research Bulletin,* February 1990, p. 9542.

45. In February 2006, British Defence Secretary John Reid confirmed that the British Armed Forces are getting prepared to meet water wars. See Ben Russell and Nigel Morris, "Armed Forces Are Put on Standby to Tackle Threats of Wars over Water," *Independent,* February 25, 2006.

46. Simon Fairle, "Fisheries: Confrontation and Violence in the Management of Marine Resources," in *Ecology, Politics and Violent Conflict,* ed. Mohamed Suliman (London: Zed Books, 1999), p. 139.

47. Ibid., pp. 153–54.

48. There is the need to point out that fishing is taken to denote the process of getting living resources out of water. Consequently, it transcends fishes to include other living materials that are sourced and sold for profit.

49. *African Research Bulletin,* October/November 2000, p. 14555.

50. Ibid.

51. Kenya also has some vessels but not adequate for its needs and certainly not comparable with those of Nigeria and South Africa.

52. *African Business,* June 2002, p. 20.

53. *African Confidential* 39, no. 20 (October 9, 1984): 4.

54. *Daily Nation* (Nairobi), August 29, 2003.

55. Ibid.

56. The United Nations Food and Agricultural Organisation (FAO) assisted these communities to get the fishermen back to business by distributing canoes to them.

57. Paul Goldsmith, Lydia A. Abura, and Jason Switzer, "Oil and Water in Sudan," in *Scarcity and Surfeit: The Ecology of Africa's Conflict,* ed. Jeremy Lind and Kathryn Sturman (Pretoria: ISS, 2002), pp. 204–5.

58. For example, a number of Francophone African countries have had it since the 1960s.

59. This does not include an additional $27 per household to install water meters in houses that do not have meters.

60. For example, the water multinational company, Biwater, withdrew from a water project in Zimbabwe on the grounds that it is commercially unsound.

61. *Business Day,* April 7, 1999.

62. These include ARB of Sweden, which allegedly bribed to the tune of US$40,410; Bouygues of France, which had an allegation of US$733,404 attached to it; and the Suez-Lyonnaise des Eaux, also of France, with a charge of US$82,422.

63. In particular, they cite the pledge of £10 million for the improvement of the water system in Kumasi. See *African Socialist: A Journal of World Socialist Movement,* January–March 2003, p. 8.

64. For a more detailed discussion on the problems associated with these laws, see A. T. Wolf, "International Water Conflict Resolution: Lessons from Comparative Analysis," *International Journal of Water Resources Development* 13, no. 3 (December 1997).

65. "Water: the 21st Century's Oil?" *African Economist* 8, no. 23 (March 2004): 44.

66. The protocol was signed by all the members of the SADC except the Republic of Angola.

67. "Zambezi River Basin States Sign Agreement," *South African News Features,* no. 62 (July 2004), p. 1.

68. Ibid.

69. For example, in January 2001, the IUCN, WWF, and the World Bank organized a workshop in Gland, Switzerland, which was founded by the Rockefeller Foundation.

70. The African Water Vision initiative was first presented at the Second World Water Forum in The Hague in 2000.

71. The framework envisages an annual investment requirement of US$12 billion until 2025 in order to achieve the targets on water supply and sanitation.

72. The idea was mooted by the African Water Task Force, but it was subsequently endorsed by the Accra African Water Stakeholders Conference in April 2002.

Chapter 7

Epigraph Two. Emeka Achebe, former senior corporate adviser, Shell International and former Director, Shell Nigeria. Quoted in John Mcmanus, "Shell Damage Limitation Tours Offers No Easy Answer," *Irish Times* (Dublin), February 2, 1996.

1. There may, however, be dangers in overgeneralization, as there are some countries where the first set of elected leaders tried, within the limitations under which they existed, to ensure that proper structures were laid for future generations. One such example is Tanzania, where governance, even at the early stages of independence, had become synonymous with some form of accountability and careful management of state resources. The late President Julius Nyerere was in fact quoted as thanking "providence" for his country's lack of natural resources. This was against the backdrop of the role natural resources were playing as a cause of conflict in many other states.

2. Julius Ihonvbere, "Towards a New Constitutionalism in Africa," CDD Occasional Paper Series No. 4, London, April 2000, pp. 22–23.

3. The constitutional review panel was under Dr. Amos Sawyer, who was later to become the president of the country during the civil war.

4. There is an irony about the call for a sovereign national conference in Nigeria. Even those who clamored for it while in opposition soon modified their stance once they found themselves in power or at the corridors of power. There are also fears in some circles that the hidden objective of the conference is to discuss the ultimate separation of the country. The potential implications of this possibility have made the incumbent government of President Obasanjo wary of the conference. After persistent pressures, the government agreed in 2004 to a "National Conference" but not a "Sovereign National

Conference." The opposition is quick to dismiss it as a charade. By the beginning of 2005, the politics of the national conference assumed a new dimension when two opposing conferences were being put together, one by the government and the other by a group of individuals who are opposed to the government's initiative.

5. There is a court case on resource control, where oil-producing communities in Nigeria sued the federal government over control of offshore oil.

6. Some of the countries that have attempted to set up commissions on land use include Ghana, Nigeria, Tanzania, and Uganda.

7. The tribunal that condemned Ken Saro Wiwa and others was the Ogoni Civil Disturbances Special Military Tribunal, headed by Justice Auta.

8. Jeremy Gauntlett, "Mugabe's Broken Bench," *Counsel*, February 2004, p. 16.

9. Ibid.

10. This has been a major issue in the ongoing civil war in the country. Mr. Quattara was prevented from contesting election in the country on the technical ground that he is not an Ivorian "citizen."

11. See Jotham Tumwesigye, "Tackling the Problem of Corruption in the Judiciary" (Paper presented at the 7th Biennial Conference of the International Women Judges, Entebbe, Uganda, May 11, 2004).

12. The committee was created in 2003, and it was headed by Justice Aaron Ringere.

13. The advice was given by the WAC Global Services, a conflict management firm commissioned by Shell.

14. *This Day* (Lagos), July 22, 2003, p. 19.

15. *Skyways Magazine* (Pretoria), September 2000, p. 34.

16. Faysal Yachir, *Mining in Africa Today: Strategies and Prospects* (London: UNU/ZED, 1998), p. 1.

17. Ibid.

18. Discussion with the author, May 1999.

19. *African Business,* June 2004.

20. There has been precedence. During the 1980s, Des Wilson, who ran Friends of the Earth in England, jumped to a corporate job as head of Public Affairs of BAA Plc., the company that managed London airports and has been the target of activists. After the carpet crossing, Wilson noted that the contribution he could make from within far "outweighs standing outside in the streets and waving banners at them." Another recent example is that of Tricia Caswell, the former head of the Australian Conservation Foundation and a fierce opponent of the logging industry, who, in April 2004, became the chief executive of the Victorian Association of Forest Industries.

21. *Wall Street Journal,* November 17, 2004.

22. For more on SAP in Africa, see, among others, Nicolas Van de Walle, Nicole Ball, and Vijaya Ramachandran, eds., *Beyond Structural Adjustment: The Institutional Context of Africa's Development* (London: Palgrave Macmillan, 2003); Julius Nyang'oro and Timothy Shaw, eds., *Beyond Structural Adjustment in Africa: The Political Economy of Sustainable and Democratic Development* (New York: Praeger, 1992).

23. See William Reno, *Warlord Politics and African States* (Boulder, CO: Lynne Rienner, 2000).

24. Apart from the activities of ECOWAS, civil society groups in West Africa have formed the West African Network on Small Arms (WAANSA).

25. Halliburton has been allegedly involved in bribing Nigerian officials in an oil contract. See *Newsweek,* February 4, 2004. In August 2004, Nigerian parliament voted

unanimously that Halliburton should be disqualified from bidding on future government projects in the country.

26. See David Leigh and David Pallister, "Revealed: The New Scramble for Africa," *Guardian* (London), June 1, 2005.

27. David Pallister, "Alarm Bells Sound over Massive Loan Bank-rolling Oil-rich, Graft-tainted Angola," *Guardian* (London), June 1, 2005.

28. Michael Fleshman, "The International Community and the Crises in the Oil Producing Communities—A Perspective on the US Role," in *Boiling Point: A CDHR Publication on the Crises in the Oil Producing Communities in Nigeria*, ed. Wumi Raji, Ayodele Ale, and Eni Akinsola (Lagos: CDHR, 2000), p. 188.

29. There are evidences of this in the process of privatization in Kenya.

30. This, for example, was the case in Uganda, where ministers were indicted for corruption in deals over water privatization.

31. This was at a press conference before the WTO Ministerial Conference in Cancun, Brussels, September 4, 2003.

Conclusion

Epigraph One. Bimpe Aboyade, "Governance and Development," *This Day* (Lagos), May 5, 2004. The reference to the "happiest people on earth" is sequel to a report by the UK's *New Scientist Magazine* that Nigerians are the happiest people on earth.

Epigraph Two. Olutayo Adesina, "Diamonds, Democracy and Constitutional (Dis) Order in Sierra Leone," in *Africa's Experience with Liberal Democracy*, ed. S. C. Saxena and Kunle Amuwo, forthcoming.

1. Richard Dowden, "Cynical Politicians, Pipedreams and How We Can Make a Difference," *Independent* (London), June 1, 2005.

BIBLIOGRAPHY

Abdel Rahman, Maha. "The Politics of 'unCivil' Society in Egypt." *Review of African Political Economy*, no. 91 (2002).

Abdullai, Ibrahim. "Bush Path to Destruction: The Origin and Character of the RUF." *Journal of Modern African Studies* 36, no. 2 (1998).

———. "The Lumpen Proletariat and the Sierra Leone Conflict." *Journal of Modern African Studies* 36, no. 2 (June 1998).

Adebajo, Adekeye. Building Peace in West Africa: Liberia, Sierra Leone and Guinea Bissau, Boulder Co: Lynne Rienner, 2002.

———. Liberia's Civil War: Nigeria, ECOMOG and Regional Security in West Africa, Boulder Co: Lynne Rienner, 2002.

Adebanwi, Wale. "Nigeria: Shell of a State." *Dollars and Sense Magazine*, July/August 2001.

Adebayo, Akanmu. G. "Fulani and Yoruba Farmers in Iwo." *Journal of Asian and African Studies* 32 (1997).

Adedeji, Adebayo, ed. *Comprehending and Mastering African Conflicts*. London: Zed Books, 1999, p. 364.

Adejumobi, Said. *Globalisation and Africa's Development Agenda*. Occasional Paper 12, Addis Ababa, Ethiopia: DPMF, 2003.

Adeleke, Ademola. "The Politics and Diplomacy of Peacekeeping in West Africa: The ECOWAS Operation in Liberia." *Journal of Modern African Studies* 33, no. 4 (1995).

Adigun, Olajide, and A. A. Utama. "A Decade of Land Reform in Nigeria: The Land Use Act, 1978 in Perspective." Nigerian Association of Law Teachers: The Proceedings of the 26th Annual Conference. Lagos, 1979.

———. "Land Use Decree: A Critical Review." *Nigerian Judicial Review* 2 (1979).

Adisa, Jimi. *The Comfort of Stranger: The Impact of Rwandan Refugees on Neighbouring Countries*. Ibadan: UNHS, 1996.

Akinrinade, Sola, and Amadu Sesay. *Africa in the Post-Cold War International System*. London: Cassell, 1997.

Alao, Abiodun. *African Conflict: The Future Without the Cold War*. London: Centre for Defence Studies, 1994.

———. *Brothers at War: Dissidence and Rebellion in Southern Africa*. London: British Academic Press, 1994.

———. *The Burden of Collective Goodwill: The International Involvement in the Liberian Civil War*. Aldershot: Ashgate Publishers, 1996.

———. "Diamonds Are Forever . . . But So Also Are Controversies: Diamonds and the Actors in the Sierra Leone Civil War." *Journal of Civil Wars*, Autumn 1999.

Alao, Abiodun, and Comfort Ero. "Cut Short for Taking Short Cuts: The Lomé Peace Agreement in Sierra Leone." *Journal of Civil Wars* 4, no. 3 (Autumn 2001).

Alao, Abiodun, and Funmi Olonisakin. "Economic Fragility and Political Fluidity: Explaining Natural Resources and Conflict." *Journal of International Peacekeeping* 7, no. 4 (Winter 2000).

Alao, Abiodun, John Mackinlay, and Funmi Olonisakin. *Peacekeepers, Politicians and Warlords: The Liberian Peace Process.* Tokyo and New York: United Nations University Press, 1999.

Albert, I. O. "Ife Modakeke Crisis." In *Community Conflict in Nigeria: Management, Resolution and Transformation*, edited by O. Otite and I. O. Albert. Ibadan: Spectrum Books, 1999.

Areola, Olusegun. *Ecology of Natural Resources in Nigeria.* Aldershot: Avebury, 1991.

Atkinson, Philippa. *The War Economy in Liberia: A Political Analysis.* London: ODI, 1997.

Barnett, Jon. "Destabilizing the Environmental Conflict Thesis." *Review of International Studies* 26, no. 2 (April 2000).

Baylis, John, and Steve Smith, eds. *The Globalisation of World Peace.* Oxford: Oxford University Press, 1997.

Bennett, O. *Greenway: Environment and Conflict.* London: Panos Institute, 1991.

Berdal, Mats, and David Malone, eds. *Greed and Grievance: Economic Agendas in Civil Wars.* Boulder, CO: Lynne Rienner, 2000.

Blench, Roger. *Resource Conflict in Semi Arid Africa: An Essay with Annotated Bibliography.* Working Paper, London: ODI, 1997.

———. *Conflict in Protected Areas of Africa: Livestock and Conservation of the Rwenya Wildlife Management Area, North East Zimbabwe.* London: ODI, 1998.

———. *Hunter-Gatherers, Conservation and Development: From Policy Institute to Policy Reform.* Resource Briefing Paper 43, London: ODI, 1999.

Boateng, E. A. *A Political Geography of Africa.* Cambridge: Cambridge University Press, 1978.

Boit, Stephen. "Oil, Africa and the US: The Dangers." *West Africa* (London), December 2–8, 2002.

Bookchin, M. *Rethinking Society.* Montreal: Black Rose, 1989.

Boulding, Elise, ed. *New Agenda for Peace Research: Conflict and Security Re-examined.* Boulder, CO: Lynne Rienner, 1992.

Bradbury, M., S. Fisher, and C. Lane. *Working with Pastoralists NGOs and Land Conflicts in Tanzania.* Pastoral Land Tenure Series No. 7, London: International Institute for Environment and Development, 1995.

Bridgland, Fred. *Jonas Savimbi: A Key to Africa.* London: Hodder and Stoughton, 1988.

Burkett, Paul. "Value, Capital and Nature: Some Ecological Implications of Marx's Critique of Political Economy." *Science and Society* 60, no. 3 (1996): 32–59.

Buzan, Barry. *People, State and Fear: The National Security Problem in International Relations.* Brighton: Wheatsheaf Books, 1983.

———. *People, State and Fear: An Agenda for International Security Studies in Post Cold War Era.* Boulder, CO: Lynne Rienner, 1991.

Carpenter, Susan, and W. J. D. Kennedy. *Managing Public Disputes: A Practical Guide to Handling Conflict and Reaching Agreements.* London: Jossey-Bass Publishers, 1988.

Chabal, Patrick. "Africa in the Age of Globalisation." *African Security Review* 10, no. 2 (2001).

Chabal, Patrick, and Jean-Pascal Daloz. *Africa Works: Disorder As Political Instrument.* Bloomington: Indiana University Press, 1999.

Christie, Sarah, and Madhuku Lovemore, eds. *Labour Dispute Resolution in Southern Africa.* Cape Town: Friedrich Ebert Stifting and the Institute of Development and Labor Laws, University of Cape Town, 1996.

Cilliers, Jakkie, and Dietrich Christian. *Angola's War Economy: The Role of Oil and Diamonds.* Pretoria: Institute for Security Studies, 2000.

Cilliers, Jakkie, and Peggy Mason, eds. *Peace, Profit or Plunder: The Privatisation of Security in War-Torn African Societies.* Half-Way House: Institute for Strategic Studies, 1999.

Clarke, J. "Marx Inorganic Body." *Environmental Ethics* 2 (1989): 243–58.

Collier, Paul. "Doing Well Out of War: An Economic Perspective." In *Greed and Grievance, Economic Agendas In Civil Wars,* edited by Mat Berdal and David Mallone. Boulder, CO: Lynne Rienner, 2000.

Collier, Paul, and Hoeffler Anke. *Greed and Grievance in Civil Wars.* Working Paper, Oxford University Centre for the Study of African Economies, 2002.

Collins, Robert. *The Waters of the Nile.* Oxford: Clarendon Press, 1990.

Conton, Paul. "The Battle for Freetown." *West Africa* (London), March 2–15, 1998.

Copley, Gregory. "Diamonds Are Not Forever." *Strategic Studies: The Journal of the International Strategic Studies Association* 19 (1999).

Copson, R. *Africa's Wars and Prospects for Peace.* New York: M. E. Sharpe, 1994.

Cousins, Ben. "Conflict Management for Multiple Resource Users in Pastoralists and Agro-Pastoralists." *Context* (IDS Bulletin) 27, no. 3 (1996).

Crocker, Chester, ed. *Managing Global Chaos.* Washington, DC: USIP Press, 1996.

Daniels, Anthony. *Liberia Mon Amour: A Visit to Liberia.* London: John Murray Publishers, 1992.

Davies, Victor A. B. "Sierra Leone: Ironic Tragedy." Ad Hoc Expert Group Meeting on the Economics of Civil Conflicts in Africa, Addis Ababa, Ethiopia: Economic Commission for Africa, 2000.

Deng, Francis. "Anatomy of Conflict in Africa." In *Between Development and Destruction: An Enquiry in the Causes of Conflict in Post Colonial State,* edited by Luc Van de Goor, Kumar Rupesinghe, and Paul Sciarone. The Hague: The Netherlands Ministry of Foreign Affairs, 1996.

Desmond, Davies. "Peacekeeping: African Style." *West Africa* (London), May 4–17, 1998.

de St Joree, John. *The Nigerian Civil War.* London: Hodder and Stoughton, 1972.

de Waal, Alex. *Who Fights? Who Cares? War and Humanitarian Action in Africa.* Trenton, NJ: African World Press, 2000.

Dorney, Sean. *The Sandline Affair: Politics and Mercenaries and the Bougainville Crisis.* Sydney: ABC Books, 1999.

Duffied, Mark. "Post-Modern Conflict: Warlords, Post Adjustment States and Private Protection." *Journal of Civil Wars* 1, no. 1 (Spring 1998).

Duffied, Mark. "Globalisation and War Economies." *Fletcher Forum of World Affairs* 23, no. 2 (Fall 1999).

Ellis, Stephen. *The Mask of Anarchy.* London: Hurst, 1999.

Emunyu, Charles Ocan. *Pastoralism and Crisis in North East Uganda: Factors That Determined Social Change in Karamoja.* Working Paper No. 2, CBR Publication, June 1992.

Esterhuysen, Pieter, ed. *South Africa in Sub-Equatorial Africa: Economic Interaction.* Pretoria: Africa Institute of South Africa, 1994.

Falk, Richard. *This Endangered Planet.* New York: Random House, 1970.

Falkenmark, Malin, and C. Widstrand. "Population and Water Resources: A Delicate Issue." *Population Bulletin* 47, no. 3 (1992).

Falola, Toyin. *Violence in Nigeria: The Crisis of Religious Politics and Secular Ideology.* Rochester: University of Rochester Press, 1998.

Falola, Toyin, and Ann Genova. *The Politics of the Global Oil Industry: An Introduction.* London: Westport, 2005.

Fernie, J., and A. E. Pitkethly. *Resources: Environment and Policy.* London: Happer and Row, 1985.

Feyide, M. O. *Oil in World's Politics.* Lagos: University of Lagos Press, 1986.

Franck, George. "Diamonds: No Stone Unturned." *Business Africa,* February 2000.

Frynas, Jedrzet George. "Political Instability and Business: Focus on Shell in Nigeria." *Third World Quarterly* 19, no. 3 (1998).

Garcia, E. *A Time of Hope and Transformation: Sierra Leone Peace Process Report and Reflection.* London: International Alert, 1997.

Garvey, Gerald, and Lou Ann Garvey, eds. *International Resource Flow.* Lexington, MA: Lexington Books, 1977.

Gauntlett, Jeremy. "Mugabe's Broken Bench." *Counsel,* February 2004.

Gberie, Lanasana. *West Africa: Rock in a Hard Place, The Political Economy of Diamonds and Regional Destabilization.* Occasional Paper No. 9, The Diamonds and Human Security Project, 2003.

———. *Sierra Leone: Destruction and Resurgence.* London: Hurst, 2005.

Gleick, Peter. "Environment, Resources and International Security and Politics." In *Science and International Security,* edited by Eric Arnette. Washington, DC: American Association for the Advancement of Science, 1990.

———. "Water and Conflict: Fresh Water Resources and International Security." *International Security* 18, no. 1 (Summer 1993).

———. *The World's Water: The Biennial Report on Freshwater Resources, 1998–1999.* Washington, DC: Island Press, 1998.

Gore, Al. *Earth in the Balance: Forging a New Common Purpose.* London: Earthscan Publication, 1992.

Greene, William N. *Strategies of the Major Oil Companies.* Ann Arbor: UMI Research Press, 1986.

Gurr, Ted. "On the Political Consequences of Scarcity and Economic Decline." *International Studies Quarterly* 29, no. 1 (March 1985).

Hamilton, Adrian, ed. *Oil: The Price of Power.* London: Michael Joseph Limited, 1986.

Hance, William. *The Geography of Modern Africa.* New York: Columbia University Press, 1969.

Harvey, David. "The Nature of Environment: The Dialectics of Social and Environmental Change." In *Socialist Register,* edited by Ralph Miliband and Leon Panitch. New York and London: Monthly Review Press, 1993.

Heilbroner, Robert. *An Inquiry into the Human Prospect.* New York: Norton, 1980.

Hendrickson, Dylan, Jeremy Armon, and Robin Mearns. "Conflict and Vulnerability to Famine: Livestock Raiding in Turkana, Kenya." *Dryland Issues Paper,* no. 80 (1998).

Herbst, Jeff. "Economic Incentives, Natural Resources and Conflict in Africa." *Journal of African Economies* 9, no. 3 (2000).

Hildyard, Nicholas. "Blood, Babies and the Social Roots of Conflicts." In *Ecology, Politics and Violent Conflicts,* edited by Mohamed Suliman. London: Zed Books, 1999, p. 21.

Hirsh, John. *Sierra Leone: Diamonds and the Struggle for Democracy.* Boulder, CO: Lynne Rienner, 2007.

Hodges, Tony. *Angola: Anatomy of an Oil State.* London: James Curry, 2003.

Hogan, Michael, ed. *The End of the Cold War: Its Meaning and Implications.* Cambridge: Cambridge University Press, 1992.

Holdgate, M. W. A. *A Perspective of Environmental Pollution.* Cambridge: Cambridge University Press, 1979.

Homer-Dixon, Thomas. "Environmental Scarcity and Violent Conflict: Evidence from Cases." In *Global Dangers: Changing Dimensions of International Security,* edited by Sean M. Lynn-Jones and Steven E. Miller. Cambridge, MA: MIT Press, 1995.

Howe, Herbert. "Private Security Forces and African Stability: The Case of Executive Outcome." *Journal of Modern African Studies* 36, no. 2 (1998).

Huband, Mark. *The Liberian Civil War.* London: Frank Cass, 1998.

Ibeanu, Okechukwu. "Aguleri-Umuleri Conflict in Anambra State." In *Civil Society and Ethnic Conflict Management in Nigeria,* edited by Thomas Imobigbe. Ibadan: Spectrum Books, 2003.

Ihonvbere, Julius. "Towards a New Constitutionalism in Africa." London: CDD Occasional Paper Series No. 4, April 2000.

Ikein, Augustine. *The Impact of Oil on a Developing Economy: The Case of Nigeria.* New York: Praeger, 1990.

Jackson, Paul. "Warlord as Alternative Form of Governance." *Small Wars and Insurgencies* 14, no. 2 (Summer 2003).

Jacobson, Jodi. *Environmental Refugees: A Yardstick of Habitability.* Worldwatch Paper No. 86, Washington, DC: Worldwatch Institute, 1988.

Jones, Gareth, and Hollier Graham. *Resources, Society and Environmental Management.* London: Paul Chapman Publishing, 1997.

Joseph, Richard. "Africa, 1990–1997: From Abertura to Closure." *Journal of Democracy* 9, no. 2 (April 1998).

Kaplan, Richard. "The Coming Anarchy." *Atlantic Monthly,* February 1994.

———. *The End of the Earth.* New York: Random House, 1996.

Kay, Geoffrey. *Development and Underdevelopment: A Marxist Analysis.* London: Macmillan, 1975.

Keen, David. *The Economic Functions of Violence in Civil Wars.* Adelphi Papers 320. London: IISS, 1998.

Kibble, Steve. *Land, Power and Poverty: Farm Workers and the Crisis in Zimbabwe.* London: Catholic Institute of International Relations, 2001.

Kofman, E., and G. Young. *Globalisation: Theory and Practice.* New York: Pinter, 1996.

Kufour Kofi, Oteng. "The Legality of the Intervention in the Liberian Civil War by the Economic Community of West African States." *African Journal of International and Comparative Law* 5, no. 3 (1993).

Lecomber, Richard. *The Economies of Natural Resources.* London: Macmillan, 1979.

Lederach, John Paul. *Preparing for Peace: Conflict Transformation across Culture.* Syracuse: Syracuse University Press, 1996.

Lewer, Nick, Jonathan Goodhand, and David Hulme. "Social Capital and Political Economy of Violence: A Case Study of Sri Lanka." *Disasters* 24, no. 4 (2000).

Lewis, L. Al, and L. Berry. *African Environment and Resources.* Boston: Unwind Hyman, 1988.

Lind, Jeremy, and Kathryn Sturman. *Scarcity and Surfeit: The Ecology of African Conflicts.* Pretoria: ISS, 2002.

Liodakis, George. "The People-Nature Relations and the Historical Significance of the Labor Theory of Value." *Capital and Class,* no. 73 (Spring 2001).

Lomborg, B. *The Sceptical Environmentalist: Measuring the Real State of the World.* Cambridge: Cambridge University Press, 2001.

Lund, Christian. *Land Tenure Dispute and State, Community and Local Law in Burkina Faso.* Issue Paper No. 70, International Institute for Environment and Development, May 1997.

Lynn Karl, Terry. *The Paradox of Plenty: Oil Booms and Petrostates.* Berkeley: University of California Press, 1997.

Mackinlay, John. "Warlords." *RUSI Journal* 143, no. 2 (April 1998).

———. *Globalisation and Insurgency.* Adelphi Papers 352. London: IISS, 2002, p. 15.

Maiga, Idrissa, and Gouro Diallo. *Land Tenure Conflicts and Their Management in the 5th Region of Mali.* Issue Paper No. 76, International Institute for Environment and Development, Dryland Programs, April 1998.

Malaquias, Assis. "Diamonds are a Guerrilla's Best Friend: The Impact of Illicit Wealth on Insurgency Strategy." *Third World Quarterly* 22, no. 3 (June 2001).

Mandel, Robert. *Conflict over the World Resources: Background, Trends, Cases Studies and Considerations for the Future.* New York: Greenwood Press, 1988, p. 13.

Manger, Leif. "East African Pastoralism and Underdevelopment: An Introduction." In *Pastoralism and Environment: Experiences from the Greater Horn of Africa,* edited by Leif Manger and Abdel Ghaffar M. Ahmed. Addis Ababa, Ethiopia: OSSREA, 2000.

Markakis, John. *Resource Conflict in the Horn of Africa.* London: Sage Publication Ltd., 1998.

Marongwe, Nelson. *Conflict over Land and Other Natural Resources in Zimbabwe.* Harare: Greenwood Park, 2003.

Mbaru, Jimnah. *Transforming Africa: New Pathways to Development.* Nairobi: African Educational Publishers, 2003.

McNamara, Robert. *The Essence Of Security: Reflections in Office.* London: Hodder and Stoughton, 1968.

Meredith, Martin. *Mugabe: Power and Plunder in Zimbabwe.* Oxford: Public Affairs Limited, 2002.

Metz, Steven. "A Strategic Approach to African Security: Challenges and Prospects." *African Security Review* 9, no. 3 (2000).

Montague, Dena. "The Business of War and the Prospect of Peace in Sierra Leone." *The Brown Journal of World Affairs* 9, no. 1 (Spring 2002).

Morrison, R. "Two Questions for Theory and Practice: Can You Be Marxist and Green? Can Marxism Be Green?" *Rethinking Marxism* 7, no. 3 (1994).

Morton, Paul. "Sudan Lurches towards Peace." *Federations* 14, no. 1 (March 2004).

Mountjoy, Alan, and David Hilling. *Africa: Geography and Development.* London: Hutchinson, 1988.

Moyo, Sam. *The Land Question in Zimbabwe.* Harare: SAPES, 1995.

Moyo, Sam, and Daniel Tarera. "The Environmental Security Agenda in Southern Africa." *SAPEM,* June 2000.

Moyo, Sam, P. O'Keefe, and Michael Sill. *The Southern African Environment: Profile of the SADC Countries.* London: Earthscan, 1993.

Musa, Abdel-Fatau, and Kayode J. Fayemi. *Mercenaries: An African Security Dilemma.* London: Pluto Press, 1999.

Myers, Carl. "Water Co-operation in Southern Africa." *World Water and Environmental Engineering,* August 1997.

Nathan, Laurie. "Trust Me, I am a Mercenary: The Lethal Danger of Mercenaries in Africa." *African World Review,* November 1997–March 1998.

Nest, Michael. "Ambions, Profit and Loss: Zimbabwe's Economic Involvement in the DRC." *African Affairs,* 2001.

Nicholson, Michael. *Conflict Analysis.* London: English University Press, 1971.

Nyang'oro, Julius, and Timothy Shaw, eds. *Beyond Structural Adjustment in Africa: The Political Economy of Sustainable and Democratic Development.* Westport, CT: Praeger, 1992.

O'Connor, A. M. *An Economic Geography of East Africa.* New York: Frederick A. Praeger, 1966.

Ofuatey-Kodjoe, W. "Regional Organizations and the Resolution of Internal Conflicts: The ECOWAS Intervention in Liberia." *International Peacekeeping* 1, no. 3 (Autumn 1994).

Ogunsanya, Mobolaji, and S. O. Popoola. "Intervention in the Conflict between the Yoruba Farmers and Fulani Herdsmen in Oke-Ogun, Oyo State." In *Building Peace, Advancing Democracy: Experience with Third-Party Interventions in Nigeria's Conflict,* edited by Isaac Olawale Albert. Ibadan: John Archers, 2001.

Okonta, Ike. "The Disease of Elephants: Oil Rich 'Minority' Areas, Shell and International NGOs." Paper presented at Oxford University, Nigeria Foreign Policy after the Cold War: Domestic, Regional, and External Influences, 2003.

Olanijo, Mobolade. *Doe: The Liberian Tragedy.* Ikeja: Sahel Publishing and Printing, 1990.

Olonisakin, Funmi. "Mercenaries Fill the Vacuum." *World Today,* June 1998.

———. "Nigeria and the Peacekeeping Mission in Sierra Leone." *Jane's Intelligence Review,* July 1998.

Onadipe, Abiodun, ed. *Neither War Nor Peace: Perspectives on the Karamoja Problem and Its Effects on Neighbouring Communities.* London: Conciliation Resources, 2002.

Oosthuysen, Glen. *Small Arms Proliferation and Control in Southern Africa.* Johannesburg: South African Institute of International Affairs, 1996.

Ophuls, William. *Ecology and the Politics of Scarcity.* San Fransisco: W. H. Freeman, 1970.

O'Riordan, Timothy. *Perspectives on Resource Management.* London: Pion Limited, 1971.

Osaghae, Eghosa. "The Ogoni Uprising: Oil Politics, Minority Agitation and the Future of the Nigerian State." *African Affairs* 94 (1995).

Osborn, Derek, and Tom Bigg. *Earth Summit 11: Outcome and Analysis.* London: Earthscan, 1998.

Osuntoku, Akinjide. *Environmetal Problems in Nigeria: With Special Emphasis on Northern Nigeria.* Ibadan: Davidson Press, 1999.

Oyebade, Adebayo, and Abiodun Alao, eds. *Africa after the Cold War: The Changing Perspective on Security.* Trenton, NJ: Africa World Press, 1997.

Oyediran, Oyeleye. "Modakeke in Ife: Historical Background to an Aspect of Contemporary Ife Politics." *Odu,* no. 10 (July 1974).

Pankhurst, Donna. *A Resolvable Conflict? The Politics of Land in Namibia.* Bradford, UK: University of Bradford Department of Peace Studies, 1996, p. 1.

Panter-Brick, K., ed. *Soldiers and Oil: The Political Transformation of Nigeria.* London: Frank Cass, 1978.

Paton, Bill. *Labour Export Policy in the Development of Southern Africa.* London: Macmillan, 1995.

Pearce, Fred. *Climate and Man: From the Ice Age to the Global Green House.* London: Vision Books, 1989.

Perman, Roger, Ma Yue Ma, and James McGilvray. *Natural Resources and Environmental Economics.* London and New York: Longman, 1996.

Peters, Krijn, and Paul Richards. "Why We Fight: Voices of Youth Combatants in Sierra Leone." *Africa: Journal of International African Institute* 68, no. 2 (1998).

Porto, Joao Gomes. "Cabinda: Notes on a Soon-to-be-forgotten War." ISS Paper 77, Pretoria, August 2003, p. 3.

Raji, Wumi, Ayodele Ale, and Eni Akinsola. *Boiling Point: A CDHR Publication on the Crisis in the Oil Producing Communities in Nigeria.* Lagos: CDHR, 2000.

Rees, Judith. *Natural Resources: Allocation, Economics and Policy.* London: Routledge, 1990.

Reno, William. "The Business of War in Liberia." *Current History* 95, no. 601 (May 1996).

———. *Humanitarian Emergencies and Warlord Economies in Liberia and Sierra Leone.* Helsinki: UNU World Institute for Development Economics Research, 1997.

———. *Warlord Politics in Africa.* Boulder, CO: Lynne Rienner, 1998.

Richards, Paul. "Rebellion in Liberia and Sierra Leone: A Crisis of Youth?" In *Conflict in Africa,* edited by O. Furley. London: I. B. Tauris, 1995.

———. *Fighting for the Rain Forest: War, Youth and Resources in Sierra Leone.* Oxford: James Curry, 1996.

Rothchild, Donald. "Ethnic Bargaining and State Breakdown in Africa." *Nationalism and Ethnic Politics* 1 (1995).

———. "Structuring State-Society in Africa: Towards and Enabling Political Environment." In *Economic Change and Political Liberalization in Sub-Saharan Africa,* edited by Jennifer Widner. Baltimore: The Johns Hopkins University Press, 1994.

Rothchild, Donald, and Naomi Chazan, eds. *The Precarious Balance: State and Society in Africa.* Boulder: Westview, 1988.

Said, Ali. "Resource-Use Conflict between Pastoralism and Irrigation Development in the Middle Awash Valley of Ethiopia." *Eastern Africa Social Science Research Review* 10, no. 2 (1994).

Saro Wiwa, Ken. *Genocide in Nigeria: The Ogoni Tragedy.* Port Harcourt: Saros International Publishers, 1992.

Sawyer, Amos. *Dynamics of Conflict in Liberia.* Accra: Institute of Economics Affairs, 1997.

Sesay, Max Ahmadu. "Civil War and Collective Intervention in Liberia." *Review of African Political Economy,* no. 67 (1996).

Shawcross, William. "In Praise of Sandlines." *The Spectator,* August 1998.

———. *Deliver Us From Evil: Warlords and Peacekeepers in a World of Endless Conflicts.* London: Bloomsbury, 2000.

Shearer, David. *Private Armies and Military Intervention.* Adelphi Papers 316. London: IISS, 1997.

Shima, Vandama. "Resources." In *The Development Dictionary,* edited by Wolfgang Sachs. London: Zed Books, 1995.

Simmons, Ian. *The Ecology of Natural Resources.* London: Edward Arnold, 1974.

Solomon, Hussein, and Anthony Turton, eds. *Water Wars: Enduring Myth or Impending Reality.* Pretoria: Accord, 2000.

Suliman, Mohamed. *Alternative Strategies for Africa.* Vol. 2, *Environment/Women.* London: The Institute for African Alternatives, 1991.

Suliman, Mohamed, ed. *Ecology, Politics and Violent Conflict.* London: Zed Books, 1999.

Tegegn, Melakou. "Political Marginalization vs. Good Governance: The Case of Pastoralists in Ethiopia." In *Breaking Barriers, Creating New Hopes: Democracy, Civil Society and Good Governance in Africa,* edited by Abdalla Bujra and Said Adejumobi. Addis Ababa, Ethiopia: DPMF, 2003.

Thom, William. "Congo-Zaire's 1996–97 Civil War in the Context of Evolving Pattern of Military Conflicts in Africa in the Era of Independence." *Journal of Conflict Studies* 19, no. 2 (1999).

Thomas, Caroline. *The Environment in International Relations.* London: Royal Institute of International Affairs, 1992.

Tomori, S., ed. *Oil and Gas Sector in the Nigerian Economy.* Lagos: Faculty of Social Sciences, University of Lagos, 1991.

Tovar, Michael. *Economic Development in the Third World.* New York and London: Longman, 1989.

Turton, Anthony. "Water and Conflict in an African Context." *Conflict Trends,* no. 4 (1999).

Udo, Reuben K. "Environment and the Peoples of Nigeria: A Geographical Introduction to the History of Nigeria." In *Groundwork of Nigerian History,* edited by Obaro Ikime. Ibadan: Heinemann, 1999, p. 10.

Ullman, Richard. "Re-defining Security." *International Security* 18, no. 1 (1983): 133.

Van de Goor, Luc, Kumar Rupesinghe, and Paul Sciarone, eds. *Between Development and Destruction: An Enquiry into the Causes of Conflict in Post Colonial States.* The Hague: The Netherlands Ministry of Foreign Affairs, 1996, p. 2.

Van de Walle, Nicholas, Nicole Ball, and Vijaya Ramachandran, eds. *Beyond Structural Adjustment: The Institutional Context of Africa's Development.* London: Palgrave Macmillan, 2003.

Van Wyk, Jo-Ansie. "River Dry Mountain High: Water Security in Southern Africa." *Conflict Trend,* October 1998.

Westing, Arthur, ed. *Global Resources and International Conflict.* Oxford and New York: SIPRI/OUP, 1986.

Wirth, David. "Climatic Chaos." *Foreign Policy,* no. 74 (Spring 1989).

Wihbey, Paul. "The Oil Power behind New US African Policy." *Africa Analysis,* no. 357 (October 6, 2000).

Wolf, A. T. "International Water Conflict Resolution: Lessons from Comparative Analysis." *International Journal of Water Resources Development* 13, no. 3 (December 1997).

Woodman, Ian. "War of Scarcity: Myth or Reality? An Examination of Resource Scarcities as a Cause of Conflict in Africa." In *Seaford House Papers,* edited by J. E. Spence. London: Royal College of Defense Studies, 2002.

Yachir, Faysal. *Mining in Africa Today: Strategies and Prospects.* London: UNU/ZED, 1998.

Zhou, Emerson. *Socio-economic Implications of the Current Farm Invasion in Zimbabwe.* Harare: Friedrich-Stiflung, 2002.

INDEX

337

ROCHESTER STUDIES in
AFRICAN HISTORY and the DIASPORA

Toyin Falola, Senior Editor
The Frances Higginbotham Nalle Centennial Professor in History
University of Texas at Austin

(ISSN: 1092-5228)

Power Relations in Nigeria:
Ilorin Slaves and their Successors
Ann O'Hear

Dilemmas of Democracy in Nigeria
Edited by Paul Beckett and
Crawford Young

Science and Power in Colonial Mauritius
William Kelleher Storey

Namibia's Post-Apartheid Regional
Institutions: The Founding Year
Joshua B. Forrest

A Saro Community in the Niger Delta,
1912–1984: The Potts-Johnsons of Port
Harcourt and Their Heirs
Mac Dixon-Fyle

Contested Power in Angola,
1840s to the Present
Linda Heywood

Nigerian Chiefs: Traditional Power in
Modern Politics, 1890s–1990s
Olufẹmi Vaughan

West Indians in West Africa, 1808–1880:
The African Diaspora in Reverse
Nemata Blyden

The United States and Decolonization in
West Africa, 1950–1960
Ebere Nwaubani

Health, State, and Society in Kenya
George Oduor Ndege

Black Business and Economic Power
Edited by Alusine Jalloh and
Toyin Falola

Voices of the Poor in Africa
Elizabeth Isichei

Colonial Rule and Crisis in Equatorial
Africa: Southern Gabon ca. 1850–1940
Christopher J. Gray

The Politics of Frenchness in
Colonial Algeria, 1930–1954
Jonathan K. Gosnell

Sources and Methods in African History:
Spoken, Written, Unearthed
Edited by Toyin Falola and
Christian Jennings

Sudan's Blood Memory: The Legacy of War,
Ethnicity, and Slavery in Early South Sudan
Stephanie Beswick

Writing Ghana, Imagining Africa:
Nation and African Modernity
Kwaku Larbi Korang

Labour, Land and Capital in Ghana:
From Slavery to Free Labour in Asante,
1807–1956
Gareth Austin

Not So Plain as Black and White:
Afro-German Culture and History,
1890–2000
Edited by Patricia Mazón and
Reinhild Steingröver

Printed in the United States
131804LV00003B/69/P